# Search for the Summit

# *Search for the Summit*

## AUSTIN COLLEGE
## THROUGH XII DECADES

# *1849-1970*

## By
## George L. Landolt

*Printed in United States of America
by Von Boeckman-Jones Co.
Austin, Texas*

# Dedication

**TO THE MEN WHO MADE AUSTIN COLLEGE**
The Trustees and Faculty
and especially to

**THE FAMOUS FOUR HORSEMEN OF AUSTIN COLLEGE**
Thomas E. Craig of McKinney, Texas
Patrick E. Hooks of Itasca, Texas
Hoxie H. Thompson of Houston, Texas
C. Stanly Roberts of Sherman, Texas

# Acknowledgments

*Search for the Summit* includes much that has been written by others about the men who made Austin College. I have borrowed freely from the diary of Dr. Davis Foute Eagleton, Professor of English at Austin College from 1889 until his death in 1916. I have used many excerpts from the Session Minutes of the Presbyterian Church of Huntsville, Texas, and Minutes of the Brazos Presbytery, the Synod of Texas and the Board of Trustees of Austin College. I have verified, used or corrected statements concerning the College history made by P. E. Wallace in his Master's Degree Thesis on Austin College, and Dan Ferguson's two treatises "Antecedents of Austin College" and "Austin College at Huntsville."

A great deal of information has been obtained from articles in *The Southwest Historical Review;* from Mrs. Josephine Bush, archivist of the Sam Houston State University, and Bowen C. Tatum, of Huntsville, Texas; from the University of Texas Library; from the Archives Division of the Texas State Library; from the Rosenberg Library of Galveston, Texas; and the General Assembly's Historical Library at Montreat, North Carolina, and the Houston, Texas, Public Library; and for research assistance by Mrs. Yasuko Takata in the Historical Library of the University of Texas.

On the campus here at the College I am indebted to John G. Hall, Librarian; Mrs. Lena Kolb, archivist; Mrs. Carolyn Squires, Secretary of the College; Mrs. Amateene Sewell in the Records Office for assistance in gathering historical data. Credit must be given to Betty Joe Hough for typing and to my wife, the former Doris Eagleton, for typing and proofreading; and for pictures by Willie B. Jacobs, Director of Public Relations.

Personal interviews with grandchildren and great grandchildren of early trustees, Presidents and Professors of Austin College have been extremely helpful and I am deeply appreciative of these. I particularly want to thank Mrs. Edwina Cook Brewer, of Little Rock, Arkansas for information about her grandfather, Abner Cook, and A. J. Burke, a charter trustee; to

vi

George C. Red of Houston, Texas, grandson of Dr. George C. Red; to Mr. and Mrs. W. T. Robinson of Huntsville, Texas, for a picture and information concerning their great grandfathers, Henderson Yoakum and Robert Smither, charter trustees; for a picture and information given me by Mrs. Jennie Morrow Decker and Mrs. Edward Everett of Houston, Texas, relating to their grandfather and great grandfather, Gen. Sam Houston; to Richard A. Houston of Woodward, Oklahoma, grandson of Gen. Houston; and to Rev. Tom Cunningham of Denton, Texas, for a biography of his grandfather, Hugh Wilson, pioneer Presbyterian minister and teacher.

Sources of numerous news items, quotations and books are noted at the end of related paragraphs, but I am sure there are omissions. If so, I apologize now and these omissions and any errors brought to my attention will be corrected in the next edition of this book.

George L. Landolt

# Foreword

Texas is a graveyard of educational institutions started with great hopes. The state is dotted with foundations of old college buildings where once the doors of higher education were open to aspiring youth.

Grayson County alone has lost Kidd-Key and Carr-Burdette Colleges in Sherman, and Grayson College of Whitewright.

> Of the one hundred and thirty-five institutions of higher learning chartered by the Texas legislature, from the time Texas became a state in 1845, until the close of the Civil War — only one survived and that one was Austin College (Eby, *Education in Texas* — Source Material, p. 206)

Dr. Eby might have added that the original Austin College building is also the only one completely in use today for the purpose for which it was so well constructed in 1851. In the center of the campus of Sam Houston State University it rises in magnificence, its beautiful Grecian columns attesting to the skill of architect and builder. Continuously in use for college instruction one hundred and eighteen years, it is still thought by many to be the most beautiful building on the campus.

This book reveals the many crises in the history of Austin College, how they were overcome and gives credit to those who so well planned and brought the College through twelve decades to the "Summit of Excellence" that it enjoys today. "Search for the Summit," written by Dr. George L. Landolt, who has been an active participant in this history making institution for the last five decades, brings to life the true extent of this legacy.

The book reveals the determination of Daniel Baker, Sam Houston, Anson Jones, Henderson Yoakum, Judge Abner Lipscomb and other notable trustees to build an institution where the motto always is: "The Best Today is not Good Enough for Tomorrow."

*Old Prospect
Presbyterian
Church
Washington County*

*First College
Building
Huntsville
(In Use Today)*

*First College
Building
Sherman
Burned in 1913*

# LEGACY OF STEPHEN FULLER AUSTIN

Austin College, named in honor of Stephen Fuller Austin, was founded in 1849, after ten years of planning and thirteen years after Austin was appointed first Secretary of State of the Republic of Texas. His few weeks in office before he succumbed to the rigorous pioneer life and energy-consumming responsibility of those early days of the Republic were packed with ideas and plans for the development of a land won to independence at San Jacinto.

Shortly before his untimely death this selfless patriot, still unmarried said: "I have no house, not a roof in all Texas that I can call my own . . . I have no farm, no cotton plantation, no income, no money, no comforts. I have spent the prime of my life to colonize this country . . . my health, my strength and time have gone to the service of Texas and I am therefore not ashamed of my present poverty."

However, the "Legacies" he bequeathed Texas were more than the undeveloped lands which he left to his relatives. The heritage of ideas which he envisioned for the development of the Republic and so successfully imbued into the lives of thinking fellow Texans enabled this region to quickly take its place in international affairs.

Austin College was one of these legacies, for Austin put high on his list plans to provide the means to obtain academic excellence for the children of the pioneers who settled his colonies.

Eugene Barker, in his excellent *Life of Stephen F. Austin* states: "Without Austin there is no reason to believe that Texas would differ today from the Mexican states south of the Rio Grande. There would have been no settlement of Texas, no revolution, no annexation, no Mexican war." Red River would probably be the boundary between Mexico and the U.S. And of course there would never have been an Austin College.

*Stephen F. Austin*

*Father of Texas*

*Daniel Baker*

*Father of*
*Austin College*

# List of Illustrations

*Sam Houston*

*Charter Trustee*
*1849-1863*

*Steamboat House—Huntsville Final Home of Sam Houston*

# Contents

*Henderson Yoakum*

*Shepherd's Valley
Home of the Author
Who Wrote the First
History of Texas*

# Excerpts from First Published Catalog

# REGULATIONS, 1853

## Text Books.

Arrangements have been made with a merchant in the village, for keeping a good supply of books, used both in the *preparatory* and *Collegiate* Departments.

## Religious Worship

Students will be expected to attend public worship, in the College chapel, or elsewhere, on Sabbath morning, and the Bible class in the afternoon, unless excused by their parents or guardians, or from conscientious scruples.

All immorality, such as profane swearing, obscenity, playing cards, and intemperance, is expressly prohibited; and also, all visiting of groceries or gaming-houses; and loitering in the village.

## Government and Discipline.

The government of the College shall be parental; *mild,* but *firm.* In the College Department, punishment for the offences shall be reprimand, suspension or expulsion, as the nature of the case may demand.

## Pledge Required.

Every student, at the time of his admission, shall sign the following PLEDGE: "I, A. B., promise, on the honor of a gentleman, that I will faithfully observe and keep the Rules and Orders of Austin College so far as I can, whilst I continue a student of the same."

## Week-Day Chapel Exercises.

Every morning and evening, at a stated hour, upon the ringing of the College-bell, the students are required to assemble in the College-chapel; the roll will then be called, and absentees recorded; after which, a portion of Scripture shall be read, and prayer offered by the President or some other person who may be called upon to perform the service.

*Abner H. Cook*

*George Clark Red*

*Anson Jones*

# 1855-56

# AUSTIN COLLEGE.

## BOARD OF TRUSTEES.

## FACULTY

# 1855-56
# COLLEGIATE CLASSES.

### Senior Class.

William A. Allen (Walker Co., Texas), George W. Davis (Walker County), Hanibal H. Boon (Rock Island), James S. Harrison (Walker Co.), John B. Rector (*Irregular*, Bastrop).

John T. Hamilton (Huntsville), William L. Hume (Walker Co.), William B. Smither (Huntsville).

### Sophomore Class.

George W. Barber (Austin), Lewis B. Hightower (Walker Co.), William Hill (Walker Co.), Champion T. Hill (Walker Co.), Henry G. W. McDaniel (Huntsville), Robert F. Mathews (Austin), Ewin C. Thom (Huntsville), John W. Mayes (Walker Co.).

### Freshman Class.

Frederick Z. Buckley (Fort Bend), Andrew J. Burke (Houston), Jacob M. Fullenwider (Huntsville), Tilford A. Hamilton (Huntsville), Francis C. Hume (Walker Co.), J. Adair Murray (Walker Co.), Richard S. Sims (Walker Co.), Samuel Y. Smith (Huntsville), Kenner K. Rector (Bastrop), William B. McClintock (Walker Co.), Marcellus B. Woodall (Huntsville).

### Law Department

Joab H. Banton (Huntsville), L. O. Black (Brazoria), H. H. Boon (Rock Island), P. P. Porter (Huntsville), John R. Peel (Danville), Benton Randolph (Walker Co.), Marton Royston (Washington), L. E. Trezevant (Nashville, Tenn.), ____ Waller (Washington).

## Preparatory Department

Thomas F. Alston (Anderson), Angus D. Alston (Houston Co.), Robert H. Alston (Houston Co.), Charles T. Besser (Huntsville), Thomas M. Blakely (Fort Bend), Jacob W. Blakely (Fort Bend), Sylvester F. Check (Wheelock), William Clark (Houston), Isaac Cox (Walker Co.), William H. Crawford (Huntsville), Christopher Dart (Houston), William H. Day (San Marcos), Joseph A. Desha (Franklin, Louisiana), Jesse T. Fenn (Fort Bend), Charles A. Fowler (Montgomery), Alexander Fullenwider (Huntsville), John T. Garrett (Washington Co.), John A. Green (Walker Co.), Robert F. Green (Walker Co.), William F. Hardin (Liberty Co.), Lemuel B. Hatch (Walder Co.), Thomas K. Hatch (Walker Co.), Sam Houston (Huntsville), William Leigh (Huntsville).

# Introduction

## REV. BENJAMIN CHASE, D.D.

The Rev. Benjamin Chase was the first Presbyterian minister to visit Texas, though there is no record of his having preached during his visit. While an agent of the American Bible Society, he visited Nacogdoches and Austin's Colony in the summer of 1833. He was also the first large contributor to the founding of Austin College. For his generosity, a gift of nearly 30,000 acres of land, the Board sought to honor him with endowed scholarships named after each of his five children. These two facts give him a place in any history of Texas Presbyterianism which can be occupied by no other.

In a letter to Henderson Yoakum, dated April 24, 1851 Chase said:

> I purchased the lands with the intention of moving to Texas . . . new difficulties soon arose . . . and I abandoned all idea of removing there. But I never abandoned the desire to do what I could to promote the temporal and eternal welfare of the people of Texas . . . In devoting my valuable interests there toward the endowment of an institution of learning, I wished to do it in such a manner as will best promote the end.

Benjamin Chase was born of English ancestry in the township of Litchfield, New Hampshire, November 20, 1789. After a course at Salisbury Academy he entered Middlebury College, graduating in 1814. Having taught in New Jersey for a time, he went to New Orleans, where he continued teaching and also studied theology under his college friend, Sylvester Narned, the first settled Presbyterian pastor in New Orleans. He was licensed by the Presbytery of Mississippi and ordained by an Association of the Congregational Church in Connecticut. He returned to Mississippi and spent most of his life in mission work, and as agent for the American Bible Society.

Upon his death in 1870 his Presbytery said: "The eminent services of Dr. Chase, in planting and sustaining the religious and educational institutions of the Presbyterian Church in this portion of our land, entitle his name to a foremost place among those whom, as a Church, we delight to honor, and ought to insure its grateful commemoration for generations to come." (J. H. Hutchison, *Reminiscences, Sketches, and Addresses.*)

# CHAPTER I

# Search for a Site

## Brief History of Presbyterian Interest in Education in Texas

MUCH of the zeal for establishing a Presbyterian college in Texas came from Presbyterian teachers in the private academies which sprang up in pioneer communities. As early as 1829 Stephen F. Austin enlisted the aid of T. J. Pilgrim to teach at San Felipe. Josiah H. Bell built a school at Columbia. D. B. Edwards started a school at Gonzales in 1830. Rev. P. H. Fullenwider taught in Austin's colony, 1834-1835. The same year a Miss Trask opened a boarding school for young ladies at Independence. J. M. Rankin started an academy in St. Augustine in 1837. Rev. Hugh Wilson arrived in 1838 to add his influence. In 1840 Rev. Francis Rutherford became Principal of Velasco Institute at the mouth of the Brazos. Rev. W. L. McCalla, formerly a chaplain in the United States Navy, came to Galveston in 1839 and immediately set out to start a school there. In 1840 Rev. Hugh Wilson built a school at Gay Hill, near his Prospect Presbyterian Church, second oldest in the State. This effort was turned over to Rev. J. W. Miller who founded the Live Oak Seminary for Girls, and Dr. George Red moved from Independence to the school to become one of its famous teachers. (Dr. George Red, Revs. Hugh Wilson and J. W. Miller became charter trustees of Austin College, and Rev. Fullenwider joined the trustees in 1857). Professor M. A. Montrose opened La Grange Institute in 1848.

San Augustine University came out of Rankin's Academy in 1842 but closed in 1847 when its President Russell was assassinated.

Nacogdoches University, founded in 1845, closed in 1847.

Austin College, founded at Huntsville in 1849, was operated by the Brazos Presbytery of the Presbyterian Church U.S.A. until 1851 when the Synod of Texas was formed.

Chapel Hill College was opened by the Cumberland Presbyterians in 1850 at Daingerfield.

Aranama College, called the "College of the West" was established in 1851 by zealous Presbyterians at Goliad but was never chartered. It closed in 1856.

Larissa College was founded in Cherokee County in 1855 by Rev. F. L. Yoakum, brother of Henderson Yoakum, Texas historian. It closed in 1861.

Ewing College succeeded LaGrange Institute in 1859 under the Cumberland Presbyterian Church.

Trinity University was founded at Tehuacana in 1869, requiring each trustee to be a member of the Cumberland Presbyterian Church.

Austin College moved to Sherman from Huntsville in 1876.

Daniel Baker College was founded in Brownwood by the Northern Synod of the Presbyterian Church U.S.A. with Rev. B. T. McClellan as President in 1888. It operated until bankrupt in 1893 when the Synod of Texas of the Southern Presbyterian Church took it over from the receivers and operated it until the depression closed it in 1929.

The Synod of the Cumberland Presbyterian Church met in Sherman, Texas, November 1900 and decided to move Trinity University to Waxahachie.

Texas Presbyterian College for Women at Milford was founded by the Synod of Texas, Presbyterian Church U.S., in 1902. It was consolidated with Austin College in 1929.

Trinity University united with the University of San Antonio of the Methodist Church in 1942 at San Antonio.

One interesting fact about Austin College and Trinity University, the only two surviving institutions, is that Austin College was originally founded by the Presbyterian Church U.S.A. and is now under the Presbyterian Church U.S., while Trinity originally was operated by the Cumberland Presbyterians and later came under control of the Presbyterian Church U.S.A.; and finally under the United Presbyterian Church in the U.S.A.

# The Planting of the Presbyterian Church in Texas and the Antecedents of Austin College

WHEN Stephen F. Austin succeeded in getting his land grant from Mexico in 1828, the opportunity for Presbyterian missionaries to come to Texas from the United States became a possibility. The American colonists heard their first sermon from the old-school Presbyterian, Rev. Henry R. Wilson, in the fall of 1833, at Doaksville. Rev. Peter Hunter Fullenwider and his wife came to Texas in 1834, commissioned as missionaries, settling near San Felipe de Austin, where they taught school for the children of Austin's colony. Due to the Catholic influence in the Mexican government it was forbidden for Protestant ministers to actively engage in preaching.

The spreading of the Presbyterian doctrine since coming to American soil has always been one of missionary zeal coupled with the establishment of seminaries and schools of higher learning (out of Princeton came many of the pioneer missionaries to Texas). However, the governing bodies of the Presbyterian Church took no official notice of Texas until 1837. Jurisdiction of the territory west of the Mississippi was claimed by the Presbytery of Mississippi in 1834 and by the Mississippi Synod in 1835. An executive committee headed by Rev. Benjamin Chase was set up at Natches, Mississippi and through it all mission work to this region was to be channelled. In 1837 the Presbyterian Assembly's Board of Domestic Missions approved the screening of all missionaries for the colonists, stating that . . . "under the especial patronage of the Synod of Mississippi, whose Executive Committee from their location at Natchez, will have many facilities for the instruction of good and faithful men into Texas."

One must give credit to the missionaries who embarked from the port of Natches to labor among the pioneers of Texas for the growth of the Presbyterian Church and eventually the establishment of Austin College. And to Benjamin Chase, who supervised their commissioning and who later played an active role in the financial affairs of the College, we give the position of prime mover in its destiny. Chase had visited Texas in the summer of 1833 as an agent of the American Bible Society. He was accompanied by Sumner Bacon, a layworker who had been in Texas since 1827, and the two reached Austin's colony between the Brazos and Colorado rivers. This is probably the time when Chase obtained his large land acquisition which he later donated to Austin College. There was then, according to the report of the Bible Society in 1834, only one Bible for every ten families. In 1835, through the influence of Mr. Chase, Sumner Bacon was ordained by the Cumberland Church in Louisiana.

Spanish statutes barred Protestant ministers and church services on Mexican soil and prevented Presbyterian ministers from entering Texas until 1834. In May of that year Rev. Peter Hunter Fullenwider brought his bride of two months to San Felipe de Austin to teach school. Fullenwider was the first Protestant minister to take up residence in Texas; the statutes forbidding it not being enforced any longer. He preached in what is now Washington, Burleson and Austin Counties under the direction of the Missionary Committee of the Presbytery of Mississippi.

In the spring of 1836, after the fall of the Alamo, and before Santa Anna's defeat at San Jacinto, only two Presbyterian ministers resided in Texas. The Rev. P. H. Fullenwider was still here with his wife. He had been commissioned by General Sam Houston, as soon as Houston became commander of the Texas forces, to collect the women and children at Fort Sam Houston near Palestine, while the fathers and brothers went to meet Santa Anna. Sumner Bacon, a Cumberland Presbyterian who had spent six years in Texas as a lay missionary at his own expense, had returned with his bride in January 1836, as an ordained minister. He hastened to join the Texas army on its way to San Jacinto; but General Sam Houston commissioned him as a diplomat and securer of military supplies in the States. (*Texas Colonist and Religion* pp. 84, 135)

The next Presbyterian minister to come to Texas was the Reverend William Whitty Hall, M.D. of Kentucky. He had studied medicine with a view to self-support while preaching as a foreign missionary. He says in his autobiography: (taken from the *Presbyterian Reporter* Nov. 1858.)

"Thinking it better to clinch my medical knowledge and practice, I went directly to the sickliest regions of the Union, the Bayous of Louisiana, where I practiced and preached, day and night, all summer and winter and fall; when, being near the Texian border, and the country becoming famous, through the battle of San Jacinto, I concluded in October 1836 to go over there. Meeting with General Sam Houston, near Nacogdoches, who himself was going on to Southern Texas to be inaugurated President, we joined company and traveled and camped together until we reached Columbia, where I was elected Chaplain, and continued in office, following the Congress over to Houston, where we lived and slept in tents. I opened the House and Senate.

While dozens of Methodist and Baptist colleges, as well as colleges chartered by stock companies and independent boards, were dying on the vine, the Presbyterians launched a group of educational institutions, whose survival was equally short.

LaGrange Institute (female) opened 1845 and chartered May 11, 1846, was rechartered as LaGrange Collegiate Institute February 14, 1852. It closed and was again rechartered as Ewing College February 11, 1860; none of the three ever granted a degree.

Aranama College at Goliad to be the Presbyterian college of the West, was chartered January 25, 1854. Rev. Stephen F. Cocke was appointed its financial agent by the Presbytery and for several years it seemed to prosper. In a lengthy oration November 24, 1857, made before the legislature, Representative A. B. Norton made a plea against state universities, mentioning that:

I commend Austin College, at Huntsville, and many other worthy ones in successful operation, such as Baylor University at Independence, Aranama College, represented here by one of the brave survivors of Fannin's Massacre, Dr. Bernard of Goliad, and others of like character, called into being by citizens of the State impelled by a laudable desire for the increase of knowledge and dissemination of literature, religion and sound morality throughout the land. (Aranama College never issued a college degree.) Allusions have been made by several of the gentlemen who have preceded me, to the gray-haired, venerable President of Austin College. He is now here, soliciting at our hands aid for an institution already located and at work disseminating sound learning in the country. Shall his petition be heeded, or will we turn a deaf ear to the respectful request thereof? (*State Gazette* Appendix 1857, Vol. 2, 27, 29)

On August 4, 1856, R. W. Bailey, agent for the college, had a one page "Broadside" in three columns printed in the Huntsville *Item*: To Hon. P. W. Kittrell, chairman of the State Legislature Committee on Education (In support of the Memorial before you, presented by the President of the College.)

The answer to Norton's plea and Kittrell's was of no avail. The legislature passed first and second readings and turned a deaf ear to the required third.

Thus ten years of planning were required before Austin College was launched into a sea of educational institutions that came into being between the establishment of the Republic of Texas and the Civil War.

Desiring to do his evangelistic labors near the center of Texas, the Rev. Hugh Wilson, a Presbyterian missionary to Texas from Tennessee, took his family, accompanied by the family of a carpenter named John McFarland, to Independence in Washington County. Wilson only a year previously had organized the first Presbyterian church at San Augustine, then called Bethel Church.

Hugh Wilson had graduated from Princeton in 1819, remaining for three more years for the Master of Arts Degree and for his ministerial training in the Princeton Seminary, established largely as the result of dedicated labor of his uncle, Dr. James Hall. At Independence Mr. Wilson joined the faculty of Independence Female Academy, first school to be chartered under the Republic of Texas, later to become Baylor Female College.

In February 1839, Rev. Wilson formed the second Presbyterian church in Texas with twelve members, at a community called Chriesman Settlement near Mt. Prospect, about eight miles west of Independence, the historic spot where Austin College was founded ten years later.

Dr. George C. Red, a Presbyterian physician neighbor, writes of Mr. Wilson's move to the new location at Prospect:

By 1840, having located a tract of land two hundred and forty eight acres and half mile southeast of Mt. Prospect, he began his home, a cedar log house erected a little north of a spring. This move placed him in the midst of his congregation. Here the brethren who came to join with him in organizing the Presbytery of Brazos found him hard at work on his school house. Then began a series of heartbreaking experiences which might have discouraged a less noble spirit.

Rev. Fullenwider had left for his home state after independence but was commissioned to return to Texas to work under Rev. Hugh Wilson, who on Nov. 1837 was sent for one year as a "Missionary and General Agent of the Missionary Cause." Rev. Wilson, who was destined to play an important role in establishing churches in Texas, came to be known as the "Father of Old School Presbyterianism in Texas."

Rev. Benjamin Chase came again to Texas for two months in 1838 to look over the mission field and soon thereafter the Mississippi Synod directed "Rev. W. C. Blair, Hugh Wilson, W. Y. Allen and John McCullough to meet together at such time and place in the Republic of Texas as may be convenient to themselves and organize a presbytery which will on due application be admitted into the Synod."

The idea of a Christian college was first conceived at Chriesman's Schoolhouse, near Independence, Washington County at this organizational meeting of the Presbytery of Brazos.

### *First Meeting of Brazos Presbytery, April 3-6, 1840 at Chriesman's Schoolhouse*

The Reverend Daniel Baker, of Presbytery of Tuskaloosa, being present, was invited to sit as corresponding member, produced a commission from General Assembly's Board of Foreign Missions author-

izing him to labor as a mission agent in the bounds of
the Republic of Texas to preach the Gospel, to organize churches, etc., wherever he may think it expedient. Resolved therefore that Brother Baker has our
cordial approbation.

John McCullough, Moderator
Wm. Y. Allen, Stated Clerk

The split between the old and new schools and other adversities made the missionaries to this raw outpost realize that
the only effective solution to the problem of leadership was
the founding of a frontier institution for Christian Education,
which might raise up a ministry sufficiently hardy for this
crude, primitive land.

It was not, however, until the sixth session of Brazos Presbytery that the matter of an educational institution received
serious consideration.

### Sixth Session of Brazos Presbytery, April 4, 1844
### Columbia

W. C. Blair, Hugh Wilson, I. J. Henderson, J. Mc-
Cullough, ministers and J. McCormick, elder from
Columbia Church. H. P. Fullenwider of Mississippi
Presbytery was present and received into Presbytery
as was his church at Point Pleasant in Montgomery
County, and also its elder, B. F. Irvine.

A resolution on the subject of education was proposed: viz, Resolved that the ministers of Presbytery
be requested to present the subject of education to
their respective congregations, and endeavor to secure funds for establishing an Institute of Learning at
some convenient place in the country to be under
control of Presbytery, and report at our next meeting.

Hugh Wilson, Moderator

### Seventh Session of Presbytery of Brazos

### Meeting at Point Pleasant November 7, 1844

Application having been made to this Presbytery
for some action in relation to an Institution of Learning to be located at Nacogdoches, Rev. Hugh Wilson,

J. M. Becton, and J. D. Sharp were appointed a committee to report on the subject. This group recommended that if Presbytery joined in establishing a college, nine of fifteen trustees should be Presbyterian; and J. M. Becton, J. D. Sharp and T. J. Rusk represent Presbytery in nominating trustees to be named in the charter, and to assist in drawing up the charter.

Rev. J. M. Becton had been ordained in April 1840 at Mt. Carmel, Tennessee, the church Hugh Wilson organized, and that fall he visited Texas. The following year he returned to Texas with his family, settling at San Augustine, where he commenced to teach and preach. He applied and was admitted to Brazos Presbytery in November 1844. He presented the memorial from the citizens of Nacogdoches, looking to the establishment of a university under the control of the Presbytery of Brazos.

Becton's previous efforts to establish San Augustine College had failed. In the spring of 1842, he and Rev. P. W. Warrener were joined by Marcus A. Montrose, another Presbyterian minister who was put in charge of its operation. Rev. Montrose was a Scotchman and a graduate of the University of Edinburgh. He had come to the United States in 1839 and had just arrived in Texas. Controversial teaching policies led to the resignation of Montrose in 1845, and was the contributing factor to the assassination of his successor, James Russell, another Presbyterian minister; and the sudden end of San Augustine College in 1847. The efforts of the Presbyterians to establish Nacogdoches University were also too feeble and it closed the same year without either school conferring a single degree. Though his two efforts to establish a Presbyterian college had failed, Becon lived to see Austin College founded. He died on July 14, 1853.

Dr. J. D. Sharp, a brother-in-law of Rev. Becton was an elder in the Bethel Church near San Augustine, founded by Hugh Wilson, June 2, 1838. This was the first Presbyterian church organized in Texas and it is still active today. Dr. Sharp, a practicing physician, was licensed to preach by Brazos Presbytery in 1844, holding pastorates at Alto, Rusk and Kaufman. He was chaplain for the 18th Texas Regiment during the Civil War.

T. J. Rusk, the third member of the nominating committee, was Secretary of War under Gen. Sam Houston. He was later co-senator with Houston in the U. S. Senate until his death by suicide, April 23, 1856, caused by grief over the early death of his wife.

### *Eighth Session of Brazos Presbytery* *Victoria, Texas, April 3, 1845*

Rev. J. W. Miller, from the Presbytery of Steubenville, Ohio, was present and invited to sit as corresponding member. The agent to solicit funds for the college reported and the report was accepted. J. M. McCormick and J. W. Miller were added to the committee to draw up a charter for the "college of the West." Boundaries previously set for "Western College" at the November meeting were rescinded.

### *Nineth Session of Brazos Presbytery* *Seguin, Texas, April 14, 1845*

I. J. Henderson, Moderator; J. McCullough, Stated Clerk.

The Committee appointed to select a site for the location of the College in the West, beg leave to report that they have examined most of the country on each side of the Guadalupe from Caporti to Old San Antonio and recommend that the college be located within ten miles of Seguin and that Charles D. Sayre, J. M. McCormick and J. J. Tinsley be appointed to obtain the best site according to their judgment and authorized to begin as soon as possible the necessary buildings. (This closed Voume I of the Brazos Presbytery Records.

*(The first seed corn of the Austin College of the future)* However, for years nothing was done except to appoint committees, and from time to time change prospective locations, until in 1848 when the committee on education reported the purchase of a site at Goliad. In 1845 the rapidly increasing Baptist denomination had founded Baylor College at Independence, only a few miles from Prospect, which forestalled

the placing of a Presbyterian college on the beautiful location first agreed upon. This spot was on the main road from East Texas through Huntsville to Washington-on-the-Brazos and on the Independence and Gay Hill, thence west to Austin. Today the density of population in a five-mile radius of Prospect Church is almost zero, much less than it was 130 years ago. The main highways bypass this spot and it can only be reached on a narrow black-topped road, impossible to find except by one who has been there before.

The Presbyterians were not completely discouraged by previous failures to provide higher education in Texas but became active in the Texas Literary Institute, an interdenominational effort to arouse public interest in the subject of general education in the State. The Institute published a monthly *Public School Advocate*. Presbyterian ministers J. W. Miller and I. J. Henderson took part in the Institute and made addresses, while Elders H. E. Lillie, James Bailey, Abner Cook, J. M. McCormick and James Burke were members, the latter being the corresponding secretary. (Miller, Cook and McCormick later became trustees of Austin College). Small notice was taken by the public over the resolution, unanimously adopted by the Institute which declared: "That every child being the property of the State, the State is imperatively bound to provide for its Education." Three years later James Burke wrote, "We are aware that the Institute has been denounced as impractical and selfish; having embarked in this enterprise we are determined to persevere." It was thirty-five years later that his perseverance succeeded. (When Texas University was founded)

The Mexican War halted efforts of Presbytery in regard to founding a college and it was not until the summer of 1849 that they convened again at Washington on the Brazos, June 21, with Revs. Hugh Wilson, P. H. Fullenwider, J. M. Becton and J. W. Miller; and Ruling Elders Hugh McCain and W. L. Gresham present. Daniel Baker, after ten years, had returned to Texas and was received on the second day of the meeting.

On page 534(35-36) of Vol. 2 of his "History of Texas," Henderson Yoakum gives an account of the Presbyterian Church in Texas, beginning with the arrival of Hugh Wilson in 1838. He gives a brief account of Daniel Baker and others interested in "the educational movement made by the Presbyterian church, ending in the establishment of Austin College in 1849, through the instrumentality of Dr. Baker, and now in a flourishing condition." Although a member of the Methodist church, Yoakum was a charter member on the Board, with the men he mentions, — Rev. Wilson, Rev. Baker and Rev. P. H. Fullenwider. He was frequently in meetings with the other charter trustee Presbyterians, Dr. George Red, Rev. Miller, Rev. Samuel McKinney, all of whom he knew well.

This led him to eloquence: "In education, as in organization of the churches, the Presbyterian interest may seem slow in its operation, but it is *sure*. The denomination, like the Texas live-oaks, gradually, almost imperceptibly, extends its branches to the light, the air and the dew; but it tends to a sturdy, magnificent growth, whose evergreen glory, by the blessing of God, knows no alternation of season."

## The Synod of Texas and Austin College With Excerpts from Synod's Minutes

AUSTIN, Texas, October 30, 1851. The Synod of Texas of the Presbyterian Church U.S.A. was organized with two presbyteries, Brazos and Western Texas. The meeting was held in the church built by Abner H. Cook, one of the two elders of that congregation.

(Abner H. Cook was the builder who designed and furnished the brick for the first Austin College building at Huntsville while he was first superintendent of the State Penitentiary there. He also erected the first two governors' mansions, the first University of Texas building and the first capitol building. He is given credit for erecting the dome and constructing all of the woodwork of the present capitol. Abner Cook became a member of the Austin College Board in 1854).

The elder representing his church at this first meeting of Synod was charter trustee, Wade Hampton, Editor of the Austin, Texas, newspaper. This first Synod of Texas had eighteen ministers, twenty-two churches and seven hundred communicants. Rev. Stephen F. Cocke was made a trustee of the College at this organizational meeting. Other trustees present were: Rev. Daniel Baker, P. H. Fullenwider and J. W. Miller.

According to the Minutes of the Synod of Texas, on Saturday, November 1, 1851: "Synod proceeded to the second order of the day, the transfer of Austin College — at the request of Brazos Presbytery, and also the Board of Trustees — and this college is now hereby received under the care of this body."

It is an interesting fact that the Synod of Texas met again on this exact spot eighty-one years later, December 13, 1931 in an adjourned meeting for the sole purpose of deciding what to do with Austin College. This time, with only six elders and twenty-seven ministers present from nine presbyteries, this small membership representing approximately the same number of churches that assumed its control in 1851, again held the destiny of the College in its hands. However, this time Synod was acting for over sixty-thousand communicants. The small group present at this meeting were about to close the College but adjourned for lunch. Two hours later the question of closing came up again, and after lengthy committee meetings, voted to keep the College open, because there was no way available to pay its debts and still maintain Synod's other institutions.

Hon. Anson Jones resigned as trustee and (Judge) R. T. Wheeler was elected to fill out the unexpired term in Class 2 Huntsville, April 8, 1854 at a called meeting of the Synod. Austin College was instructed to turn over to recently established "college in the West" money originally collected for that purpose but loaned to Austin College.

On April 10, 1854 Synod recommended that Austin College establish five perpetual scholarships for five children of Benjamin Chase, in view of his liberality to the College.

On November 2, 1855 Rev. Daniel Baker presented the report of the Trustees of Austin College. Hon. Guy M. Bryan was elected to the Board in place of Rev. Hugh Wilson, resigned; James Sorley in place of G. C. Red, M. D. resigned; and Synod required each minister except those connected with Aranama College (College in the West) to present the claims of Austin College, and take up a collection and subscriptions and send scholars to the College, reporting annually what had been done. (Aranama College opened at Goliad, Texas, but was never chartered and closed in 1856).

At Huntsville, November 6, 1858 Dr. P. W. Kittrell was elected in place of Rev. Daniel Baker, Class 2, deceased.

On December 6, 1867 D. MacGregor and Wm. C. Somerville declined to serve as trustees, Class 3, and Wm. McClintock and T. C. Bell (two former students of the College) were elected instead.

Waco, November 4, 1871 Mr. A. T. McKinney, Dr. T. L. C. Means, Rev. R. H. Byers, Rev. R. F. Bunting and Rev. L. Tenney were elected Class 1, and Gen. John Besser Class 2.

In the College there were reported: "43 students, one professor and one assistant. The pecuniary embarrassment of the college keeps the students away. The debt is $10,000." The interests of the Church in this State suffered greatly from the condition of the College. Interest, honor and religion, bind the Synod to provide for the payment of the debts.

Palestine, Texas, November 8, 1872. The Committee on Austin College was heard. A commission of 24 members, 3 ministers and 3 elders from each Presbytery in the Synod, was appointed to take into consideration the whole question of the removal of the College, and to invite propositions, and, if the way be clear, select a location. The following trustees were elected for class 2: Joab Banton, J. C. Smith, Benton Randolph (all graduates) E. H. Cushing (editor of the Houston paper) and John S. Besser (Financial agent of the State Penitentiary).

Houston December, 1873. The Committee on Removal of the College reported that no sufficient offer has been received.

It was determined that no proxy of the trustees of Austin College shall be voted by any person not a trustee.

Synod ordered the "Chase lands" to be sold to endow the "Chase Professorship of Language" thought sufficient to endow the chair richly and leave $3000 surplus.

An amendment to the Charter of Austin College, passed by the last legislature, authorized the Synod to move Austin College to another location, Synod appointed a comittee of nine persons, with full power vested in it to take into consideration the subject of removal of the College, select a location and complete the removal if the way be clear.

A resolution of thanks to Rev. S. M. Luckett for a gift of $600 in coin to Austin College.

Jefferson, Texas November 5, 1874. Synod expressed the opinion that Austin College ought to be moved immediately. Rev. W. K. Marshall, Rev. John Smythe and Rev. John W. Neill were elected a committee to secure bids for location of the college.

Austin, Texas, November 4, 1875. The Committee on Austin College reported it still in debt $7500, but arrangements made to pay same in installments. The largest offer made for location of Austin College (Sherman) was $36,000.

November 7, 1873, Marshall, Texas. Every communicant in the church in Texas was asked to contribute one dollar to the College. The trustees are warned against incurring debts for any purpose. A statement of assets shows: Austin College buildings and campus $25,000; Land notes $12,000, Endowment notes $5,000; Land, 1800 acres-value $2700; Total $44,700. The College has a President, two professors and 53 students and a budget of $4000.

The uncollected subscriptions due from Sherman citizens is $9000. The death of E. H. Cushing, editor of the Houston paper, a long-time Treasurer and trustee was reported.

Ft. Worth, Texas, November 10, 1979. "The Committee on Austin College reported "The old debt of the college reduced to $2800." Synod commended the Board of Trustees for its foresight, wisdom and skill, commended also the President and faculty and ratified the removal of the College to Sherman.

Waco, Texas, November 18, 1889. The trustees were requested to appoint a Financial Agent to visit all the churches for the purpose of collecting funds for the College. A. J. Burke, charter trustee, was re-elected. (His son, A. J. Burke, Jr., B.A. 1859 died May 5th that year.)

Corsicana, October 21, 1881. The hope was expressed that the financial crisis of the College was past, that the College would live and do a great work. The Committee was deeply impressed with the importance of maintaining the institution, and that every proper effort ought to be made to do so.

Weatherford, Texas, October 2, 1882. A subscription was taken up in open Synod to liquidate the debt of the College and $3785 was subscribed.

Victoria, Texas, November 8, 1883. Synod recommends that the Trustees devise some plan for 3 annual subscriptions, in small amounts for gifts and patronage of all of our people. Gen. John Besser was re-elected and Rev. E. D. Junkin, D. MacGregor, W. N. Scott and Elder C. N. Roberts elected trustees Class 2.

Belton, Texas, October 20, 1884. The Committee on Austin recommended that Synod raise annually $4000 for current expenses, and pay off the bonded debt of $12,000. During the discussion of the affairs of Austin College, the following trustees resigned: Capt. C. N. Roberts, Rev. L. B. Chaney, J. S. Moore, C. S. M. See, W. N. Dickey, D. MacGregor, E. D. Junkin, A. P. Smith, T. W. Erwin and W. W. Taylor. Several nominations were made to fill the vacancies, but no election was had; whereupon it was resolved that the above named trustees who have resigned be re-elected in order to have a conference. The resolution was adopted, and permission was given to the trustees to retire. Rev. E. P. Palmer, D. D. resigned the Presidency of the College and Synod expressed its appreciation for his service, Rev. D. MacGregor was nominated to the Presidency of the College by the Board of Trustees after resigning as trustee. Synod recommended that the Presbyteries raise $3000 annually for 6 years to pay off the debt of the College to President Palmer, resigned.

Austin, Texas, October 21, 1885. Synod appointed a Committee to suggest amendments to the charter so as to make Austin College a "denominational Presbyterian College, and especially to repeal Sec. 7 of the original charter," (which forbade religious tests to trustees or faculty).

In answer to an overture from Paris Presbytery, Synod refused to turn Austin College over to those Presbyteries that would support it, as "impracticable and as raising insurmountable legal difficulties."

Galveston, Texas, November 4, 1886. The Trustees of Austin College were directed to have stricken from the original charter sections 7 and 12. The College reported only 27 students against 45 the year before. Assets were campus and 3,324 acres of land, cash on hand $3500 and $11,500 debt.

Paris, Texas, October 27, 1887. Synod concurred with the Board in expression of sorrow at the death of the late President of the College, Rev. D. MacGregor D. D., and approved the action of the Board in its election of Rev. S. M. Luckett President and Financial Agent of the College.

San Antonio, Texas, October 16, 1890. A petition from the Faculty and students of Austin College for more buildings was read and referred to the committee. The trustees are urged to use all proper efforts to complete the addition to the building and Synod will gladly co-operate in pushing the matter to success. A subscription of $500 was taken up for the College.

Houston, Texas, October 22, 1891. The report of the Board of Trustees was read. With profound gratitude to God the names of the liberal donors, Mrs. H. A. MacGregor, Mrs. S. M. Luckett, Mrs. C. A. Allen and Mr. J. H. Chadwick are mentioned as signal blessings of God to the college; also the fact that many of the students are preparing for the work of the ministry.

Corsicana, Texas, October 20, 1892. All conditions in our state call for exertion; intelligent, earnest and persevering, in order to meet the increasing demands on the College, *that it may not be second to any college in the State or Southwest.* These demands specified are the erection of an East wing, to furnish two more classrooms, a library room, a room for a museum, and another Literary Society Hall; the erection of a dormitory; additional apparatus for these four departments,- philosophical, chemical, physiological and astronomical,- and increased endowment to enable the College to increase its teaching force. The Board of Trustees are authorized to raise money for these purposes in and out of Synod's bounds.

Ft. Worth, Texas, October 21, 1893. The College Committee reported $760 income from the Chadwick Farm used according to the provisions of the gift to the College to aid in the education of candidates for the ministry, numbering 20.

The MacGregor property has been leased to Ed Kiam for 50 years at $250 per month net, and he has already erected a good five-story brick building on it (corner of Fannin and Main Streets in Houston). Elder John Besser, long-time treasurer and trustee of the College for 35 years died at Hunstville.

Brownwood, Texas, October 12, 1894. Special attention is called to the condition of the College, there being no longer any indebtedness to hinder its usefulness. The College was authorized to solicit funds for endowment.

Marshall, Texas, December 3, 1897. The action of the trustees in abolishing military training was heartily commended. The fitting up of the Gymnasium was approved. The Board is asked to preclude membership on the Board to any whose family is represented in the faculty and to dispense with proxies, and that the President of the College not serve as President of the Board of Trustees.

Weatherford, Texas, October 27, 1898. A marked increase in attendance and interest in physical training is noted. The plan of the Board, the faculty, the alumni association and the student body to celebrate next June the semi-centennial of Austin College is most heartily commended.

Temple, Texas, October 20, 1899. An overture from the Presbytery of Brazos touching the change of the name of Austin College was read: Resolved that the Synod advise the Board of Trustees to change the name of the College to "Stephen F. Austin College."

Synod returned thanks to Mrs. Sarah C. Ball for her munificent gift of $5000 to the College. Synod notes with pride that the University of Texas officially recognizes Austin College on the list of first-class institutions and that one graduate (C. Stanly Roberts, B. S. 1898) has been admitted to the senior class of Princeton University.

Cleburne, Texas, October 9, 1902. Synod recommended the abolition of the Preparatory Department and expressed its high appreciation for the largehearted liberality of Rev. S. M. Luckett and J. Lewis Thompson for the gift and equipping of athletic grounds for the students.

Austin, Texas, October 20, 1904. Through the Twentieth Century Fund Drive for $150,000 Austin College will receive $30,000, but of the first $30,000 raised the College will receive only $1800. (The College got almost nothing from this drive).

Houston, Texas, November 23, 1905. Synod endorsed the plan to erect the dormitory to be called "Luckett Hall" and authorized the Board of Trustees to adopt and carry out such financial policies as shall be adequate to meet the needs of the College, provided that in so doing they shall not disregard Synod's former action forbidding incurring of debts. The value of property belonging to Austin College is listed as follows: Building and campus, $60,000; Athletic Park, $5,000; Lands in Brazoria and Pecos Counties, $2,000; Houston and Dallas property-endowment-$81,000; total, $150,000. Debts are $2,000 and annual expense estimated at $11,500.

Dallas, Texas, October 18, 1906. A permanent committee on schools and colleges was created to apportion all funds according to a scale fixed by the committee.

Texarkana, Texas, October 15, 1908. The permanent committee on schools and colleges reported that Austin College received $201.50 from $1755 collected as designated funds, and nothing from $1432 received as undesignated funds. Pastors and churches are urged to do everything possible to clear away the $40,000 debt of the College.

San Angelo, Texas, November 20, 1909. The report of the College shows it to be in the best condition in its history. Special need is money to complete the Y.M.C.A. building. Representatives of the College are given free access to our churches and people.

Synod's plans for supporting the College in the Seventh Decade were very disheartening. Sherman citizens came to the rescue after the disastrous fire that destroyed the main building in 1913. They erected Sherman Hall and the Power House (now the Cern Building). Unable to redeem its promise to the College by matching this effort, Synod on October 14, 1915 "authorized and enpowered Austin College to execute a note in the amount not to exceed $275,000 for which the members of the Board of Trustees of Austin College shall in no way be individually liable for said sum nor any part thereof." Dr. Davis F. Eagleton, Professor of English at the College, was host and retiring moderator of the Synod which met at the College for this 1915 session, which featured popular meetings on foreign and home missions and an educational rally.

The depression of the 1930's practically ended financial support by Synod and resulted in a $40,000 skeleton building as evidence of it. This projected administration building became known as the Austin College "Skeleton" and remained so until 1943.

The Minutes of Synod of July 26, 1934; Vol. VII No. 5, page 275 read:

> The plan adopted last year by Synod for raising $15,000 to be applied on Synod's obligations of $157,156 yielded no results. The Field Secretary appointed to raise this amount reported no receipts. The Field Secretaries' salary and expenses left a deficit of $1,525 in this operation. The result of the failure of our liquidation scheme increased Synod's indebtedness to $158,389.

The total receipts from Synod for 1932 amounted to $2,321 and in that entire decade (1930-39) Synod contributed $33,000 to maintain Austin College. In the Tenth Decade, Synod contributed $128,700. From 1950 to 1959 Synod's Presbyterian Educational Fund provided $280,000 and Synod's Treasurer $617,000. From 1960 to 1969 Synod's support amounted to $860,000.

At the present time the Presbyterian Foundation Book Value is approximately seven million dollars, from which Austin College receives as its share about $60,000 per year.

## Change the Name of Austin College?
## Move? Merge? Close?

THERE have been numerous attempts to change the name, merge, close or move Austin College and only once has any of these efforts succeeded — the moving of Austin College to Sherman from Huntsville in 1876. This removal to Sherman came about on account of two epidemics that decimated the population of Huntsville and refusal of Huntsville to bring a railroad into the town. Sherman was selected because it was a rail center, an important shipping point on the H&T.C. Railroad; and the county seat of Grayson, the most populated county in the State of Texas at that time.

The first effort to change the name of Austin College came when the College was not yet two years old. The minutes of the Board of Trustees on June 1, 1851 read: "On motion resolved that the President of the College (Samuel McKinney at the time) is hereby required should he deem the interests of the Institution to require it, to apply to the Legislature to change the name of the College to 'The Texas University.' An amendment to the College charter June 16, 1877 provided that the name of the college could be changed by three-fourths of the trustees."

The Board of Trustee Minutes, page 332 of Nov. 3, 1884 read: "The Board met at ½ past 2 pm at the request of Synod and unanimously elected Rev. D. MacGregor, President and Financial Agent of Austin College. Rev. MacGregor was added to the Committee for the revision of the charter; This Committee was instructed to have the name changed to "Texas Presbyterian College."

The Board Minutes, page 430, Oct. 28, 1898 read: "The Board unanimously voted to change the name of Austin College to 'John Knox College.' This name is to take effect at the close of the semicentennial celebration next meeting."

The Board Minutes of one year later, Oct. 1899 page 440 read: "A communication was received from the Ben Milam chapter No. 8 of the Daughters of the Republic of Texas touching the change of the name of Austin College."

On the pending question of the change of name of Austin College, the role was called for votes on change to "Stephen Austin College," and the following vote was recorded: Ayes; Russell, Brownson, Aldrich, Wilson, Roberts, Hutton, Fullcnwider, McMurry, Moseley, Butte (by proxy) Wiggins, French; Nays-Wharton (by proxy) Moore (by proxy) absent Scott and Ralston.

The motion to change the name to "Stephen Austin" received affirmatively the votes of three-fourths of all the Trustees, and the name of Austin College was changed to Stephen Austin College. (This action was completely ignored by the succeeding Board)

It was Jan. 17, 1906 before the matter of changing the name of Austin College cropped up again. Relatives of Stephen F. Austin—the Bryan and Perry families (four nephews) desired to perpetuate his name by endowing "The Stephen F. Austin Fellowship in History" and one of them, Guy M. Bryan, Jr. placed in his will a legacy of his 11,000 acre ranch in Brazoria County. However they exacted a letter from the Secretary of the Austin College Board of Trustees to Col. Guy M. Bryan "That there was no likelihood of ever changing the name of Austin College."

The possibility of a move from Sherman to Dallas came in 1910 when that city was seeking an institution of higher learning. The Board Minutes of April 10, 1910, page 599, state that further consideration by the trustees committee was abandoned when the offer of the Dallas Chamber of Commerce was found to be unattractive and of insufficient financial inducement.

The depression at the close of the seventh decade ended Synod's support of Daniel Baker College and closed Texas Presbyterian College at Milford. Daniel Baker College was given to the city of Brownwood and the meager assets of T.P.C.

transferred to Austin College, the graduates of that institution thereby becoming affiliates of Austin College. In this manner the possibility of a change of name and location was avoided.

The attempt of a small group at a called meeting of Synod in Austin in Dec. 1932 to close the college failed because there was no way to liquidate its indebtedness — saved by debt.

However, a decade later, after the campus mortgage was liquidated and all external debts paid, two fruitless attempts were made at Synod's meetings to merge Austin College with Trinity University. Some give credit to the Japanese attack at Pearl Harbor for quashing the first attempt, and a tie vote by Synod at Ft. Worth decided the second.

When these two attempts failed, the Hulen Black scheme to close Austin College at Sherman and to establish a Presbyterian College adjacent to the University of Texas at Austin was pushed vigorously by a determined group, mostly from Austin. At Synod's meeting Sept. 1, 1943 (see minutes of the Synod of Texas Vol. VIII No. 4, 1943, (p.p. 212, 216). This idea drew little support but considerable tension and delayed the financial campaign by Synod for support of all of its institutions. Mr. Black publicised it as "A Bold Step Forward" and similar to the Thomas Jefferson Plan.

Thus, after ten years (1840-1849) of search for a location and a charter (1849), Austin College in 1970 enters Decade Thirteen on its "Search for the Summit." Judge Francis Charles Hume, an 1859 graduate, addressed the Alumni Association at Austin College in Sherman June 3, 1903 "On The Great Stride Upward of the Men and Events in Austin College History." In this hour long speech he alluded to efforts to rename the College:

> I have heard with surprise of some suggestions to change the name of this institution. I pray leave of speech upon that theme. In 1849 Austin College was chartered. That was over half a century nearer than we are now to the imposing and heroic period of our history — and so, with pride and love, and as if it were a benediction, the name of him whom men called the "Father of Texas," was bestowed upon the infant institution, and not without honor, it has borne that name for fifty-four years. The name is part of its life,

and with it are interwoven its traditions, its ideals —
and, more than all, the interest and love of the people
of Texas. Take the name away and half the significance of the birth, the history and the hopes of the
College is lost. No Texas institution can safely break
any link in the chain that binds it to the glorious past
— and the less so when the link is the golden one of
Austin's name. My friends, there is magic in the great
names, and immortal events that distinguish Texas
from the very dawn of her history. Let me, in conclusion, revive your memory of some of these. . . .(Austin
College Quarterly, Vol. 2, No. 2, p. 10).

## The Best Today is Not Good Enough for Tomorrow

THE cause of education, though delayed, was not to be neglected altogether, and the task fell to individual educators. Recognized as one of the outstanding teachers of the
State, Hugh Wilson, in 1840, threw his personal powers into
this field and built up one of the most efficient private schools
in the Republic at Prospect, a rapidly growing community.

With the return of Daniel Baker to Texas in 1849, the cause
of Presbyterian education was speedily revived. At Presbytery that fall a committee consisting of Daniel Baker, Hugh
Wilson, and W. L. Gresham reported in favor of a site near the
center of the State's population, preferably at Huntsville, and
recommended inviting Dr. Samuel McKinney, of Holley
Springs, Mississippi, to aid in founding the school and become
its president. This report was adopted. After communication
with the citizens of Huntsville, it was found that they were
most agreeable to the plan; showing their interest by subscrib-
in $8,000, and by overturing Presbytery to give the name of
Daniel Baker to the institution. This honor Daniel Baker declined, and Presbytery chose the name of Austin College in
honor of Stephen F. Austin, the father of Texas.

A few weeks later, October 13, 1849 in Hugh Wilson's study,
a called meeting of Presbytery received a report of the committee which had drawn up a charter for the college. Some
wished to postpone the matter until the brethern from the

western part of the State might be present. But Daniel Baker, in characteristic decisiveness, insisted that "postponement will be a death blow, for the legislature meets biennially, and if we do not get a charter at the coming session of legislature, we cannot get it for two years." Accordingly a charter was adopted and a committee was appointed to present it to the Legislature. With two amendments by that body, it was signed by Governor Wood, November 22, 1849. The physical resources of the college were pitifully small, but its intangible assets, represented by the hopes, the faith and the courage of its founders were amazingly large.

Hugh Wilson was elected to the first Board of Trustees, and this Board met in Huntsville for the first time April 5, 1850 — just ten years from the first proposal for founding a college made in his church by the first meeting of Brazos Presbytery.

The two other ministers of the charter Trustee group were Rev. James Weston Miller, pastor of the Houston Presbyterian Church and Daniel Baker himself. The Presbyterian elders on the Charter Board were Daniel D. Atchison, of Galveston; Andrew Jackson Burke, of Houston; Dr. George Clark Red, of Washington on the Brazos; Judge Abner S. Lipscomb of Gay Hill; Joseph M. McCormick of Columbia; Dr. John Branch, Joseph Wade Hampton, and John Hume of Huntsville. The other charter members of this Board were J. Carrol Smith, a Baptist and Sam Houston, first and third President of the Republic of Texas, later to become a Baptist; Anson Jones, fourth and last President of the Republic, and Robert Smither; Episcopalians and Henderson Yoakum, Texas historian, who was a Methodist.

Dr. Wm. S. Red, first graduate to enter the ministry, son of a charter trustee and himself a later trustee said:

> The responsibility of Trustees who lay the foundations of an institution is so notable that all successors should honor the memory of those into whose labors they have entered.

Only the loyalty, persistence, patience and self-sacrifice of its sturdy trustees kept the College in its early days from going the way of many similar undertakings in the State; for, of the one hundred and thirty five schools chartered by the Texas

Legislature prior to 1861, Austin College is the only one to survive the Civil War and to continue its existence to the present time.

The Board of Trustees adopted almost the exact curriculum offered by time honored Princeton University. The two-fold purpose of the College was set forth as: (1) To offer an opportunity for the young men of Texas to obtain an education, (2) To give suitable training for Presbyterian ministers.

The emphasis in the solicitation for operating funds and endowment for the College was most often placed on the second of these objectives and Daniel Baker was very diligent in his travels and speeches to this approach.

> "The one idea of the founders, that for which they wept, and prayed, and toiled, and gave their means, was that it might be an institution wherein there might be raised up for Texas, generation after generation, a native ministry."

And yet, in spite of this chief objective, so often heralded in the churches and church courts, it was over thirty years before Austin College turned out one minister of the gospel. The first were Wm. Stuart Red and James I. McCullough, the entire graduating class of 1882, both licensed to preach in 1884. Of the next sixty graduates half entered the ministry. At Huntsville the College had granted 27 B. A. degrees, six M.A. dedegrees, and six Law degrees but not a graduate chose the ministry. After moving to Sherman in 1876, law gave way to the ministry, medicine and teaching, and at last the College had attained its two primary goals. President-Elect Rev. Rufus Bailey, D. D. said in his inaugural address; just ten years after the College was founded:

> We will ever keep before the minds of the youth who may resort here for instruction, that the founders and early friends of Austin College were religious men — men of prayer, whose liberal charities came warm gushing from souls who waited daily in devotion at that throne whence issues the streams of divine love, and the light that shines with exceeding brightness on the evil and on the good. The history of Austin College shows that it was the child of prayer, and traces its paternity to praying men.

I but state a historical fact when I say that Presbyterians plant the Church and the Schoolhouse wherever they emigrate, wherever they abide. Wherever, in a new country, "they lift up the axe mightily upon trees," there the log cabin, the meeting house, and the school house spring forth from the forest, and are raised in succession by the first labors of their hands. They do not wait to become rich before they contribute to these objects; they contribute to these objects that they may be rich. Everywhere and always, they have been the liberal patrons of learning, the unflinching advocates of an open Bible, of religious liberty, a separation of Church and State, and universal toleration. Hence, in the organization of this College, as of all their Schools and Colleges, intended to unite a general patronage, the only claim they have asserted is for an open Bible and an exposition of the great principles of morals as there defined.

When we speak of Austin College as founded in prayer by religious men, and for religious education, we do not mean that it is, or was, designed to be other than a Literary Institution; but certainly for the cultivation of the mind in all its powers, faculties and relations, laws, responsibilities and obligations. The cultivation, then of the moral sense, of the religious element of our nature, which holds us to the Throne of God, must be essential to a well-balanced mind, and necessary to secure its efforts in the right direction. We hold that the education of a human being should be adapted to his entire constitution and suited to the whole duration of his being. The cultivation of the intellect, ruled and controlled by his passions, would make him worse than before. The affections, left without the influence of a well instructed judgment, would mistake their proper objects. The mind and heart, then, must be suitably disciplined, and taught to act in harmony and correspondence.

Here we take our stand. We demand for our sons an education on religious principles; an education which seeks first and always to correct the moral disorders of the heart, and then to give knowledge, vigor and activity to the mental energies, restrained by the centripetal force on an enlightened and tender conscience. Youth cannot be adequately controlled by any other discipline. An enlightened and educated conscience secures a ready subjection to good laws. Intellect, cultivated at the expense of the moral sense, gives power to do evil with no corresponding restraint. Hence the schools which have been best sustained in this country have ever been those organized under religious supervision and controlled by religious men.

For Austin College, founded by the labors of Presbyterians — organized, watched and watered under the supervision of the Synod of Texas — a monument of their zeal and pious effort in the cause of learning, we claim that its entire construction has been made with reference to a wholesome religious influence in the education of our youth. We do not teach Presbyterianism, but we do seek to lead the minds of our young men to "fear God and keep his commandments" -- to feel their obligations to God as the only security to fidelity in their duties to men. We desire it to be distinctly understood that the young men, who are educated here, have been made to feel a religious influence by "line upon line and precept upon precept." When we cannot occupy this ground, we shall retire from the labors of education, believing that all we can do without it would be worse than nothing.

The religious aspects of this College, then, and the objects at which we aim are patent and palpable. While we enforce no dogmas, and seek to instill no creed, we do seek to educate our youth religiously. The Bible is installed as a text-book — that is our creed — God's written constitution for the government of our race, the great moral code of the universe, the revealed will of the King of Kings. We educate our sons to read it, to value it, to have it.

In our theory, then, the basis of all sound education lies in the parallel and coincident training of the mind and heart, of the intellect and moral sense, not neglecting a physical discipline that will present the "mens sana incorpore sano." In Texas, however, where our youth live so much out of doors, and are early attracted by the hunt and the chase with horse and hound — where they are conversant with the wide-spread paternal acres, and where an ordinary neighborhood of families embraces a territory equal in area to a common principality of the old world, a healthy constitution of physical habits naturally fostered, renders attention to physical discipline less a matter of definite education. Yet even here we encourage athletic exercises in the campus and gymnasium, suited to the leisure hour and intervals of study. Our principal labor, however, lies in leading to mental application, acquisition and discipline.

This, then, is our introduction to a new era in the history of Austin College. With the lights of past experience, an improved and improving conditions of our finances, a faculty devoted exclusively to the duties of the recitation and lecture-room, we need only the material, rough-hewn, on which to try our hand and prove our skill."

Dr. Bailey summed up his inaugural address by saying that if the faculty and students worked together with heart, mind and soul on these aims and these goals in the "Search for the Summit" a mark of greatness would be the reward. Let our motto ever be "The Best Today Is Not Good Enough For Tomorrow."

# CHAPTER II

# The Men Who Made Austin College

## The Charter Trustees

### DANIEL DENNISON ATCHISON

DANIEL D. Atchison (April 7, 1820-December 23, 1898) was born in Fayette County, Kentucky, four miles from Lexington. He was the son of John and Elizabeth Atchison, who both died in 1833, leaving the boy an orphan. He was educated at Center College, Danville, Kentucky, and at the Harvard Law School, from which he graduated with the class of 1844. He returned to Lexington, Kentucky, and opened his law office. There he practiced his profession until 1846, when he decided to move to Texas. Arriving in Texas, May 1, 1846, he settled in Galveston, and became the partner of William Alexander; some years later he became associated with George W. Brown, United States District Attorney.

Atchison took little hand in politics, but from the time of his arrival in Texas was an admirer of Sam Houston, and stood with him in his views on most of the public matters of his time. He was one of the "Old Guard," who formed Houston's personal escort at the time of the celebrated speech at Tremont Hotel in 1861.

Atchison practiced law in Galveston for a long time, and during this time he filled several positions of public trust, the longest of these services being that of clerk of the Supreme Court of Texas for twelve years. Scholar and linguist that he was, he never sought distinction on the public platform, nor in print, for he preferred a quiet life devoted to professional duties.

Mr. Atchison was editor of the *Galveston Standard*, which at times was a strong Sam Houston backer. He campaigned in Texas and New York State to get Houston nominated for the Presidency of the U. S. in 1860 (*New York Herald, May 30, 1860*) He was a regular contributor to the budget of Austin College and after the death of Henderson Yoakum did much of the legal work in land sales for the College.

On January 20, 1847, he was married to Frances Alexander, daughter of J. R. Alexander, of Woodford, Kentucky. She died at Galveston in July of 1847, and in 1863, Atchison married Lucy Holt, of August, Georgia. He was a deeply religious man, and served as elder of the First Presbyterian Church of Galveston for many years. See Lewis Publishing Company, *History of Texas, with Biographical History of Houston and Galveston* (1895), pp. 716-718.

D. D. Atchison and another elder, S. D. C. Abbot, and Rev. J. W. Miller, were appointed a committee by Presbytery and by authority of the Board of Trustees to secure the legislature's approval of the charter. They rode horseback to Austin to obtain this and the charter was signed by Governor Wood on the 22nd day of November, 1849.

Mr. Atchison was also interested in free public schools and was the moving spirit in establishing the Atchison Free School at Navasota.


## JOHN BRANCH

DR. John Branch came to Texas from Virginia soon after he completed his medical education. He was a graduate of Hampden Sydney, class of 1840. He began his practice in Huntsville in 1847. His wife was a principal of the Huntsville Brick Academy. He served on the first executive committee of the Board with Henderson Yoakum and Robert Smither till June 21, 1852, when J. Carroll Smith was added and the four served until February 23, 1853. On June 27, 1853, Dr. Branch, Sam Houston and Yoakum became the Executive Committee. It was the Action of this Committee in calling a meeting of the

Board of Trustees that caused Rev. Samuel McKinney to resign the Presidency.

Dr. John Branch, on registering as a delegate to the Whig
Party Convention at Huntsville in 1848, recorded that he owned lands to value of $600, had five slaves and was a physician
fifty two years old. There were only twelve delegates, three
doctors, three merchants, one lawyer, one farmer and four
craftsmen; the Whig Party being very small in Texas. (*Southwestern Historical Quarterly* (Vol. 73, No. 1, July 1969, p. 33)

Col. G. W. Rogers, one of the merchants, donated five acres
of land for the college campus. (Lane, J. J., *History of Education in Texas*, U. S. Bureau of Education Circular No. 2, p. 89)

Dr. Branch and General Sam Houston were neighbors and
cordial friends, although at opposite poles politically. Senator
Sam Houston said during the campaign of 1848: "There are
but six men belonging to the Whig Party in Texas, one of
whom was a horse thief, another a black-leg, a third a land
grabber, and the other three mere tools of the first three
named, ready to do their bidding at all times for a glass of grog
or an old suit of clothes." (*Galveston Civilian* and *Galveston
Gazette*, Aug. 17, 1848).

Dr. Branch was on the original committee with Henderson
Yoakum, J. Carroll Smith, John Hume and Robert Smither
to raise subscriptions for the College at Huntsville. He
pledged only $20 but the other four pledged $100 each. The
subscriptions amounted to $10,000 and five acres of land.
All five were then made charter trustees.


## ANDREW JACKSON BURKE

QUOTING from the Alumni Record edition of the *Austin
College Quarterly*, July 1903:

### HON. A. J. BURKE
### THE PASSING OF THE LAST OF THE FATHERS

The session of Brazos Presbytery held in Washington, June
21st, 1849, transacted an item of business, the full effect of
which is not yet appreciable, after the lapse of more than half
a century. The report of the committee on the location of
Austin College was adopted and the institution decreed for

Huntsville. On another notable date, April 5, 1850, the Board
of Trustees convened in Huntsville and set the machinery in
motion. This was an immortal band of heroes. Just think for
a moment of the significance of the very conception of a high
grade college for Texas, away back yonder in the fifties! —
with desperadoes galore, Mexicans sullen, Indians rampant,
and even our Federal government offish! What were the
prospects?

One by one has this body passed from the stage of action.
Daniel Baker, J. Branch, Sam Houston, J. W. Miller, G. C.
Red, J. C. Smith, R. Smither, H. Wilson, H. Yoakum — until
one sole survivor remained in the person of the late Andrew
Jackson Burke, reputed to be the oldest man in Houston,
when the summons finally came to him to join the silent majority on March 22, 1903.

Of his career it behooves Austin College to take more than
a passing notice. The following items are compiled from
an article which appeared in the *Houston Post* of March 23,
1903: Mr. Burke was born October 10, 1813, in Giles County,
Tennessee, the seventh son of Benjamin and Drucilla Burke.
He spent his boyhood amid scenes which at that time constituted an almost unbroken wilderness. The death of his
father in 1830 threw him on his own resources. Inspired by
the same resolution that doubtless led Houston and Austin
and Crockett into the great unknown west, he started for
Vicksburg as his first objective point. Following the mercantile business here and at Amsterdam for several years with
some acquisition of property, he was attracted to the newly
formed republic across the great river. So, selling his interests
in Mississippi, he came to San Augustine in the spring of
1837. In the fall of this year he married Miss Eloise Lusk,
daughter of Mr. George V. Lusk, who had the year before
moved with his family from Alabama. She died in 1886.
Thirteen children were the result of this union, only three
of whom are living; Hon. Frank S. Burke, a prominent member of the Houston bar; Mr. Edmund L. Burke, a railway
engineer; and Mrs. Annette Bringhurst, wife of Prof. George
Bringhurst of Houston.

Shortly after his marriage he moved to Houston and again
embarked in the mercantile business. For fifty years he was
thus engaged, sometimes with a partner, sometimes without,

amassing independent property and exhibiting public spirit in various enterprises of his fellow townsmen. He served two terms as County Commissioner, one term as Mayor of Houston, and was for some time a member of the Board of Directors of the Houston and Texas Central Railroad.

Mr. Burke was a Democrat of the old type, an ardent admirer of General Andrew Jackson, for whom he received his name. He united with the Presbyterian church early in life and cast his lot in with the First Presbyterian Church in Houston in 1843. Two years later he was ordained and installed elder in that church. He became a Mason in 1844 and at the time of his death was one of the oldest members of the organization in the State.

But that for which he will longest be remembered by the friends of Austin College is the fact that he served the institution so promptly and so faithfully in those early days. Dark, uncertain and appalling were those days. Political conditions were discordant; society disintegrated; the church in an almost infantile state; educational concerns merely projected into the future . . . —what could those old heroes have hoped for as they launched such a frail bark upon such a stormy main? But there was a master pilot and a dauntless crew at the oars! Read the ringing appeal of the revered Daniel Baker, Leader, as he made his first report, one of glowing success to his Board of Trustees! Mr. Burke and the others seem to have caught the enthusiasm, for those master workers builded more wisely than they knew. All honor to these intrepid pioneers! Fifty-three years attest the wisdom and permanency of their judgments. Subsequent generations have arisen to call them blessed.

Mr. Burke's epitaph may well be found in the words of the poet:

> His life was innocent: his riper age
> Marked with some act of goodness every day,
> And watched by eyes that loved him. Calm and
>     sage
> Faded his late declining years away;
> Cheerful he gave his being up and went
> To share the holy rest that waits a life well spent.

Mr. Burke was a consistent donor to Austin College, often

guaranteeing salaries of professors. He rarely missed trustee meetings and was one of three trustees who served on the Board from charter time until long after the College was established in Sherman—from 1849 until 1884. Three times he represented his Presbytery at the General Assembly of the Presbyterian Church U.S.

## JOSEPH WADE HAMPTON

MR. Wade Hampton was born July 7, 1813 in North Carolina. He graduated from Yale University with the M.D. degree. Returning to North Carolina, he bought a partnership in the paper "Carolinean" with Ashbel Smith who was the editor. Smith left for Texas in 1837 leaving the paper in the hands of Hampton who was appointed postmaster of Charlotte N.C. December 9, 1844. This appointment was a reward for his good job as editor of his paper *The Jeffersonian*. He resigned the partnership February 17, 1845 and returned to *The Jeffersonian*. He became widely known Democrat before he came to Texas, arriving at Montgomery, December 28, 1848, and at Huntsville, January 1, 1849. Both Hampton and his wife suffered from tuberculosis. His wife and two children were still in North Carolina when he was notified of a third daughter. Hampton obtained a job with the County Clerk and began to study Law. He wrote to Ashbel Smith at Galveston that he had joined the new organized Sons of Temperance and the Masonic Lodge of Huntsville. He also taught English at the Huntsville Male Academy. A cholera epidemic caused the death of a close friend, Tillet, which shook him emotionally and Daniel Baker became his friend.

Though the 1840's were horseback or boat days for travel, the lure of this new land of Texas was so great that men from every state in the union and for every conceivable reason were wending their way southwestward. Hampton came to win health and Daniel Baker to win souls—the travels of these two eventually brought them together in Huntsville.

On Aug. 1, 1849 Hampton wrote his wife Cynthia: "There is a protracted meeting (Presbyterian) to begin here tomorrow night by a Mr. Daniel Baker, one of the ablest ministers in the South. I trust he will do good."

Dr. Baker was delayed for a few days. On Aug. 10, 1849 he wrote his son: "Did you ever! rain, rain, rain! Streams swollen, bridges gone, the whole land flooded! I have had to 'rough it' indeed; with great difficulty I managed to reach this place on Sunday morning in time to preach, after riding until near nine o'clock the preceding night, and fourteen or fifteen miles in the morning. Many had given me out, yet we had a very large congregation and I never saw people more eager for preaching. I broached the idea of our locating a college here. People wonderfully in favor of it and will subscribe, as I am told, liberally. This meeting has been blessed with the conversion of a few souls, one of whom was Major W. Hampton."

The Minutes of the newly founded Huntsville Presbyterian Church reveal the inspiring power Baker had over men. In the space of three months Joseph Wade Hampton became the first convert in the First Presbyterian Church of Huntsville, ordained and installed an elder, made clerk of the session, delegate to Presbytery and charter trustee of Austin College. Page 2, the Minutes of August 13, 1849: "The Session consisting of Reverend Daniel Baker, and Sam A. Moore, only elder, met at the church and after examination received into full communion of the church Major Joseph W. Hampton. Concluded with prayer, Daniel Baker, Moderator."

"The session met at the church Monday August 20, 1849. Present as before. The following persons were received on examination: Mrs. Margaret I. Hume, Col. A. H. Cook, Mr. Flavius Taylor, Mr. Alex McCilvey. On motion the session agreed to recommend to the Presbytery, meeting Friday, Oct. 12, at Independence, that the name of the contemplated college, should it go into operation, be San Jacinto College. Concluded with prayer, Daniel Baker, Moderator."

The session records (page 3) read: Oct. 6, 1849: "This day after the sermon, Major Hampton and Colonel Abbot having been elected, were according to the forms of our church, ordained and installed ruling elders in the Huntsville Presbyterian Church.

Minutes of Nov. 19, 1849: "Major Hampton was appointed to represent the Church at Presbytery Meeting in Houston, Nov. 22. Daniel Baker, Moderator." Hampton's conversion and baptism by Daniel Baker led him to write his wife from Houston November 24, 1849: "I have enjoyed more substantial peace and happiness in the past two weeks than in all my life and I pray daily that the same peace and happiness might be give you and our children." (From *Life and Labor of Daniel Baker,* p. 388)

Hampton became assistant to the postmaster in Huntsville and Daniel Baker soon had Hampton actively engaged in church work. He moved to Austin in April 1850 to become editor of the *Texas State Gazette* at $15.00 per week and was appointed clerk of the Committee of Senate and House in August 1850, and clerk of the Legislature in October at a salary of $100 per month. He purchased a third interest in the *Gazette* in December 1851 and sent for his wife and children who joined him on June 11, 1851.

Hampton and his wife were charter members of the First Presbyterian Church of Austin, Texas, and he served on the Board of Austin Female Academy. He resigned from the Board of Trustees of Austin College in 1854 and died of tuberculosis June 14, 1855. Previously (June 5, 1849) he wrote his wife:

> We are to have a Grand Temperance Jubilee here on the 4th of July. It is estimated that there will be 600 Sons of Temperance from different parts of the States in the Procession and at least 6000 persons at the barbecue. I have been appointed to read the Declaration of Independence, and the famous General Sam Houston to deliver the oration. We will have a grand time of it.

Hampton was a close friend and strong supporter of Sam Houston and boosted Austin College in his paper. A typical example follows: *Texas State Gazette* (Austin), May 11, 1850, p. 1, Col. 2

## TO THE PUBLIC

> The Board of Trustees of the Austin College, avail themselves of this medium to inform the Public of their organization, and the pleasing auspices under which they have entered upon the task confided to their care.
> The object in founding this institution, is to afford the youths of this State the literary advantages en-

joyed at institutions in the older States, and thus obviated the necessity imposed upon parents, of sending their sons so far from home, at vast expense, and exposing them to climates more severe, and to modes of thinking different from their own.

With a view of accomplishing so desirable an object, the board have unanimously resolved to make the course of study, as extensive, and to require, in those receiving the honors of the institution, a proficiency equal to that of the most respectable Colleges of the older States.

While the Board have determined that the Alumni of this institution shall compare favorably with those of the most respectable institutions of the older States, they assure the public that a moral and religious influence will be thrown around the literature, in order that the heart, as well as the head, may be educated in that plastic and favorable season, (the morning of youth.) and thus become deeply imbued with those principles of rectitude and virtue taught in the Bible, which alone can sanctify all human attainments, and give them their permanancy, their usefulness, and their ornament.

A neat and commodious edifice will soon be erected, and when completed, the Faculty will be organized by the election of professors.

The College is located at Huntsville, a village distinguished for its healthy location, and the enterprise, intelligence, and morality of its inhabitants.

Here, fellow citizens, you may, in this great and growing State, by your generous contributions, and fostering influence, build up an institution of enduring usefulness, from which may emanate men of extensive literary attainments and virtuous principles, to ornament the public, private, and social walks of life.

And where was there ever a finer field or a larger demand for a host of young men of regenerated purified hearts, and well disciplined minds, young men of burning zeal and eloquence, whose love for doing good "many waters cannot drown, nor floods quench?"

Parents, your sons are fast ripening into manhood, and are demanding of you, with perhaps a silent, but thrilling eloquence, the opportunities to enable them to answer the demands, and realize the hopes of their country, in maintaining the honor and permanency of her glorious institutions. You will not, we hope, permit minds to remain uncultivated, which, under proper discipline, might prove an honor to their friends, a blessing to their country, and exert an influence, which like *a zone of mercy,* might be felt around our globe.

Whatever diversity of sentiments, professions, or pursuits there may exist in the members of the Board, there is perfect unanimity in this one, high holy enterprise, and we go forward, relying upon your co-operation fellow-citizens, in a matter which deeply interests every parent who has a son to educate, every friend of religion and letters, and every lover of his country.

SAMUEL McKINNEY,
President of the College, and of the Board, ex-officio.

H. YOAKUM, Sec. of the Board
*******************

### TRUSTEES

| | |
|---|---|
| Rev. Daniel Baker, D. D. | Dr. John Branch |
| J. McCormic | Sam Houston |
| John Hume | Anson Jones |
| Robert Smither | Rev. Hugh Wilson |
| A. S. Lipscomb | J. C. Smith |
| Rev. J. W. Miller | Joseph W. Hampton |

P.S. The Rev. D. Baker, D. D. is the general agent to solicit donations in money, books, etc., for the present, in the older States, and the Rev. J. W. Miller and the Rev. J. M. Beckton for this State.

While the College edifice is being erected, the President will aid the executive committee in carrying into successful operation the plans of the board, and also prepare such young gentlemen as may desire it, for entering the College classes as soon as they can be organized. Already a number of interesting youth are in a state of preparation, so that an elegant edifice, the necessary professors, and an interesting number of pupils prepared for membership may be expected in the course of two or three sessions.

## SAM HOUSTON

SAMUEL E. Asbury in his "The Amateur Historian" states: "One great way to solve a mystery is to study the lives of all participants, both before and after the event." Mystery surrounds the rise of a small-town, uneducated country Tennessee boy who loved to live with the Indians, to the governor's mansion of his State; eventually to become the cunning commanding general of an undisciplined army that routed an organized one ten times larger; chosen to be the first and third President of the Republic of Texas; elected Senator three times when Texas gained statehood and finally governor of a second state. In all history there is no parallel, no man who has written more or who has had more written about him than Sam Houston. A dozen writers have portrayed his "wine, women and wars" accomplishments, as well as his political successes. Eight huge volumes of his own letters and speeches and more than two dozen biographies do not fully solve the mystery. Somehow, though, the qualities of a self-taught teacher, lawyer, military genius, gifted orator and shrewd politician were blended to fulfill his destiny. One simply concludes that Samuel Houston was "A Man of Destiny" and "A Man for All Seasons."

How could this man leave a lovely bride in the governor's mansion to live with the Indians, taking one for a wife, establishing a wigwam and gaining citizenship among the tribe; abruptly leaving all to seek out a new career in a raw, rough frontier Mexican State? Brilliant in using men who chose to throw obstacles in his path to fame, he used them as stepping stones to accomplish his purposes without seeming to be ambitious. In a day he could fight a duel and pen a poem to a lady, or inspire a lady to write a poem about him. In a day he could deliver an oration or pen a letter that could end the political career of a politician and that same day write appealing letters to gain help for some friend or deserving person. A man whose only education was experience, yet a friend of presidents who enlisted his aid and sought his intuitive advice. Many brilliant men have become forgotten men rushed to oblivion by doing the right thing at the wrong time, but here was a man who rose to fame by doing the wrong thing at the right time. Even in his youth he had quit school to live with the Indians near his Tennessee home. He developed a love and trust for these people who always trusted him. Had he never left his wife and the governorship of Tennessee he might have become President of the U.S.A., but Texas would probably today just be another Mexican state. His retreat day after day before Santa Anna brought calumny, cries of cowardice and even "traitor" by those who desired premature battle before fateful "San Jacinto." The turn of events April 21, 1836 in less than an hour elapsed time—630 enemy dead, 730 prisoners, including General Santa Anna captured, a new republic—The Lone Star, in the making with a loss of only two lives and 23 wounded, including Houston himself, had a mark of destiny.

Houston's ancestry was definitely Presbyterian, as recently recalled in Huston's "Bold Journey." Marquis James infers that the Cherokee theology he gained from the Indians was responsible for the picturesque idioms of the Indian speech and the maxims of the headman which time never eradicated from Houston's vocabulary. Perhaps this was because Dr. William Hume, the Presbyterian minister who had united Houston and Eliza Allen in marriage had refused Houston the rites of baptism after their sudden separation. Rev. Obadiah Jennings, another Presbyterian pastor, also refused to baptize Houston for the same reason. While with the Indians, he protested to his friend, General Jackson, President of the United States, that he lacked "that evangelistic change of heart so absolutely necessary to a man to proclaim to a lost world the mediation of a blessed Saviour," before he could become a missionary to the Indians. James says: "Sam Houston joined the Catholic Church in 1833 because it was required by the Mexican government to obtain a land grant." This "Muldoon Catholicism" had no visible effect in any future actions of Houston.

Sam Houston was a man who made friends easily and enemies with like ability. He did make efforts to overcome this latter tendency and was sometimes successful. After he had fought one duel, he aided his wounded adversary and refused thereafter to accept at least ten other challenges on the grounds that he "didn't want their blood on his hands," or that "they would have to wait their turn as others were ahead of them." Angered at remarks of a U.S. legislator named

Stanberry, Houston was fined $500 for whipping Stanberry with a cane on the streets of Washington, D.C. (President Jackson remitted this fine.) Records show that Houston was challenged to a duel by Gen. Albert Sidney Johnston, Ex-President Mirabeau Lamar, Commodore Edwin W. Moore, Provisional President David G. Burnett, a Dr. Archer, Gen. Felix Huston and two Fisher brothers.

In his earlier life Houston was quite a drinker and his enemies referred to him as "Big Drunk." Houston gave up drinking in May 1840 when he married Margaret Lea. Soon thereafter he delivered the first temperance lecture in Texas, followed in later years by temperance talks at Boston, New York, Philadelphia and Washington.

Fortune brought Sam Houston and Daniel Baker together in the summer of 1849. Houston was back in Texas making temperance speeches and defending his position on national matters brought up in the previous senate meetings in Washington. He had been a U.S. senator from Texas since 1845.

Daniel Baker was back in Texas after ten years trying to organize a Presbyterian college. He wrote to his son from Huntsville August 10, 1849:

> "I had never before been in Huntsville, middle Texas, but having heard a favorable account I came here and held a protracted meeting and broached the idea of locating a college here. People wonderfully in favor of it and will subscribe, I am told, liberally. One gentleman of standing says he thinks 10,000 acres of land can be obtained and a large amount of money. And General Houston says that it would be a greater advantage to have a Presbyterian college located here than to have the place made the capitol of the State. God grant that I may be enabled to give a new and great impulse to the cause of religion and education." (*Life and Labours of Daniel Baker,* pages 390-391)

## SAM HOUSTON AND AUSTIN COLLEGE
### 1849-1863

Houston was placed in Class I of the charter Trustees at the first meeting of the Board in Huntsville early in 1850.

He had built a home called "Raven Hill" about seven miles from the College but he maintained an office very close to the campus. While away on senatorial duties in Washington, Henderson Yoakum shared that office as the two were law partners. The Yoakum home, "Shepherd Valley," was about nine miles away. Houston was present for the laying of the cornerstone of the first permanent building in June 1851. He held an umbrella over Dr. Samuel McKinney to protect him from the sun while President McKinney made the dedication address. A few weeks before this, through Henderson Yoakum, Houston had rented a small tract of land to McKinney on shares to raise a crop of corn. Failure on the part of McKinney to fulfill this agreement led to the handwritten letter printed below:

> At Home
> 1st Sept. 1851
>
> Dear Sir
>
> Until Col. Yoakum returns, I object to any more fodder being removed. It will not be injured in the field and I have much to say before its removal. So soon as I can this evening, I will be happy to call over, and see to (it) in Town or at the Schoolhouse.
>
> Professor McKinney        Your Friend
> Sam Houston

At the time of the Trustees meeting in June 1853, Houston, as Chairman of the Executive Committee of the Board, called a meeting of his committee to discuss the condition of the College. Dr. McKinney objected to the procedure of having an Executive Committee meeting when he could not be present, because of a previous commitment in Galveston. This led to Dr. McKinney's resignation as he felt that Sam Houston as Chairman of the Executive Committee of the Board had assumed Presidential duties. The whole matter was further aggravated when the husband of Houston's niece, Rev. N. A. Penland, was placed on the faculty of the College and put on trustee committees.

Houston, in the U. S. Senate on February 8, 1850 had used the striking phrase "A Nation divided against itself cannot stand:, (Abraham Lincoln used it eight years later, substituting only "house divided" in his campaign for senator).

Cedar Grove
1st Sept. 1857

Dear Sir.

Until Col. Saunders
returns, I object to any more
fodder being removed.
It will not be injured
in the field, and I have
much to say before it's removed
Val. As soon as I can this
evening, I will be happy to call
and see to in town
or at the Schoolhouse.

Professor                    Your Friend
E. B. Kenning-             Sam Houston

There is no doubt that Houston's oratorical ability was responsible for getting the issue settled quickly. It took only one session to hear Dr. McKinney's objection; accept his resignation; elect Daniel Baker President of the College and to appoint Rev. N. A. Penland President pro-tem until Baker returned to Texas.

Dr. McKinney returned to Alabama almost immediately and in October of that year Houston moved from Raven Hill to Independence. The whole incident had become more embarrassing to Houston when the Board of Trustees accepted the resignation of Prof. Penland after he had been dismissed as supply pastor of the Huntsville Presbyterian Church for "ardent use of spiritous liquors."

There were other irksome occasions for Houston that summer and fall of 1853. An exchange of letters between Houston and Guy M. Bryan, nephew of Stephen F. Austin turned out to be a battle of words. Enemies of Houston including Anson Jones had convinced Guy M. Bryan that Houston was partly responsible for the fatal illness of Stephen F. Austin when he was Houston's first Secretary of State. Bryan was convinced that his uncle Stephen F. Austin, would be alive and probably President of Texas if Houston had been his true friend. Houston finally tired of Bryan's questioning and insinuations and closed the matter by telling Bryan to name names or drop the matter which Bryan reluctantly did. (See Houston to Bryan, Nov. 15, 1852, May 1, Aug. 3, and Nov. 1, 1853, *Writing*, V. 364-69, 447, 454-55, 459-463.)

Anson Jones and Guy M. Bryan, both Episcopalians and busy trying to establish St. Paul's College at Anderson, had resigned or refused to serve as trustees of Austin College and one apparent reason was that they couldn't serve with Houston.

Houston was baptized at Rocky Creek November 1854 by Rev. Rufus C. Burleson, a Baptist minister, thereby joining his wife's church.

Houston's interest in Austin College was sustained by endowment of a scholarship, evidenced by a letter to the faculty in 1861, requesting that his grand-nephew, Samuel Penland, have the benefit of it. Previously he had enrolled Sam Houston, Jr., his oldest son, in the Preparatory Department of the College at the age of twelve.

Houston was again in Washington, D.C. when the Board met October 30, 1854, but voted proxy by Daniel Baker. At the January 23, 1858 meeting his proxy was J. Carroll Smith. Houston was a busy man that year, mending his political fences and preparing for the governor's race against incumbent Runnels (which he won by a considerable majority). Nevertheless, he attended the November 4, 1858 meeting of the Board and at this time made the College a loan of $2000 for much needed funds. (The Minutes of the Board meeting November 4, 1874 reveal that the College still owed Houston's heirs $1200.) At a called meeting of the Board in Galveston, Rev. R. H. Byers voted proxy for Houston, Busy in the governor's chair at the time of the next three meetings of the Board in 1859 and 1860, he entrusted his proxy vote to Joab H. Banton, first graduate of Austin College and later trustee from 1867 to 1874.

On the 25th of August 1861 from Huntsville, the deposed governor of Texas wrote:

> Huntsville
> 26th Aug 1861

To the Faculty of Austin College, Texas

Gentlemen
    You will please admit Samuel Penland a student of Austin College by virtue of a Scholarship held by me, until further orders

> I am Your
> Obt Servant
> Sam Houston

*(The original letter is in the Samuel Penland Collection of Letters now in the possession of the Rosenberg Memorial Library, Galveston, Tex. Reference to this letter on page 310 of Vol. VIII, "The Writings of Sam Houston" incorrectly transcribes Penland as Pintieno: Poor penmanship of Houston probably was the cause of a similar error by Andrew Jackson Stevens who transcribed Penland's name as Pentano (in the Barker Collection).*

*[handwritten letter]*

After being ousted from the governor's mansion Houston went to Huntsville and purchased "Steamboat House" which had been the home of the President of Austin College, Rev. R. W. Bailey. It was in this home that his last child was born and where he spent his remaining days surrounded by all of his family except young Sam, who was away at War in the Confederate Army.

When Houston read Lincoln's Proclamation that all slaves were free after January 1, 1863, he didn't wait; he immediately read the proclamation to his slaves, explained it and told them that they were free men and women at that moment. Previously while in office as President of the Republic and later while Governor of Texas, Houston refused to permit payments to bounty hunters of escaped slaves. He also forbade slave ships to traffic in Texas, though he owned twelve on which he placed a value of $10,500 in his will.

We find General Sam shortly before his death writing in the interest of an Austin College graduate to one of his severest critics and political enemies:

There is a young gentleman of this neighborhood, now a nurse in one of the hospitals in Richmond, whose name is James Harrison. He was wounded in his left hand in a night march, when he fell, and endeavoring to recover himself, his hand accidentally was on the muzzle of the gun, when it went off accidentally wounding him. It is the desire of his friends that he should obtain a discharge. It is understood, that he could obtain one if he could hire a substitute. If he is rendered unfit for service, it is but fair that he should receive his discharge. He has a servant there with him. Since he left home one of his negroes has killed another and run away. His mules on his plantation took a distemper and are nearly all dead. Mr. Harrison is a young gentleman who graduated at Austin College. He is of most respectable conexions. His uncle is a representative from Cherokee county in the Legislature; his brother-in-law Mr. Rhodes, sends him a certificate of deposit with Smith, Walker, & Company, of this place for $1,500. They are perfectly responsible gentlemen, and if needful may I ask you to have the kindness to aid him in negotiating the certificate. I will also write to Hon. P. W. Grey in relation to Mr. Harrison.

If it is convenient for you to send me some sketches of the debates in Congress and any other news, I would be much obliged to you.

I am truly your sincere friend,
Sam Houston

Huntsville Feb. 24, 1863

*Letter written to Hon. Williamson S. Oldham, Senator to the Confederacy from Texas, Proprietor of the Texas Gazette, a paper, unfavorable at one time to Houston. They later became friends. Houston's letter was in behalf of James S. Harrison who had received the A.B. degree in 1856 and the A.M. degree in 1859.)*

General Houston also made loans to the College and to the Finance Committee to tide it over the Civil War crisis. At the time of his death these loans amounted to several thousand dollars, according to his will. The debt was partially settled by payment to his heirs. The Board of Trustees Minutes of June 1875 record that the College "still owes $600 on the Sam Houston note, a part of $8720 total debts."

Even Houston's closest friends often misjudged him. When he mentioned his attraction for Margaret Lea, Ashbel Smith and Barnard Bee in particular sought to convince Houston that his "temperament" was unsuited to the quiet of married life. Col. Bee wrote Houston: "In view of your terrific habits, I implore you to resort to any expedient rather than marry." After the marriage Col. Bee wrote to Dr. Smith: "In all my acquaintance with life I've never met with an individual more totally disqualified for domestic happiness — he will not live with her six months." No man could have been more in error. Margaret gave him six daughters and two sons and never was there a more loyal and happy family. Col. Bee was killed at Manasses in 1863 and thus lived long enough to see his error. David Burnett, the Provisional President of the Republic, who had sent a spy into Houston's Military Advisory Group at San Jacinto, and who later challenged Houston to a duel, said before he died: "In my heart dwells no bitterness toward General Houston. He is a Christian, blest with a Christian lady with many fine children, while I am bereft and alone."

In his remaining retirement days Houston became reconciled to many old enemies and with young Sam off to the battle field, he said in March of 1863 on a visit to Houston, Texas, where to his surprise he was hospitably received: "Let us go forward, nerved to nobler deeds — Let us bid defiance to all the hosts that our enemies can bring against us. Can Lincoln expect to subjugate a people this resolved? No!"

Marquis says in "The Raven": "Many were the men from whom Sam Houston parted in anger but he hated as he loved, in hot blood, and with few conspicuous exceptions, bitterness lapsed on this side of the grave." Such was certainly true of Houston on his deathbed.

Even Guy M. Bryan, in Huntsville on a mission for the Confederacy, suddenly falling ill himself and learning of

Houston's need for certain medicine, generously shared his own remedy.

And Mrs. Anson Jones, whose suicide husband had so disliked Houston, learning from her son, Samuel Edward, at the battlefront that young Sam was wounded but safe, sent consoling word to the General and his wife. Anson Jones had given the name Sam Houston Jones to his first born, but because of Houston's political views and actions, friendship turned to enmity between them and Jones changed his boy's name to Samuel Edward Jones when the child was only eight years old.

When the time came for Houston to face his Maker, he sent for Dr. Kittrell and Rev. Samuel McKinney. Young Black Jeff, Houston's youthful slave, was dispatched fifteen miles to get Dr. Kittrell, a political adversary but also a friend and fellow trustee at Austin College. Rev. Samuel McKinney, now President of Austin College for the second time, was called to Houston's bedside. The family gathered around the couch and Dr. McKinney offered a prayer. He asked Houston how it was between him and his Maker and the General replied: "All is well, all is well." He died at sunset July 26, 1863.

Houston had made his will April 2, 1863, reflecting his confidence and dependence upon many of his fellow Board members. His executors included J. Carroll Smith, charter trustee with him for 14 years, and Anthony M. Branch, then a trustee in place of his brother, Dr. John Branch, deceased. Houston listed among his assets a note from Austin College for $1,002.59; notes from Dr. P. W. Kittrell and several other Board members. It also included 20,000 acres of land valued at $60,910. (Vol. VIII, pp. 339-343 *Writings*)

In the cemetery at Huntsville, the monument that marks Houston's resting place rises in splendor amidst towering oaks, The front bears the inscription of Andrew Jackson's tribute to him: "The World Will Take Care of Houston's Fame."

The inscription on one side of Houston's monument reads:

A Brave Soldier, A Fearless Statesman, A Great Orator, A Pure Patriot, A Faithful Friend, A Devoted Husband and Father, A Loyal Citizen, A Consistent Christian, An Honest Man.

To this could be added truthfully, A Champion of Education.

A memorial page recalling Houston's continuous loyal devotion to the College was placed in the Minutes of the Board of Trustees, Vol. 1, page 158 on November 3, 1863. A resolution of the Texas House of Representatives, and speech of Joab H. Banton, the member from Walker County was ordered to be transcribed and forwarded to Mrs. Houston. Joab Banton was the first graduate of Austin College, in 1854, and received the first law degree in 1856. He was a witness to Houston's will made April 2, 1863 and testified to its authenticity when filed on August 17, 1863. He began his speech with: "General Sam Houston is no more. A great man has fallen. Texas' most distinguished citizen has ceased to exist among us and it is but fitting and just that we give expression to that deep feeling of regret which pervades the whole country in consequence of its bereavement—We might say of Texas, that she was his handiwork—and as long as her glorious history is read, the name of Houston will be honored and revered and his noble deeds emulated by a grateful people."

Wm. Carey Crane, in his "Life of Sam Houston" page 237, erroneously states that Houston "conversed freely on his soul's welfare with Rev. Cockrell, pastor of the Huntsville, Presbyterian Church." The pastor of the church was Rev. John Morton Cochran, who succeeded Rev. Rufus W. Bailey, the supply pastor of the church and retired President of Austin College. Rev. Bailey died suddenly April 26, 1863, exactly two months before Houston's death. It was Rev. Samuel McKinney, President of the College, who attended Houston's bedside at the time of his death. (See M. K. Wisehart's "Sam Houston—American Giant," page 650; or Marquis James' "The Raven" page 432.)

Houston's death occurred in the midst of the Civil War when the South was fighting gloriously. Three days after his death E. H. Cushing, Editor of the Houston, Texas, *Tei-Weekly Telegraph,* printed "An Editorial Appreciation of Houston:"[1]

[1] From the *Tri-Weekly* (Houston) July 29, 1863

E. H. Cushing served on the Board of Trustees of the College from 1869 until the College was moved to Sherman in 1876; and it was in his newspaper office that the Trustees finalized this move.

It is with deep and heartfelt sorrow that we announce the death of General Sam Houston. It took place at his residence in Huntsville, on the 26th inst.

Thus has passed away one of the great men of the age. Say what we may of General Houston, we can but accord to him the merit of having filled his full share of the history of the last forty years. His life has been a remarkable one, — whether as Governor of Tennessee when he was but a little over thirty years of age, as chief of the Cherokees, or as hero of the Texas revolution, or still later in the political arena of these last past years, he has always occupied a high place in the public consideration.

What were the springs of action in his mind; who dare undertake to tell? What drove him when he was on the high road to fame and the enjoyment of life, the Governor of a great State, the idol of a great people, to cast himself loose from them all and plunge into the wilderness of the West to become the companion of savages? What led him afterwards, reinstated in the paths of civilization, the honored Senator of another great State, and the beloved idol of its people, again to cast himself loose from their convictions of right, and in defiance of their feelings yield his assent to the designs of their enemies? Who can tell. Whatever it was, the ease with which he regained the confidence of his fellow-citizens, both these instances, is among the most remarkable incident of history.

After being lost for years in the wilderness, he revisited Tennessee, and was received with the most flattering attentions by the whole people. He entered Texas, twenty years later, denied his seat in the Senate, cast off by many who had always before voted for him, he, only two years later, took the field again against a powerful and well-organized party, and again the people flocked to his support, and by an overwhelming vote made him their Governor. Such power over men is unquestionably the most remarkable trait of his character.

To write a history of the life of Sam Houston is not our part. His history is too well known to make it necessary. We pity the heart that could now conceive evil of him. His noble qualities will ever stand out clear before the people.

So, let us shed tears to his memory, tears that are due to one who has filled so much of our affections. Let the whole people bury with him whatever of unkindness they had for him. Let his monument be in the hearts of those who people the land to which his later years were devoted. Let his fame be sacredly cherished by Texans, as a debt not less to his distinguished services than to their own honor of which he was always so jealous, and so proud.

E. H. Cushing

Perhaps the sincerest tribute of all came from the pen of Houston's niece, Phebe G. Moore Penland:

From P. G. Penland to Uncle Sam,

### A WISH FOR SAM HOUSTON

Not the victor's wreath above,
On the field of battle won
But the peace the pure possess
And the pure in heart alone.
Not the name of mighty deeds
In the high career of life
But a heart at peace with heaven
Though surrounded by with strife
And a crown of fadeless light
In the regions of the blest
Where the wicked trouble not
And the weary are at rest.

The original poem is in the "Sam Penland Collection"[2] at the Rosenberg Library in Galveston, Texas. Samuel M. Penland wrote that he obtained his mother's poem from Marion Williams, granddaughter of Houston, on August 8, 1910.

#### A SHRINE FOR SAM HOUSTON

*Life and times of dynamic frontier soldier and states-man depicted for public in two homes and museum at Huntsville*

AMONG the pine-clad hills of historic Huntsville, just 70 miles north of Houston on Highway 75, stands a shrine dedicated to a remarkable pioneer, soldier, and statesman—

---

[2]The *Galveston Daily News* of July 30, 1922, page 5, erroneously states that Penland's mother was the sister of Sam Houston (his mother was a daughter of Houston's sister).

Sam Houston. Here, in the buildings and on the grounds which once served as home for Houston, his wife, and their eight children, has been assembled a collection of items which reflect Houston's active life and his service to state and country.

Now, the old home place of the Houston family, just across the highway from the Sam Houston State Teachers' College in Huntsville, Texas, is the Sam Houston Shrine. Included are a fine museum with many exhibits and collections of early Texas; Houston's original family home, built in 1847; his old law office; and a restoration of the log kitchen in which the Houston family meals were prepared. The old "Steamboat House" to which Houston retired after serving as governor of the state in 1861 was moved across town in 1936 to become part of the shrine. Gifts from the Houston family have made it possible to provide most of the rooms with original furniture and personal belongings.

Steamboat House had been the Austin College home of Dr. Rufus W. Bailey, President of the College to which General Sam Houston gave the last fourteen years of his life in service as charter trustee on its Board.

He died at Sunset, July 26, 1863, and was buried in the cemetery at Huntsville. Surrounded by the tombstones of many of the fellow trustees who preceded him in death is the graceful monument that bears the inscription of Andrew Jackson's tribute to him: "The World Will Take Care of Houston's Fame."

## JOHN HUME

JOHN Hume was born August 1, 1802, in Culpepper County, Virginia. He moved first to Mississippi then to New Orleans where he was one of the first elders in the Lafayette Presbyterian Church (1843). Six years later we find him a prosperous farmer at Huntsville, and a charter member of the Austin College Board of Trustees. There was no more faithful attendant at the meetings of the Board than he. A perpetual scholarship is still treasured as an heirloom by the family. True to the faith of his fathers, he was a Presbyterian until his death in 1864. His death was memorialized in the Minutes of the Board of Trustees on the same page with that of Sam Houston (Board Minutes, p. 158).

*In the Sam Houston Museum, seen through archway, are rare reminders of the man who was U. S. Senator, governor of Tennessee and of Texas, twice president of the Texas Republic, Charter Trustee of Austin College.*

## ANSON JONES

And what of Anson Jones? Third and last man to become President of the Republic of Texas, he occupied a very important role in the history of Texas. Yet when statehood was obtained his political life was abruptly ended due to his own arbitrary and contentious claims. From that day he was destined to disappointment, overlooked at the ballot box, blaming Houston for lack of support, jealousy offended by the success of what he termed "were less worthy men," he withdrew from public affairs "seeking only the *plow* and the *pen* and the *scalpel*" to prevent oblivion.

Anson Jones came to Texas a failure in every thing he previously had attempted. Arriving at the mouth of the Brazos in October 1833 at the age of 35, he almost did not start a new life in Texas. A few days inspection of Brazoria seaport which, if he remained was to be his home, held no appeal and he wanted no part of it: "I forthwith engaged my passage back to New Orleans on the return trip of the vessel I came in." He had in his wallet just two dollars more than the price of return passage. That he missed the boat was definitely the good fortune of Texas. He opened his medical office and in his own words: (page 10 of his private Memoirs) "I devoted myself exclusively and earnestly to business and soon had to ride over a space of 20 to 40 miles in each direction from Brazoria." Jones prospered and by 1835 we find him "an anxious observer of the political life of my adopted country." He bacame interested in organizing Masonic lodges and in advocating steps for Texas Independence from Mexico. Events transpired quickly — on March 1836 Dr. Jones enlisted as a private for the duration of the war of independence. He was with Houston's Army, a private in the medical corp at the Battle of San Jacinto. Thirteen years later, Jones wrote twenty pages (57 to 77) of the events leading up to the battle and the battle itself with very little but condemnation and condescension for Houston. After the battle, Jones became surgeon general and medical purveyor of the Army. Later, Provisional President Burnett confirmed his appointment with the title "Apothecary General." He accompanied twice wounded Houston and Santa Anna down the Bayou to Galveston Island. (Anson Jones "Republic of Texas")

Very soon thereafter Anson Jones began his political career. Elected from Brazoria district September 4, 1837 he took his seat at the called meeting of the Second Congress, September 25, 1837. In the House Jones was soon successfully battling for a procedure for examining and licensing all persons qualified to practice medicine; means for the establishment of a general and uniform system of education, under the control and direction of Congress; and dedication of public lands for the ultimate endowment of a University.

During Houston's two year term as President of the Texas Republic Jones and Vice President Mirabeau Lamar organized the Philosophical Society of Texas and were elected vice president and president respectively modelled after Franklin's American Philosophical Society. Under authority of the Masonic Order of Louisiana he began organizing Masonic lodges wherever he could find sufficient interest.

Dr. Anson Jones' biographer, Herbert Gambrell, states that "during the twenty-five years Jones had been a Texan he had been a leader of the independence struggle, an outstanding Congressman, ablest diplomat at Washington (So Calhoun said) in 1838-1839, senator and de-facto vice president of the Republic during part of Lamar's administration, Secretary of State, and, for the last two years of the Houston regime, de-facto President. Twenty one numbered paragraphs enumerated the achievements of his own brief presidency." And then oblivion!!

The *Texas Ranger* declared:

> And what of his reward? Rudely thrust aside in 1846, when he had . . . saved the country . . . Traduced and wounded, he retired to private life, where he has quietly remained ever since.

Not quite. He was elected a charter member of the Board of Trustees of Austin College in August 1849. And what did he do for Austin College? Nothing, absolutely nothing. He never attended a single meeting. His name is on two pages of the Austin College Minute Book. Page one lists his name as one of the original sixteen members of the Board. The June 20, 1852 records (page 20) reveals that the Prebytery has received a letter of resignation from Dr. Jones. One naturally asks why? What was Jones doing those two years? He had purchased a farm near Old Washington on the Brazos which he called "Barrington." Here he retired to write his "Private Memoirs" which he began June 28, 1849; and his "Republic of Texas" which were published posthumously by Act of Congress in 1859.

Jones was also very busy trying to found St. Paul's College at Anderson, only a few miles from his plantation. In this latter project he was joined by another Episcopalian Texas pioneer, Guy M. Bryan, who also had been elected to the Austin College Board. Jones and Bryan had another thing in common, both of them held Sam Houston in disdain.

Lawrence L. Brown's "The Episcopal Church in Texas 1838-1874" (Page 257) shows that Anson Jones was lay delegate to the Diocesan Council from St. Paul's, Washington Church in 1851, 1852, 1853, 1854, 1855. The same author relates that Guy M. Bryan was a lay member of a committee to select a site, find a teacher, and put a school into operation. (p. 54) This Dr. Jones and Guy M. Bryan materially aided and St. Paul's College was opened at Anderson, Texas January 1852 tho it was not chartered until February 4, 1853. The College was doomed from beginning. Anderson was a very small community, mostly Catholics and almost geographically isolated. Attempts to move the school first to Austin and later to Brenham failed and it closed its doors.

Gambrell in "Anson Jones" page 422 states: "He had been a trustee of St. Paul's College at Anderson—had contributed heavily to the college, helped draft its charter, had sent his sons there. He had made an appeal for its support at the Triennial Convention of the Church in New York, but support had not come. He had allied himself with a small and unpopular sect that the unecclesiastical Texans confused with the Catholics. The College withered and died. It was regretable—but the doctor had seen so many things he was connected with wither and die."

Jones was to suffer two more great disappointments. When Sam Houston chose to run for the governorship of Texas in 1857, he felt hopeful of being selected to take Houston's place in the Senate. The *Austin State Gazette* published the following from a citizen who "deemed it not inappropriate to suggest Anson Jones as the logical successor to Houston, and to point out that the General, jealous of Jones' intellect and business capacity . . . had publicly defamed and slandered him . . . which, by-the-way, is one of the best evidence that we have of Jones' purity."

This was the only notice given to Jones support though he had come early to Austin with high hopes. When the legislature balloting began behind closed doors, after ten hours Chief Justice John Hemphill was chosen and Anson Jones got not a single vote. Unnoticed Jones packed his bags and started toward Barrington.

Back home he applied his energy disheartedly to the farm which was beginning to be a chore, and was delaying him in completing his writing efforts. The delay cost him the fame he secretly coveted, as Henderson Yoakum's comprehensive two volumes of "Texas History" were now off the press and acclaimed throughout the nation as a stupendous accomplishment. And the most unkind cut was that Henderson Yoakum had given great credit to Houston's part in it, quite at variance with the skimpy critical version by Jones.

All this was too much for Jones — failure and disappointments in his efforts at *politics, plow* and *pen* led him to reflect that at least in medicine he was a success. He quickly sold the plantation at a sacrifice and left Barrington to start medical practice anew at Galveston or Houston. At the old Capitol Hotel he received an encouraging letter from his wife: "I feel confident this little trip will be of service to you . . . I trust we will soon be together again . . . Blot out the past, forget you were engaged in the promotion of the best interest in Texas and above all, try to forget her ingratitude to you. I pray you will do this. . ."

Blot out the past and forget? This he could not do. He was old and weary and terribly tired. His heart was not in opening a medical office. Four days he brooded — no doubt he recalled the plight of other notable acquaintences, Grayson, Collingworth, Rusk, and Childress — all dead now — suicides.

Next morning — in the same hotel where the historian Henderson Yoakum had succumbed to his fatal attack of pnemonia they found Anson Jones with a bullet thru his head. A year later his faithful wife sent the bulky manuscript he had labored on so long to a New York publisher, and its 648 pages were printed without a single change.

# ABNER LIPSCOMB

A BNER Smith Lipscomb (February 10, 1789-November 30, 1856) was born in Abbeville District, South Carolina. His parents were natives of Virginia but had immigrated to South Carolina prior to the American Revolution, in which war the father fought. Young Lipscomb was educated in the common schools of his State, but had the advantage of studying law in the office of John C. Calhoun. Intimate association with that distinguished statesman was an important factor in the formation of the young man's character, and in the foundation of the profound professional learning which placed his name, in his later life, in the ranks of the distinguished jurists of Texas. He was admitted to the bar in 1811, and located at St. Stephens on the Tombigbee River in Alabama, where he successfully engaged in the practice of law. In 1812 he served in a campaign to suppress Indian hostilities fomented by England in the war of that year. Therefore he served as a member of the Territorial Legislature of Alabama. Upon the organization of the new state government in 1819, he was appointed Circuit Judge. In 1823, he was chosen Chief Justice of the Supreme Court of Alabama, in which position he served eleven years. He resigned this position in 1835 and removed to Mobile, where he resumed the practice of law. In 1838 he was elected a member of the Alabama Legislature, but in 1839, resigned that office to move to Texas, where he was appointed as Secretary of State by President Lamar. He was a member of the Convention of 1845, and introduced into that body a resolution accepting the terms of annexation that had been submitted by the United States. In 1846, Governor Henderson appointed him a justice of the Supreme Court of the State, a position he held at the time of his death. In 1813 Judge Lipscomb was married to Elizabeth Gains, the daughter of a planter in the Mississippi Territory; she died in 1841, and he was married in 1843 to Mary P. Bullock, the daughter of Dr. Thomas Hunt of Austin, Texas; She survived him. His death occurred at Austin during the session of Supreme Court, November 30, 1856. See E. W. Winkler (ed.), *Secret Journals of the Senate, Republic of Texas,* 1836-1845, pp. 174, 177; James D. Lynch, *Bench and*

*Bar of Texas,* 85-90; J. H. Davenport, *The History of the Supreme Court of Texas,* 30-49.

Lipscomb introduced the subject of homestead tax exemption in the Texas Convention and was instrumental in perfecting the homestead laws of Texas; (p. 103, Vol I, p. 446 Vol 57 — *Southwest Historical Quarterly*); Tax laws and Laws of Contracts (p. 48, Vol. 25 and p. 118, Vol. 40 *SHQ*) He was largely responsible for the development of the Texas Judicial System. (P. 140-144 *SHQ*).

Lipscomb was a commissioner of the Republic's Sinking Fund by Loan Act of Jan 14, 1840.

He was honored by having a town and county named after him; Lipscomb, county seat of Lipscomb County, in the Panhandle.

Judge Lipscomb lived near Gay Hill where he was a member of the Prospect Presbyterian Church. He and Daniel Baker made the favorable committee report to the Board of Trustees which led to the establishment of the Law Department at Austin College.

Dudley G. Wooten in his *Texas History,* vol. 2, pages 5 and 8 says: "Lipscomb and Royal T. Wheeler are considered two of the triumvirate of legal worthies of the Supreme Court of Texas — the dii-majores of Texas juriprudence. Lipscomb was made Chief Justice by choice of bar and the people."

## JOSEPH M. McCORMICK

JOSEPH McCormick became an elder when the Presbyterian Church at Columbia, Texas, was organized. He was considered a lay missionary or colporteur — selling Bibles and distributing religious tracts. We find McCormick attending Presbytery at Columbia April 4, 1844, when first official action was taken looking toward the founding of a college. "Resolved, that the ministers of Presbytery be requested to present the subject of education to their respective congregations and to endeavor to secure funds for establishing an institution of learning, at some convenient place in the country, to be under control of the Presbytery, and to report at our next meeting."

Mr. McCormick was a member of the Literary Institute organized in 1846 to arouse public interest in the subject of education. Two other members of the Institute who also became trustees of Austin College (Rev. J. W. Miller and Elder A. H. Cook) joined him in presenting a memorial to the Legislature in November 1847 seeking to get land grants for schools. (*Texas Presbyterian,* Feb. 13 to Nov. 13, 1847, passim)

Though he was elected a charter member of the Board by Brazos Presbytery, and his name is in the charter, on account of bad health McCormick never attended a Board meeting and resigned April 5, 1852. He was replaced by Rev. Stephen F. Cocke. However, his interest in Austin College was sustained for he gave Austin College one-fourth league of land in June 1857. (*Trustee Minutes,* p. 90)

## JAMES WESTON MILLER

JAMES Weston Miller, one of the Presbyterian missionaries who played an important part in the organization of the Church and also in the creation of Austin College, was born in a two-story farm house, on the west bank of beautiful French Creek, near Mill Village, Erie County, Pennsylvania, on November 15, 1815. He attended public schools a few winters and then entered the old academy at Waterford where he was the best student and was long remembered for his brilliant record. He was awarded the first honor at the end of two years and granted free board and tuition at Jefferson College, Canonsburg, Pennsylvania. He graduated in 1840 with first honors and valedictory in a class of 32 members. He finished his course at Allegheny Theological Seminary in 1844.

Rev. Miller came to Texas in December 1844 and entered upon the discharge of his duties as supply for the First Presbyterian Church in Houston. In 1847 the church at Houston became self-supporting and issued a unanimous call to Rev. Miller to become its pastor. The installation services were conducted November 2, 1847, the first installation service to be held in a Presbyterian church in the Republic of Texas. Due to bad health he found it necessary to resign his pastorate, and in January 1850 he moved to Washington County.

Upon reaching his new home he began preaching to the churches in Washington County; in addition to his church work he opened a school for young ladies, Live Oak Seminary. This institution was for many years one of the leading female schools in Texas.

Dr. Miller attended the June meeting of Presbytery in 1849 and was appointed on the committee with Revs. Baker and Blair to find a suitable location for the contemplated college. At the called meeting of the Presbytery at Prospect Church, he was appointed on the committee with D. D. Atchison and S. D. C. Abbott to secure a charter for Austin College. Among the names of the trustees of this new college appears that of Rev. J. W. Miller. With the resignation of Dr. Daniel Baker in 1857, Miller was offered the presidency of Austin College. His election to the presidency occurred without his knowledge or consent, as appears by letters communicating to him the action of the trustees. In a letter, dated June 25, 1857 from Huntsville, W. C. Somerville informed Miller of his unanimous election to the presidency of the College and urged him to accept. In a letter dated June 27 of the same year, Baker also informed Miller of his unanimous election and urged him to accept. The minutes of the Board of Trustees, however, show that Professor Thom acted as President while the Board was finding Baker's successor. In 1869 Austin College conferred upon Rev. Miller the degree of Doctor of Divinity.

James Weston Miller was a great educator, and as a minister he ranked with the best of the State, both in ability and popularity. Throughout his life he was ever anxious and watchful regarding the interest and welfare of Austin College.

The Rev. J. W. Miller is buried at Oaklawn Cemetery near Prospect Presbyterian Church, Old Gay Hill, Washington County, about eight miles from Independence. On the right side of his tombstone is that of his first wife Elizabeth McKennan, born Nov. 1, 1824; died Jan. 17, 1850. On the left side is the tombstone of his second wife, Elizabeth Scott Stewart, born Nov. 25, 1825; died August 30, 1908. To the side of these markers is that of his son, Dr. Robert Finney Miller, author of "A Family of Millers and Stewarts." He was born Jan. 9, 1866 and died April 4, 1935.

Adjoining the Miller family plot is that of the Sara Williams Massie family where the author's grandmother, his Aunt Emma Massie Eldridge and Uncle Robert Massie are buried. The author's mother, Lonie Massie Landolt, attended the Live Oak School its last year before the school was moved to Austin to become the Stuart Seminary.

Dr. Miller loved the outdoors and it was his custom to prepare his sermons while he fished at a place which came to be known as Miller Hole on the Yegua River. This was a favorite place for picnicing and fishing, but swimming was hazardous on account of water moccasins. The author still remembers the picnics and camping out over night at this famous fishing spot just two miles from his birthplace, and especially being scared to death while seining for fish when the net was raised with four or five writhing snakes among the catch. He remembers Dr. Robert Miller treating him for a copperhead snake bite when only four years old.


## GEORGE CLARK RED

DR. George C. Red was born in Newberry, South Carolina, Dec. 16, 1820. When his two parents died he was only fifteen. An uncle invited him to come and live in his home and attend the United Presbyterian College at Zenia, Ohio. With his only belongings on his shoulder, he walked all the way. His early education had been under an Associate Reformed Presbyterian minister. After two years he decided to be a physician, attended South Carolina Medical School from which he graduated in 1844. It is said that on his final examination he answered all Latin questions in Greek and all Greek questions in Latin. Nevertheless, when he sought to marry he proposed to his fiancee by letter. He had met and had fallen in love with Miss Rebecca Stuart, Principal of the Live Oak Female Seminary, whom he married in 1854.

After a year's medical practice in Newberry, S. C., he came to Texas in 1845, settling first at Washington-on-the-Brazos where he bacame an elder in the Presbyterian Church. Soon thereafter he bought land at Old Gay Hill between Chriesman's School House and Prospect Presbyterian Church Hugh

Wilson had organized in 1839. This location, about eight miles from Independence, Texas, was on La Bahia Highway, the main artery from San Augustine and Nacogdoches (through Huntsville) to Austin and San Antonio. A well travelled road from Houston joined the La Bahia and this area became known as the "hub of culture" and the center of Presbyterian work in Texas. Rev. James Weston Miller chose this spot to build his Live Oak Female Seminary in which Dr. George C. Red became instructor of the physical sciences, physics and chemistry. He at once built a large two-story home with an outside stairway to his office, clinic and laboratory on the upper floor. It was to this place that the students from the girls' school had to come after a good walk for their science classes. Today this home and clinic have weathered twelve decades. The good doctor's instruments, account books and laboratory are still intact. A grandson, George Red, of the law firm of Red and Kemp, at Houston, Texas, has preserved his grandfather's home just as it was in the 1850's. His plantation now includes the land where Prospect Presbyterian Church (second in Texas) formerly stood and the Oakrest Cemetery where Dr. George Red is buried. Nearby is the monument of Rev. James Weston Miller, his intimate friend and associate for half a century. It is an interesting fact that Rev. Miller's son, Dr. Robert Miller, became the outstanding medical practitioner of this area. Dr. Red's son, Rev. Wm. Stuart Red, D.D., who wrote the "History of the Presbyterian Church in Texas," was the first Austin College alumnus to enter the ministry.

Another son, Dr. Stuart Clark Red, attended Austin College, then Jefferson College, and entered Texas University as an upper classman when it opened in 1883. He was the first and only graduate of Texas University in its first graduating class, 1885.

Dr. Red was devoted to the College but his medical practice and teaching were extremely confining and made it difficult to attend trustee meetings. The Board meetings were held at Huntsville, more than fifty miles away. It was quite a trip in those days by horseback and crossing the Brazos was often hazardous. Consequently Dr. Miller, his colleague and employer at Live Oak Seminary, often voted his proxy. When the two attended together they were either late or left early. At the end of his six-year term Dr. Red chose not to be re-elected. He assisted in writing the charter and in publicizing the College, and was also active at Presbytery meetings. He was an elder at Washington where he practiced medicine until his marriage in 1854, then an elder at Prospect Church until 1875.

Dr. Red was opposed to the Secession and the Civil War, was shot at from ambush, persecuted and charged with treason. He pleaded his own case and was exonerated.

Soon after he arrived in Texas, Dr. Red volunteered for service in the Mexican War. However, while on a professional call (in those days a physician often remained at the patient's bedside until all danger had passed), his troop marched away to war, leaving him behind. Now with statehood, he could see no future in secession. In this respect, Dr. Red and Sam Houston stood alone and were constantly criticized for their stand.

When the Santa Fe Railroad was built through Washington County the new Gay Hill station was more than three miles from Live Oak Seminary. The number of white families living near the Seminary became almost non-existent. Consequently Dr. George Red bought land in East Austin and opened the Stuart Female Seminary in 1876. This school closed soon after Dr. and Mrs. Red died and was donated to the Synod of Texas for a theological seminary—now Austin Theological Seminary, successor to Austin School of Theology. (Barkley, *History of Travis County and Austin,* p. 173)

Dr. George Red died in 1881 and at his own request was buried in the cemetery near his 100-acre farm from which he went each day for twenty-five years to heal the sick or to teach the young of that area.


## J. CARROL SMITH

J. CARROL Smith, son of Samuel and Sara (Long) Smith, was born in Giles County, Tennessee, in 1815. The father died in 1844, and the mother, with her twelve children, moved to Texas to join her eldest son, J. Carrol, who had gone there in 1838. When J. Carrol Smith first reached Texas, he settled at Houston and engaged in the mercantile business; but on account of the frequency and fatality of yellow fever epidemics at Houston, he moved to Galveston, where he lived for twenty-one years, engaged in the commission business. He then moved to Ennis, Ellis County, and bought a farm, on which he lived for some time; later he moved to Huntsville. During the Civil War, he gave a thousand bales of cotton to the State Penitentiary to be made into clothes for the Confederate soldiers.

In 1840 J. Carroll Smith married Mary Cotton, a native of Mississippi. They had six children. Smith was a Democrat and a member of the Baptist Church. See Lewis Publishing Company, *A Memorial and Biographical History of Ellis County, Texas,* 512-520.

Although J. Carroll Smith was a Baptist, his interest in establishing Austin College was strong, chiefly through the influence of Daniel Baker. He was a substantial and consistent donor to the budget of the College, both operation and endowment. With his fellow trustees from Galveston, James Sorley and D. D. Atchison, provisions were made to endow several professorships. Smith and his brother, S. Y., were large landholders in Walker County and with Robert Smither and Henderson Yoakum, many enterprises were developed for the growing town of Huntsville. They raised subscriptions for a brick courthouse and other county buildings, thus securing a county seat. In quick succession a newspaper, *The Huntsville Item;* the state penitentiary, and the Cumberland Presbyterian Church, the first Presbyterian church in Huntsville, were established (1850). Through the efforts of J. Carroll Smith, Yoakum and Smither, funds were raised from Huntsville citizens to provide land for a campus and an attractive building for Austin College.

Smith early became a loyal friend and political backer of Sam Houston, who also was a fellow Baptist. Houston made J. Carroll Smith one of the executors of his estate and in his will delegated Smith Testamentary Guardian of his children if they became orphans. *(Writings of Sam Houston,* Vol. 8, pp. 340-341)

## ROBERT GOODLOE SMITHER

A BRIEF Sketch of Major Smither is given on page 85 of *Writings of Sam Houston* Vol II:

> Robert Goodloe Smither (November 21, 1811-September 10, 1853), was born at Washington, Rappahannock County, Virginia. He was a merchant of ordinary education who gave his whole attention to his business. Like most of the pioneers of his day he moved westward but he reached Texas in the early 1830's, locating in Walker County, a few miles from Huntsville. He later moved to the town and became one of the leading merchants of the place. During the Texas revolution he served in the Texas army with the rank of major. He also participated in the campaigns of 1842 against Vasquez and Woll, who invaded Texas in the spring and the fall of that year. Robert G. Smither married Elizabeth Emmeline Calmes of South Carolina. They had seven children, six of whom became worthy citizens of Huntsville, Texas. Robert Smither was a Democrat, an Odd Fellow, and an Episcopalian. He died at Grand-Encore, Louisiana, while returning from New York where he had gone to purchase goods for his store. See Johnson-Barker, *Texas and Texans*, IV, 1767.

Robert Smither was one of that trio whose civic pride and energy organized Walker County and secured the county seat for Huntsville. Smither, a devout Episcopalian, was joined by Henderson Yoakum, a Methodist, and J. Carroll Smith, a Baptist in raising subscriptions for a town market house; a newspaper (*The Item*), founded in 1846; a courthouse; a state penitentiary and Austin College.**

Joined by John Hume and Dr. John Branch (all of whom were later made charter trustees), they raised $10,000 and five acres of land for the College. At the organizational meet-

---

**The *Year Book for Texas*, page 317, gives annual reports of R. Smither and John Besser, Directors of the Penitentiary of the State of Texas to Gov. P. H. Bell, July 11, 1859 and November 10, 1851.

ing of the Board of Trustees, April 5, 1850, he was elected Treasurer of Austin College and never missed a meeting until his death four years later. The report of the Finance Committee of February 23, 1853, carries the statement:

> Thus far our labors have been successful. Let it not be by our own neglect that they not so continue. The important business in which we are engaged requires vigilance, patience and a hearty union and cooperation of all. Let no selfish spirit enter into our proceedings, no indifference to the high trust—let nothing be set down as impossible when necessary to complete what has been so well begun; and with the smiles of a kind providence, our children and our children's children will have cause to rejoice over this noble institution.
>
> Huntsville, Texas. Signed: R. Smither,
> H. Yoakum, John Branch, J. C. Smith
> Board of Trustees Minutes, page 33)

Robert Smither came to know General Sam Houston when he took orders under Houston as Major, 3rd Regiment, 2nd Brigade, of the Texas Republic Army. (page 85, *Writings of Sam Houston,* vol. II) His untimely death cutting his services as trustee to four years was a great blow to the administration of the College, but many of his family received their education at the institution he loved.

## REV. HUGH WILSON

*The Father of Texas Presbyterianism*

HUGH Wilson was the center about which Presbyterians in Texas in the early days grouped themselves. He lived on the main highway from Nacogdoches to Austin. The Presbytery of Brazos was organized at Chreisman's schoolhouse, which was near his home at Gay Hill in Washington County. The first five meetings of his Presbytery were held in his parish. One who knew him well says: "He always had a beef or a fat mutton and it was surprising how many his log house could entertain. People came twenty or thirty miles to these meetings and stayed for days. A blanket was a bed and a live oak was shelter, and plain food was abundant."

This hardy pioneer was born on March 16, 1794, in Bethany congregation, North Carolina. His father was a Presbyterian minister of English West Indian stock. His mother, Margaret Hall, was the granddaughter of James and Prudence Hall, who by 1875 could number twenty-five Presbyterian ministers among their descendants. He was literally a minister by heritage.

Hugh Wilson went to Princeton, graduating from both the college and seminary, and two years later received his master's degree. Hardly was he out of college when he hastened home to wed, on June 12, 1822, his childhood sweetheart, Ethalinda Hall, the sister of Revs. William A. and Davidson Hall. Three months later he was before Concord Presbytery with a certificate of licensure from New Brunswick Presbytery. Whereupon the Presbytery made all haste to ordain him, that he might "enter fully upon the discharge of his duties as a missionary amongst the heathen." His ordination took place at Fourth Creek Church, the home from which Mary McKenzie had gone out just three years before to wed Josiah H. Bell. In a few weeks Mr. and Mrs. Hugh Wilson were on their way as regularly commissioned missionaries of the Synod of South Carolina and Georgia, to the Chickasaw Indians, then located in Northern Mississippi and Western Alabama.

Mr. Wilson received an urgent request from the Board of Domestic Missions to go into their service to Texas. To this he returned a prompt refusal; but to his surprise, a second and more earnest application was made by officers of the Board. The importance of his accepting the call was more strongly represented, and as it was difficult to say what would be the expenses of a family in Texas, the Board offered whatever he should find necessary for his comfortable support, without limiting him to any fixed salary.

Hence Wilson made a tour of inspection of Texas in the summer of 1837. His route lay through Natchez, to Natchitoches, Louisiana, and thence along the King's Trail, via San Augustine and Nacogdoches, to Robinson's ferry at Old Washington on the Brazos.

Stopping for a few months at San Augustine, on June 2, 1838, Mr. Wilson organized Bethel Presbyterian Church, in Goodlaw's schoolhouse, four miles west of town, with twenty whites, two negroes, and two elders. H. G. Alexander and J. D. Sharp, M.D. This was the first Old School Presbyterian Church organized in Texas.

On the second of October, the family started for Independence, Washington County, where Wilson lived for two years, teaching in "Independence Female Academy," the first school chartered under the Republic. It had more than fifty students who boarded around the neighborhood, paying from $12.00 to $20.00 tuition for a five months session. J. P. Coles was president of the Board, of which Mr. Wilson was also a member.

By 1840, having located a tract of land of two hundred and forty-eight acres a half mile southeast of Mount Prospect, he began his home, a cedar log house. The move placed him in the midst of his congregation. Here the brethren who came to join with him in organizing the Presbytery of Brazos found him hard at work on his schoolhouse. When Sam Houston moved the Capitol of the Republic of Texas to Washington-on-the-Brazos, Rev. Hugh Wilson was made Chaplain of the House of Representatives in 1844.

In 1850, the Rev. J. W. Miller, pastor of the Houston Presbyterian Church, and also a charter trustee with Hugh Wilson at Austin College, was forced to leave Houston for a higher climate on account of his health. He came to Prospect to establish a school for girls (Live Oak Seminary) and the Miller family joined Wilson's church. Very soon thereafter Mrs. Miller became stricken and died, leaving the father with two small boys. Hugh Wilson's deep friendship for Miller led him to relinquish his home, school and pastorate to his closest friend and to seek new fields of endeavor further West. When Hugh Wilson left Prospect he was not alone. Like the patriarchs of old, the retinue of this Prince of Israel included a large train of followers; moving by ox carts, his wife, four daughters, two sons-in-law, grandchildren and a large group of friends. This band of immigrants landed fifty miles further westward up the Yegua, a tributary of the Brazos River. Here a settlement called Spring Prairie in Lee County Wilson built the first of several churches. He began to raise sheep and cattle, and served a large area with his pastoral devotion. Governor Elisha M. Pease, in recognition of Mr. Wilson's public benefactions, as a pioneer minister and educator, issued him a headright grant of 1280 acres, 100 miles further west. Mrs. Wilson passed away on Independence Day 1856.

At Commencement in 1857 Austin College conferred its first honorary degree, the Doctor of Divinity, upon Mr. Wilson. The same year the Synod of Texas made him the fifth Moderator of that body. In 1858 he married again and his second wife bore him one son. Today more than 260 descendants are living, 18 of whom have entered the ministry of the Presbyterian Church. On March 8, 1868 Rev. Hugh Wilson ended his earthly ministry and his remains were laid to rest at Tanglewood, Lee County.

Rev. Tom M. Cunningham, one of the eighteen who entered the ministry, graduated from Austin College in 1914. Dr. Cunningham was the Y.M.C.A. Secretary and the Austin College band and Glee Club Director at the College in the 1920's. This grandson of Hugh Wilson has published a 150-page biography of his grandfather, with the title *Hugh Wilson — a Pioneer Saint*. (Wilkinson Printing Co., Dallas, Texas, 1938).

## HENDERSON YOAKUM

H ENDERSON Yoakum, the Texas Historian, oldest son of George Yoakum, and his wife Mary Ann Maddy, and who was born at "Yoakum's Fort" or Station in the famous Powell's Valley section of Tennessee on September 6, 1810; at the age of 17, or in 1827, was appointed to West Point Military Academy, where he graduated in 1832. He married Miss Eveline Cannon, daughter of Robert Cannon. They were married near the little town of Philadelphia, Roane County, Tennessee, in 1883.

Soon after his marriage Henderson Yoakum moved to Murfreesboro, Tennessee, and entered the office of Judge Mitchell as a law student, soon was admitted to the bar and began the practice of his profession in that town. He entered the military service again in 1836 and served against the Indians on the Western frontier, serving as the captain of a company under General Gaines.

In 1838 he commanded another company in the Cherokee war. Then on October 7, 1839, having been elected to the office, he took his seat as a member of the Senate of the State of Tennessee. He made a splendid record in the Legislature, supporting both Jackson and Polk, and stood strongly in favor of the annexation of Texas, and on October 6, 1845 he and his family and relatives arrived in Huntsville, Texas then a part of Montgomery County. The following year he volunteered as a private, but was soon made a first lieutenant in the company of Captain James Gillespie, and took an active part in the war with Mexico, distinguishing himself at the battle of Monterey, etc. After the close of the war with Mexico he returned to Huntsville and resumed the practice of law.

Prior to his entrance into the Mexican War and after his arrival in Huntsville, Captain Yoakum conceived the idea of writing a comprehensive history of Texas and had begun the work. He formed a close friendship with Peter W. Gray, who encouraged him in the enterprise and to whom the two volumes were dedicated.

In 1853, Yoakum established a home seven miles out from Huntsville, called 'Shepherd's Valley,'' and it was here that most of his work on his famous history was done. (The above was taken from *Southern Historical Research Magazine,* Dallas, Texas. April 1936)

Another trustee and early graduate and teacher at Austin College, Judge A. T. McKinney, son of the first and fourth president has appended the life of the historian to Wooten's edition of Henderson Yoakum's "History of Texas."

Yoakum is reported to have gotten Sam Houston to go with him to the San Jacinto Battle field where he took down verbatim the strategy of the retreat, the plan of attack and the diversive action leading up to the final rout of Santa Anna's Army and his capture. Some of Yoakum's critics have opined that his close friendship to Houston with whom he shared the same law office in Huntsville allots Houston too much glory in the victory. Certainly the only resemblance between Yoakum's account and that of Anson Jones in the skimpy two pages (p.p. 15-16) of his "Republic of Texas" is that the Texans won the battle, capturing Santa Anna. Jones'

"History" is mostly a history of Jones. There are only three parallels in the lives of these two historians of Texas. They were both Charter trustees of Austin College and both died in the Old Capitol Hotel in Houston. Yoakum had gone to Houston, tho ill, to make an address, caught pneumonia and died while talking to his friend, Peter Gray. Jones died by his own hand in the same hotel fifteen months later. Both men have been honored by having county seats and counties named after them using both first and last names.

Yoakum and his wife, Eveline Cannon, were the parents of nine children, five daughters and four sons. His son, George Yoakum, died near Richmond, Virginia, a casualty of the Civil War. Henderson Yoakum, Jr. died of yellow fever in Huntsville during the epidemic of 1867. Houston Yoakum, named after Henderson Yoakum's best friend, was connected with San Marcos schools until his death there in 1912. Another son also lived at San Marcos and died there in 1923.

A daughter, Mary, married W. T. Robinson in Huntsville and their son, Wilburn T. Robinson, Jr. has presented Austin College with a copy of the only portrait of his grandfather. Mr. and Mrs. W. T. Robinson, Jr. have the Yoakum family Bible which includes the genealogy of the family back to 1608. The Yoakum family came near to complete extinction when Henderson Yoakum's grandfather, Valentine Yoakum, his wife and children, except one son, were slain by the Indians. Only Henderson Yoakum's father, George, managed to escape after running the gauntlet and slaying several with the handle of a cooking vessel.

Henderson Yoakum's brother, Dr. Franklin L. Yoakum, teacher at Tehaucana and President of Larissa College, was also a practicing physician. He was also a noted astronomer, theologian and horticulturist. Henderson Yoakum was the uncle of the famous railroad president, B. F. Yoakum.

Henderson Yoakum's influence in the history of Austin College began when he and several other Huntsville citizens began to raise funds for a college in the summer of 1849. With the help of four other men who later became charter members of the Board of Trustees (J. Carroll Smith, John Hume, Robert Smither, and Dr. John Branch) $10,000 and five acres of land for a campus and three one acre lots were donated for a college within one mile of Huntsville.

Although a Methodist, Yoakum immediately joined Daniel Baker in the project to found a Presbyterian college in Huntsville. In quick succession he became a benefactor, chief designer of the charter, charter trustee, secretary of the Board of Trustees and a member of the Executive Committee. And very soon he became chief legal council with the responsibility of title and deed work of all land transactions, and first librarian of the college.

When money was raised for the first building at the College, he was on the building committee. He was also one of the first directors of the newly established state penitentiary which provided the college with many bricks for the structure.

At the first meeting of the Board of Trustees after incorporation, held in Huntsville April 5, 1850, Yoakum voted as proxy for Sam Houston who was then on national senate duty in Washington. Later he was the go-between and unsuccessful adjuster in the first rift between the Board of Trustees' Executive Committee of which he and Sam Houston were members, and President McKinney, which led to McKinney's resignation as president.

At the June 24, 1851 meeting of the Board (page 15 of Board Minutes) Yoakum and Dr. John Branch and Robert Smither, were the Executive Committee. They reported that a communication had been received from the Smithsonian Institute with reference to the purchase of suitable instruments for teaching science and for keeping daily meteorological records. These were to be ordered at once. As a member of the Permanent Building Committee, Yoakum reported: "The Committee had purchased 300 thousand brick from Connor and Royal, delivered and all paid for. Also a kiln of brick was purchased from the State Penitentiary."

## The First Crisis in Huntsville

At the June 27, 1853 meeting General Sam Houston, Dr. Branch and Yoakum were placed on two committees: (1) On unfinished business (2) To inquire into the internal condition of the College. At the same meeting Yoakum, Dr. Branch and Rev. N. A. Penland were made a committee on Education. This Rev. N. A. Penland had been employed at the February

1853 meeting as Chase Professor of Foreign Languages. He was stated supply of the Huntsville Presbyterian Church, having recently arrived from Alabama. This was an unfortunate choice even though Rev. Penland was the husband of Sam Houston's niece.

In order to have a quorum several professors including Penland cast proxy votes for absent trustees. This was in violation of Sec. 8C of the Charter and later was declared illegal. When the Executive Committee with Houston as chairman called a meeting it was resented by President McKinney, who tendered his resignation June 29, 1853. Minutes of that meeting (page 48) show that McKinney's resignation was accepted and that Daniel Baker was immediately elected to take his place, and that until Baker could return from his trip East, Rev. N. A. Penland was elected president pro-tem.

Dr. McKinney insisted after handing in his resignation that he had a right to file a protest and did so, stating: "That in the estimation of the President, there was want of comity to absent members, and a haste which he could not now sanction in the calling of a meeting of the Board of Trustees by the Executive Committee without his consent. (page 48, 49, 50, Vol 1. *Board Minutes.*)

At the annual meeting of the Board June 28, 1854, Yoakum as Secretary and Chairman of the Committee on the state of the College, recommended that A. B. degrees be granted to L. O. Black and Joab N. Banton, the first degrees earned in a Texas college. At the same time the committee recommended that because of lack of progress J. W. Mayes should continue in the Freshman class for another year. They further recommended that the name of each of the children of Benjamin Chase be ascertained and that scholarships to Austin College be awarded each child (*Minutes of the Board* p. 61).

At the October 31, 1854 meeting a resolution was passed that three trustees be appointed to look into the matter of need for, cost, professors required and additional buildings, and a law library for a law department. They were also to determine the extent of patronage it would receive. The three men appointed to report at the next meeting were Yoakum, Judge Abner Lipscomb and Judge J. A. Baker, all lawyers (*Minutes*, page 67).

The 1855-56 college catalog, page 13, advertised the new Law Department to open on the last Wednesday in June 1855, with Judge R. T. Wheeler as Professor of Law at a salary of $100 per month. Judge Wheeler had been a trustee but resigned to accept this teaching responsibility.

The Law Department was an immediate success, possibly because six members of the Board were lawyers and such well known men as Houston, Yoakum, Col. John Hill, D. D. Atchison, Judge J. A. Baker and Supreme Court Judge Abner S. Lipscomb would naturally have favorable influence.

Henderson Yoakum was absent from the June 27, 1855 meeting, his first to miss. He was on a trip back East securing the much needed library and science equipment. He was back again for the January 17, 1856 and May 28, 1856 sessions. In his state of the College report (with John Hill) he stated:

> The committee therefore approves heartily of the disciplinary measures adopted by the faculty in regard to the few who have been refractory and disobedient. They append a resolution in regard to one of them—Resolved that upon recommendation of the Faculty of Austin College and the Board being satisfied with their moral worth and literary attainments, the Acting President be directed to confer upon William A. Allen, George W. Davis, and James S. Harrison the degree of "Bachelor of Arts." Resolved further upon like recommendation that the degree of "Bachelor of Laws" be conferred upon L. E. Trezevant, L. O. Black, Joab H. Banton and Benton Randolph. Resolved that upon recommendation of the faculty—and the Board believing the good morals and discipline of the institution require it—Joshua B. Byrd is hereby expelled from the College. (*Board Minutes*, page 78)

This was Yoakum's last Board meeting. In the fall of 1856 he went to Houston to deliver a Masonic address, became ill with pneumonia and died Nov. 30, 1856, in the Old Capitol Hotel (where the Rice Hotel now stands.).

In the testimony of the high appreciation of his character as a man, his usefulness as a citizen and his ability as a lawyer, his fellow citizens of Huntsville have erected this monument:

To the memory of
Col. Henderson Yoakum
who was born on the
10th of September, 1810
and died the 30th of November
A.D. 1856
Age 46 years, 21 months, 20 days.

Henderson Yoakum is buried in Huntsville, Texas, in the same cemetery where Robert Smither, John Branch, J. Carroll Smith, John Hume and General Sam Houston are buried. The monuments of John Besser and many other notables in the making of Austin College make this spot a shrine of Texas heroes.

## OTHER FIRST DECADE TRUSTEES

### James A. Baker

JUDGE James A. Baker was a First Decade trustee serving from 1854 to 1858, but was re-elected in the Second Decade from 1864-1867 and again in 1873, serving this last time until Austin College moved from Huntsville to Sherman.

Coming to Huntsville in the late 1840's, he promptly married Miss Rowena Crawford, the Principal of the Huntsville Female Brick Academy, (*S.W. Historical Quarterly*, Vol. 3, p. 263) and began his law practice.

At the October 31, 1854 Board meeting Judge Baker, judge Abner L. Lipscomb and Henderson Yoakum were appointed the Law Department Committee as follows: "Resolved that a committee of three be appointed whose duty it shall be to enquire into the propriety of erecting a law department in connection with and dependent upon this *corporation*, and that they report to the regular meeting of this board in June next. Resolved that this committee report as to the probable expense for additional buildings, for a law library, and also as to the number of professors necessary in such department; and the probable extent of the patronage it would receive."

At a Board meeting March 17, 1855 the Law Department was established with Judge Royal T. Wheeler, Professor of Law, at a salary of $1000 per year.

## CHARTER TRUSTEES OF AUSTIN COLLEGE

| 1849 to | | Origin | To Texas | Education | Church | Occupation |
|---|---|---|---|---|---|---|
| 1867 | D. D. Atchison | Kentucky | 1846 | Harvard | Presbyterian | Lawyer-Editor |
| 1857 | Daniel Baker | Georgia | 1840 | Princeton | Presbyterian | Minister |
| 1857 | John Branch | Virginia | 1847 | Hampden Sydney | Presbyterian | Doctor |
| 1884 | A. J. Burke | Tennessee | 1837 | Self | Presbyterian | Merchant |
| 1853 | John W. Hampton | N. Carolina | 1849 | Yale | Presbyterian | Editor |
| 1863 | Sam Houston | Tennessee | 1832 | Self | Baptist | Farmer |
| 1864 | John Hume | Mississippi | 1841 | Self | Presbyterian | |
| 1852 | Anson Jones | Massachusetts | 1833 | Jefferson Med. | Episcopalian | Doctor-Statesman |
| 1856 | Abner Lipscomb | S. Carolina | 1839 | Common School | Presbyterian | Lawyer-Judge |
| 1852 | J. W. McCormick | | 1839 | Self | Presbyterian | Bible Colporteur |
| 1874 | James W. Miller | Pennsylvania | 1844 | Jefferson | Presbyterian | Minister-Educator |
| 1855 | George C. Red | S. Carolina | 1845 | College of South | Presbyterian | Doctor-Educator |
| 1876 | J. C. Smith | Tennessee | 1838 | Self | Baptist | Merchant |
| 1853 | Robert Smither | Virginia | 1839 | Self | Episcopalian | Merchant |
| 1855 | Hugh Wilson | N. Carolina | 1837 | Princeton | Presbyterian | Minister |
| 1856 | Henderson Yoakum | Tennessee | 1845 | West Point | Methodist | Lawyer-Historian |

## JOAB BANTON

JUDGE Joab H. Banton came to Huntsville, Texas, from Tennessee in his early years. He graduated as valedictorian of the first class that earned the A.B. degree from Austin College, which also were the first A.B. degrees awarded in Texas. In 1856 he received with three others the first Bachelor of Law degrees awarded in Texas and in 1857 he and Livingston O. Black received the first two A.M. degrees awarded in Texas.

Mr. Banton married Miss Imogene Hamilton in 1856 and to this family were added two sons and two daughters, all of whom became residents of New York City, where Joab Banton, Jr. practiced law. Judge Banton was the idol of the people of the 33rd district, known and honored over the State. He died in 1874 at the age of forty. The *Alumni Quarterly* eulogizes him with the statement, "When a Hall of Fame swells the proportions of Austin College, with historic form and "animated bust" adorning the scene, in some niche consecrated by its presence the sweet, classic expression of Joab Banton, moulded in marble will smile as a loving benediction upon his cherished Alma Mater."

Judge Francis C. Hume of Houston, a college school mate gives the following testimony: "Banton was, perhaps, of all the sons of the College, the most distinguished lawyer. He outlived the application of the generally accepted saying that denies honor to a prophet in his own country; strong, proud and assertive, he won the reward of his deserving: he had become a prophet *with* honor in his own country."

## THADEUS C. BELL

THADEUS C. Bell was the son of Josiah Bell who came to Texas in 1821, one of the Stephen F. Austin's "3000" colonists. He settled on a 4,428-acre allotment at what is now Columbia on the Brazos River. Later J. H. Bell founded West Columbia, afterward the "Cradle of Independence" and the first capitol of the Republic of Texas. The Bell home provided accommodations for President Sam Houston, Stephen F. Austin and other prominent men. For awhile Houston had his headquarters in a small building in the yard, and the "great hall of the home wore the air of a sovereign court." (From A. P. McCormick, "Scotch-Irish in Ireland and America") Thadeus Bell's father died in 1838, but his mother carried on the hospitality of the family and it was in this home that he became acquainted with the famous men of early Texas. The Bell home was also a favorite stopping place for colporteurs of the American Tract Society.

Bell made law his chosen profession, moving to Huntsville where he could study under the best legal talent of the State. It was here that he met and married Elizabeth Cornelis, daughter of Dr. Samuel McKinney. They had one son, John Randolph Bell, who now lives at Salida, Colorado.

## GENERAL JOHN S. BESSER

GENERAL John S. Besser was born in Pennsylvania in 1802. At the age of 21 he made a trading expedition to the Rocky Mountains. He was Justice of the Peace in Lincoln County, Missouri, in 1830, and State Legislator of Missouri in 1834, coming to Texas in 1841. Except for twenty months during the governorship of Sam Houston, Besser was director or financial agent for the Texas Penitentiary in Huntsville from 1850 to 1863. Because he and Sam Houston were of different political parties, Houston asked for his resignation as soon as Houston became governor. Houston refused to swear allegiance to the Confederacy and was deposed in 1861, and Besser was reinstated as superintendent. Houston later stated that the only mistake he had made as governor was his dismissal of Besser as financial agent.

General Besser was co-director of the penitentiary with Robert Smither and Henderson Yoakum, both charter members of the Board of Austin College. In this double role, to keep the peace with the citizens of Huntsville, it was necessary for the three to see that the *escapades* of the college students gave no more trouble than the *escapees* of the adjoining institution. A special citation and memorial resolution of sorrow at his death, on page 384 of the Austin College Minutes, states that he served Austin College over forty years.

In 1878, Besser was elected Judge of Walker County. He was married four times, was a Royal Arch Mason, and an elder in the Huntsville Presbyterian Church. He gave the church bell to call the faithful to worship in 1856. Besser died May 19, 1893, and was buried in Oakwood Cemetery at Huntsville, Texas.

He had begun his services to Austin College January 17, 1851 as chairman of a committee to regulate the Preparatory Department. He, A. J. Burke and James Sorley were the only three men of the first decade of trustees to serve on the Board after Austin College moved to Sherman.

## ANTHONY M. BRANCH

A NTHONY Branch came to Texas with his older brother, Dr. John Branch, M.D., in 1847, settling in Huntsville where he began his law practice. When General Sam Houston made his will April 2, 1863, he appointed his wife, Anthony Branch, and J. Carrol Smith, another trustee of the College, executors of his estate. Houston went further to see that his wife and children were provided for by making A.M. Branch one of the "testamentary guardians of my estate" (*San Patricio County Records* Vol. G., p. 518). He was a graduate of Hampden Sydney College in 1842.

The first American "Branch" was a member of the House of Burgesses in 1639. The paternal grandfather of Anthony Branch was an ensign in the War of 1812 and his maternal grandfather was a lieutenant under Washington. Anthony was a member of the Confederate Congress and a colonel in the Civil War. He began serving on the Board of Trustees June 24, 1857, while his brother, Dr. John Branch, was closing his term of service. With the death of Yoakum, his law partner, he assumed the financial committee chairmanship and was often entrusted with the proxy vote by Sam Houston and others. Anthony Branch was never married. He was an Episcopalian and was Diocese delegate from the Huntsville St. Stephens Church in 1856.

After the Civil War he was the first elected representative to the national legislature (3rd Cong. District of Texas) and did much to get rid of carpet baggers in Texas and to restore statehood.

## GUY MORRISON BRYAN

G UY Morrison Bryan was born in Jefferson County, Missouri, January 12, 1821. He was the youngest of three sons of Emily Margaret Austin and James Bryan whom she married August 31, 1813. Emily Austin was the sister of Stephen Fuller Austin, father of Texas, and in whose honor Austin College is named. Mr. James Bryan died September 24, 1824 and Mrs. Bryan married James F. Perry. The family moved to the Stephen F. Austin land grant in Texas in 1831.

Guy M. Bryan was educated in private schools in Texas and at Kenyon College, Ohio, where he was the classmate and close friend of Rutherford B. Hayes, afterward President of the United States. Correspondence with his step-father during his college days indicated that he lived too extravagantly and was put on a fixed budget. After graduating from Kenyon College in 1842 he studied law under William H. Jack, but had to give up his plans for a law career on account of eye trouble. He turned his attention to ranching and farming but after serving in the Mexican war with the Texas volunteers began his political life, having been elected to the State House of Representatives in 1846.

Guy M. Bryan's first interest in Austin College came in November 1849, when the bill to incorporate Austin College was sent to the Committee on Education, of which he was chairman. This bill exempted Austin College from taxes but passed the House only after an amendment was added to section six with the words "while the property of the College."

In 1851 Guy M. Bryan and his half brother, Stephen Perry, agreed to give Austin College the claim of General Stephen F. Austin amounting to $2200 due him for pay as Commander-in-chief and Secretary of State when Texas was a Republic. While a member of the State Legislature, Mr. Bryan was assigned the task of supervising the restoration of a painting of Stephen F. Austin, then hanging in the House of Representatives. Bryan commissioned the famous English artist, Flintoff of New Castle-upon-Tyne to paint two copies of an original portrait of Austin painted in New Orleans in 1832 for his sister Emily, mother of Bryan. One of these he gave to hang in the Senate chambers and the other he promised Daniel Baker for Austin College. Daniel Baker wrote his son on September 6, 1855,

"Another thing I must tell you is this: Mr. Guy Bryan has made the College a donation of a splendid painting, a fine likeness of Stephen F. Austin, large as life. It cost three hundred dollars. He had two painted by an English artist, one was designed for the Senate chamber, the other for the House of Representatives, at Austin; but one has been given to our College. A fine present this. It will be a fine and very appropriate adornment to our College chapel. Daniel Baker."

However, it was not until 1890 that Bryan presented this portrait to the College. It now hangs in Hopkins Library on the campus. (*Board of Trustees Minutes,* p. 364, June 11, 1890.)

In 1857 Moses Austin Bryan gave a 300-acre tract of land in Brazoria County to the College and his nephew, Guy M. Bryan, Jr., gave two tracts in Anderson County, both of which have brought considerable oil revenue to Austin College.

Mr. Bryan served six years, 1846 to 1852, as Representative from Brazoria County and as Senator from his district for the four years 1852-56. At the request of Rev. Daniel Baker, the first Guy M. Bryan was elected trustee of Austin College November 2, 1855. (P. 86 *Austin College Board Minutes*). There were several good reasons why he soon resigned, namely: (1) He was an Episcopalian actively sponsoring St. Paul's College, an Episcopal school at Anderson, Grimes County. He was drawn into this by Anson Jones, also an Episcopalian and an early trustee of Austin College. Jones had resigned from the Austin College Board because of his dislike of fellow board member Sam Houston. In spite of the fact that both Jones and Bryan were liberal benefactors of St. Paul's College which opened in 1851 and was chartered February 4, 1853, they were unable to prevent it from closing in 1856. He was elected as a Democrat to the thirty-fifth United States Congress and served from March 4, 1857 to March 3, 1859. During this term he married Laura H. Jack, daughter of his old law preceptor, on October 20, 1858. In 1859 the Houston forces gained political control with the election of Houston over Runnels and this with his wife's dislike of social demands of Washington, determined his return to Texas where he made Galveston his home. He re-entered political life in 1873 serving as Speaker of the Lower House 1873-74 and was elected again in 1879, 1887, 1891.

Bryan was led by several of his Episcopalian friends (probably Anson Jones and Williamson Oldham) into believing that Sam Houston had been responsible through neglect in the early death of his uncle Stephen F. Austin. An exchange of lengthy correspondence on this subject was terminated when Bryan refused to divulge the names of his informants. This estranged relationship was alleviated somewhat in October 1862 in the city of Huntsville when both men became seriously ill. Major Bryan was at the time on a mission for the Confederate Army. Houston had just purchased the Steamboat House from Dr. Bailey, retiring president of Austin College, and had moved from the governor's mansion in Austin to Huntsville, after having been deposed as governor of Texas. Bryan's biographer, George P. Garrison, states:

> Major Bryan's illness proved typhoid pneumonia, and for weeks he lingered in a most critical condition; but by the careful and tireless nursing of his wife and the two servants his life was finally save. During his convalescence, however, he was stricken with rheumatism from the knees down, to which he remained subject at intervals throughout his subsequent life.

In treating Major Bryan during his illness, it became necessary for him to have brandy administered by teaspoonfuls constantly. This was furnished by Mrs. Bryan's brother-in-law, W. P. Ballinger, of Houston, who sent first several bottles, and later, on two different occasions, a five-gallon demijohn. Meanwhile Major Bryan was informed by his physician, Dr. Rawlins, that Gen. Sam Houston, who was then living in Huntsville, was also seriously ill with pneumonia, and that he needed brandy, but could get none. Thereupon Major Bryan sent him a bottle and received in return the general's most grateful acknowledgements.

At the time of his death June 3, 1901, Guy Morrison Bryan was president of the Texas Veterans Association and vice-president of the Texas State Historical Association. He is buried in the Texas State Cemetery at Austin.

On January 16, 1907 the Board, recognizing the importance of establishing a chair of History and Political Science, appointed President T. S. Clyce, and Board members E. E. Bryan and J. M. Fullenwider to formulate plans to this end.

This chair was to bear the name of Stephen F. Austin and it was hoped that the heirs of Stephen F. Austin would endow it. Guy M. Bryan, briefly a trustee in the first decade of the College and the nephew of Austin, did not accept this opportunity. His son, Guy M. Bryan, Jr., and a nephew by the same name, with two other nephews, Lewis R. Bryan and E. L. Perry, did endow the "Stephen F. Austin History Fellowship" for four thousand dollars.

On the first day of January, 1906, Guy M. Bryan, Jr., son of Wm. Joel Bryan, made a will in which he stated, "If my daughter dies without any children I want the balance of my estate left given to some worthy college like Austin." He died September 3, 1921 and the will was filed September 9, 1921. Later, to satisfy the request of an oil company who chose to lease a part of the estate, Austin College executed a quit claim deed to an 11,000 acre Ranch in Brazoria County at the request of his daughter, Mrs. Lucy Bryan Hervey, upon verbal agreement that she would honor her father's bequest when she herself died. During her lifetime Mrs. Hervey was to receive all the income from the estate but in 1934, 1935 and 1936 she gave a portion of the lease rental for three scholarships each year to Austin College.

Mrs. Hervey died at Bryan, Texas, in 1968 and Austin College has since become the owner of this 11,000 acre ranch sixty-two years after the bequest was made.

In Mrs. Hervey's will, made December 14, 1964, she bequeathed "to Austin College, at Sherman, Texas, all the rest of and residue of the real estate of which I die possessed, situated in Brazoria County, Texas, to be used by said Austin College at Sherman, Texas, in the erection of a building to be known as the 'Guy M. Bryan, Jr. Building.' I am making this provision and request with reference to the erection of a building because I know, from talking with my father, that it was his desire to have done this during his lifetime, but he did not have the means to make such a gift to the College."

## STEPHEN F. COCKE

STEPHEN Frederick Cocke was born in Springfield, Kentucky, January 1, 1810. His early education was in Centre College.

He first attended Union Theological Seminary, Virginia, but was graduated from Princeton Seminary in 1832. He was licensed by the West Hanover Presbytery on October 22, 1832, and ordained two years later by the same Presbytery. For two years he was pastor of Bethany Church in Virginia; and at Fincastle until 1844, when he went to Little Rock, Arkansas. In the latter part of the year 1846, he appeared in Texas as the supply of Victoria Church. From there he moved to Port Lavaca, where he organized a church in 1854, also one at Green Lake. In this latter place he made his home and there he remained until his death, at the age of forty-six years.

Rev. Cocke was a strong believer that the Presbyterians needed two colleges in Texas, one in the East and one in the West. His Presbytery appointed him to the agency of Aranama College which was to have been established as the "College of the West." This Presbyterian college at Goliad was chartered by the Fifth Texas Legislature January 25, 1854. Though Rev. Cocke was efficient in his labors to undergird the institution financially, it closed before graduating any students. The people of the area surrounding Goliad were mainly Mexican Catholics.

His daughter, Ella, married Rev. J. M. Cochran, Pastor of the Huntsville Presbyterian Church, the minister who attended Sam Houston during his last illness. Another daughter married Rev. W. L. Kennedy. His son, Frederick, gave his life for the Confederacy.

## A. H. COOK

REFERENCES to Abner H. Cook, trustee of Austin College during its first decade begin with a letter to President Mirabeau Lamar, August 13, 1839: "that Col. A. H. Cook from Austin will visit Galveston Island to see him in a day or two and to defer sending up the Republic Archives until Sept. 15—because the building was not ready." Lamar planned to remove the government seat to Austin.

At the age of 21, Cook left his North Carolina home beginning his career as a master builder at Macon, Georgia, and two years later at Nashville, Tennessee. He came to Texas at the age of 25 in 1839. From that date until his death there was hardly a city block in Austin on which he had not built at least one structure.

In 1848 he was chosen to build the first State Penitentiary at Huntsville by Governor T. Wood and appointed its first superintendent. Coincidentally this venture brought him into a definite relation with another institution which was also laying its cornerstone just a few blocks away. Austin College, chartered in 1849, needed the bricks supplied by the prison inmates and needed the architectural supervision of a master builder. In fact, one might say truthfully that the brains that supplied the planning for both institutions came largely from the same individuals, for Henderson Yoakum, who wrote the charter of Austin College, was the first director of the penitentiary and charter member of the Board of Trustees of Austin College, and R. Smither was also.

John Besser, later a trustee of Austin College, was the first financial agent of the penitentiary serving under Cook. Two other Austin College Board members, James H. Murray and later Thaddeus C. Bell, succeeded Cook as Superintendent of the penitentiary. In fact, in these early days of Austin College the people of Huntsville frequently compared the enrollment of A. C. with that of its sister institution on the adjoining hill and the students at A. C. made wagers on which would have the largest number of inmates when school opened each Fall. And sly remarks were often made by students about the appearance of some of the individual members of the Board as to whether or not they were *Trustees* of A. C. or *trusties* of the neighboring institution.

Free board and room at the penitentiary with no study, no chapel were topics compared and it didn't help matters when the superintendent of the penitentiary published: "Utilizing the appropriation for the purpose, I bought last year a cane mill and evaporator pans and made 1300 gallons of molasses and have constructed a large cemented pool, well housed where the boys can bathe winter or summer." It can be said, however, from the record according to the *Texas Almanac* that A. C. led in enrollment each year until the Civil War took most of the student body.

On observing some of the characters lolling on the campus of the Sam Houston State University during a recent visit to inspect the old A. C. Main building still in use there, one finds it hard to tell whether they might be escaped trusties of one institution, or students from the other.

According to Wm. Stuart Red (*The History of the Presbyterian Church in Texas,* pp. 95-96), Abner H. Cook was one of the six members who were organized into a church by W. Y. Allen in Bullock's Hotel, Austin, in 1839. Mr. Cook was the most experienced and talented builder in Texas and was appointed to construct many of the public structures from 1840 until his death. He accepted the superintendency for the construction of the State Prison at Huntsville in 1848 and began its erection in 1849, simultaneously with the founding of Austin College there. The first page of the Minutes of the Presbyterian Church in Huntsville states: "Aug. 20, 1849. The session met at the church. The following people were received on examination: Col. A. H. Cook, . . . On motion, Major Hampton was appointed Clerk of Session. Concluded with prayer. Daniel Baker, Moderator."

Cook returned to Austin early in 1850 and was one of five persons who assembled in the old log capitol May 26, 1850 to be reorganized into a church by Rev. W. M. Baker, son of Daniel Baker. Mr. Cook became one of the two ruling elders; Wade Hampton who had also moved from Huntsville was the other.

Mr. Cook had erected the first Presbyterian church building of logs in 1841; in 1851 he bought two lots, now the present site of the USUPA church on 7th and Lavaca Streets and built a frame structure. It was here in the frame meeting house that the Synod of Texas of the Presbyterian Church was organized.

Of the dozen ministers and elders present at this meeting three (Daniel Baker, Wade Hampton and J. W. Miller) were charter members of the Board of Trustees, and four others, Stephen F. Cocke, J. M. Becton, P. H. Fullinwider, and A. H. Cook were soon to be Trustees. Rev. J. W. Miller moderated this first Synod of Texas which officially took over Austin College.

In Austin, Abner H. Cook became a friend and neighbor of Sam Houston during the general's second term as President of the Texas Republic. Later this association was renewed when both Cook and Houston were living in Huntsville 1848-1850. Cook returned to Austin and in 1853 built the beautiful home Woodlawn, later to become known as the "Old Pease

Place" now the present home of Allen Shivers. He built the present governor's mansion with columns and front very much like the original Austin College in Huntsville. The resemblance of the warden's home in Huntsville to the governor's mansion is also striking with the "Neo-Classic" or "Greek Revival" style of both.

It was in Cook's own old home at 502 W. 13th Street that O'Henry lived and left the name of Athol Estes carved on the second window sill, while waiting for her to visit the Smith family with whom he boarded. Later Cook built a home across from the governor's mansion at 1104 Colorado Street and was living there when Houston was deposed as governor in 1861. The Houston and Cook children were backyard playmates and it was one of Cook's sons who carried the message from the meeting of the legislature in 1861 to Houston, telling him he had been deposed and the lieutenant-governor elevated to take the governor's chair. Cook's interest in education led him to become a trustee of Austin Collegiate Female Institute in 1875.

Cook built the City Hall on the site of the old capitol building in 1870. He designed and constructed the dome and most of the woodwork of the present Capitol building. His last great work was "Old Main" the first building on the State University Campus, built in 1884. He died that year on February 21, and was buried in Oakwood cemetery, Austin.

## PETER HUNTER FULLINWIDER

PETER H. Fullinwider was of Swiss ancestry. His grandfather, a Swiss reformed minister, had come to Maryland in 1752. Peter was born in Shelbyville, Kentucky, June 6, 1797. He received his early schooling in the old field schools of that state, took his college work at Centre College, and crowned three years of theological study at Princeton, which he completed in 1830, by applying to the Board of Missions for a commission to labor under the Presbytery of Mississippi when Mississippi, religiously speaking, included everything between it and sunset. His remuneration was $100.00, less anything collected on the field. He was instructed "to endeavor, by all Scriptural means, to win souls for Christ; . . . .

avoid all unprofitable controversy; abstain from unfriendly reflections upon other denominations of Christians and never become a political partizan."

He was of rather robust form, five feet, ten or eleven inches tall, and strongly built. He limped a little in walking, because of a defective foot. His eyes were of a light gray. His hair, which was never cut short, was sandy and curly. His face was round and full, with intelligent expression. He was a man of fine education and a good preacher.

Mr. Fullinwider was licensed shortly after by the Presbytery of New Brunswick; and eight months later, on October 30, 1831, he was receiving ordination as an evangelist in the Presbytery of Mississippi. He did not press westward at once, for the next year he supplied Zion Church, Jaynesville, Mississippi; and in 1833, we find him reaching out to include Sharon and Hopewell churches in his parish. He married Miss Belinda McNoir, March 18, 1834; two months later he and his wife were located at San Felipe de Austin. His activities as a missionary were very limited, as the Mexican government did not allow Protestant preaching, so he supported himself by teaching, assisted by his wife. However, he took part in a camp meeting near the home of Rev. John Wesley Kinney, on Caney Creek that fall, and again in September, 1835.

In the meantime he and his wife must have gone back to Mississippi, for they returned to Texas with their little girl in 1835. Affairs in Texas were then shaping up for the Revolution. The next spring we find the Old Ranger with his wife and child at Fort Sam Houston, near Palestine where his little girl died and was laid away in an unmarked grave to prevent Indian pillage. During the "runaway scrape," he was commissioned by Houston to conduct the families under his care to the "Stone Fort" at Nacogdoches. But while they were en route, a messenger brought the glad news of San Jacinto. Immediately he carried his grief stricken wife back to Mississippi, where she remained while he returned to Texas the next year.

Probably he went to Mississippi again, for in September 1838, he met W. Y. Allen in Natchez, on his way to Texas on horseback. Back in Texas he attended a Cumberland Presbyterian camp meeting near Summer Bacon's home. Then he went to San Augustine and met Hugh Wilson and John McFarland, as they were about to depart for Washington County.

After some months of preaching he returned from Texas to preach from 1838 to 1843 at Jaynesville, Mississippi and did not go back to Texas until he brought his little family to make their permanent home in the Republic, in the fall of 1843.

For nine years the Old Ranger roved about, preaching first at Montgomery, then Danville, Huntsville, Anderson, Bethel, until at last he settled at Jaynesville. At each place he preached, he had sought to awaken an interest in a college; so when Austin College was located at Huntsville, he realized the fulfillment of his dreams, and called it home.

In the meantime, Peter Fullinwider had been admitted to Brazos Presbytery by correspondence, and a year later in April 1844, appearing in person, he was received. That summer he organized Bethel (now Madisonville) Church, and continued to minister to it for more than twenty-five years, for half-time at a salary which never exceeded $200 per year. Marlin, Centerville, Point Pleasant, Concord, Harmony and Oak Island churches were also supplied by him at various times. Ruling Elder Byers of Bethel Church describes his habit: "The greater part of the time he lived at Huntsville, and came to Bethel twice each month. Often, leaving home late in the evening, he would ride eighteen or twenty miles, then stake his pony and, with his saddle for a pillow, and 'the angels of the Lord encamped round about' him, lie down in the lonely woods to rest awhile. Then, rising before day, he would come into the neighborhood for his breakfast and be at the church on time."

His son declares, "It was not an uncommon thing for him to ride fifty or one hundred miles to fill an appointment. I have seen father leave home when the snow was falling; neither winter's cold nor summer's heat, rain nor flood stopped him. Swollen and overflowed streams were no serious obstacle. If need be, and need often came, all night rides were made. At all events, under any possible conditions, appointments must be met."

Peter Fullinwider died of yellow fever at Huntsville in 1867, at the age of seventy years and a few months.

Rev. P. H. Fullinwider was elected to the Board November 6, 1857 and was President of the Board from June 28, 1858 to September 1858, at which time he was made Secretary of the Board until June 15, 1863. His consistent efforts toward influencing the youth of his parishes to enroll at Austin College was one of his greatest accomplishments. One of his sons, Jacob M. Fullinwider received his entire education from Austin College — Preparatory Department and four years of college work at Huntsville — for a B.A. degree in 1860, and the A.M. degree from Austin College in Sherman twenty-one years later.

The son followed in his father's footsteps by serving as a Board of Trustees member from 1897 until his death in 1910.

## JOHN HILL

COL. John Hill was elected to the Board November 3, 1855 and served until June 29, 1866. He was added to the Finance Committee on June 23, 1858. Being a lawyer he was frequently called upon to shoulder some of the legal burden left by Henderson Yoakum. Hill and Yoakum were responsible for keeping the other members of the Board informed concerning the state of the College *(Board of Trustee Minutes,* Jan. 17, May 28, 1856). Hill and Yoakum also composed the Finance Committee.

John Hill married Mary L. McKinney, granddaughter of Rev. Samuel McKinney, first president of Austin College and daughter of A. T. McKinney. Much of his law career was in partnership with his father-in-law in the firm of McKinney and Hill.

## HON. P. W. KITTRELL, M.D.

DR. P. W. Kittrell came on the Board of Trustees November 6, 1857. This was a crucial time in the life of the College. Henderson Yoakum, who was depended upon to guide the school through all land sales and legal matters was now missing. Daniel Baker had also passed away after a week's illness (Dec. 10, 1857) in Austin where he failed to get a land grant for Austin College. The bill before the legislature to finance Austin College and for which Baker was on the scene as lobbyist, succeeded through the first and second reading but never reached the third.

This task now fell to Dr. Kittrell by request of the Board since he was now a state legislator. The Board now urged him to push through a bill for financial aid by legislative act. Kittrell was one of the most noted debators in the legislature but unfortunately the establishment of a state university consumed that body's deliberation at the time.

Lubbock (Texas governor from 1861 to 1863) in his *Memoirs* states that: "Kittrell was the leading advocate for establishment of one universtiy; that Geo. W. Chilton contended for two and A. B. Norton didn't want any." Thus Kittrell's interest was divided. Lubbock reports further:

> Mr. Kittrell, on offering a resolution of respect to the memory of Rev. Daniel Baker, said among other things: "His death, sir, was a beautiful commentary on life. When his physician's skill failed and the solemn truth burst upon him that in a few minutes he must die, he calmly and peacefully folded his arms on his breast and said, 'Lord Jesus, into thy hands I commend my spirit.' Thus, sir, the spirit of this great and good man, on the very incense of hope, faith, and prayer, was borne to the bosom of his Heavenly Father. Sir, let gentlemen vaunt their cobweb system of infidelity, but give me that pure system of Christianity which will enable me, when the last moment comes, to calmly and quietly consign my spirit to Him who gave it as did our friend."

Politics in Texas during the gubernatorial race of 1857 became quite warm as the agitation to reopen slave trade was advocated by Governor Runnels, who had defeated Houston. Dr. Kittrell was of Runnel's party and strongly supported him. In one heated session he stated "to call the African slave trade piracy was an insult to Southern men, and ought to be left to the States to decide." (*Southwest Historical Review,* Vol. 60, p. 254)

This called for a strong letter from Houston to Kittrell and 60 other Huntsville citizens, Nov. 20, 1860, in which Houston gave all of his political views. (*Southwest Historical Review,* Vol. 49, p. 568)

P. W. Kittrell made a stirring speech on the occasion of the inauguration of Rev. Rufus W. Bailey, D.D. to the Presidency of the College (*Austin College Quarterly,* October 1859)

At this time his son, Norman G., was a student at the College preparing himself for a notable career in the legal field. Addressing the newly elected president, he said:

You have immortal minds commited to your care. Every impression here made on the mind, every mental effort or activity called forth, all moral or mental expansion in whatever form, will be lasting as the imperishable minds which you teach. The character of your work gives honor to your position, from the fact, as you have justly said to-night, that you intend to "prosecute it within the claims, and according to the true morality of the Bible," a sentiment, sir, worthy of your calling. And here I may be permitted to add my humble endorsement to that sentiment and determination of yours; for I have been long since convinced that it is only when agencies *human* and *divine*, operate in unison, cultivating the intellect and the moral elements of our nature, and the better feelings and affections of our heart, that education can be made a blessing to mankind.

Another thought which the occasion suggests, is, that your position, though honorable, is one of heavy responsibility and attended with great difficulties. You have a great variety of minds to operate upon. Associations of this kind must necessarily bring together a variety of elements, each member of which has some peculiarity of mind, manners and disposition, to which attention must be paid in the administration of the government of your institution. For no association of this kind can succeed — can operate harmoniously and successfully without a proper system of discipline. A large share of practical, sound wisdom, founded upon a knowledge of human character, is necessary in adapting proper rules and regulations to the peculiarities of each and all who may be placed under your care. Promptness and decision, combined with prudent forbearance, are also necessary to secure the ends of government. Your position is important and difficult, from the peculiar nature of the business of teaching. In consequence of the great variety of minds you have to operate on, your instruction, or rather your mode of instruction, must be so varied, as to suit the temper, disposition and peculiarities of each. The timid and self-distrusting must be encouraged and inspired with a laudable ambition for success. The forward and self-reliant must be taught to know that self-confidence will not supercede a long course of laborious industry and persevering toil. The indolent and inactive must be stimulated to study and close application. The excitable and impatient, to close investigation and patient thought. This whole work is to be so performed as to be suited to the peculiarities of all, so as to render the business of teaching and governing successful in the development of the whole man, moral, mental and physical, in all the symmetrical strength and beauty of which he is susceptible, so as to fit him for the highest circles of distinction and usefulness in human society.

Dr. Kittrell was a political adversary of Sam Houston, although they were personally and neighborly friends. General Houston, on his deathbed, summoned Kittrell from his plantation fifteen miles away. Because both Kittrell and Houston were often in Washington, D.C., and Austin, Texas, respectively, about national and state legislative affairs, they frequently used proxies at the Board meetings. The *Minutes of the Board* of September 2, 1862 (page 150) state that "P. W. Kittrell appeared in person and took his seat."

Sam Houston's will included as one of his assets, a note for a loan to three of his fellow trustees, P. W. Kittrell, J. C. and S.R. Smith, money loaned to help Austin College through the Civil War years.

A life size portrait hangs in the hall of the Tower Library of Texas University with this inscription: "Hon. P. W. Kittrell— 1805-1867"

## ANDREW TODD McKINNEY

JUDGE A. T. McKinney was Professor of Mathematics at Austin College from 1862 to 1864. He had completed an extension course of instruction during the war years from Princeton University. In fact, with his brother, Robert A. McKinney, assistant professor, and their father, Dr. Samuel McKinney, the three McKinneys did nearly all of the teaching from September 1862 to June 1864.

Andrew McKinney was elected to the Board in 1867 and was Secretary of the Board from 1869 to Nov. 7, 1876. As secretary of the Board, he notified Sherman that their offer was accepted and that Austin College would open its doors for college work in the Fall of 1876. This was the result of a called meeting by President S. M. Luckett in Houston, January 4, 1876.

On January 5 Judge J. A. Baker, E. H. Cushing, Rev. S. M. Luckett and Rev. Daniel MacGregor, were appointed to draft a new charter. McKinney attended the first meeting of the Board in Sherman February 9, 1876.

On May 10, 1876, the Board again met in Houston and only old-timer A. J. Burke was present and three others who had recently come on the Board. These four acted as proxies for seven absentees. Before the meeting was over only three trustees were voting eight proxies. One resolution to borrow $500 at 8% to wipe out the remaining debt ($600) to Sam Houston, now owned by Mr. Morrow, one of Houston's heirs, caused a heated discussion. When the full report was adopted, Rev. D. MacGregor filed a written protest as follows:

> Houston, Texas, May 10, 1876 . . . I protest against the first resolution in the series which has just been adopted by a majority vote of this meeting, because in attempting to liquidate an old debt, made by previous trustees, it creates a new debt thereby shifting a debt made by previous trustees to the present trustees. I therefore protest against such action and against being bound or held responsible for any effect growing out of said action of a majority of the trustees. 'Signed' D. MacGregor, a member of the Board of Trustees of Austin College.

Nevertheless, the money was secured and the debt of $2000.00 to Houston, mentioned in Houston's will as a loan to Austin College, was finally liquidated after fifteen years.

After Austin College moved to Sherman, Judge A. T. McKinney became a trustee for Sam Houston State Normal School which had taken over the Austin College building and campus in Huntsville. His name is on the cornerstone of the Peabody Library Building of that institution. He was author of *A Comprehensive History of Texas, 1685 to 1897* in two volumes (1898) edited by D. G. Wooten.

## BENTON RANDOLPH

JUDGE Benton Randolph received the B. S. degree in 1856 and the Bachelor of Law degree in 1857. Ten years later he was elected to the Board of Trustees of Austin College. He joined his brother-in-law, Judge A. T. McKinney, son of Rev. Samuel McKinney, first president of the college, in establishing a law firm that became one of the strongest in the State. His first wife was Miss Elenor McKinney, who died shortly after their wedding. His second wife was Miss Wood. Benton Randolph was the last survivor of his class of five.

Randolph was active in the conservative party and supported President Johnson in his reconstruction policies. He was named on a caucus to push the candidacy of J. W. Throckmorton for governor against incumbent E. W. Pease. Throckmorton was elected over Pease by a 4 to 1 majority. Randolph was joined by A. M. Branch, another board member, in easing reconstruction tension when Branch was elected to the national legislature. By the beginning of January 1868 the state government was again on a stable basis. *(Wortham,* Vol. 5, page 17)

## WILLIAM STUART RED

REV. Wm. S. Red was born in Gay Hill, Washington County, Texas, the son of Dr. George Red, charter trustee of the College. He graduated with the A.B. degree from Austin College in 1882, Austin College School of Theology in 1886. He taught school for two years, spent one year at Leipsic, and was Chaplain at A. & M. College for two years. He was editor of the *Texas Presbyterian* for five years. He was the first alumnus to enter the ministry as a life work. He was Moderator of the Synod of Texas in 1902 and served on the Austin College Board from 1901 to 1917.

He was honored with the D.D. degree by his Alma Mater in 1907. He served churches at Navasota, Houston, Columbia and Velasco, Hempstead, Free Church of Glascow, Scotland (1908-09), Mexia and Austin. He died in Austin July 8, 1933 and is buried there. He was the author of *Texas Colonist and Religion* and *History of the Presbyterian Church in Texas* published posthumously in 1936.

## S. R. SMITH

S. R. SMITH and his brother, James Carroll Smith, were born in middle Tennessee; came first to Houston in the 1840's and engaged in merchandising. Later they moved to Huntsville, operating Smith Brothers Wholesale Company. Before S. R. Smith came on the Board he and his brother, J. Carroll, who was a charter Trustee, bought a part of the Chase lands from Austin College for $5,000 in 1857. After Daniel Baker, financial agent for the College, learned that a Mr. James Sorley of Galveston would pay three times as much for the land, the Smith brothers donated it back to the College. The College then deeded it to Mr. Sorley for $15,000 with which the Daniel Baker Chair of Mathematics was established. These three men came to be close friends while on the Austin College Board and became partners in the coton business in Galveston, widely known for their integrity and generosity. Mr. Sorley gave the land back to Austin College in 1867 to help the College reestablish itself after the Civil War.

Mr. S. R. Smith was a member of the Episcopal Church and served as Diocese Delegate from the Huntsville St. Stephens Church in 1858.

(*The Episcopal Church in Texas* by Lawrence Brown, p. 257)

## JAMES SORLEY

JAMES Sorley was elected to the Board on November 2, 1855, to take the place of Dr. George C. Red. He was one of three trustees who served the College until after it moved to Sherman.

Sorley was a Galveston importer-exporter and cotton was one of his chief interests. During the Civil War he, with Guy M. Bryan, formulated and inaugurated the Texas State Cotton

Bureau. Through details worked out by these two, Texas was able to nullify the blockade of Gulf ports by the Federal gunboats. Cotton, floated down the Trinity River to Trinity Bay and also from Anahuac, was rolled over the narrow coastal strip of land at what is now called Roll-Over Beach, then reloaded on Gulf boats for export, thus by-passing Galveston. Cotton from the Valley was taken into Mexico and shipped to France and England from Tampico.

Rev. J. R. Hutchison, pastor of the First Presbyterian Church in Houston from 1861 to 1868 wrote: "I became interested after the war in reorganizing the church work in reference to the spiritual desolation of the villages and churches within the bounds of the Brazos Presbytery that were accessible by railroads from the city of Houston. In the fall of 1866, in a conference with some prominent members of the church, I was urged to carry out my purpose. Mr. James Sorley, of Galveston, placed in my hands $50.00 as salary for the month of January 1867, to justify me leaving my home and commencing my work." This work he continued for ten years through financial aid, chiefly from James Sorley.

During the early spring of 1857 the Galveston *Civilian* kept up a steady press campaign in behalf of promotion of bonds to build a bridge to the mainland. The *Civilian* issue of May 12, 1867 stated, "The cotton merchant, James Sorley, has composed a special 'Bridge Song' to the tune of 'Wait for the Wagon' which is being used effectively to liven the publicity." Shortly thereafter the Galvestonians obtained victory by voting 741 for the bridge and only 11 against.

Daniel Baker recounted in a different way another side of Mr. Sorley. To the Board of Trustees in his annual report and also in a letter to his son (May 30, 1857, page 529 of *Life and Labors of Daniel Baker)* he relates how the College had sold a tract of land to one of the trustees, J. C. Smith, for five thousand dollars and when Mr. Sorley heard of it, offered to pay fifteen thousand to the College for the land, if Mr. Smith was agreeable. Baker said, "If I were not principled against dancing, I would dance for joy," for the next day he received a written communication containing the following words: "We agree to re-convey the land—in so doing we are well aware that we surrender that which would result very profitably to us. At the same time, we cannot resist our great desire to see

Austin College placed upon a permanent footing." It was thus that James Sorley endowed the Baker Professorship of Mathematics.

## REVEREND JEROME TWITCHELL

R EV. Twitchell came from New Orleans to Houston in April 1855 to be the minister of the First Presbyterian Church. He was elected to the Board of Austin College by Synod action November 3, 1855 and took his seat January 17, 1856.

In his book, *Sketches and Addresses,* Rev. J. R. Hutchison, D.D., Pastor of the First Presbyterian Church of Houston, states that "Reverend Jerome Twitchell was lost on the 'Nautilus' in the Gulf of Mexico during the storm of August 10, 1856 after a ministry in Texas of little over a year.

The Austin College Minutes record in Daniel Baker's report to the Board of Trustees that "Mrs. Twitchell has made known her desire to give Rev. Twitchell's library to Austin College." In a letter to Rev. James Weston from Austin on November 23, 1857, Dr. Daniel Baker added a postcript with these words: "Mrs. Twitchell has most generously made a donation of her late husband's library to our college with the cases which contain the books. This donation is a valuable one." *(Southwest Historical Quarterly,* Vol. 19, p. 182) Among the rare volumes now in the Austin College archives are a number of Twitchell's sermons.

## ROYAL T. WHEELER

R OYAL T. Wheeler was born in Vermont, in 1810. He was reared in the State of Ohio, and after being admitted to the bar in that State in 1837, he emigrated to Arkansas and settled at Fayetteville, where he practiced his profession. In 1839, he married Miss Emily Walker, and then removed to the republic of Texas and settled at Nacogdoches. Here he practiced law successfully, as the partner of the distinguished Kenneth L. Anderson, who was cut off in the flower of his fame while holding the office of vice-president of the Republic of Texas.

Sam Houston appointed Royal T. Wheeler to district attorney for the Fifth Judicial District Court on Jan. 15, 1842 (page 430, vol. 2, *Writings of Sam Houston*).

In 1846, he was appointed one of the associate justices of the supreme court. In 1851, he was elected to the same office, and re-elected in 1856. In December, 1857, when Chief-Justice Hemphill was elected to the United States senate, he became chief justic of Texas. He died in April, 1864 by his own hand, while holding that office. He was the survivor of those who constituted the first supreme court of Texas. In a short sketch of Judge Wheeler occurs the following allusion to his two distinguished associates, which it is deemed appropriate to insert here: "Judges Hemphill, Lipscomb and Wheeler have now passed away from us. The subject of this imperfect sketch was the last of that illustrious trio, who constituted the original supreme court of the State of Texas. Their names are imperishably connected with the judicial history of our State. They constitute the *dii majores* of Texas jurisprudence."

Judge Wheeler aided in securing from Secretary of State Abner Lipscomb a proclamation to liberate free negroes who had been sold into slavery. (P. 105, Vol. 41, *S.H.Q.*)

In the "Secession Convention" held February 1, 1860, the vote was 166 aye and 8 no. Sam Houston, the governor, insisted this convention was illegal and Judge Wheeler called for a state-wide election, resulting in 42,129 ballots for secession and 14,697 against.

Judge Wheeler is honored for his work as Chief Justice of the Supreme Court of Texas by having a town and county named after him; Wheeler, the county seat of Wheeler County in the Panhandle.

## JACOB M. FULLINWIDER

J ACOB Fullinwider was the son of Rev. P. H. Fullinwider, pioneer Presbyterian missionary who taught and preached in Texas before Texas gained independence from Mexico.

He obtained his education from the preparatory department of Austin College in Huntsville and later received the B. A. degree in 1860. He then enlisted as a private in the Civil War serving until 1865. Returning, he began his teaching career while studying law, and combined his law practice with a real estate and insurance business in Palestine, Texas. He married Mrs. Francis Arnold Lewis November 16, 1868.

He received the M.A. degree from Austin College in 1881, twenty-one years after graduating with the B.A. degree; and has the distinction of being the only one to graduate from the Austin College Preparatory Department, from the College at Huntsville and from the College in Sherman.

He followed in his father's footsteps by becoming a member of the Board of Trustees in 1897, serving until his death in 1910.

## EDWARD HOPKINS CUSHING, Editor of the Houston Telegraph

IN his "Appreciation by His Son" Mr. E. B. Cushing makes no reference in his biography of his illustrious father, Edward Hopkins Cushing, to the fact that his father was a trustee of Austin College, and that he served as Treasurer of the College from 1869 until his death in 1879.

Neither does Mr. Emory M. Thomas in his *Rebel Nationalism: E. H. Cushing*. Nor does Earl Wesley Fornell in *The Galveston Era*.

Perhaps we can excuse Mr. E. B. Cushing for the omission of his father's important role in the destiny of Austin College because he waited until June 1921, forty-two years after his father's death to write the biography. The son does recall that his father "was an earnest advocate of education in both grammar school and university . . . all through his ownership of the Telegraph, the columns were open to communications on educational matters and there are many editorials which evidence his deep and sincere appreciation of the value of education."

Emory Thomas cites E. H. Cushing as a writer and publisher of books and concerning education quotes Cushing: "We must not forget, amid the beauties, the excitement and confusion of the hour, (the Civil War) that all this sacrifice and effort will be in vain if we fail to bequeath our liberties when gained, to an intelligent and devoted posterity."[2]

Fornell writes that Edwards Hopkins Cushing was a severe critic of education, a former school teacher in Galveston, a publisher of textbooks and quotes Cushing: "It is time the Legislature stopped giving college charters to common schools . . . let us give up this art of shamming and come back to the first principles."

Edwards Hopkins Cushing married Matilda Burke, daughter of Andrew Jackson Burke, a charter trustee of Austin College. Burke served the College for thirty-five years — until his death in 1884. He was one time mayor of Houston and was a great benefactor of Austin College, at times paying the full salaries of two of the professors. It was in Burke's home that Cushing came to know Sam Houston, Henderson Yoakum, also charter trustees of the College, and Rev. Daniel Baker and other pioneer Presbyterian ministers. Cushing and A. J. Burke were both elders in the Houston Presbyterian Church.

After Cushing married Matilda Burke, they built their home "Bohemia" which became a showplace in the early days of Houston and a gathering place for aspiring writers and poets of Texas.

In the midst of the Civil War when the South was still fighting gloriously, Gen. Sam Houston died and Cushing was the only one to publish a memorial — his famous "An Editorial Appreciation of Houston."

E. H. Cushing was elected to the Board of Trustees of Austin College on November 6, 1868 and was elected college treasurer a year later. He was re-elected to this position three times and was Treasurer of the College at the time of his death, January 15, 1879.

Cushing and A. J. Burke were leaders in getting Austin College moved from Huntsville to Sherman. Epidemics of yellow fever and other diseases had taken a great toll of the coastal area in the 1850's. Cushing had lost his wife and a son during these epidemics. When the Board of Trustees decided to move the College to a higher location, a site on the H & TC railroad was favored. A. J. Burke was a director of this railroad. It was at first thought that a new charter would be required to move the College and Judge J. A. Baker and Cushing were appointed to draw up this new charter. Later it was decided that only an amendment to the charter would be required and at a Board of Trustees meeting in the office of the bookstore of E. H. Cushing, June 13, 1877, the Board met to sign the amendment. E. H. Cushing, with seven proxies, and A. J. Burke with four proxies, composed the legal quorum, signed the amendment and sent it to Austin where the Secretary of State certified it on June 18.

The action to accept Sherman's offer of ten acres of land and $35,000 for a new building was taken in Cushing's office on February 1, 1876, but the College continued to operate in Huntsville for another year under Prof. C. P. Estill. The College President, S. M. Luckett, presided at this meeting which was attended by A. J. Burke, E. H. Cushing, and two ministers, Rev. MacGregor and S. A. King. These four with ten proxies held by them made the important decision of accepting the offer to transfer the College to Sherman if its citizens could raise the money by February 10, 1876. A well attended Board meeting in Sherman on that date consummated the deal.

A memorial resolution in the Minutes of the Board of Trustees of Austin College, page 295, reads:

> June 18, 1879   It is with sincere regret that as a Board of Trustees we have heard of the death of Mr. E. H. Cushing, who for many years has been a member of this Board and the trusted Treasurer of the College.
>
> Be it therefore resolved: 1st, That in the death of Mr. Cushing Austin College has lost one of its most diligent members. 2nd, That we will ever treasure a memory of his many noble traits of character, and that we express our warmest sympathy to his family in this their hour of affliction, and that the President of the College be instructed to send them a copy of this resolution.

## The Board of Trustees of Austin College

IN addition to the original or charter trustees, there were 21 replacements during the First Decade. The average age of the charter trustee in 1849 was over 50 years and largely because of death, new trustees were elected by the Synod quite often. The number of famous men who gave their time, prayers and money during this founding period was double the number of graduates (17), 1849 to 1859, and equalled the total number of degrees granted (37), prior to removal of the College to Sherman in 1876.

Only seven new trustees were called to service in the Second Decade which included the Civil War period and nearly all of these were graduates or ex-students of the College—men who made Texas history after the war.

Six of the First Decade trustees; namely, Houston, Yoakum, Jones, Wheeler, Lipscomb and Bryan had Texas counties named after them.

### Some Interesting Family Relationships of Trustees:

Four sets of brothers served on the Board during the First and Second Decades: J. Carroll and S. R. Smith; John and Anthony M. Branch; J. P. and W. G. Bagby; Rev. Daniel and Rev. Evander McNair.

Two wives followed their husbands on the Board: Mrs. Thomas E. Craig and Mrs. E. E. Shelton.

One son followed his mother—Robert L. Wood succeeded Mrs. Robert F. Wood.

There were at least seven sets of father-son trustees:

| Father | Son |
| --- | --- |
| Charter trustee George C. Red | Rev. Wm. Stuart Red, B.A. 1882 |
| Rev. P. H. Fullenwider | J. M. Fullenwider, B.A. 1860; M.A. 1881 |
| C. N. Roberts | C. Stanly Roberts, B.A. 1898 |
| Rev. Wm. M. Anderson | Rev. Wm. M. Anderson, Jr., B.A. 1911 |
| A. A. Aldrich | A. A. Aldrich, Jr., B.A. 1914 |
| E. T. Fant | James Fant |
| Capt. J. Thompson | J. Lewis and Hoxie H. Thompson, B.A. 1901 |
| A. N. Leecraft | B. M. Leecraft. |

## CHARTER BOARD

*1st Class:* Rev. Daniel Baker, Hon. Sam Houston, Rev. Hugh Wilson, Rev. James W. Miller, Joseph McCormick.

*2nd Class:* Robert Smither, J. Carroll Smith, Hon. Anson Jones, Abner S. Lipscomb, J. W. Hampton.

*3rd Class:* Henderson Yoakum, John Branch, John Hume, George C. Red, A. J. Burke, Daniel D. Atchison.

## OTHER FIRST DECADE TRUSTEES

Judge Jas. A. Baker, Rev. Joseph G. Boone, Col. A. M. Branch, Guy M. Bryan, Rev. R. H. Byers, Stephen F. Cocke, A. H. Cook, P. H. Fullenwider, Col. John Hill, Hon. P. W. Kittrell, Dr. J. A. Lawrence, Col. W. A. Leigh, Rev. Donald MacGregor, Rev. Daniel McNair, Rev. Evander McNair, Col. J. H. Murray, James Sorley, Wm. A. Stewart, Rev. Jerome Twitchell, Judge R. T. Wheeler, Rev. James Wilson.

## SECOND DECADE

Joab H. Banton, T. C. Bell, B. Campbell, E. H. Cushing, William McClintock, Judge Benton Randolph, S. R. Smith.

## THIRD DECADE

J. P. Bagby, W. G. Bagby, John S. Besser, Rev. H. B. Boude, Rev. W. W. Brimm, Rev. R. F. Bunting, Rev. J. D. Burkehead, Rev. W. E. Caldwell, Josephus Cavitt, Dr. S. E. Clement, Rev. W. N. Dickey, Judge E. P. Gregg, A. F. Hardie, Rev. S. A. King, H. A. McDonnald, T. L. C. Means, Rev. John S. Moore, Rev. Hilary Moseley, Rev. R. E. Sherrill, A. P. Smith, Rev. R. K. Smoot, R. C. Stewart, W. W. Taylor, Rev. Levi Tenney, T. F. Willis, Rev. J. H. Ziveley.

## FOURTH DECADE

Dr. T. J. Bell, Rev. R. S. Burwell, E. H. Carter, Rev. L. P. Chaney, J. J. Dimmitt, Rev. C. R. Dudley, Rev. T. W. Erwin, Rev. William George, Judge S. P. Greene, J. W. Gulick, W. S. Johnson, Rev. E. D. Junkin, Rev. S. M. Luckett, W. K. Marshall, C. M. Moore, Andrew T. McKinney, Rev. R. H. Nall, Rev. H. R. Raymond, Captain C. N. Roberts, Rev. W. N. Scott, Rev. C. S. M. See, J. H. Skinner, G. T. Thompson, J. E. Wharton, A. W. Wilson, T. P. Young.

## FIFTH DECADE

Judge A. A. Aldrich, J. B. Baldwin, Jr., J. M. Brownson, George F. C. Butte, Rev. Junius B. French, J. M. Fullenwider, M. C. Hutton, Rev. Josephus Johnson, Rev. W. H. Leavell, Rev. W. L. Lowrance, John Martin, Rev. A. M. Milster,

Rev. J. N. McFarlane, Rev. S. J. McMurray, C. P. McNeill, Rev. C. J. Ralston, Rev. J. J. Read, H. L. Moseley, James P. Robertson, Jerome P. Robinson (Rev.), G. A. Russell (Rev.), Rev. A. Walker White, Rev. J. H. Wiggins, Rev. John A. Williams.

## SIXTH DECADE

Rev. William Stuart Red, G. T. Reynolds, Fred S. Robbins, R. S. Rose, W. McB. Smith, J. Lewis Thompson, Capt. J. M. Thompson, G. E. Wilson, Judge J. M. Blanding, Erin E. Bryan, Rev. C. T. Caldwell, W. A. Vinson, R. W. Coffin, Dr. C. P. Coleman, Rev. Brooks I. Dickey, Capt. W. L. Donnell, W. L. Estes, Capt. J. L. Greer, D. W. Gulick, Col. P. B. Hunt, W. T. Ivy, John S. Kerr, Henry Moore, J. E. Morrison, Capt. D. D. Peden.

## SEVENTH DECADE

Rev. W. M. Anderson, Rev. W. M. Anderson, Jr., J. L. Cunningham, Rev. E. B. Fincher, Rev. W. F. Galbraith, Rev. Jas. F. Hardie, Hon. A. N. Leecraft, Dr. Ed Link, Hon. A. L. Randall, Albert Sledge, Judge Sam H. Smelser, J. B. Thomas, Joseph Wilson.

## EIGHTH DECADE

Judge Rhodes S. Baker, R. B. Binnion, William Bryce, Benjamin Clayton, J. P. Critz, G. B. Dealey, E. T. Fant, Rev. P. B. Hill, Pat E. Hooks, W. B. Morrison, Rev. T. D. Murphy, E. A. Peden, C. Stanly Roberts, Rev. W. A. Rollee, Hoxie H. Thompson, W. M. Whitenton.

## NINTH DECADE

Rev. W. A. Alexander, Rev. M. L. Baker, Rev. Frank C. Brown, Rev. R. L. Cowan, Thomas E. Craig, Mrs. J. W. Culver, Rev. H. W. DuBose, Eugene Elder, T. M. Gribble, Rev. Gaines B. Hall, Rev. Robert Hill, J. E. Jarratt, B. M. Leecraft, Rev. J. M. Lewis, Mrs. Dean Lide, Walter E. Long, Mrs. E. M. Munroe, Rev. L. L. McCutchen, W. H. McCarley, Jr., E. C. McDanald, R. L. Morrison, R. A. Partlow (Rev.), Mrs. G. T. Ralls, Mr. and Mrs. E. E. Shelton, Frank G. Trau, C. T. Wharton (Rev.), Mrs. Robert F. Wood.

## TENTH DECADE

Fred W. Adams, A. A. Aldrich, Jr., Rev. John F. Anderson, Rev. A. V. Boand, Dr. W. W. Bondurant, Jr., Rev. R. R. Craig, Shem P. Cunningham, Rev. Wm. M. Elliott, Jr., James A. Fant, R. A. Farnsworth, A. H. Ferguson, Rev. A. F. Fogartie, Houston Harte, Rev. Charles L. King, Rev. R. Gage Lloyd, Rev. P. D. Miller, John E. Mitchell, Jr., Mrs. Frank Phillips, B. Coleman Renick, Reid V. Robinson, Mrs. A. L. Slaughter, Mrs. George M. Smith, Rev. J. L. Spears, Mrs. J. Percy Terrell, Joe D. Warren, W. C. Windsor, Robert L. Wood, Toddie Lee Wynne.

## ELEVENTH DECADE

Rev. Tom B. Anderson, Dr. D. A. Angus, W. H. Avery, Rev. Walter A. Bennett, Rev. Joe M. Brown, Mrs. Thomas E. Craig, Clay Chiles, Elmer Danner, Lamar Fain, O. H. Grissom, Rev. Paul D. Hanna, John F. Henderson, J. Marshall Huser, Rev. Robert F. Jones, Mrs. J. A. Little, Rev. George Mauze, Mrs. Denman Moody, Rev. Leland Murphy, A. M. Pate, Jr., Bert Pfaff, Geo. R. Reese, Jr., Rev. S. P. Riccobene, Louis Rochester, Mrs. John W. Russell, Dr. George J. Seibold, Dick Simpson, Frank S. Thompson.

## TWELFTH DECADE

Crowdus Baker, A. L. Barnett, Murphy H. Baxter, Lewis H. Bond, John R. Brown, Jerry L. Brownlee, Mrs. Leo Corrigan, Sr., Cecil H. Green, David Hannah, Jr., John A. Huebner, J. Erik Jonsson, R. W. Kline, Matthew Lynn, E. Clyde McGraw, Stewart E. Meyers, W. C. Miller, Will A. Morriss, Jr., Mrs. E. J. Mosher, Cecil E. Munn, Dewitt C. Reddick, Mrs. Will M. Richardson, K. E. Smith.

# The Famous Four Horsemen of Austin College

A T the turn of the century four men left the campus armored for battle for a place in a not too inviting world. These men soon became known as the "Four Horsemen of Austin College" and even before they left their studies began to lead the way upward to the summit for their Alma Mater.

*"Tec" Craig*

*"Pat" Hooks*

*C. Stanly Roberts*

*Hoxie H. Thompson*

For further preparation, Thos. E. Craig, "Tec," obtained a Civil Engineering degree from the University of Tennessee. Stanly Roberts studied at Princeton University and Hoxie Thompson at Cornell University. Pat Hooks entered the graduate school of experience.

All four of the "Horsemen" were ruling elders in the Presbyterian Church and many were the battles they fought together to preserve and sustain Austin College on the floor of the Synod of the Presbyterian Church.

**THOMAS EDGAR CRAIG** (B.S. 1898) was born at Sulphur Springs, Texas. He was an engineer for the General Electric Company in its pioneer days and it was while building the Texas Electric Railway (Interurban between Dallas and Denison) that he met and married Kathryn Heard of McKinney, Texas, which has been their home. "Tec" Craig quickly found a challenging objective in developing McKinney into a strategic agricultural and industrial center. Thomas Edgar and Kathryn Heard Craig have sustained Austin College with their interest in every phase of college life by establishing scholarships, fellowships, permanent endowments and buildings. Mr. Craig served on the Board of Trustees from 1934 until his death and Mrs. Craig came on the Board soon after.

Resolution in the Minutes of the Board of Trustees, Mar. 12, 1962, page 512.

> Whereas; Thomas Edgar Craig, A.B. 1898, a Trustee of this college for almost a quarter of a century, and his wife, Kathryn Heard Craig, her husband's successor as trustee, have endeared themselves to the entire College family by warm friendship, unfailing loyalty, wise leadership and generous benefaction, be it, Resolved: that the Austin College Board of Trustees, as evidence of affection and gratitude, hereby order that this (music) building be named Craig Hall, and called no other name.

**PAT E. HOOKS** (1902) entered Austin College in 1900 and played on the football team. After two years he entered the banking business in Itasca, Texas. Though his interest in Austin College was originally in developing intercollegiate athletic activities, he became a trustee in 1920 and served until his death in 1950. He became known as the father of athletics at Austin College—even the Kangaroo mascots always being named "Pat." During the last eighteen years as trustee he was Chairman of the Board, a period in which the College was beset with adversities and crises, and often hampered in its upward progress by attempts to close, move or merge Austin College. This steady, determined and loyal helmsman brought the College through rough waters. He not only contributed financially to sustain the College but worked vigorously to obtain support from the alumni and the Presbyterians of the Synod of Texas. For twenty five years Pat Hooks personally financed the athletic program at Austin College and is credited with providing scholarships and loans for more than a hundred students.

**CHARLES STANLY ROBERTS** (B.S. 1898) was born at 915 South Crockett Street, in Sherman, July 27, 1878 and still lives at that address. From the Preparatory Department of Austin College he entered the Freshman Class in 1894. He was a charter member of Tri Phi fraternity founded at Austin College Nov. 4, 1894. He was valedictorian of his class, and at this writing is the oldest living alumnus of the College. He married Leska Murphy, also of Sherman, and their two sons, Royston and Stanly, Jr. are also graduates of Austin College.

Following in the footsteps of his father, Capt. C. N. Roberts, he became a member of the Board of Trustees in 1921 and served until 1966—longest term of service in twelve decades of the College history. Most of this time he was Chairman of the Executive Committee or Secretary of the Board.

At the Homecoming Game which also celebrated the Hundredth Anniversary of intercollegiate football, Mr. Roberts was recognized as the only one present who also attended the first Austin College game in 1896.

This Sherman civic leader has always had a leading role in getting financial support for Austin College from citizens of the Sherman area. The College has bestowed upon him the Doctor of Humanities in 1950 and the Austin College Distinguished Service Award in 1963.

**HOXIE HARRY THOMPSON** (B.S. 1901) was born at Kilgore, Texas, July 15, 1880. He entered the freshman class in 1897, after graduating from the Preparatory Department of Austin College. He graduated with the B. S. Degree in 1901 and later studied Civil Engineering at Cornell University. He and his brothers owned the Thompson Bros. Lumber Company. They donated the lumber for the Luckett Athletic Park in 1903, financed Thompson Science Hall in 1913, Cawthon Gymnasium and Cashion Field in 1923.

Mr. Thompson served on the Board from 1921 to 1946, succeeding his brother, J. Lewis Thompson, who had served on the Board from 1902 to 1922. His wife, the former Goree Gregg, daughter of Judge E. P. Gregg, who himself was a trustee (1876-1880) perpetuated her husband's memory through a bequest for construction of the Hoxie Thompson Auditorium.

Mr. Thompson was awarded the Austin College Distinguished Service Award and the Alumni Association Award in 1957.

These four valiant champions of the Austin College cause were directly responsible for securing most of the funds needed for the college to progress during the Eighth, Ninth and Tenth Decades. On April 12, 1923, Hooks, Roberts and Thompson were authorized to arrange a $90,000 loan from the Mississippi Valley Trust Company of St. Louis. The same three were appointed a committee on June 1, 1925 to appear before Synod's Executive Committee of Schools and Colleges to urge Synod to fulfill its obligation and promises to Sherman of twelve years standing. The three men were made the finance committee of the College and for the next thirty years Thompson and Hooks pushed the drive for funds out in the Synod while Stanly Roberts engineered the drives in Sherman, and Mr. Craig procured funds in the Dallas and McKinney areas.

# The Presidents of Austin College

## REV. SAMUEL McKINNEY, D. D., 1850-1853.

## REV. DANIEL BAKER, D. D., 1853-1857.

## THE REVEREND RUFUS WILLIAM BAILEY
*December 15, 1858-1862*

RUFUS Bailey was born April 13, 1793 at Yarmouth, Maine. His father, Lebbeus Bailey, was the son of Colonel John Bailey, who commanded a Regiment of Massachusetts "Minute Men" through the Revolutionary War. His mother's name was Sarah Sylvester.

He graduated at Dartmouth College in 1813, was fitted for college partly at Hebron Academy, and partly by Rev. Dr. Francis Brown, afterwards President of Dartmouth College. He became a member of the Junior Class in 1811.

He took his Masters Degree in 1816, was appointed Tutor in Dartmouth College in 1818, was returned as "Phi Beta Kappa" Orator in 1821 and was subsequently invited to preside over two other colleges. He was a Trustee of Williams College while residing in Massachusetts; at one time was Trustee of the University of Vermont.

After graduating from Dartmouth he entered the office of Daniel Webster as a student of Law. Before commencing practice of it, he changed his purpose, and repaired to Andover Theological Seminary as a student of Divinity. In 1818 he was ordained pastor of the Congregational Church at Norwich Plain, Connecticut, and at the same time was Professor of Moral Philosophy in the military Academy there. In 1823 he succeeded Dr. Humphrey as Pastor of the Congregational Church at Pittsfield, Massachusetts. In 1827 failing health compelled him to seek a southern climate, and he relinquished this pastorate.

He has always been connected with the cause of Education. In 1825 he originated, and led in the organization of the "Pittsfield Female Seminary"; established in South Carolina the "Richland (Normal) School"; taught a Female School in

Rev. Daniel Baker, D.D.
1853-1857

Rev. Samuel McKinney, D.D.
1850-1853    1862-1871

Rev. R. W. Bailey
1858-1862

Rev. T. S. Clyde, D.D., LL.D.
1900-31

Rev. S. M. Luckett, D.D.
1811-1818    1887-1897

Rev. K. B. Boude, D.D
1878-1881

Rev. Donald MacGregor, D.D.
1885-1887

Rev. E. P. Palmer, D.D.
1882-1885

E. B. Tucker, LL.D
1931-1943

Rev. T. R. Sampson, D.D.
1897-1900

*Rev. Wm. B. Guerrant, Ph.D.*
*1944-1953*

*John D. Moseley, LL.D*
*1953-*

Fayetteville, North Carolina. In 1842 he founded the "Augusta Female Seminary" (now "Mary Baldwin Seminary") at Staunton, Virginia. He continued to preside over that flourishing institution until 1848, when failing health again required him to relinquish his labors.

In 1854 he came to Texas and to Huntsville. He was appointed Professor of Languages in Austin College in February 1855. On December 14, 1858, at a meeting of the Trustees of Austin College at Houston, he was tendered and accepted the presidency of Austin College in which he continued to labor until 1862 when the condition of his health would not permit his continuance.

He died in Huntsville, Texas, April 26, 1863 at the age of seventy years and two weeks. He was sick only a few days of pneumonia.

(From a biographical sketch compiled partly from biographical notices of members of Alumni of Dartmouth College in 1813, and partly from records in his "Diary" kept by him for a number of years.)

## SAMUEL MAGOFFIN LUCKETT
*1871-1878—1887-1897*

REV. Samuel Magoffin Luckett was born in Russelville, Kentucky in 1839. He received the B.A. degree from Central College of Kentucky in 1859, attended Danville Theological College and was licensed and ordained in the Presbyterian ministry in 1866.

After serving Kentucky churches for five years, Rev. Luckett was elected President of Austin College in 1871. He held that position throughout the difficult times in Austin College history leading to its removal from Huntsville to Sherman in 1876. Two years later he turned over the Presidency of the College to Rev. H. B. Boude.

Rev. Luckett served the Milford, Texas, Church from 1878 to 1880, and the Palestine Presbyterian Church from 1880 to 1887. He married Mary J. Link of Palestine, Texas, in 1875 and both he and his wife became substantial benefactors of Austin College, often saving the College from financial embarrassment. Rev. Luckett was a Fourth Decade trustee.

In 1887 the College honored Rev. Luckett by bestowing upon him the D.D. degree and re-electing him President of the College. This second time in the presidency Dr. Luckett spent a whole decade in elevating the College to an enviable position among Southwestern institutions of higher learning. Graduates of Austin College were eagerly sought to head institutions of all levels, to form banks and commercial enterprises.

Dr. Luckett retired from the presidency in 1897 but both he and his wife continued their deep interest in Austin College with substantial gifts. He served pastorates at Beeville, Texas, in 1897-1902 and at Pine Street Church in San Antonio until his death in 1905.

Dr. Luckett gave the land for the first Austin College Athletic Field named Luckett Park, located on Luckett Avenue four blocks north of the main college campus. All intercollegiate football, baseball and track events were played on this field until removed in 1924 to Cashion Field (now Louis Calder Stadium) adjoining the campus.

Austin College again honored Dr. Luckett by naming the first men's dormitory "Luckett Hall" in 1907. Today this building is the oldest landmark on the campus and now newly renovated serves 150 students.


## HENRY BUCKNER BOUDE
*1878–1881*

REV. Henry Buckner Boude was born in Mayslick, Kentucky in 1833, received the B.A. degree from Central College of Kentucky in 1857, attended Danville Theological College and was ordained in the Presbyterian Church in 1861. He was a soldier and chaplain in the Confederate Army for four years; pastor of the Gallatin, Tennessee Church until 1872; of Columbus, Mississippi Church 1872-75; of Paris, Texas church 1875 until 1878, when he became President of Austin College, having previously been elected to the Board of Trustees of the College.

Rev. Boude was directly responsible for getting Austin College permanently established in Sherman. His energy and forcefulness was needed to pressure Sherman citizens to comply with their commitment to the College and the first main building on the campus was dedicated through his untiring efforts. (This was the building which was destroyed in 1913, set afire by a recalcitrant student.)

Dr. Boude married Eleanor Chambers in 1860. Their daughter married Rev. J. W. Moore, missionary to Japan, the father of Boude and Lardner Moore, both A. C. graduates and also missionaries to Japan.

Rev. Boude was honored by Arkansas College with the D.D. degree in 1878. He became pastor of Central Presbyterian Church in Kansas City, Missouri in 1881 and served Missouri churches until he died in Independence, Missouri in 1912.

## EDWARD PORTER PALMER
*1882–1885*

R EV. Edward Porter Palmer was born in Summerville, South, Carolina in 1826. He attended the University of Georgia and Columbia Theological Seminary and was ordained in 1849. He married Annie Buchanan of Winnsboro, S. C. in 1850. He served as pastor of a number of churches in South Carolina and Alabama until in 1869 when he became a professor at Louisiana State University. While there he was honored with the D.D. degree in 1874.

At the time of his election to the presidency of Austin College in 1882 he was serving as pastor of the Presbyterian Church at Mobile, Alabama. After three difficult years in the presidency, he accepted the pastorate of the Abilene, Texas, church for a year. Rev. Palmer left the State to serve in churches of Louisiana, Mississippi and Virginia until his death in 1905.

Synod's Minutes reveal that Rev. Palmer had the loyal support of Trustees John S. Besser, Rev. E. D. Junkin, Dr. Donald MacGregor and Elder C. N. Roberts in getting contributions of $3785 in 1882; and a promise of $4000 each year to support Austin College in 1884. The entire Board of Trustees of the College resigned at Synod's meeting October 30, 1884 at Belton, Texas and refused to be re-instated until Synod complied with a promise of annual financial support.

## DONALD MACGREGOR
*1884–1887*

REV. Donald MacGregor was born in Glasgow, Scotland. He came to Houston, Texas in 1849 after four years in the mercantile business in New Orleans. He became an elder in the First Presbyterian Church of Houston, Texas in 1850 where he first sustained an interest in Austin College and was soon elected to the Board of Trustees. His aspirations to study for the ministry had been delayed on account of business reverses but he overcame this difficulty and was ordained in 1871. After serving the Presbyterian Churches of Chapel Hill and the Lamar Street (now Second) Church of Houston, he was elected President of Austin College in 1884. He was the only President of the College to die while in office (Oct. 10, 1887).

Rev. MacGregor had continued as supply pastor of the Houston church and it was in Houston that he passed away after a short illness. A deed issued to James A. Baker, President of the Board of Trustees of Austin College, from the Glenwood Cemetery Association shows that he was interred there in Lot 261.

Rev. MacGregor married Mrs. Henrietta A. Speake in Jefferson, Texas in 1876. They were both great benefactors of Austin College. The five-story building on the corner of Fannin and Main Streets in Houston now leased to the estate of Jesse Jones until 2042 is one of their legacies. It is a part of the College Endowment and bears a net income of $5500 per year.

## THE REVEREND THORNTON ROGERS SAMPSON
*1897–1900*

THE Reverend Sampson was born at Hampden Sydney, Virginia, on October 9, 1852, and was reared in an educational environment. He received his education at Hampden Sydney College, University of Virginia, Edinburgh and Leipsig. After his ordination in 1878, he went to Europe and served as missionary for Greece until 1892. He became Secretary of Foreign Missions in 1892-4, and President of the Assembly's Home and School in 1894-7. Dr. Sampson became President of Austin College on June 10, 1897 and served in that capacity until June 10, 1900.

These years immediately following the military regime of the College were years of readjustment. Dr. Sampson emphasized the importance of the College Y.M.C.A. and advised all the students to become members of it. Everyone who knew Dr. Sampson understood the value which he placed upon college athletics. He was an ardent advocate of "a sane mind and a sound body" and believed all kinds of proper athletics contributed to that end. The beginning of real athletics dated from the beginning of his connection with Austin College. During the first year of his administration the only gymnasium the College had ever had was started, and during this time the first athletic director was procured for the College.

In May 1900 Dr. Sampson was elected President of the Austin School of Theology and on June 10th became its first President. He served in this capacity until 1905 when ill health made his resignation necessary. He served as Professor of Church History and Polity until his death in 1915.

In the summer of 1915 Dr. Sampson went to Colorado for a short vacation and rest. He was an experienced mountain climber, and on September 2nd he was seen alone, on foot going in the direction of Rocky Mountain Park. From this trip he did not return. Every possible effort was made to find the lost traveler or to recover his body, but no trace of the missing man was found. It is supposed that he was lost in a severe wind and snow storm which occurred on September 3rd, and which old residents of the mountains said it would have been impossible for even an experienced mountaineer to survive without shelter.

Ten years elapsed before the skeleton of Dr. Thonrton Sampson's body was found in the mountains of Estes Park. Thus ended the career of a close friend of Woodrow Wilson and a man who in just three years played a decisive role at Austin College in its "Search for the Summit."

*From "The History of Austin College" by Percy Wallace, and "Thornton R. Sampson-A Life Sketch" by Arthur G. Jones "Austin College Scrapbook" Jan. 11, 1925.*

# THOMAS STONE CLYCE
## 1900–1931

R EV. Thomas Stone Clyce was born in Kingsport, Tennessee, September 12, 1863. Dr. Clyce was educated at King College, where he received his B.A. in 1887 and in Columbia (then in South Carolina) and Louisville seminaries. He did graduate work in the University of South Carolina and held the honorary degree of LLD from King College, Baylor University and Austin College.

He was ordained in 1890 by the Presbytery of North Alabama and served pastorates in Decatur, Alabama; Louisville, Kentucky (where he met and married Miss Mayde Perrin October 1892); and Jackson, Alabama. During this last pastorate he was also President of Jackson Agriculture College.

Dr. Clyce came to Sherman in 1900 in the joint capacity of President of Austin College and Stated Supply of Grand Avenue Presbyterian Church. He relinquished the latter duty three years later, but offered the college a loyal and aggressive leadership as president for more than a quarter of a century, retiring in 1931 to become President Emeritus and Professor of Philosophy.

The Church conferred its greatest honor on this noted educator when Dr. Clyce was elected Moderator of the General Assembly in 1912. He had served as Moderator of the Synod of Texas in 1909.

During his thirty one years at the helm of the College the ten-acre campus was increased to thirty acres and six substantial buildings were erected or begun, all but one of which (YMCA) are in full use in 1970. Enrollment increased fivefold and financial support, especially from the alumni, quadrupled. Realizing the importance of science courses in the curriculum for developing medical and technological leaders for the Southwest, Dr. Clyce sought out qualified Christian professors to direct the science training program on the campus. These soon established an enviable record and after Thompson Science Building was constructed with complete laboratory facilities in 1913. Austin College took the leadership in this field.

Foreign languages, social and economic sciences were not neglected, nor were pre-ministerial, pre-law and pre-engineering. Intercollegiate athletics and forensics thrived and the College was making tremendous steps upward in its Search for the Summit when the depression at the close of the Eighth Decade brought it all to a halt.

No greater man of heart or spirit ever held the firm hand on the Austin College ship of state than Dr. Clyce. Affectionately called "Big Doc" and sometimes "Big Bull", he always held the respect of everyone in the College community. During his forty-seven years of service to Austin College he left his impress on thousands of those who passed through its halls.

Dr. Clyce died March 6, 1946. He was survived by his widow and two children, Wallace Perrin ("Pep") Clyce, '13, of Dallas; and Mrs. Allan G. (Dorothy) Smith of Houston, Texas.

## EVERETT BRACKIN TUCKER
*1931–1943*

D R. Everett Brackin Tucker was born in Tennessee near Smyrna where he was educated before entering Vanderbilt University, from which he received the B.A. degree in 1905. After several years of teaching he joined Jim Peoples in organizing a preparatory school at Springfield known as Peoples-Tucker School. Ill health forced him to give up school work and he retired to his father's farm to raise pigs for three years.

In June 1913, Dr. Tucker began eighteen years of service in the public school system of Arkansas, first as Superintendent of Searcy and later at Helena.

In 1923 he became President of Arkansas College at Batesville, which awarded him the L.L.D. in 1925. He served there until he was elected President of Austin College in 1931.

(From the Shelbyville, Tennessee *Times Gazette*, Vol. 95, No. 15, July 11, 1968)

Dr. Tucker did not find it easy to overcome the many serious problems confronting Austin College which started with the depression of the early thirties, the bank moratorium of 1933, a Synod divided in regard to the future of Austin College, and a Board of Trustees not in harmony with his aims. In his last three years as president he gave much of his time to the proposed merger of Austin College with Trinity University. Synod voted against the merger and Dr. Tucker resigned February 9, 1943.

Dr. Tucker returned to Tennessee and the Shelbyville *Times-Gazette* write-up continues:

> Unable to stop what he was best at doing, Dr. Tucker came to Webb School and for 14 years taught there, sometimes as many as seven classes a day and night school as well.
>
> In 1959 he retired from teaching and now makes Bell Buckle, Tennessee his home. He was awarded The Founder's Medal by the Board of Trustees of Austin College in 1963.

## THE REVEREND WILLIAM BARNETT GUERRANT
### 1944–1953

WILLIAM Barnett Guerrant was a native of Danville, Kentucky, and a descendant of French Calvinists and educators known particularly for mission work in Kentucky and Tennessee. In 1913 he was graduated from Centre College at Danville with a Bachelor of Arts degree, and in 1914 he received a Master of Arts degree, with English major, from the same school. He holds the Bachelor of Divinity degree from Kentucky Theological Seminary and graduate degree of Doctor of Sacred Theology from New York City Bible Seminary, and Doctor of Divinity from King College, Bristol, Tennessee.

After being licensed to preach in 1917, Dr. Guerrant was pastor of Highland Church and Superintendent of Highland Institute at Guerrant, Kentucky for ten years. From 1927 to 1929 he was President of Stonewall Jackson College at Abingdon, Virginia, going from this position to the Chair of Bible and pastorate of the University Church at Harrogate, Tennessee. His service as Superintendent of Bachman Memorial School and Home, Farner, Tennessee, followed.

Dr. Guerrant was called to the Austin College Chair of Bible in the fall of 1939 and served as Professor of Bible until 1943. He became Acting President in June 1943 and served in that capacity until June 1944 when he became President of Austin College. His appointment and acceptance were announced at graduating exercises.

Under the direction of Dr. Guerrant Austin College made outstanding gains, including admittance to the Southern Association of Colleges and Secondary Schools on December 13, 1946. A major building project was launched which included the completion of a $350,000 Administration Building in May 1947, and the start of a $500,000 construction program.

Paul Coffin Dormitory for girls was completed in 1948. The greatest gift ever made to Austin College up to this time was provided by M. B. Hughey who left to Austin College oil properties valued at $1,000,000. A new $250,000 Hughey Memorial Gymnasium was completed in the fall of 1949. The Alumni and Ex-Students Association established a campaign to raise funds to assist in the building of the Memorial Student Union Building as a memorial to students who lost their lives in the two World Wars. This building was completed in the fall of 1951. A $25,000 gift from Mr. and Mrs. Fred Adams made possible the construction of an infirmary, The Adams Health Center, completed in the fall of 1951.

A Department of Fine Arts was added in 1946; and a Department of Home Economics was added in 1952, made possible through an anonymous gift.

The Austin College Centennial was celebrated in 1949-50 during the administration of Dr. Guerrant. He resigned in the summer of 1953.

From: *Austin College Bulletin* (June 1944 and July 1944, *The Presbyterian Outlook*, September 26, 1949 (002.20).

EDITORIAL PAGE     Sherman Democrat     Aug. 23, 1953
### GUERRANT AND MOSELEY

There is a tinge of sadness in the welcome Sherman gives to John D. Moseley, new president of Austin College. For in welcoming the new president we bid farewell to the old, Dr. William B. Guerrant.

For 14 years Dr. Guerrant has been in the flow of Sherman events, first as professor of Bible and then as one of the most successful presidents the 103-year-old Presbyterian school has ever had.

The quiet gray-haired minister with the gentle philosophical manner and gay spirit is neither the cloistered scholar nor the big-shot college president interested only in the financial program of his school.

Barney Guerrant is a Sherman citizen, a part of the community, church and social life. He has performed marriage ceremonies, and conducted funeral services. He has seen the sons of many of his friends as well as his own sons go to war and faced with them the problems that came when the battle was over. He has served as a worker in the Community Chest, the Boy Scouts and the Rotary Club.

Mrs. Guerrant has become "Susie" to a host of friends. She has contributed much to church and social life and clubwork. The Guerrant family has been a Sherman family, as well as a college family.

The changed appearance of the Austin campus, the handsome new buildings, the enlarged faculty and expanded curriculum, — all are evidences of Dr. Guerrant's wise leadership and acute understanding of the place the small liberal arts college has in the field of American education. There must have been times when this Bible scholar and teacher longed to leave the administrator's post for the quiet of the classroom and study. But he filled with courage and industry as well as wisdom the post to which he had been called.

With his achievements as a banner, Dr. Guerrant can now return to the teaching he loves, enriched by his contact with the more practical side of educational problems. Our regard and best wishes go with him in his return.

John Moseley comes to fill a big gap but he brings with him a reputation of being able to do big things. He is young, vigorous and capable. His experience in research and government affairs, in particular in advising the State Legislature in college budgeting matters, will undoubtedly prove invaluable to Austin College. His strength and leadership as a Presbyterian layman should be an inspiration for educational service to others of his church.

Sherman bids farewell to the Guerrant family and welcomes that of John Moseley, new president of the school that has a glorious heritage in Christian education in the South.

## JOHN DEAN MOSELEY
*1953—*

JOHN Dean Moseley was born in Greenville, Texas, November 17, 1915. He received his B.S. degree from the East Texas State College in 1936, his LL.B. degree in 1940, and M.A. degree in 1942 from the University of Texas. He received the LL.D. degree from Midwestern University, and from Trinity University in 1954. Dr. Moseley's special field of study was Political Science, Public Administration, and Law. He had a wide variety of experience in research and organization work. He helped organize the war-time Office of Price Administration in Dallas, and became Director of Administrative Services for the OPA in Washington, D.C., 1942. As Director in the OPA, he was in the immediate management staff of the Administration. He helped reorganize the state government of Connecticut and was employed by the United States Bureau of the Budget before accepting the directorship of the newly formed Texas Legislative Council. He left this position to become President of Austin College on September 1, 1953.

Two things particularly fitted Dr. Moseley for the presidency of Austin College — his work in the Legislative Council and his church activities. As Executive Director of the Texas Legislature Council he completed a study of higher education in Texas. He was active in church work from his youth, serving as President of Youth Council in the Presbytery, Synod, and General Assembly of the Presbyterian Church, U.S. He helped reorganize the Synod of Texas administrative set-up, then served on the first Synod's Council. As Chairman of the Division of Research, he directed surveys and studies which pointed up the need for a long range program for the development of Synod's agencies and institutions. As a result the Long Range Planning Committee was established. Out of this came the TFC drive from which Austin College received a larger share than any other single institution.

Dr. Moseley has held the office of President of the Sherman Chamber of Commerce, the Sherman Area Council of the Boy Scouts of America, the United Fund Drive, the Texas Council of Church–Related Colleges, Presbyterian Educational Association of the South, Council of Protestant Colleges and Universities, Association of Texas Colleges and Universities, and served as Moderator of the Synod of Texas.

Since coming to Austin College, Dr. Moseley has accomplished much in the development of the academic and physical aspects of the College. A Self-Study was made of the management and of the academic program of the College, and improvements resulted in both areas. The Austin College Plan, underwritten by the Ford Foundation, resulted in major changes in the academic program, bringing all elements of the college program into a coordinated unit, the academic, chapel and campus activities. Changes were made in the scholarship program in discontinuing "category" scholarships— ministerial, athletic, and faculty children. This helped to solve the problems of the subsidized athletics, and Dr. Moseley took the lead in organizing the Church College Amateur Athletic Association and became its first President. This plan has brought about a great stability in the problems of operating a full scale athletic program.

Master Plans have been drawn up for the future development of the College. Ten new buildings resulted—four dormitories, Library, Science Building, Chapel, President's Home, Dean's Home, Music Building. Additions have been made to two buildings, and extensive remodeling to four other buildings.

Texas Christian University honored Dr. Moseley for his contributions to higher education in Texas and for his services to the Presbyterian Church by awarding him an honorary Doctor of Laws degree during the summer commencement of 1969.

# CHAPTER III

# The Twelve Decades

## The First Decade — A Crisis

SAMUEL McKinney (March 10, 1807-November 27, 1879), an early Texas educator, was born in County Antrim, Ireland. He was the son of Samuel McKinney and Margaret Findlay McKinney, who immigrated with their family to America and settled first at Philadelphia in 1812. After a few months they moved from Philadelphia to Radgerville, Tennessee. In 1829, young Samuel entered the University of Pennsylvania, and graduated from that institution in 1832. While at the university he studied medicine, but during the latter part of his university course, he changed his major study from medicine to theology, for he had decided to become a preacher. Upon finishing his preparation for the ministry, he went to Illinois, where he served as pastor of the Oakdale Covenanter Church from 1834 to 1840; in Illinois he also did a great deal of missionary work among Indians and "backwoods settlers." For the next two or three years he taught and preached in Shelby County, Tennessee. Gradually he gave up ministerial work to devote his entire time to teaching. During this period of his residence in Tennessee, he taught for some years in Denmark Academy, and was President of the West Tennessee College at Jackson, Tennessee. His next work in the educational world was as President of Chalmers Institute in Holly Springs, Mississippi. There he met Dr. Daniel Baker, who was a member of the Board of Trustees of Chalmers Institute. When Dr. Baker went to Texas and secured a charter for Austin College, he persuaded Dr. McKinney to come to Texas to assist him in the organization of the new college. So the McKinney family arrived in Huntsville, Texas in February, 1850, and on April 5, 1850, Samuel McKinney was elected President of Austin College, a position he held until June 29, 1853.

Dr. McKinney had preceded his family to Texas and upon arrival at Huntsville began immediately to take charge of Stovall Academy in a building previously used by Huntsville Male Institute chartered privately in 1848. When he took over the presidential reins of Austin College he continued to teach in the Academy, deriving part of his salary from the Academy until the end of the school year. Thereafter the Academy became the Preparatory Department of the College and McKinney's salary was set at $1500 per year by the trustees, January 25, 1850. At that time President McKinney "had charge of the *Classical Department* of the preparatory school and exercised general supervision over the English branch of the same." (*Minutes of Board*—p. 19). He was a man of great energy and devotion, and loyal to his convictions; a strong man physically and mentally endowed with fine executive ability, and was eminently fitted for his position at this period of ripe scholarship. He was also an effective disciplinarian.

At this first Board of Trustees meeting General Sam Houston was placed second after Daniel Baker in class one of the Board. He was present for the annual meeting June 24, 1851 which marked the laying of the cornerstone for the first permanent building (page 9 of *Minutes*). The account in the Huntsville newspaper states that "General Sam Houston held an umbrella over Dr. Samuel McKinney while the college president addressed the assemblage."

> This being the day for laying the cornerstone of Austin College, the Secretary presented to the Board the following list of deposits which he had prepared to be laid in the cornerstone of the new building, namely: A copy of the Constitution of the United States and the State of Texas. A copy of the Charter of Austin College. History of the admission of each State into the Union, Washington's farewell address, the names of the Officers of the Federal and State government, names of the officers and trustees of Austin College, specimens of the Revolutionary paper currency of the old 13 states, and of the Texas

Republic, Disturnell's map of North America with the new boundaries up to the present year, Congressional Directory, pamphlets on various subjects, a bundle of the latest newspapers, names of the architect and workmen engaged on the edifice and a copy of the Sacred Writings.

The time having arrived for the formation of a procession to proceed to the College Grounds, the Board, headed by Col. James Gillispie, Grand Marshall of the ceremony, were followed in procession by the Grand Master of the Grand Lodge of the State of Texas, the Knights Templar, the Grand Royal Arch Chapter of the State of Texas in a body, and the members of Forrest Lodge and many visiting brethern under their Grand Marshall, Adolphus Stern. The teachers and students of the Huntsville Female Academy, under the protection of John H. Calhoun, Deputy Marshal; the students of the Huntsville Male Institute under the direction of Mr. Brown, and a large and respectable number of visiting ladies and gentlemen. Having arrived at the place designated, the blessings of Heaven were invoked upon the Institution in a prayer by the Rev. Chaplain R.E.B. Baylor, the deposits made, and the corner-stone laid in due and ancient form by the Most Excellent Grand Master Neal, after which the entire concourse repaired to an adjoining grove on the college grounds where an address was delivered by President McKinney and the meeting dismissed by a benediction from the Rev. J. W. Miller, and the Board joined the large assembly in a bountiful repast prepared for the occasion. The Board took a recess until 5:00 o'clock P.M. (*Minutes of Austin College Board*, Vol. 1, p. 9)

Soon thereafter a very disconcerting affair occurred between Senator Houston and President McKinney. Houston, through Yoakum his agent, had rented several acres of land near the College to "Professor McKinney" on shares. Returning to Raven Hill, his plantation home several miles from Huntsville, Houston noticed that much of the crop of corn had been gathered without leaving every third row, which was his rent. The following letters give the details:

At Home, Sept. 1, 1851

Professor McKinney,

Dear Sir, Until Colonel Yoakum returns I object to any more fodder being removed. It will not be injured in the field, and I have much to say before its removal. So soon as I can, this evening, I will be happy to call over, and see to it in Town, or at the School.

Your friend,
Sam Houston

On the same day he wrote Henderson Yoakum:

Huntsville, Sept. 1, 1851

Dear Col. There is no news. Doctor McKinney and I disagree about the fodder of the corn. I insist on *one-third of the produce* of the *land*. We have agreed to leave it to you. You can be ready to say what was your understanding when it was rented. By pulling the fodder when he did, I suppose he injured the crop one-fifth. Say what you think right but make your decision before you leave for Montgomery. I hope to see you on your way. I write in your office with an infernal pen.

Houston was again in Washington D.C. when the Board met February 23, 1853 but had his friend Sam Hay present to vote his proxy. At this meeting several vacancies on the faculty were to be filled, among them the Chair of Foreign Languages. Rev. N.A. Penland was elected professor of that department. (p. 46, *Minutes*). Rev. Penland had recently come to Huntsville from Alabama and was the husband of Houston's niece, Phebe Moore Penland.

Houston was present at the June 27, 1853 meeting and made chairman of two committees, (p. 48 of Minutes) the Executive Committee with Yoakum and Dr. John Branch to inquire into the internal condition and progress of the College; and a committee on unfinished business with the same two trustees. The only other members present were Robert Smither, John Hume and J. Carroll Smith. Four professors were allowed to vote by proxy for Atchison, Red, Burke and Judge Lipscomb—an illegal procedure since faculty were disqualified by Section 8 of the

Charter. To add to this irregularity of No Quorum, the committees met and reported June 28. In the business transacted by the Board a resolution from the Committee on Education to exempt ministerial candidates from paying tuition was adopted (provided the number did not exceed thirty).

The Minutes of the next day, Wednesday, June 29, 1853 read:

> Board met accordingly to adjournment, and was opened with prayer.
>
> Present as at the former session. The President, Rev. Samuel McKinney, then tendered his resignation, whereupon it was resolved that the resignation of the President be and hereby is accepted, to take effect upon the termination of the present meeting of the Board.
>
> The report of the Committee on Education (Dr. Branch, N.A. Penland and H. Yoakum) being read was adopted: Resolved that the Board proceed to elect a President of the College to take the place of the late President resigned. The election being entered into resulted in the choice of the Rev. Daniel Baker D.D. The Trustees then proceeded to elect a professor of Mathematics which resulted in the choice of Rev. A. E. Thom. Resolved that Professor N. A. Penland be appointed and requested to act President Pro-tem of Austin College in the absence of President Baker.

McKinney then entered his protest:

> Whereas the Executive Committee did in the estimation of the President and without his consent, call a meeting of the Board of Trustees when it had adjourned to meet at the call of the President, and when he had definitely stated his purpose to call a meeting in accordance with the adjourned at Galveston, that in the estimation of the President there was a want of comity to absent members, and a haste which he cannot now sanction.
>
> Samuel McKinney

Further Action by the Board was then taken:

Resolved that the Executive Committee be allowed to reply to the above protest entered by the President, Rev. Samuel McKinney.

Resolved that a vote of thanks be tendered to Dr. McKinney for the able and dignified manner in which he discharged his duties while president.

Motion to adjourn until the date of the next meeting according to rules and regulations.

Some historians have suggested that the resignation of President McKinney was to become so embarrassing to Houston that it was the cause of his moving his family to Independence in the fall of 1853. Houston had previously provided a home in Independence for his wife's mother, Mrs. Nancy Lea, who was an ardent Baptist and "ran the Baptist Church" there. Houston's wife, Margaret, suffered from asthma. In a letter to Washington D. Miller on September 13, 1853 Houston states that "he bought the Hines place and a tract of timbered land for a new location for his family as he felt Independence held educational advantages for his children." He moved them from Raven Hill on October 25, 1853. It was well that he did as Dr. McKinney had many friends in Huntsville and more unpleasant events were soon to occur.

Dr. McKinney returned to Alabama after his resignation. Rev. N.A. Penland did not serve as President Pro-tem very long. The *Board Minutes* of 1854 (p. 70) state:

> Whereas Professor Penland has tendered his resignation of the chair of Languages in Austin College, the Board of Trustees of said College in view of the many charges and reports which have been in circulation to the prejudice of said professor, and to the interest of the college, have received his resignation; and in doing so they are not influenced by the truth or falsehood of the charges or slanderous reports against Professor Penland, but in view of the interest of the college resolve that the Executive Committee procure an assistant teacher to supply the vacancy caused by the above resignation, till the chair is regularly filled.
>
> The Board then adjourned *sine die*
> R. H. Byrd
> Pres. Pro-tem
> H. Yoakum, Act. Sec.

*Note:* Rev. N. A. Penland had come to Texas from a church in Alabama where he had been accused of "ardent use of spirituous liquors and opium." He was charged by the session of the Huntsville Church for excessively using alcoholic beverages and suspended. This charge was sustained by Presbytery and a year later April 6, 1855, the Presbytery of Brazos records (Vol. II, page 3) read:

> Rev. N. A. Penland having made application to the Presbytery by letter and by some of the Citizens of Huntsville to be restored to ministerial fellowship v 'th the body; on motion his case was taken up. The letters relating to his case and the testimony taken during his trial having been read, the following minute was adopted: "As the Presbytery has not had sufficient evidence of his repentance and reformation during the short period of time which has elapsed since the suspension of Mr. Penland Resolved that his *Request* be not granted at this time."

(Records show that Prof. Penland died at Woodville, Texas, the next year).

Some historians state that Dr. McKinney returned to Mississippi in 1853 "because his family had never been satisfied to live in Texas." The truth is that Dr. McKinney was a man of strong convictions. He could not tolerate actions of the Executive Committee of the College chaired by Sam Houston in calling a meeting of the Board which he termed "a want of comity to absent members, and a haste which he would not sanction." Thus ended the first crisis at Austin College.

## THE REVEREND DANIEL BAKER
*Trustee and General Agent 1849-1853*
*President 1853-1856 Agent 1857*

BAKER, in his autobiography, states that his attention was first drawn to Texas in 1838, by Rev. John Breckenridge, who had recently visited Texas. In a glowing account of Texas as an unusually promising field for missionary enterprise, before members of Tuskaloosa Presbytery, Breckenridge turned to him and said, "Brother Baker, you are the man for

Texas." A few months later Baker again met Breckenridge and again was urged to "go to Texas." It was not long before he felt the call and was appointed by Assembly's Board. He preached 33 sermons in various towns on the way before he reached New Orleans, where Rev. Breckenridge was pastor of the Presbyterian Church. A month was used in preaching in Mobile and other cities.

Daniel Baker, whose activities made Austin College a reality, descended from noble Puritans who felt that education and religion were sisters. He was born at Midway, Liberty County, Georgia, August 17, 1791. He was converted at the age of 14 and resolved he would become a minister of the Gospel. His early education was largely gained through private reading, most of which was of a religious nature. He entered Hampden-Sydney for the first two years of his college education, and completed his senior year at Princeton in 1815 as one of the five honor members.

He married Miss Elizabeth McRobert, March 28, 1816. He held pastorates at Harrisonburg and New Erection, Virginia, and Second Presbyterian Church, Washington, D.C., other pastorates in Savannah, Georgia, and did missionary work in South Carolina, Georgia and Florida. Work in Ohio and Kentucky did not prove so successful, due in all probability to the fact he was not an Abolitionist, and he returned to Alabama. It was about this time that he became interested in The Republic of Texas. He left his family in the East and reached Galveston, February 1840 where he served as a missionary.

Baker preached as he had opportunity for several weeks, publicly baptizing several converts, the first on the island by a Protestant.

A month later Baker was in Houston where he first met Rev. Benjamin Chase, who was later to become the prime benefactor to Austin College. His travels soon led him to Independence where he became acquainted with Rev. Hugh Wilson, who formerly had been laboring with the Chickasaw Indians. In the spring of 1840 (April 3rd) Brazos Presbytery was organized at Chriesman School House near Independence with four ministers and one elder present. It was here that the brethern first discussed the hope of establishing a Presbyterian college, and here that Baker obtained his first subscription — 1500 acres of land from Captain Perry — who married Stephen F. Austin's sister.

In May Baker returned to New Orleans on the brig "Sam Houston" preaching here and there. It was not until June 1848 that he "perceived that his preaching in Holly Springs, Mississippi, was not doing much good' and he became restless and unhappy. A note from Rev. Stephen F. Cocke of Lavaca, Texas, with a glowing account of a promising field sent him off again and he arrived in the Lone Star State (now the name for Texas) on June 26, 1848. He accepted a call to the church at Galveston, was chosen to become a missionary to Texas and began his active work.

Dr. Baker had two very famous maxims to guide his life; namely, "Do good on a large scale! on a small scale! on any scale!," and "Don't worry about the clouds, they are in good hands."

In July 1849, Baker, Revs. Miller and Blair were appointed to select a place for making a renewed effort to found a college. On visiting Huntsville for the first time a few days later he preached and "converted a few souls, of whom one, Major Wade Hampton, was subsequently made an elder." The citizens at Huntsville were so pleased with his talk of a college that they immediately subscribed eight thousand dollars "for the creation and support of a college by the Presbyterian Church, at or within a mile of Huntsville, Walker, Co., Texas, to be called Baker College." This honor he instantly declined. Rev. Daniel Baker, D. D. was #1 charter member of the Board of Trustees serving as such until he became the second President of the College June 29, 1853. He was president pro-tem until Rev. McKinney arrived in Huntsville to become officially the first president, April 6, 1850. Actions of the Board on this day made:

> Dr. Baker permanent agent of Austin College with full power to receive donations for the use of same "resolved that he be fully authorized to give receipts, to make deposits in favor of our Treasurer, or to do any act necessary in the promises for aid on behalf of the college. Resolved, that for his services he be allowed at the rate of one thousand dollars per annum, and his expenses incurred traveling and in forwarding books, etc., from the point received." (*Minutes of the Board* page 7)

One of the first acts was to donate a lot to President McKinney on which to build a home, to be selected by him from three donated to the College by Col. G. W. Rogers. Evidently Dr. Baker lost no time in beginning his task. He immediately launched a series of trips throughout the States soliciting funds. From Savannah, Georgia, November 18, 1850, he writes, "I have set my heart upon making Huntsville, as far as I have influence, the Athens of Texas, in building up there a college of high character, one that shall be a credit to Texas, and an honour to the Presbyterian name." Later he writes: "On this tour I obtained maps, books, globes and $4,165. I went to Natchez, saw Brother Chase, and received from him a relinquishment of all the lands which he owned in Texas, amounting to nearly 15,000 acres." In 1851 he made his second trip in the interest of the college, going as far as Baltimore, this trip netting about $5,000. In February 1852, he began his third trip which netted another $6,000 from collections taken up after his preaching of twenty sermons and converting 67 persons. It was on this trip that he was robbed of nearly one thousand dollars, most of which he recovered through prompt help of an ex-sheriff and marshall.

His fourth trip as financial agent before he became president of the college was begun early in 1853, traveling as far as New York. His preaching often drew crowds between two and three thousand.

Dr. Baker was away on a field trip and did not attend the June 27, 1854 meeting and Rev. R. H. Byers was called to the chair. Sixty one preparatory and 23 college students constituted the student body. All the claims against the College were met without having to sell any land. The secretary of the Board, Henderson Yoakum reported for the Executive Committee, "Our general agent is now in the Southern States and is indefatigable in his efforts in behalf of the College. With the fostering care of the Board, the committee feel confident that we have nothing to fear as to the ultimate success of the Institution." Six long pages are required for Daniel Baker's report to the Board read to them by the secretary. It became the duty and pleasure of Yoakum and president pro-tem R. H. Byers to issue the first two diplomas for B.A. degrees ever issued in Texas, to Joab H. Banton and L. O. Black.

By October 31, 1854, President Baker was still absent from the college for the Fall Board meeting. It was at this meeting called by the executive committee that the Board appointed Henderson Yoakum, Abner Lipscomb and James A. Baker (all lawyers):

> A committee of three whose duty it shall be to enquire into the propriety of erecting a law department in connection with and dependent upon this corporation, and that they report to the regular meeting of this Board in June next.
>
> Resolved that said committee report as to the probable expense for additional buildings, for a law library etc: also, as to the number of professors necessary in such department, and the probably extent of patronage it would receive.
>
> Also at this meeting the Board accepted the resignation of Prof. N. A. Penland who had been discharged as stated supply pastor of the Huntsville Presbyterian Church for ardent use of spirituous liquor." (*Board Minutes*, pages 65-66)

Dr. Baker was present March 17, 1855 for a called meeting of the Board of Trustees for the express purpose of creating the first Law School in Texas. Judge R. T. Wheeler was elected professor of Law and Henderson Yoakum, Secretary and assistant professor.

This meeting also "authorized Col. Henderson Yoakum to purchase additional apparatus and chemicals as deemed necessary when he went north." Action of the Executive Committee and president in hiring Rev. R. W. Bailey (later to become president) to fill the language chair vacated by N.A. Penland's resignation was confirmed.

There was no regular June meeting for lack of a quorum.

> June 28, 1855—Trustees met, but not having a quorum was obliged to abandon the idea of a meeting—Had a free conversation on matters pertaining to the interest of the Institution without any legislation. (Nevertheless the faculty issued one B.A. degree to S. A. Hume—Flood conditions and an epidemic had prevented all but seven trustees from reaching Huntsville). (*Board Minutes,* page 69.)

Dr. Baker did assemble a quorum for the January 17, 1856 meeting, resulting in his being instructed to:

> proceed as soon as possible to the Older States, and in the earnestness of truth and want, apply for aid from those who can and will help us to build up in this new country a flourishing institution of moral and intellectual culture. That Professor Bailey be appointed agent for the college in this state to collect funds, receive subscriptions for endowment, scholarships, lands and students. (*Board Minutes*, page 73)
>
> Business conditions everywhere and especially at the college were getting rough-President Baker "was authorized to sell a sufficient of land if indespensable, to meet the present and pressing want of the professors, or if advisable to mortgage lands for that purpose.
>
> To cut down on expenditure the School year was shortened by one month — to end last Wednesday of May instead of June as formerly.
>
> The Board also united in a written request to Jesse Givens, F. A. Palmer, P. W. Kittrell and John Sayler, members of the Legislature to use their influence and efforts to procure an endowment for the law Department of Austin College. (*Board Minutes*, p. 74)

The Board met May 28, 1856 without Dr. Baker, who was away searching for funds. Three Bachelor of Arts degrees were awarded to W. A. Allen, G. W. Davis and J. S. Harrison. The first Bachelor of Law degrees ever awarded in Texas were issued to Joab Banton, B. Randolph, L. O. Black and L. E. Trezvant. Banton and Randolph later became Trustee and Judges.

Early in 1857 Dr. Baker returned to the campus from his travels for the College in the East and at a called meeting January 16, 1857 addressed the Board:

> Gentlemen:
>
> Matters touching the vital interests of our beloved Institution have in my judgement made it necessary that you should be called together at this time. I am no alarmist; but Gentlemen, let me tell you plainly, that the present condition of Austin College imperatively demands on your part, prompt and efficient action. Not mere paper resolutions; not any more ex-

pressions of good wishes but *prompt and efficient action.* It is true—we have a beautiful College Edifice; nearly a full corps of teachers, and for the present session eighty six students enrolled; thirty three in the Collegiate and fifty three in the preparatory department. Moreover, Austin College has a good name at home and abroad. These things are all very pleasing, very encouraging, but after all, it is my deliberate opinion, that without something effective done, and speedily done, our sky cannot long remain bright as it is now. Without something effective done speedily, our institution cannot become what is was originally intended to be, a credit to Texas and an honor to the Presbyterian Church—

Gentlemen, Money is needed—is needed now! Our debts are increasing! Your agent has not been slumbering. He has been much from home, he has done what he could. Since commencing this noble enterprise seven years ago, besides large contributions of lands, cash of more than 26 thousand dollars, paying for our College edifice and other things we have scarcely sufficient to meet our current expenses, indeed not that, for the treasury is empty and we owe our professors—The treasury must be relieved and relieved at once! These professors who are embarrassed must be relieved and now!

Having made this statement of facts, permit me, Gentlemen, to make some respectful suggestions:

(1) Reduce the number of teachers. I respectfully tender my resignation, wishing to devote myself exclusively to the ministry. This will relieve the treasury of thirteen hundred dollars.

(2) That Governor Swain, the present very popular and successful president of the University of North Carolina be elected to supply my place

(3) Call upon Huntsville citizens for aid at once.

(4) That each trustee, present or absent give some present aid in money or available notes as a donation or loan, in order that the professors should have some relief without delay from the pecuniary pressures they are under.


Dr. Baker had many other suggestions before that meeting was over. He requested his own accounts which he had handed to the Treasurer to be audited at once, He expressed thanks to the Board for their kindness while he was president and after imploring God's blessing upon them, tendered his resignation.

Before the meeting was over, all of Dr. Baker's suggestions were acted upon. (Governor Swain however, refused to accept the call to the presidency.)

J. Carroll Smith and S. R. Smith deeded 2000 acres of land worth $5000, and $1400 in cash was donated by seven of the members of the Board that day.

At the June 24, 1857 meeting with Rev. A. E. Thom acting president in the Chair, Daniel Baker still acting as agent for the college reported large gifts of land from James Sorley, and J. M. McCormick, former Board member, Benjamin Chase and Andrew Cunningham of Alabama and Austin Bryan.

At Commencement only three degrees were earned—the B.A. by W. E. Smith and the M.A. by Joab Banton and L. O. Black. The honorary D.D. degree was conferred upon Rev. Hugh Wilson charter trustee. (*Board Minutes* page 99). The *Minutes* of June 24, 1858 state:

> Mr. Byers presented a report on the death of Rev. D. Baker, DD., which was on motion received and adopted as follows:
> To the Board of Trustees of Austin College.
> Your committee in reference to the death of Dr. D. Baker, would respectfully submit—That it is needless for them to say anything in reference to Dr. Baker's connection with Austin College. Nothing which we can say would adequately express the values of his services, or the estimation in which they are held by the friends in the College. Of the number of those who first moved in this enterprize; he remained until his death, the fast friend of the College—More abundant in his labors in its behalf than all others. His praise is in the mouth of all. And his highest and best memorial is in the hearts of the friends and students of the College.
> Dr. Baker's death took place in the City of Austin December 10, 1857. He had gone there as General Agent for the College to endeavor to secure aid from the State in its behalf. His death was peace, and full of hope. And in view of this dispensation of Providence, your committee would present the following resolution:

Resolved, that in the death of Dr. Baker, the agent of the College, we feel that we have lost one of the most efficient friends of our Institution, and that while to us, its seems almost an irreparable loss, yet we bow to the decree of Him who doeth all things well; "And can but do right," in the trust that he will order this and all things for good and the prosperity of the college.

R. H. Byers]
John    Hill    ]    Committee
W. A. Leigh]

(*Board Minutes*, page 102.)

"It becomes my painful duty," said Dr. P. W. Kittrell, a leading statesman upon the floor of the Legislature on that occasion, "to announce to this house the sudden and unexpected intelligence of the death of one of Texas' public benefactors' the Rev. DANIEL BAKER is no more! This sad intelligence burst upon us so suddenly and unexpectedly, that it has been difficult to realize the truth. I could not believe it until I visted the chamber where this great and good man, this venerable father in Israel, died. I have laid my hand on that cold and marble brow, have gazed on that face which I have so often seen lit up with animation and life, but now stamped with the cold impress of death. I have pressed that hand which I have so often grasped before in the warmth of friendship and affection, but now stiffened and cold. I know that he is dead. As a general thing, I am opposed to the obtrusion of our private griefs on this house to the interruption of business; but I consider the death of Dr. Baker a public calamity. He is justly entitled to the claim and rank of one of Texas' benefactors. His exertions and usefulness were confined to no particular locality, no limited sphere. Possessed of a catholic spirit, of universal love and benevolence towards his fellow-men, he was prompted thereby to extend his sphere of usefulness as wide as possible. There has been scarcely a State in the Union but has heard his eloquent pleadings in behalf of religion and all the great moral interests of society. Twenty years ago I knew the deceased in Alabama. He was then the same devoted, enterprising, assiduous man and minister that he has been here; and since the scene of his usefulness has been transferred to this State, we all know with what untiring efforts he has exerted himself, not only in the cause of his Heavenly Master, but especially in the cause of education. He has left proud monuments in proof of these truths, and in honour to his memory. There stands not two hundred miles from this place, on the brow of a lofty summit, a beautiful edifice, surrounded by shady groves and academic walks. In it is opened a fountain of science, at which near one hundred youths daily drink. This edifice is Austin College, reared principally by the noble exertions of the lamented deceased, whose loss we are this day called to mourn. But, while these monuments stand, and I hope they may long continue so to do in honour of Dr. Baker, he is gone."

"The confidence in the purpose and favour of God with respect to the College, meant, with him, only an assured confidence in the divine blessing upon all efforts in its behalf; and from the first he made every possible endeavor that was suggested to him by others, or conceived by himself. Were the lands of the College to be looked after — though in a remote part of the State? — At the earliest moment he was there, guiding his travel-worn horse through almost impenetrable cedar-brakes, searching for the confused corners and almost obliterated bearings; or, in the nearest surveyor's office, poring over musty and bewildered records, more difficult to trace on the paper page than upon the corrugated bark of live-oak and blackjack. Was anything to be accomplished by correspondence? — By the first mail went forth his letters, each written with an accurate precision, to obviate any possible misapprehension."

"As to his efforts for the College during his six tours, we have seen how he toiled and how he succeeded. Six tours to beg for the College out of the State! He became more and more reluctant to beg in this way. It was very well when he first began; Texas was then smaller in population, and indefinitely deep in debt; but when that population so swiftly doubled itself when that debt disappeared, leaving Texas with millions in its chest for present use, and incalculable resources for the future, with the steward in Scripture, it was his feeling (to beg I am ashamed.) Two resources were left him: one was a visit to England, Ireland, and Scotland; and he felt confident that if God led him east of the Atlantic, He would bless him, as He had so richly west of it. But he regarded this only as a last resort; his other resource, in which he had the strongest hope, was in aid from the State. How he hoped, and how he strove, session after session of the Legislature, to obtain this, has already been seen. On his return from Eastern Texas, he remained at home more than a month, making all possible arrangements to prosecute his plans at a meeting of the Legislature to take place at Austin in a few weeks."

For those who would like a fuller study of the life and work of Daniel Baker there are two volumes of *Sermons* printed in Philadelphia, 1847 and 1854, and the book *Life and Labours of the Rev. Daniel Baker, D.D.* by his son Rev. Wm. M. Baker; written as an autobiography from Dr. Baker's diary. This 560 page volume was printed by the Presbyterian Board of Publications, Philadelphia in 1858, less than a year after Dr. Baker died at the home of his son in Austin, December 10th, 1857, when his son was pastor of the Austin, Texas, Presbyterian Church. A few excerpts from this book are given below which reveal how he met the "men who made Austin College.":

Galveston, Texas, February 21, 1840, "Here I think I first met with the *Rev. Benjamin Chase*" (page 239)

Houston, Texas, March 9, 1840, "From Washington I hurried to Independence and had the pleasure of becoming acquainted with *Hugh Wilson.* (page 247.)

Prospect Church Chrisman Settlement, April 6, 1840, "When the brethern were together (Brazos Presbytery) we had some talk about establishing a Presbyterian College in Texas. Later, calling upon Captain Perry, who married the sister of S. F. Austin, he was much taken with the idea and promised to make a donation of 1500 acres of land." (p. 251.)

Port Lavaca, June 26, 1848, "Here I am in Texas, and in fine health and spirits—at Brother *(Stephen) Cocke's* residence." (He preached with him here and there for two weeks) (p. 329).

Washington (on-the-Brazos) "The subject of establishing a Presbyterian College in Texas was brought up. Two years before, Rev. Mr. McCullough had been sent on to the North as Agent and had obtained a considerable number of books and about five hundred dollars in money. But Goliad had been fixed upon and this location not approved, the matter was permitted to remain without any further action. I made a speech in Presbytery in favor of renewed effort resulting in a committee of three being appointed to fix some eligible place in Middle Texas. Rev. Blair and *Rev. J. W. Miller* and myself were appointed." (p. 381)

I had never yet been in Huntsville, but having a favorable account of the place, I went there, and held a protracted meeting which lasted a few days. This meeting was blessed by the hopeful conversion of a few souls, of whom, *Major W. Hampton* was one, subsequently made an elder. I mentioned to some of the prominent citizens of the place that the Presbytery of Brazos had resolved to take measures for the establishment of a Presbyterian College — I told them I was pleased with Huntsville — a town meeting was immediately called, *Colonel Yoakum* and other gentlemen made speeches in favor of the enterprise. (p. 388)

*General Houston,* I am told, says that it would be a greater advantage to have a Presbyterian College located here than to have the place made the seat of the government. (p. 390)

Colonel Yoakum drew up the charter of the College, making some alterations as I suggested — I laid the charter before brothers (J. W.) Miller and (Hugh) Wilson preparatory to submission to Presbytery. An attempt was made to postpone final action — another member of Presbytery suggested delay until we write some of the colleges at the North to see what their charters are. I arose and said, "Moderator, we have understanding enough to frame our own charter; any such postponement will be equivalent to a complete relinquishment of the enterprise." Happily all objections were overruled and a committee appointed to secure the needful charter. (page 393)

His autobiography continued: The charter was signed by Gov. Wood on the 22nd day of November, 1849, and the first meeting of the Trustees was held in Huntsville on the 5th of April, 1850. "Present: Daniel Baker, R. Smither, J. Hume, Geo. Red, H. Yoakum, J. Branch, Sam Houston, by his proxy, H. Yoakum, H. Wilson, and J. C. Smith by his proxy, S. R. Smith." On motion I was made President pro-tem. The next day, A. J. Burke and J. W. Miller appeared, and took their seats as members. The Rev. Samuel McKinney, whom I had urged to come to Texas from Holly Springs, and for whom I had obtained the situation of teaching in the Male Institute in Huntsville, was present, and was elected President of the College. At this meeting an overwhelming majority chose Capitol Hill for the site of the College and I was appointed Permanent General Agent with a salary of $1000 per year. Shortly after my appointment I received first a verbal, and some weeks later, a written communication from Rev. Banjamin Chase — that he had some lands in Texas he was willing to donate to Austin College. (p. 414, 5, 6)

At the close of the 1858 session the first serious conflict between the faculty and students occurred. This came about when the senior class made plans for a commencement party for the student body at which there would be dancing. They were forbidden to go ahead with their plans under threat of not being issued their diplomas. Believing that they could evade supervision and control if the dance was held the day after Commencement exercises, they changed the date. This act to frustrate the faculty only served to make them stiffen their opposition and the faculty let it be known that no degrees would be granted unless they had the assurance the seniors would call off the party and dance. The senior class refused, resulting in no B.A. degrees in 1858.

Agitation of students seeking faculty allies in their approach to the Board of Trustees made matters worse and there was an investigation of the matter:

> June 24, 1858 meeting, Rev. J. W. Miller, Chairman of the Committee on the State of the College, presented a report which was received. Another motion to lay it on the table was lost. After some discussion with amendments the report was adopted, and is as follows:
>
> Your committee beg leave to report that they find a state of things which sternly calls for the prompt and prudent action of the Board. A history of the case

need not be given. Suffice it to say that there is direct collision between the faculty and the senior class. And to make matters worse the class has the general sympathy of the students and the community.

On the side of the faculty, your committee would approve the attempt made to discourage the custom of such parties given in the name of the students, or societies of the college.

The impression such parties create abroad, the expense of time and money they subject the students to, together with many of their tendencies, make it exceedingly desirable that such things be discouraged, and in time possibly stopped. And in doing this, it were desirable there should be no question of the right of the faculty; no interference with their Authority, no outside pressure brought to bear upon them in weakening their discipline.

In their arduous and responsible position they rather need all the aid and sympathy of a correct public sentiment. This we fear they have not always found.

On the side of the students, there are extenuating things. Their conduct, in the progress and origin of the thing, has been reprehensible. The steps taken at different times, to precipitate the matter, under at least a doubt of propriety and a disposition to divide the Faculty, attempted by misrepresentation and a disposition to over-awe the faculty — might demand interposition of the Board of Trustees to the extent of their power.

But the extenuations are that in this new country there are divers views about the morality of such parties and dancing, unsettled or wrong opinions as regards the province of a faculty of a College in reference to such things; the general good conduct of the class, the progress of it, the high grades of scholarship, the object in view, in giving the party; the time when it was to be given — in vacation some days after the regular college exercises were closed; as a time when many of the students supposed themselves not amenable to College supervision are extenuations.

We regret that a direct issue has occurred and are persuaded that had a more conciliatory course been pursued, the ends of discipline might have been as well accomplished. While therefore the Committee would recommend no course which would weaken the authority of the faculty, but the contrary, they recommend a conciliatory course — it is hard to interfere without injury somewhere, or appearance of injury.

On the part of the Senior Class, we think that there ought to be a written expression of certain things: "At first, there was on their part no intention to oppose the Faculty in the Administration of discipline; that after they had found the Faculty united in opposing the party on the 28th of June, they would have receeded from it if they could." We recommend upon the signature of such paper that, the Faculty be respectfully requested to receive them to their former standing in College, as Candidates for examination, recommendation and the receipt of the usual diploma of the College.

> All of which is respectfully submitted
> J. W. Miller
> Daniel McNair
> James Wilson
> James Sorley
> (*Minutes of Board*, pp. 103, 104)

There was no expression or response by the Senior Class and therefore no diplomas were issued, but the matter was to come up again several times.

In June 22, 1859 Meeting — On Motion: President Bailey was requested to continue his correspondence with Wm. T. Hill and Champion I. Hill in reference to granting their degrees and report to the Board. (*Board Minutes*, p. 111.)

On June 27, 1859 — Resolution to the Executive Committee:

In regard to the matter of conferring the A.B. on Messers. C. L. and W. I. Hill, your committee are of the opinion there is no occasion to depart from the action of the Board heretofore had. Your Committee are of the opinion that the action of the Board was liberal and conciliatory and they are informed that it has been fully explained to the Messers. Hills they therefore recommend the following resolution:

That it is inexpedient to do anything at present in the matter of the Messers C. L. and W. I. Hill.

> Fullenwider
> J. H. Banton        (Proxy for Houston)
> R. H. Byers

(*Minutes of Board,* p. 122)

At September 17, meeting, The Executive Committee consisting of A. M. Branch, J. H. Murray and S. R. Smith granted the delayed degrees to the Hill Brothers; at the request of Rev. R. H. Byers, College Agent, the diplomas to be dated 1858. Thus ended the second crisis.

At the meeting the Board thanked "Professor Thom for his valuable services as President Pro-tem, for the past three sessions." And on motion Mr. Worrall of Kentucky was unanimously selected president and the Executive Committee instructed to correspond with the President-elect informing him of his election. (*Board Minutes,* p. 106)

On November 4, 1858 at Huntsville:

The Board of Trustees met pursuant to adjournment. Only six members J. W. Miller, J. Carroll Smith, John Hume, John Hill, J. N. Murray and Sam Houston were present. They nominated Rev. Wm. Baker, son of Daniel Baker for president and adjourned to meet in Houston December 15th. At that meeting, Rev. Wm. Baker, pastor of the Austin Presbyterian Church was present but declined the nomination for the presidency of the College.

Rev. J. W. Miller was then nominated but again found reasons to decline. Rev. R. H. Byers was then nominated but declined, giving reasons that were deemed satisfactory. After much deliberation, Rev. Professor R. W. Bailey was nominated, and a ballot being had there were eleven ayes and no nays, where upon Professor Bailey was declared unanimously elected and being present, accepted the office of President of Austin College. (*Board Minutes,* pp. 107, 108)

Additional buildings were talked of at this meeting but none were ever built. Rev. R. H. Byers continued as agent for another year at a salary of 10% of all he collected up to $100 per month.

Rev. A. E. Thom, Professor of Mathematics and Natural Sciences became acting president of Austin College at the death of Daniel Baker, January 16, 1857 and served in that capacity until Rev. Rufus W. Bailey was elected president of the College December 15, 1858. Bailey found it very difficult to maintain a competent faculty.

Rev. Wm. C. Somerville, elected adjunct professor of Languages and principal of the preparatory department on February 25, 1853 was called as minister of the Huntsville Presbyterian Church after Professor N. A. Penland had been dismissed as minister by the session of that church for "ardent use of spiritous liquors." Professor Thom followed Professor Somerville as pastor and Benjamin F. Grady was elected professor of Mathematics and Natural Sciences in 1859, the first professor who was not an ordained minister.

At the end of the first decade of the college, it had endowment of $30,000, earning $2700 annually; good title to 8000 acres of land; a building costing $18,000; a library of 3,111 volumes; laboratory apparatus valued at $4,000 — Total assets $62,000 and $12,000 debts.

During his administration Dr. Bailey built "Steamboat House" which he later sold to General Sam Houston, after Houston was deposed.

> In this final home of Sam Houston which he purchased for his family immediately after being ousted from the Governor's Mansion in Austin, his last child was born. It is a state shrine and museum today. It was in Dr. Bailey's former presidential home that Houston made his peace in his last hours with Dr. Samuel McKinney and Judge P. W. Kittrell.

Dr. Bailey closed out the first decade of College history with a stirring speech — his inaugural and farewell address — printed in the entirety in the 1859-60 catalog. He had held the chair of languages since December 15, 1855 but now became Professor of Moral and Intellectual Philosophy. The other faculty members were Rev. J. H. Calvin, M. A., Professor of Ancient Languages; B. F. Grady, Professor of Mathematics and Natural Sciences; W. F. Perrie, adjunct Professor of Languages and First Division Prep. Department; and J. H. Pentecost, adjunct Professor of Mathematics and Second Division Prep. Department.

It became the painful duty of the newly elected president to ask for the resignation of Professor Grady at the end of the school year June 28, 1861. The Minutes of the session of the Huntsville Presbyterian Church state that "Professor Benjamin F. Grady—ruling elder, was excommunicated Saturday, March 22, 1862, after trial; having denied the divinity of Christ and the Bible as divine revelation." Dr. Bailey resigned the presidency in the fall of 1862, but continued the pastorate of the Huntsville Presbyterian Church until Dr. McKinney returned in January 1863. He then became financial agent of the College and died while holding that position. A memorial page to him in memory of his services and loyal devotion is placed on page 155 of the *Trustee Minutes*.

# THE SECOND DECADE

## DARK DAYS AHEAD

THE Second Decade began almost simultaneously with the War Between the States. This was the first period of great crisis for Austin College and only the devotion and intense energy of a few of its inspired leaders sustained it through these dreadful years. A graveyard of college buildings and campuses dotted the land in every section of the State. Of 135 institutions of learning, chartered by the Texas Legislature from Statehood in 1845 until the Civil War, only Austin College survived. Either prior to, or at the beginning of the War of Secession, all of the colleges or universities chartered by the Republic, except Baylor, closed forever and Baylor suspended operations, reopening for two years at Waco as Waco University.

Financial affairs were in chaos. In the conversion to Confederate money during the war and confiscation after, there was very little left for a family to use for education of the young men who survived the conflict. Lifelong friends took opposite views of secession, and its demands. Many families were divided. Sam Houston, deposed as governor because of his strong stand against secession, saw his son, Sam, march to service under the Confederate flag, and lived to learn of his son's injury and capture in battle. Young Sam was eventually exchanged and found his way back to the home in Huntsville.

The year 1863 held a few encouraging events for the College. Samuel McKinney took the helm as President again in that year. Only twenty-nine enrolled in the College that fall but the number increased to forty-three in the second semester. The tragedy of the war had left almost no boys over fifteen to qualify for college entrance; consequently, from 1861 to 1870 there were just two graduates: Robert A. McKinney in 1866, the son of President McKinney; and Wm. B. Gillespie in 1869. Only two others were awarded degrees in the Third Decade: Wm. Boyd and Wm. A. Smith in 1874. The Fourth Decade was only slightly more productive, the College issuing six B.A. degrees: Wm. H. McCullough and Wm. Stuart Red (1882), Morris Juvenat (1884), Walter W. Boone and Albert Sidney Venable (1889), Walter Vinson (1890), and one M.A. degree to Jacob M. Fullenwider.

The student body of 1859-60 included few that would not soon be called to war and many who never would return to Texas soil. It included George and Robert Yoakum, sons of historian and charter trustee, Henderson Yoakum. Also, Samuel M. Penland, Houston's grand-nephew, son of Professor Penland, illfated language teacher; and at least twenty sons of trustees of the College. Three of the six men who graduated in 1860 did not survive the War.

Jacob M. Fullenwider A.B. 1860, M.A., 1881: enlisted as a private in 1961 and served four years, and like his father P. H. Fullenwider, became a trustee serving from 1897 to 1910; lawyer.

Wm. Frank Hardin A.B. 1860 — Valedictorian — enlisted in the Confederate service for four years; merchant.

Thomas J. Peel A.B. 1860, Salutatorian, enlisted and rose to Captain in 1862, serving till war ended; merchant.

The other three graduates were James H. Murray, Lucius L. Moreland and Richard Sims. It was a lapse of six years before there was to be another graduate — R. A. McKinney in 1866; son of the man who was first and fourth President of the College.

Dr. McKinney was induced to return to Texas and was elected unanimously by the Board to succeed Dr. R. W. Bailey who resigned September 3, 1862. He took the office January 1, 1863 having arrived in the previous fall after being notified of his election by Dr. Bailey and P. H. Fullenwider. (*Austin College Minutes,* vol. 1, page 162).

His first words to the Board were:

> I have the pleasure of meeting with you again after an interval of ten years and I am glad to find some of those time honored members who met at first thirteen years ago to organize this Board, and lay the foundation of a college of learning in this great state. What melancholy evidences we have of the ravages of time. (The only charter trustees still serving were Houston, J. Carol Smith, A. J. Burke, Rev. Hugh Wilson and Rev. J. W. Miller). Many who then felt the liveliest interest in it are now cold in death.
>
> I well remember what glowing descriptions I read of and with what zeal I left a pleasant home, and a flourishing Institution to embark in this enterprise. How much disappointed when upon landing here I found we had not *a dollar* in hand, but only subscribed on paper. And it was a *gloomy* day when with seven boys we commenced in a little frame rented building near the graveyard.
>
> But my courage rose in adversity and the smiles of Heaven seemed manifestly to fall upon us. The number of pupils increased rapidly to 60, and we soon found our room too small (It was at this point that the Masonic Lodge offered their quarters).
>
> In 1852 after two years, we found accommodations in the College Edifice and friends multiplied up to 1853. In the month of June of that year, the Board concluded through other hands and under other auspices it might progress more rapidly.

Dr. McKinney presented a dismal picture "of its history since that time." The building was dilapidated, library and apparatus much injured, ravages of two years of civil war had left its mark and debt increased from $7000 to $12,000. There was little praise for the two presidents, Drs. Baker and Bailey whose terms intervened.

> In this circumstance, I found the Institution lost fame when solicited by many old friends. Re-elected by your unanimous voice, I concluded again to use

my best efforts to restore it to what it was when I left it. It was indeed an experience. The Board had offered no salary or any assurance of aid. It was the confidence expressed by the public, and the fact that the Institution seemed like a child, in distress, calling to me for aid, that had a stimulating effect, and gave assurance that I might again do what I had done before.

Dr. McKinney had assumed a greater task than he had imagined. The war was to continue two more years. In his report to the Board July 15, 1863 he stated:

There have been causes operating against the literary institutions of the Country unprecedented in its history. The war abstracted our youth of the age of seventeen and upwards from their studies; consequently we have been unable to keep together material for College classes immediately.

Just a few days after this Mrs. Houston sent a message to Rev. McKinney by Jeff Hamilton, Sam Houston's negro servant, requesting him to come to the Steamboat House. Henry Bruce in his *Life of General Houston* states that when McKinney found the General somewhat better, to avoid calling attention to the urgent errand, asked if the General's opinions about the war had changed. Houston seemed to revive and spoke with surprising energy, reflecting his youthful infatuation with the thundering lines of the *Iliad* and his mature aversion to disunion.

"My views as to the propriety and possibility of the success of this wicked revolution have undergone no changes," he said.

After a brief relapse he was again alert when McKinney asked him, "How is it between you and your Maker?" The General turned and looked the minister squarely in the face saying, "All is well, all is well." It was fitting that these two men who had labored for Austin College and who had parted enemies after two disagreeable incidents in earlier life, should come together again with this final moment of intimacy.

President McKinney requested J. H. Banton and James A. Baker to prepare a resolution in regard to the deaths of charter trustees General Sam Houston and Col. John Hume. The following was offered and adopted at the next Board Meeting, June 24, 1864:

> Whereas, Gen. Sam Houston and Col. John Hume, original members of the Board of Trustees of Austin College, have in the providence of God been removed from our midst by death since the last annual meeting of this Board—the former on the 26th day of July 1863 and the latter of the 8th day of June 1864, and whereas they were highly esteemed not only as useful members of the Board but also as citizens of the highest respectability and most honorable members of society; Therefore, Resolved, That we deeply deplore their deaths and sensibly feel the great loss the College has sustained in their death—Resolved, That our sympathies and condolences are tendered to their respective families.

At the June 29th, 1865 meeting, President McKinney addressed the Board:

> Gentlemen: I am pleased to meet you again concerned as you are to look after and foster the interest of the College. However vain the many cherished hopes are entertained respecting our country, this institution still lives, the object of so many prayers and earnest efforts of noble hearts and wise heads to cultivate the minds of the youth of the country. In the first three years it has held to even tenor of its ways. The devotion of the professors has been unremitting and for the present scholastic year there have been 120 matriculations. We now have material for three classes, Freshmen, Sophomores and Juniors. A new Epoch opens in the history of the College, a large number of young men have returned from camp and are anxious to avail themselves of the advantage here afforded.

Dr. McKinney labored hard through the war years and through the Reconstruction period. He gave three years of intensive labor as its first president and had seven years of even greater responsibility during his second administration. For several years during the latter term of service only he, his two sons, Andrew Todd and Robert Alexander, and William F. Perrie taught all the preparatory students as well as all the college classes.

The Board met at Galveston June 28, 1867. There were present: President McKinney, J. Carrol Smith, F. C. Hume, Rev. J. W. Miller, Rev. R. H. Byers, Rev. D. McNair, D. D. Achisson, Rev. P. H. Fullenwider and proxies were voted for A. T. McKinney, J. A. Baker and James Wilson. Judge Baker's resignation was accepted and Judge Joab Banton and Judge Benton Randolph (both graduates of the College with B.A. and B.L. degrees) were elected to the Board. These two latter, with Rev. P. H. Fullenwider, also an alumnus, were appointed to the Executive Committee.

There was no quorum meeting in 1868. On June 14, 1869 the president's call did not achieve a quorum, but on June 15th, meeting at the Presbyterian Church, the minutes show that E. H. Cushing, J. C. Smith and S. R. Smith's proxies were voted by Judge James A. Baker, who came on the Board to make a quorum. John Besser, Financial Agent of the State Prison was also impressed into service and voted proxy for A. J. Burke. Cushing was editor of the Houston paper, the two Smiths and A. J. Burke were all Houston businessmen and were prevented by flood conditions from attending the meeting.

The Board met in Houston November 3, 1869 but was unable to assemble a quorum.

The tragic emptiness of McKinney's ten years of labor is brought out by the fact that during his two terms as president, only two degrees were granted, the first being that of his own son, Robert, in 1866 and the second, William Gillespie, in 1869. These two were the only graduates in the entire second decade of Austin College (1860-1870).

While pastor of the Oakdale Covenanter Church in Illinois, Dr. McKinney married Nancy Woodside Todd (July 4, 1836), the daughter of Dr. Alexander and Margaret (McLean) Todd, of Chester District, South Carolina. Five children were born of this marriage: Andrew Todd McKinney; Margaret Todd McKinney, who married Albert Edwin Davis; Eleanor Louise McKinney, who married Benton Randolph; Elizabeth Cornelia McKinney, who married Thaddeus C. Bell, a descendant of Josiah H. Bell, Stephen F. Austin's friend and able assistant in settling the first Anglo-American colony in Texas. He and Cornelia McKinney had one son, John Randolph Bell, who now lives in Salida, Colorado. Dr. Samuel McKinney's youngest child, Robert Alexander, after his graduation from Austin College, studied medicine and became a physician. His eldest son, A. T. McKinney, practiced law in the town of Huntsville, Texas, for more than fifty years. He served on the Austin College Board from 1866 to 1876. At the time of his death in 1931 (age 93 years) he was the last surviving member of the Texas Constitutional Convention of 1876, and the oldest living graduate of Princeton University.

Mrs. Samuel McKinney died on September 10, 1858, while the family lived in New River, Ascension Parish, Louisiana.

Dr. Samuel McKinney died at Huntsville, Texas, and is buried there within sight of the building in which Austin College was established, the institution that he served and kept alive during the trying times of disunion and reconstruction of the nation.

For the greater part of this information on Dr. Samuel McKinney, thanks are due to Miss Cornelia McKinney, daughter of Hon. A. T. McKinney and granddaughter of Dr. Samuel McKinney.

## THE THIRD DECADE

THE Board met at Bryan, Texas, October 29, 1870, recessed the next day which was Sunday and on the following Monday, Rev. J. W. Miller, pro-tem secretary, read a letter from Dr. McKinney tendering his resignation with these words:

> From the indications of Providence I deem it proper to resign the office I have so long held in the College. In so doing I have only to say that my interest in it will be as deep as ever and I indulge the hope that I may in some way be instrumental in building it up. In it I have spent the best energies of my life and founded as it has been by the labors and prayers of devoted men now no more, may I not hope that your combined efforts will be exerted to free it from embarrassment and render it a perennial fountain for the dissemination of truth and righteousness over this extensive state.
>
> Respectfully yours, Samuel McKinney

Dr. McKinney's resignation was accepted with regret, and with the request that he continue to serve until Rev. S. M. Luckett, newly elected president, could assume the responsibility. Dr. McKinney and Rev. Miller were appointed a committee to procure changes in the charter with regard to the number of Trustees and to get the legislature to remove the individual responsibility clause. (This clause so worried Hugh Wilson that he gave it as a reason for resigning from the Board). (*Board Minutes*, pp. 177-178)

Rev. Samuel M. Luckett, D.D. called his first meeting of the Board on April 21, 1871 at Hempstead. It required five proxies to get a quorum.

Dr. McKinney was authorized to act as agent in collecting money and getting donations of money and land on the basis of 10% commission. Two heirs of Hugh Wilson, Mrs. Flanikenn and Mrs. Cunningham were released from payment of a note of Hugh Wilson to endow the Baker Professorship by payment of $160 in gold coin.

Rev. W. C. Somerville, a long-time, faithful professor was honored by having the D.D. degree conferred upon him.

A. T. McKinney was now Secretary of the Board. (*Board Minutes*, p. 180)

On November 4, 1871 the Board met in Waco, Texas. Dr. Luckett was made financial agent in addition to President, and E. H. Cushing was made Treasurer.

On November 7, 1872 the Board met in the Presbyterian Church in Palestine, Texas. Dr. Luckett reported: "I am sorry to report that Professor J. Rosamond, who had charge of the College and students in person from Nov. 1, 1871 to June 1, 1872, did not by any means give general satisfaction." The number of students reduced from 43 to 15 and there was a strong feeling of dissatisfaction. Two new teachers, Professor C. P. Estill and Professor A. C. Woodall, opened the school in August 1872 with 29 students. Charter Trustee A. J. Burke guaranteed the salaries of these two. Dr. Luckett paid $81.60 to Professor Rosamond for instructing "our ministerial candidates" (none of whom were ever ordained).

There was no meeting in June 1873, but on November 6, 1873 at Houston a quorum by using six proxies permitted the president of the College to enter into a contract with Walker County to provide teachers "for free schools for white male children of District No. 1, to be taught in the basement floor of the Austin College building for four consecutive months."

Again in Houston the Board met December 4, 1873. There were only two charter trustees left, A. J. Burke and J. Carroll Smith. First decade trustees James Sorley, S. R. Smith, Gen. John Besser and R. H. Byers; former graduates Joab Banton and Wm. McClintock; Editor C. H. Cushing, Rev. J. Wilson, R. F. Bunting, and L. Tenney made up the Board. Dr. Luckett reported little success in raising money for the College on his 400-mile horseback trip through Texas seeking payment from debtors to the College and donations from churches. Less than $300 was realized. His longer trip to Memphis; Danville, Kentucky; Nashville, New York, Philadelphia, Pittsburgh and Baltimore netted only a little over $4000. Epidemics of smallpox, cholera and yellow fever got the blame. All the money was used to pay off prior claims and left a debt to him of $1800. The meeting ended with three resolutions:

(1) Resolved that the Executive Committee be and is hereby instructed to sell the lands of the college as rapidly as possible to endow the Chase Professorship of Languages.
(2) That the Financial Agent be and is hereby directed to make any earnest effort to secure Endowment notes from the (a) officers of the college (b) from the ministers of the Synod of Texas, (c) from officers of the Presbyterian Churches in Texas and members of same (d) and from friends of Education generally.
(3) That all Ministers and Elders be requested to aid in this matter.

On August 28, 1874 the Board met at the College. Only A. J. Burke, Wm. McClintock, James Sorley, A. T. McKinney and John S. Besser were present. Eight trustees were absent and their proxy vote cast by Besser, Sorley and A. T. McKinney.

The President read his report as follows:

Huntsville, August 27, 1874

Gentlemen: I am sorry to report that the college has not been in a high state of prosperity. From several causes the students from a distance have been small: (1) The building being in need of repair was not inviting, (2) The desks and seats were old and uncomfortable, (3) There were only two active teachers on the faculty, (4) The constant expectation that the college would soon be moved from Huntsville and rumors that it had been relocated elsewhere have kept young men from coming to Huntsville to attend the college.

Until the question of location is settled you may rely upon it, the number of students will be small. It seems clear that you will not be justified in employing more than two professors and it is very questionable whether you should employ more than one.

Feeling our dependence in the Author of our being and trusting in Him for guidance, let us go forward prudently and fearlessly in discharge of duty.

With high esteem, I remain
Your obt. svt.
S. M. Luckett
President, Austin College

The A. B. degree was conferred on Wm. Boyd and the degree of graduate in mathematics on Wm. Smith.

On November 4, 1874 the Board met at Jefferson, Texas.

A. J. Burke was appointed Secretary pro—tem. Doctor Marshall and Donald MacGregor from Synod's Committee on Austin College appeared before the Board of Trustees and stated they were ready to act jointly with the Board—in any means looking toward removal of Austin College.

Trustees T. L. C. Means and A. J. Burke reported:

> We the undersigned Committee . . . are clearly of the opinion that it is to the interest of the College that it should be removed to a different point from its present location at an early a day as the same can be accomplished consistent with the best interest of the college—having in view the time, the mode and plan of permanent location as also this pecuniary inducements offered.

Action was taken to compromise an old note to Sam Houston now in the hands of a Mr. Morrow, heir of General Houston, who was pressing for payment.

On November 4, 1874 the Trustees discussed the recommendation on removal of the College. The report was adopted, the vote was 9 for removal and four against it. Three days later the Board voted to amend the charter and instructed the Executive Committee to draft and submit it.

The Board met at the Huntsville Presbyterian Church June 24, 1875; at first with no quorum, only Besser, Sorley and A. T. McKinney. However, with five proxies the meeting went on, resulting in the following resolution:

> Resolved that Rev. S. M. Luckett, President of the College, Rev. W. K. Marshall, Rev. Jno. A. Smylie, Rev. J. W. Neil and Rev. D. MacGregor be hereby appointed a special committee to invite definite propositions for the location of the College — to report to a special meeting to be called by the president in the city of Houston, on or about the 25th day of August next.
>
> Resolved that the consideration of the arrangements to be made for the opening of the Fall term of the college be postponed to the called meeting in August next.
>
> Respectfully submitted,
>
> John S. Besser, James Sorley, Committee

The financial statement presented at the close of this meeting indicated debts of $8,720 and assets of $15,000 not including the campus and building, and only $8,000 value on 8,000 acres of College lands.

The Board met in Houston August 25, 1875 — The committee on removal of the College reported visiting Austin, Wallace Prairie, Marshall and Tyler and correspondence with Waverly and Georgetown.

Letters were read from A. T. Hill of Waverly and Sam Hanna of Denison and propositions from Sherman, Tyler, Georgetown and Wallace Prairie, regarding the removal of Austin College to those places. The Board recessed til 2 p.m. and then met behind closed doors, finally deciding to decline all propositions as they were all considered inadequate, but the Board expressed a preference for some location in Northern Texas, on or near the Central Railroad. The Board was unwilling to consider any location without a valid subscription of at least $35,000 to be expended on buildings.

The next Board meeting was held at the Austin Presbyterian Church November 3, 1875. Rev. R. E. Sherrill appeared before the Board and submitted a proposition for locating the College at Sherman, and by invitation addressed the Board.

Rev. D. J. Grasty addressed the Board in behalf of Austin, Texas.

General John presented the subscriptions of the citizens of Georgetown. (*Minutes,* p. 237)

At the January 5, 1876 meeting in Houston, Rev. D. MacGregor acted as Secretary pro-tem and received the report on the committee to amend the charter. It was decided to draft a new charter and Judge J. A. Baker, E. H. Cushing, Rev. Luckett and Rev. MacGregor were assigned the task. (*Minutes,* p. 240)

The Board met again in Houston, February 1, 1876, received communications from Denison and Sherman and adjourned to meet in Sherman February 9, and informed the Sherman Committee that the offer of the citizens of Sherman would be accepted and that the College would be located there if they could raise the money by February 9th.

This was probably the reason the *Denison Daily News* carried the following item on February 7, 1876: "Major Win has called off the election to see if Denison wants Austin College to locate here, because the Council is satisfied the proposition would be overwhelmingly defeated. If Austin College wants to locate in our midst, we would suggest some other place (we hope to see it encouraged to do so)."

The issue of the *Denison Daily News* of February 12, 1876 carried this "sour grapes" item: "The Sherman people got bad sold in the Austin College deal. It can be seen that Sherman was the last chance, all the other towns having come to the conclusion that a college put up at public auction wasn't worth having."

The Board did meet February 9th and 10th in Sherman and accepted the offer of ten acres of land and a pledge to erect a new building at once. The Board then directed President Luckett to remove the College library, philosophical apparatus, desks, furniture and everything pertaining to the College to Sherman as speedily as possible. A. J. Burke, last charter member of the Board to serve Austin College, was Secretary pro—tem. Other trustees present were Rev. R. E. Sherrill, R. F. Bunting, James Sorley, J. A. Baker, E. H. Cushing, T. L. C. Means, John S. Moore, A. T. McKinney by A. J. Burke, and S. A. King and D. MacGregor by R. E. Sherrill. The Sherman committee consisted of R. A. Chapman, W. F. Summer, and C. C. Binkley. Rev. R. E. Sherrill was appointed local Financial Agent to secure additional donations from Sherman and surrounding area to be compensated by mutual agreement from time to time. (p. 241)

Dr. Luckett reported to the Board in Houston, May 10, 1876, that he needed $3500 immediately to settle debts to faculty and others, including $937 to himself, and the old Houston claim held by Morrow. E. H. Cushing was authorized to borrow $500 at 8% to pay off the Houston claim; and that the President be instructed to continue to sell college land to pay faculty and other debts; and to sign a contract with Sherman.

At this point Dr. MacGregor voiced his opposition to liquidating an old debt by making a new one, and shifting the obligation from previous trustees to present trustees. He thought the procedure illegal and requested that he be not bound or held responsbile.

In Houston, July 6, 1876, it was decided to open the College in Sherman in the Fall, but that the Executive Committee be authorized to organize and conduct a school in the College building in Huntsville for the next scholastic year at the request of Huntsville citizens.

(Professor C. P. Estill agreed to stay and conduct this school.) Judge J. A. Baker, Rev. D. MacGregor and J. Carroll Smith all resigned at this time and J. P. Bagby, Rev. A. P. Smith, D.D., and E. P. Gregg were elected to fill the vacancies.

The Board next met in Dallas November 1876. More Trustees resigned, namely J. H. Zively and B. Randolph. Rev. H. B. Boude and W. G. Bagby were elected to fill these vacancies. A. T. McKinney resigned as Secretary of the Board and H. B. Boude was elected to succeed him. The final meeting of the year was held again in Houston December, 1876, the Board consisting of:

| | | |
|---|---|---|
| A. J. Burke | Rev. S. A. King | James Sorley |
| W. G. Bagby | Rev. A. P. Smith | absent: |
| E. H. Cushing | W. E. Caldwell | T. L. C. Means |
| Rev. F. R. Bunting | R. C. Stuart | R. E. Sherrill |
| E. P. Gregg | Gen. John S. Besser | L. Tenney |
| Rev. H. B. Boude | Rev. John S. Moore | |

The Board refused to provide the Building Committee with $4000 to aid in erecting the main building.

By the April 25, 1877 meeting it was evident that only about half of Sherman's pledges were collectable. Litigation was suggested to force payment, suits were brought successfully.

In the meantime Professor T. E. Wharton was "teaching indigent candidates for the ministry" and the College was renting classroom space in town. Rev. W. W. Hill and Prof. E. F. Hoke were teaching forty-five students.

On the 13th and 15th of June 1877, the Board of Trustees met in Houston at the bookstore of E. H. Cushing, Secretary, to sign an amendment to the Charter to present to the Legislature. Cushing signed for self and proxy for seven members; and A. J. Burk for self and four proxies, thereby making a legal quorum. The amendment certified by the Secretary of State, June 18, 1877 contained three sections:

> Section 1: The President and Professors shall constitute the Faculty and shall have power to enforce rules and regulations enacted by the Trustees of said College for the government and discipline of the students and to suspend and expel offenders as may be deemed necessary.
>
> Section 2: The Trustees by a three-fourths majority of their number at any meeting legally held, may after ten days notice to all the trustees change the name of Austin College, and adopt any name they may think for the best interest of the Institution; and may change the location of said College and transfer the effects thereof, to where removed, without in either case forfeiting their legal rights and privileges under the original Charter or Amendments thereto.

Section 3: The number of trustees shall be divided into as many equal parts as there are Synods, placing equal number of trustees from each Synod except when there is unequal number, then the extra trustee may be elected from the Synod in which the college is located.

(pp. 270-271 of *Board Minutes*)

The Board met in Houston July 11, 1877 at the Presbyterian Church and passed the following resolution:

In pursuance of the expressed will of the Synod of Texas, the Board of Trustees of Austin College did on the 10th day of February 1876 at Sherman, Texas, remove the said Austin College from Huntsville, its then location, to Sherman, Texas, in compliance with a contract that day accepted and entered into by the citizens of Sherman.

Resolved therefore that the action of said Trustees in removing the said Austin College from Huntsville and locating the same at Sherman and putting the same in operation be and the same is hereby certified and confirmed to relate back and to be in effect on and from said 10th day of February 1876 and by the authority in us vested by the amended charter of said Austin College we the said Trustees do hereby declare that the said Austin College is and was on said 10th day of February 1876 removed from Huntsville and located in Sherman, Texas.

Rev. R. F. Bunting D. D., Sec. pro—tem
Attest: E. H. Cushing

At the Board Meeting in San Antonio, November 7, 1877, it was reported that the College was in successful operation; its holdings of land amounted to several thousand acres and endowment income $1500 per year. A drive for donations through Synod's help was planned.

### CIRCULAR LETTER

The Board of Trustees of Austin College to the Presbyterian Churches of Texas, Greeting:

We deem it necessary, at the outset of this Circular, to give a brief summary of the past and present condition of our Synodical Institution. As is known to many, Austin College was founded in the year 1849, by the pioneers of Presbyterianism in Texas. It was first placed under the care of the Presbytery of Brazos, where it remained until the formation of the Synod of Texas in 1851, which body then assumed its control.

At the close of the war, the College was found to be embarrassed with a debt which in 1871 had increased to $26,000.00, thus endangering the loss of the entire property.

At this critical juncture in its history, Rev. S. M. Luckett was elected to the Presidency, and accepting the responsible and arduous position, he has continued faithfully to labor for the payment of this indebtedness, and to establish the Institution on a firm basis.

These liabilities have been reduced to $4,000.00, and funds are at our command to liquidate the whole amount in a reasonable time.

In addition to this, we have an annual income from a Permanent Endowment Fund, which is sufficient to pay the salary of one Professor; also, several valuable tracts of land, that will add largely to our Permanent Endowment Fund.

We, therefore, feel warranted in assuring the friends of the enterprise, that its continuation is no longer doubtful, but is a fixed fact.

The President has heretofore labored earnestly, but under many discouragements; these considerations stimulate us to appeal to the friends of a progressive system of education for their hearty cooperation.

All future donations will be applied to increase the Permanent Fund of the College, and not for the payment of old debts. Two more Chairs ought to be endowed at once, and we make this appeal so as to attain this desirable end. To those willing to help in this important work, we would suggest that they give Endowment Notes, to be paid in one, two and three years, with six per cent interest per annum.

The sacrifices to perpetuate the Institution have been great, but they have been cheerfully borne by those upon whom the Synod has placed the responsibility.

All these facts clearly appeal to the intelligence and liberality of every member of our Church in the State. And now is the time for us, as a Church, to awake to the magnitude and importance of this enterprise, and show to the world that Presbyterians in Texas can rise to a full appreciation of this privilege and duty.

It now only remains for our people to respond liberally, and thus help the Trustees to carry on the work assigned them.

Respectfully submitted by the Trustees:

| John S. Besser, | S. A. King, |
|---|---|
| A. J. Burke, | T. L. C. Means, |
| R. F. Bunting, | J. S. Moore, |
| H. B. Boude, | R. E. Sherrill, |
| W. G. Bagby, | A. P. Smith, |
| W. E. Caldwell | James Sorley, |
| E. H. Cushing, | R. C. Stuart, |
| E.P. Gregg, | L. Tenney. |

Houston, Texas, July 12th, 1877.

The difficulties in moving all the College equipment to Sherman and the perplexing troubles over the collection of pledges and promises from Sherman citizens led Dr. Luckett to think it time for another to take the helm. He reported to the Board that there were several cities anxious to get the College who would give liberally; but, "I think we should stay in Sherman if we can get enough to complete the new building from Sherman subscriptions." (*Minutes,* Nov. 7, 1877, p. 275)

In his resignation to the Board, April 23, 1878, President Luckett expressed his desire to "devote my whole time to proclaiming the Gospel." In leaving Austin College, Dr. Luckett accepted the pastorate at Milford, Texas, 1878-80. He was pastor of the Palestine church 1881-87 and was then called back to the Presidency of the College a second time to serve ten more years. He labored tirelessly in the Synod for aid to Austin College, both as pastor and president.

Dr. Henry Buckner Boude, Secretary of the Board, who was at that time pastor of the Paris, Texas, Presbyterian Church, was elected the new president (April 24, 1878) and Rev. J. S. Moore became the new secretary. Dr. Boude had been appointed special agent to secure the money for completing the building and furnishing it, and he now became "financial agent, empowered to sell land and execute deeds and sign necessary papers." *(Minutes,* page 280).

On September 3, 1878, Dr. Boude presided at the formal opening of the College. In a ceremony on the campus, Capt. T. J. Brown delivered the keys to Rev. J. S. Moore, Secretary of the Board, who then delivered them to Dr. Boude. Dr. A. P. Smith, then pastor of the First Church of Dallas, delivered the charge to the new President. Action was taken at once to get General John Besser, Board member who was then financial agent for the State penitentiary, to ship the library and the remainder of the College furniture and laboratory apparatus to Sherman.

The new building was occupied on September 4, 1878 with fifty-three students.

Dr. Boude in his report to the Board at Marshall, November 7, 1878 stated that he personally had contracted with the builder to complete the building only partly paid for by the citizens of Sherman and that Dr. T. H. Willis had agreed also to sign the contract and to be responsible for $4000, Mr. Willis holding $4000 worth of land notes as security.

He commended his faculty as "Men of learning and men of sense. I know of none their superior."

But Dr. Boude also said, "The Board must decide how to add largely to our Endowment Fund. How can we now but develop all the energies of the Presbyterian Church for the support of the College? We want the students and we must have money and the prayers of the people. May God give the Board wisdom and grace and abundantly bless our college." *(Board Minutes,* page 286).

Some new rules were formulated for the student body namely:

(1) Every applicant for college shall report himself to the college within 24 hours after his arrival in Sherman.

(2) All students who matriculate, thereby bind themselves to obey all laws and regulations of the college.

(3) Students shall board in houses approved by the faculty.

(4) Students must take such (meal) tickets as shall be deemed best, after consultation between themselves, their parents and the faculty, and no change shall afterward be made without sanction of the faculty.

(5) At Chapel service and in class students must sit in alphabetical order and no one is allowed to leave his seat; they are also required to retire from Chapel in the same order.

(6) Students are expected to observe at all time perfect quietude in the college building.

(7) Students shall not deface or pollute the college building, whilst in it; they are not to use tobacco in any form.

(8) Every student is required to attend Public Worship at least once on the Sabbath, and to be present at morning prayer in the Chapel.

(9) No student from a distance shall absent himself from Sherman and vicinity without the President's permission.

(10) Students from a distance who are minors shall not contract debts without permission in writing from parents or guardians.

(11) Students must not engage in card playing or games of chance.

(12) Students are liable to punishment for violating any of the rules of gentlemanly deportment, in relation to each other or the Professors. (Parents are earnestly solicited to cooperate with the officers of the Institution in the enforcement of the above laws and reputation of Austin College.) (*Minutes*, Pages 288-289.)

The Board met for the first time in the library of the College June 17, 1879. There were only Rev. S. A. King, W. N. Dickey, J. S. Moore, W. W. Taylor and Col. E. P. Gregg present but with proxy votes for R. F. Bunting, Levi Tenney, John S. Besser and A. P. Smith the meeting got underway. Five small dormitories were to be constructed on the northwest corner of the campus and a Boarding House by a private party was promised to accommodate students from a distance.

Dr. Boude reported: Letters from every part of the compass indicate an increased number of students next year. I am impressed with this idea that our college has *retained* her good name and that non-Presbyterians are looking to us for solid educational privileges.

Gentlemen, we labor for God, and generations now coming in the stage of action, we must devise liberal things and I call your attention to my report as financial agent.

I now submit the facts of another year and freely say to you, my heart yearns after the pastorate, and if you know of a man of ability and name who can bring both to bear for the success of the college, my resignation is at your disposal. Nevertheless, I am your servant and feel that here lies the cause of God. May God be with the Board during this meeting. Fraternally, H. B. Boude, President. (*Board Minutes,* page 290.)

Report of Faculty: During this session sixty-three students have matriculated of which only about one-half remained to attend the final examination. A great lack of previous mental training has characterised these matriculates almost without exception. The most discouraging feature in the conduct of the college is the extreme readiness to desert their classes at examination time.

Respectfully,<br>W. D. Vinson, Sec. of Faculty

The first annual catalog in ten years was published in 1879, but of the sixty-three students matriculating, only about one-half remained to take the final examination.

The Board desired Dr. Boude to spend more time in Sherman and recommended an assistant financial agent. For a short time Rev. Thomas Washington Erwin was employed on a basis of 20% commission for all he collected in notes, new money or lands for the College. Evidently this arrangement was not satisfactory for it was revoked within the year.

The finances of the College were really in a chaotic condition for many reasons. The Treasurer of the College, E. H. Cushing, lived in Houston. His sudden death in December 1878 was a blow to Dr. Boude, especially unfortunate as his accounts were not balanced. Mr. Cushing had been very active in getting the College relocated and rarely missed a Board meeting. He has established himself as the foremost editor and newsman in the State.

The committee to draft resolutions in the death of E. H. Cushing, made the following report:

> It is with sincere regret that, as a Board, we have heard of the death of Mr. E. H. Cushing, who for many years has been a member of this Board and the trusted Treasurer of the College.
>
> Be it therefore Resolved: 1st, that in the death of Mr. Cushing Austin College has lost one of its best and most faithful friends, and this Board one of its most diligent members. 2nd, That we will ever treasure a memory of his many noble traits of character, and that we express our warmest sympathy to his family in this hour of affliction, and that the President of the College be instructed to send them a copy of this paper. (*Minutes*, p. 295)

One of the last acts at the close of the Third Decade (June 18, 1879) was the abolition of a recess at Christmas time. The College operated from the first Wednesday in September 1879 for forty continuous weeks. President Boude reported: "The session has been a successful one, no deaths, no serious illness among faculty or students, and we came to the close with fifty-five students in attendance. This is a higher average than is usually obtained by schools in the country. Our local patronage is very hard to control — parents are worse than students in inventing reasons why students should absent themselves from college." (*Minutes*, p. 299)

## THE FOURTH DECADE

At a Board Meeting June 23rd, 1880:

President Boude suggested that the Campus and buildings valued at $30,000 be mortgaged by selling bonds amounting to $12,000. He stated, "The College is fast becoming a necessity and should the present year not develop an addition to your endowment fund — then for one, I will be willing to pull the expenses within the income, which will be virtually closing the College." When the Board voted to issue $12,000 of bonds in $25, $50, and $100 denominations at 8%, there were several written protests received in the *Minutes;* namely, T. L. C. Means, H. Mosely by him, J. C. Moore and by S. E. Clement who handed in his resignation with the following: "I hereby enter my protest against any liability pecuniary or otherwise against me, of any action of the Board of Trustees whatsoever." Salaries of the College employees for 1880-81 were set as follows: Dr. Boude $1200, Professor Richardson $1200, Professor Vinson, $1000. *(Minutes of Board,* pp. 307-308)

On June 6, 1881 Dr. Boude made his report as financial agent:

> Brethren: Believing firmly that our safety was in negotiating the bonds ordered at your last meeting, I had the bonds printed here and presented them in every way I knew how. I met only with discouragement and intimations of derangement. I found little sympathy and no encouragement. After persistent effort, these bonds to the amount of $350 were taken here. I turned my attention to New York. Providentially, I opened a correspondence with Rev. W. L. Baker, Chaplain of St. Luke's Hospital, a relation of Dr. Daniel Baker, through whose personal influence I succeeded in negotiating the bonds at par value less 5% commission — and the total outlay for the sale amounted to only $687.75. *(Minutes,* p. 312)

Dr. Boude succeeded in winning back some of the much needed trust of Sherman and subscriptions, sometimes under legal pressure, were being paid, and best of all, the obligations to the faculty were all settled. He handed in his resignation which was reluctantly accepted by the Board to take effect Sept. 1, 1881. (Dr. Boude accepted the call to the Central Presbyterian Church of Kansas City, Missouri and was Presbytery's evangelist at Independence, Missouri when he died there May 6, 1912).

Two grandsons of Dr. Boude, Rev. Lardner W. Moore and Rev. Boude C. Moore, graduated from Austin College. Two great grandsons, Robert W. and John Wallace Moore are also graduates. Six of his descendants have been Presbyterian missionaries to Japan.

Dr. E. O. Guerrant of Kentucky was elected President and Financial Agent at a salary of $1200 with travelling expenses paid and 5% of all cash he collected. Temporarily Dr. Vinson was instructed to collect tuition and pay faculty salaries. Rev. J. S. Moore, pastor of the Sherman church was made Treasurer of the College.

Research indicates that Austin College issued its first diplomas in Sherman at the June Commencement of 1881, the B.A. degree to H. H. Boone of Navasota, and the M.A. degree to Jacob M. Fullenwider of Palestine. (Boone had completed most of his college work in 1859 before he joined the Confederate Army in which he served through the entire Civil War, attaining the rank of Major. He then took up the practice of law and became attorney General of the State. Three of his sons attended Austin College.) (*Austin College Quarterly,* Vol. 1, p. 49). Jacob Fullenwider, son of Rev. P. H. Fullenwider, former trustee member, had received the B.A. degree in 1860. He served four years in the Confederate Army, practiced law and taught school. He was a trustee of the College in the Fifth and Sixth Decades.

On August 3, 1881, the Board met and having received word that Dr. E. O. Guerrant could not come to Texas, elected Rev. J. B. Shearer, D.D., pastor of the Clarksville Presbyterian Church, to the presidency.

In October 1881, Professor Vinson was made President pro-tem. On Jan. 10, 1882 Dr. Shearer, refusing to accept the presidency, Rev. E. P. Palmer, D.D., then pastor of the Jackson Street in Mobile, Alabama, was elected President and Financial Agent at a salary of $1200 per year. He entered upon his duties officially at the June 13, 1882 meeting of the Board. Action at this meeting required all students of Presbyterian parents to attend the Presbyterian Church once each Sabbath. A preference expressed in writing by parents to attend another church was permitted and a report of attendance was required.

The 1881-82 year closed with one good omen. Two degrees were granted—both members of the Class of 1882 were to become ministers of the Gospel. Wm. H. McCullough and Wm. Stuart Red were the first graduates to enter the ministry as a life work. At last the dream and hope of Daniel Baker was realized. A year later, June 13, 1883, only J. C. Coit received the B.A. degree.

By June 3, 1884, the bonded debt was still $12,000 and unpaid salaries to faculty amounted to $3,427. The Board took action to request Dr. Palmer to give up his duties as Financial Agent. The faculty at that time consisted of Dr. Palmer, Professor Edward and part-time teaching by Rev. J. S. Moore. Nothing was done by the board to alleviate the empty treasury; in fact, the minutes record the following protest: "I hereby protest against any debt by note or otherwise during the present or at any future meeting of the Board of Trustees of Austin College."

Signed    W. George    Dr. McGregor<br>C. N. Roberts    Jno. S. Moore

The only graduate in 1884 was Morris Jouvenat of Monroe, Louisiana. He received both the B.A. and C.E. degrees, the first Civil Engineering degree by A.C. and the first in Texas.

Dr. Palmer resigned Nov. 3, 1884 and Rev. D. MacGregor was elected President and Financial Agent, to take office January 1, 1885. This Board took one other action: Dr. MacGregor was added to the committee on revision of the charter and this committee was instructed to have the name changed to "Texas Presbyterian College." (*Minutes*, p. 334)

The highlight of the 1884-85 year was the gift of 1232 acres of land in Austin County from J. N. Chadwick to become known as the Chadwick Farm. Only the income from this farm could be used as the gift was added to the permanent Endowment Fund. There were two important stipulations in the deed: (1) The income only was to be used to aid needy ministerial candidates to attend Austin College (2) The land was not to be sold. (Violations of this latter restriction by consent of a later Board in 1926 resulted in a loss of over a hundred thousand dollars to the College when the son and daughter, heirs of J. N. Chadwick, sued the College and settled the suit for ½ interest). Later Humble Oil Company drilled three gas wells and six oil wells on the property.

In 1886 Trustee C. N. Roberts came to the rescue with a gift of $1,000 to help liquidate the bonded indebtedness and Rev. S. M. Luckett was elected Financial Agent after Dr. MacGregor resigned June 15, 1887 on account of ill health. He was stated supply of the Lamar Street Church (now Second Presbyterian) from 1876 until his death October 10, 1887 (p. 340).

There were no graduates during Dr. MacGregor's administration. At the June 15, 1887 meeting the Board made this statement: "That the College be so conducted as to incur no further debt in the future, and, at the same time, be so manned as to make it worthy of patronage!" (page 343 of *Minutes*)

With no graduates presenting themselves, the Board conferred honorary D.D. degrees upon Rev. D. MacGregor, Rev. R. H. Nall and Rev. S. M. Luckett. Dr. Luckett was elected President and Financial Agent for the second time and again at $1200 per year. This time Dr. MacGregor had relieved him of one burden—the bonded indebtedness had been liquidated by giving the holders title to some college lands.

C. N. Roberts was made College Treasurer to further aid the progress of the College.

The Board in special session at the end of the regular meeting conferred the A.M. degree on Professor Edmonds. No doubt this was for his "holding the fort" during the serious illness of Dr. MacGregor in his last year. Trustees recorded: "We most cordially recognize the self-denying labors and success of Professor Edmonds and his assistant, Mr. C. L. Alfather, in conducting the College during the past session." (p. 343)

The Fourth Decade closed with the B.A. degree bestowed upon Walter W. Boone, who entered the McCormick Seminary and three years later became a Presbyterian minister, and Albert Sydney Venable who, after pastorates in Arkansas and Virginia, became a missionary to China.

## DONALD MacGREGOR
*Trustee 1858-1884*
*President of Austin College 1885-1897*

DONALD MacGregor was born in Glasgow, Scotland on May 18, 1818. He was fifty eight years old when he married Mrs. H. A. Speake of Jefferson, Texas. Soon after moving his mercantile business from New Orleans to Houston, he became an elder in the Presbyterian Church there and was elected to the Austin College Board in 1858. He was licensed to preach in 1873 and ordained in 1874. After two years as minister of the Presbyterian Church at Chapel Hill, Texas he served as stated supply to the Lamar Street Church, now Secone Presbyterian Church in Houston until his death in 1887.

Part of that time, from Jan. 1, 1885 to October 10, 1887, he was also President of Austin College.

A five-story business building on the corner of Fannin and Main Streets, in Houston, Texas, has become a valuable endowment asset through a legacy of Dr. MacGregor. A residuary clause in the title to this property states that the ownership would be transferred to the Board of World Missions of the Presbyterian Church if Austin College should change its name, or cease to belong to the Southern Presbyterian Church.

Dr. Donald MacGregor is buried in Glenwood Cemetery in Houston, Texas. For his loyal service as a trustee and President from 1858 to his death, the Board of Trustees have honored him by erecting a monument and providing perpetual care of his resting place.

# THE FIFTH DECADE

A NEW era in the field of education appeared on the horizon at the entrance of the Fifth Decade. With the matriculation of 123 students in 1889-90, it was necessary to increase the faculty. The Military Department added in that year with C. C. Scott as Commandant "aided in securing obedience to authority, prompt and manly discharge to duty and provided healthful exercise for the students." Dr. D. F. Eagleton was called to the English Chair and in 1890 L. J. Mitchell was elected Professor of Mathematics and Engineering; Rev. Chandler, Professor of Bible and L. Carl Koops, Professor of Military Science and Tactics.

The cadets were instructed in military practices and strict military rules were enforced during the Military Regime. In 1890-91 two companies were organized, with T. D. Collins Captain of Company A; and H. F. Sledge, Captain of B. In 1892-93, G. Boone and Alva Hardie were Captains respectively and in 1894-95 this honor was held by L. E. Selfridge and W. L. Acker. In 1895-96 R. E. Vinson and J. R. Lockett were Captains, while B. P. Edrington and J. C. Stinson held these offices in 1896-97. These were great days for the men at Austin College, filled as they were with the glamour of military routine. Much regret was expressed when this department was suspended in 1897. It also affected the enrollment as shown by the record for this decade.

| | | | | | |
|---|---|---|---|---|---|
| 1889-90 | 130 | 1893-94 | 149 | 1897-98 | 94 |
| 1890-91 | 138 | 1894-95 | 144 | 1898-1899 | 107 |
| 1891-92 | 146 | 1895-96 | 126 | 1899-1900 | 91 |
| 1892-93 | 128 | 1896-97 | 125 | | |

In the 1889-90 session, the College year was divided into three terms: Fall, Winter and Spring. Tuition and contingent fees were collected each term. It was expected this change would prevent many drop-outs. The building and grounds in Huntsville were sold to the State of Texas for $1,000 and in October J. N. Chadwick presented a check for $10,000, the largest ever received up to that time.

The June 11, 1890 meeting records thanks for: (1) The beautiful flag presented to the Cadets of the College by the Ladies of Sherman (2) The blinds for the Library by the Ladies of the First Presbyterian Church of Houston (3) The handsome portrait of Stephen F. Austin presented to the College by Hon. Guy M. Bryan (This had been promised to Daniel Baker in 1853).

Although only one senior graduated June 11, 1890 with the B.A. degree, (Walter Henry Vinson) the Commencement crowd was treated to a spectacular drill ceremony performed by the Cadets.

The *Minutes* of this meeting include: "We note with plea-sure—the increased attendance of students, the improvement in discipline, the higher education standard, and the fidelity with which the members of the faculty have discharged their duties."

"We are especially gratified at the religious interest that has been felt among the students in that many have been led to a personal consecration of themselves to Christ."

Special efforts were pledged to raise funds for an additional wing to the College building. Indeed this year for Austin College was a huge step forward in the Search for the Summit.

Another large gift was received in 1891 from Mrs. Mac-Gregor—a lot on the corner of Main and Fannin in the City of Houston. This lot was leased to Ed Kiam for fifty years at a net of $2500 per year. (After this lease had operated for seventeen years, Mr. Kiam sold it to Jesse Jones). It was the plan of Mr.

Jones to raze the five story building and to erect a skyscraper. His source of financing advised him to get a 99-year lease from Austin College. Mr. Jones offered to raise the net income to the College to $5500 in order to get the extension. Inadvertently the lawyer who drew up the lease wrote it to expire 99 years after the original 50 years, which would make it effective until 2042. After this new lease extension was drawn and filed for record, Mr. Jones was notified that no lease is legal over 99 years and his source of financing was lost. Few improvements have ever been made on this old building and only the ground floor is used. Nevertheless Austin College has received $5500 net each year since 1910 from the Jesse Jones Estate (*Minutes of Board,* p. 609).

All this good fortune led the Board to raise faculty salaries from $800 to $1000 per year.

At this time Mrs. Luckett made the College a gift of a block of land in the city of Houston which was sold and the money used to build the "Link Hall" addition to the main college building, in honor of Mrs. Luckett's parents, Dr. and Mrs. Link of Palestine, Texas (*Minutes,* p. 370). The endowment now was $21,000 on loan for $2330 annual interest.

More good fortune was to come in 1892. Mr. J. N. Chadwick wrote that he was deeding 1440 acres of land in Austin County to the College, the income from which he wanted to help educate young ministers to secure an education.

For the first time the faculty requested the Board to make arrangements for faculty members to secure leaves of absence for advanced study. The petition by Professors Eagleton, Chandler, Mitchell and Thompson was denied with regret, for lack of finances.

Four men graduated in the Class of 1892: Joseph Porter Hall, Wm. F. Junkin, James Kidd Thompson and Milton King Thompson. The first three all became renowned ministers in the Presbyterian Church and M. K. Thompson took the medical degree from Southern Medical College. A resolution on the death of Rev. E. D. Junkin, long time trustee of the College and pastor of the First Presbyterian Church of Houston from 1880 until his death in Johnson City, Tennessee, August 1, 1891, while there on a visit, was recorded in the Minutes. Rev. E. D. Junkin was the father of Wm. F. Junkin, who, upon graduating in the Class of 1892, was elected to teach at the

College (1892-93). He was awarded the M.A. degree at the 1893 Commencement at which time his brother, Tinsley P. Junkin, E. B. Fincher, F. H. Lowrance and E. S. Lowrance received the B.A. degree and Professor L. J. Mitchell was awarded the C.E. degree. A sad note at the Commencement was the announcement of the death of Gen. John Besser, who for nearly thirty years, was a faithful member of the College Board; a man instrumental in providing brick and labor to build the College at Huntsville and a charter contributor to the endowment fund.

At the June 6, 1894 meeting the Board awarded its first and only Ph.D degree to Professor Allison Thompson. The A.M. degree was conferred on E. B. Fincher and Professor C. C. Scott.

Four graduates received B.A. degrees, namely: Walter Acker, who became a school superintendent; Gordone Boone, Attorney at Law and City attorney of Navasota; Norman Cavitt, rancher; Robert Douglas Campbell, Presbyterian minister.

At the June 5, 1895 Commencement nine men received B.A. degrees and one B.S. degree was conferred, the largest graduating class in the history of the College. Geo. C. F. Butte was to become a famous lawyer, trustee and professor of the College and later Governor of Porto Rico; Brooks I. Dickey, Wm. Plummer Dickey, Frank E. Fincher, Lawrence E. Selfridge and Madison M. Slaughter, all to the ministry; Bishop Holmes, Samuel J. McFarland, Jesse E. Simmons and Thomas L. Simmons, all to become business men.

A new milestone of this decade was the action of the Board in regard to allowing Greek letter fraternities. They were forbidden and discontinued during the first decade. "The two Greek letter fraternities of Austin College were granted the privilege of organizing, and with the assurance and understanding on their part that nothing should occur to produce hurtful rivalries. It is the sense of the Board that these societies are still on probation and that their continued existence will depend upon their proving to the faculty that they are developing manliness of character and are overcoming bitterness and rivalries. It is the opinion of the Board that professors may not be members of these fraternities."

At this same trustee meeting June 3, 1896, the Board authorized tuition for sons of ministers and candidates for the ministry; and a commission of $10 to any professor for each new paying student secured by him. *(Minutes,* pp. 407, 409).

The graduates of the Class of 1896, with B.A. degrees were: Joseph F. Baird, who became a minister; Peyton Irving, who became a superintendent of schools; Joseph L. Lockett, who became a lawyer; Oscar Lusk, who became a military man; Edward H. Moseley, who became a minister; Archie Dean Rice, who became a missionary to China; Robert Ernest Vinson, who became a minister, President of Austin Theological Seminary and President of Texas University; and Wm. Ashton Vinson, who became a lawyer and Austin College Board President.

The faculty granted the students permission to begin intercollegiate athletics. In the only game Austin College was defeated by A & M 22 to 4.

Principal actions of the Board in the 1896-97 year were: Resolved to: (1) Give a quit claim deed to the Second Presbyterian Church in Houston to any residuary legatee interest on a lot given to the church by Dr. MacGregor's wife. (2) A circular was printed and distributed, calling attention to the fact that hard times had prevented many students from matriculating and that the College could not balance its budget, and that the financial stringency had curtailed endowment income. Reminding the Synod that one fourth of the College students were sons of ministers or ministerial candidates on free tuition, each church was asked to take up a collection for the benefit of the College. (3) B. P. Edrington, W. K. Hohnston, J. C. Stinson, G. T. Thompson, Jr. and Walter Thornton received B.A. degrees; A. G. Thomas and W. D. Mitchell received B.S. degrees. (4) The Board sustained the action of the Executive Committee for reversing the suspension by the faculty of three students, one of them being a senior, Hubert Atkinson. The faculty made complaints to the Board that the Executive Committee transcended its authority as established by precedent. The Board replied that the members of the Executive Committee acted for the best interest of the College. The faculty insisted on collecting damages against the three students done to the building. An appeal from action of the faculty by Atkinson's father supported by Rev. M. C. Hutton, pastor of the Georgetown Presbyterian Church and a Board member, was denied at the trial and 50% of all damage fees were retained for repairs. In reversal of its original reversal, the Board rec-ommended the case of Hubert Atkinson to the faculty for clemency.

The Board appointed Dr. Wm. H. Leavell to inform the fac-ulty that for financial reasons it would be necessary to de-crease the faculty. Quoting from Dr. D. F. Eagleton's diary:

> Through Dr. Leavell, the faculty was called and were informed that the College could not meet the expenses with so many professors and it was neces-sary to cut down the force by one man and they did not want to discriminate, that they hoped we could assist them. The readjustment provided for a Presi-dent with Bible and Philosophy, Professor of Mathe-matics, Professor of Science, Professor of Latin and Greek and a Professor of English and History. Every member of the faculty assured the Board of its hearty cooperation and all promptly offered their resigna-tion. The same astute politician thanked us in the name of the Board and bade us goodnight. (It may be said in passing that his two sons were attending an-other institution.)

The Board now had to make a decision and did so by offer-ing to keep the entire faculty for one year if the President would take a reduction in salary of 20% and each faculty mem-ber 10%. Dr. Luckett and Professor Thompson (whose father-in-law was on the Board) agreed but Professors Eagleton, Mitchell, Chandler and Bell declined.

Before adjourning to meet in Dallas the next week, the Board abolished military training and Captains (C.N.) Roberts and Wharton were instructed to take charge of the gounds and return the arms belonging to the U.S. Government.

On June 10, 1897 the Board elected Rev. Thornton R. Samp-son president at $1500 per year. The other faculty were John R. Roseboro, English and History at $700 per year; J. A. Mc-Laughlin, Mathematics at $1000 per year; W. G. Morrison, Natural Science at $800 per year; A. T. Thompson, Latin, and G. L. Bell, Greek at $1000 per year (These last two were the only old faculty retained and both were sons-in-law of Board members). Dr. Luckett in relinquishing the Presidency was elected Financial agent at $600 per year. Thus the Board now had employed one more man instead of reducing by one, as

originally planned. And salary obligations were increased 20%
instead of being reduced 10%.

Austin College was again beaten in football, this time 2 to 0.

When Dr. Sampson met with the Board for the first time at
Marshall, Texas, December 2, 1897, he was added to the
Executive Committee as Chairman and the Board decided
that the Executive Committee would have no control in the
future over discipline of the College (*Minutes*, p. 422).

At Commencement June 1, three graduates received the
B.S. degrees; namely, C. A. Lannius, T. E. Craig, and C. Stanly Roberts; one B.A. degree to Alva Hardie.

For lack of funds the building of a gymnasium was postponed. It was necessary for the Treasurer to use three thousand dollars of Endowment Funds for current expenses. Only
the "generosity of Captain J. M. Thompson, who liberally
defrayed the travelling expenses of the President, enabling
him to visit every Presbytery in the Synod" kept the deficit
down (*Minutes*, p. 425).

The Board agreed to allow the Alumni Association $100 to
aid in publishing a semi-centennial memorial volume, and
established an honor scholarship for the Sherman high school
boy with the highest grade in his graduating class.

In every decade it seems there were attempts to change the
location or name of the College or both and the Fifth Decade
was no exception.

"The Board unanimously voted to change the name of Austin College to 'John Knox College.' This name to take effect
at the close of the semi-centennial celebration next meeting."
(*Minutes of Board,* October 28, 1898, p. 430)

New rules and by-laws to govern the Board were reported
and adopted. Of note was the decision to have two annual
meetings, one in Sherman at Commencement and the other
preceeding Synod wherever it met.

A resolution on the occasion of the death of J. N. Chadwick
was a mark of sadness as the Fifth Decade closed. At the last
meeting of the fiftieth year of the College the action of the
previous Board to change the name of the College was reconsidered and after several hours of discussion simply postponed indefinitely. In order to close the year without a deficit,
Mrs. Sarah C. Bell, of Galveston, came to the rescue with a
cash gift of $5,000. (*Minutes of Board,* p. 435).

Notable, too, was the Board's gift of $100 to the *Chromascope* Committee; also, advertisements in the *Houston Post* and *Dallas News;* completion of the gymnasium and laboratory fee of $5 established. Professor D. F. Eagleton was elected Professor of English replacing Professor Roseboro.

In this last year of the Fifth Decade (and the last year of the century) Austin College graduated the largest graduating class in its history: Four B.S. degrees and seven B.A. degrees to A. M. Barton, Blaine Brown, Guy Hart Evan and Veris McInnis; F. P. Files, J. B. Files, Wm. F. Galbraith, James McCall, John Moore, James Sedgwick and John A. Williams. Five became lawyers, three became ministers, one a postmaster and one a rancher. Guy H. Evans died a month after graduation.

## THE SIXTH DECADE

T HE beginning year of the Sixth Decade had hardly opened before the matter of changing the name of the College came to the Board's attention with a request from the Ben Milam Chapter No. 8 of the Daughters of the Republic of Texas to add Stephen F. to the name of Austin College.

A committee appointed to investigate the legal requirements for actually changing the name reported that a majority of three-fourths was all that was required. At this meeting (October 20, 1899) "the roll was called for votes to change to Stephen F. Austin College, and the following vote was recorded: Ayes—Russell, Brownson, Aldrich, Wilson, Roberts, Hutton, Fullenwider, McMurray, Moseley, Butte (by proxy) Wiggins, French. Nays—Wharton (by proxy), Moore (by proxy)." So the motion to change the name to "Stephen F. Austin" received affirmatively the vote of three-fourths of all the Trustees and the name of "Austin College" was changed to "Stephen F. Austin." (*Minutes*, p. 440)

Succeeding Boards, faculty and students all completely ignored the Board's action. A special Board meeting was called in Dallas, Texas, May 3, 1900. Dissension arose between the President and members of the faculty. Internal affairs were not satisfactory. Many students did not return after the holidays. The investigating committee reported to the Board, "We realize the difficulty in the way of Dr. Sampson continuing as President and refer the whole matter to the Board. The committee feels constrained to express the opinion that it will be for the best interest of the College that Professor Thompson be asked to resign." (Thompson, Professor of Latin, was the son-in-law of one of the trustees).

Professor Sampson offered his resignation to take effect June 10, 1900. (*Minutes of Board* at Dallas, Texas, May 8, 1900, page 442)

The June 5, 1900 meeting of the Board records: "Professor Thompson appeared, made some statements to the Board, after which his resignation was accepted."

Rev. Thomas Stone Clyce, A.B., B.D. of Jackson, Alabama was elected President. The Board expressed "our entire satisfaction with the services of Professors Eagleton, McLauchlin and J. L. Bell" and re-elected Professor Charles C. Scott, a former incumbent, to be Professor of Natural Sciences. (*Minutes of Board*, p. 443).

Dr. Eagleton in his diary states:

> The fact is that the old College is about gone, and the Trustees are mainly responsible for it. The semicentennial exercises were devoid of interest. The addresses were good but students, faculty, trustees and citizens were conspicuous by their absence.
> I am returning to the atmosphere of criticism, of complaint, of jealousy and strife.

When the Fall session of 1900 opened he states:

> School has opened in earnest and a fearful condition do we find—night vandalism is of nightly occurrence. The Boarding houses are bedlam. Cheating is common. It is evident there is an organized clique for such deeds. Seeing that someone must be sacrificed to save the College I throw myself into the breach and receive calumny, insult—all but personal violence. My stable is entered and my horse sheared, my buggy put in the gymnasium.

At Commencement June, 1900 the faculty issued three B.S. and six B.A. degrees to Joseph W. Wilson, Harry Cern, John A. Martin, Jr., Motte Martin, Ernest Bradshaw, Frank B.

Spangler, Earle Carter, Wm. N. Scott, Jr. and Jessie Rosser Stitt—three lawyers, two ministers and three business men. Wm. N. Scott died a few months after graduation.

If Dr. Clyce had known the enormous task awaiting him he probably would have remained in Alabama. At the first Board meeting in San Antonio, October 17, 1900 the Board adopted unanimously the following resolution:

> Whereas the change of the name of Austin College (to Stephen F. Austin by order of the Synod) has not been a success in meeting its difficulties, we the Board of Trustees of the College restore to it the original form, and the Committee on change of charter be instructed to take no further action at this point. (*Minutes*, p. 447)

The committee on revision of the charter recommended that Section 7 which follows, be stricken out:

> Be it further enacted, that no religious test shall be required of any President, Professor, or Tutor in said college: nor, shall any student or officer be censored, suspended or expelled on account of his opinion, political or religious; provided, however, that nothing herein contained shall prevent the Trustees of said college from throwing around the instructors and students a proper moral restraint, and inflicting suitable punishment upon all immoral conduct. (Quoted from original charter)

Salaries were raised to $1200 per year, the Preparatory Department enlarged, and Dr. George Butte added to fill the chair of Modern Languages. At the June 6 Commencement of 1901 the following graduates were honored: M. A. degree to T. O. Perrin; B.A. degree to E. G. Bell, J. L. Read, A. W. Kinnard. The B.S. degrees were awarded to D. P. Brown, H. W. Head, J. B. McFerrin, Hoxie H. Thompson and E. E. McInnis. Two ministers, two lawyers, one doctor, one superintendent and three business men.

When Dr. Clyce took the Presidency in 1900 the total assets of the College were listed as follows:

| | | |
|---|---|---:|
| Buildings, fixtures, library and grounds | | $50,000 |
| 500 acres in Brazoria County | | 2,500 |
| Kiam Building—Houston | | 50,000 |
| 375 acres in Pecos County | | 875 |
| Other lots and parcels of land | | 3,300 |
| Notes receivable—good | | 2,500 |
| Notes receivable—doubtful | | 5,179 |
| | Total | $114,354 |

Chadwick Farm—1296 acres not valued. The year ended with a deficit of $809, and the abolition of Greek letter fraternities.

The year 1901-02 closed with the awarding of six A.B., one B.S. and two M.A. degrees, these latter to Professor Bell and Professor Butte for work they had done while teaching, as they both were leaving the College for more graduate work.

At the June 3, 1903 meeting the Board ruled that it would no longer award M.A. degrees except "in consequence of work done at the direction of the faculty." (*Minutes*, p. 482)

John Walker Vinson, who was martyred in China while serving as a missionary there, was one of the three B.S. and six A.B. degree awardees. The faculty was advised "that nominations for the honorary titles and degrees do not properly come from the Faculty but from Board members." (*Minutes*, p. 483)

Mr. J. Lewis Thompson was commended for his gifts and interest in equipping athletic facilities.

Dr. T. R. Sampson, President of the Austin Seminary, was refused in his request to have part of the Chadwick Farm income allotted to students at the Seminary.

Records of the 1903-04 session show that $4,092 was paid in tuition by all students and that contributions amounted to $3,800; $1800 coming from Synod's Committee.

There were 15 ministerial candidates, six sons of ministers and three honor scholarships. Total receipts were $14,191. Only three seniors were recommended for graduation: Nathan Cox, B.S., Clyde B. Moore and Wm. L. Tillman, B.A.

Dr. R. R. Harwell was appointed Professor of Languages to replace Professor W. W. Bondurant, who was given a leave of absence.

Presbyteries were requested to pay tuition for ministerial candidates recommended by each. The request was made by overture to Synod.

The 1904-05 session began with 98 students. It ended with 14 seniors, 11 juniors, 16 sophomores, 26 freshmen, 32 preparatory and one graduate student. (100)

Thirteen received B.S. and B.A. degrees and Rev. W. Fred Galbraith earned the M.A. degree.

The 1905-06 session started off with 113 enrolled, with $5,329 paid in tuition—largest in the history of the College. A drive to secure funds for a Y.M.C.A. building was in progress with $5,000 pledged on a $10,000 building. Dr. Eagleton was the sponsoring spirit in this venture.

A communication to Col. Guy M. Bryan that there was no plan or likelihood of changing the name of Austin College served to stimulate the establishment of the "Stephen F. Austin Fellowship" ($5,000) by Austin's heirs.

On January 17, 1906 the by-laws of the Constitution were amended—notable in the additions was Section 6 of Article VIII:

> The President and Professors shall be publicly inaugurated at the next annual Commencement succeeding their election, at which time the President of the Board of Trustees shall require an affirmative answer to the following questions: (a) Do you sincerely believe the Old and New Testament to be the Word of God, the only infallible rule of faith and practice? (b) Do you obligate yourself not to teach anything that is opposed to any doctrine of the standards of the Presbyterian Church while a professor of this institution? (c) Do you solemnly promise to faithfully discharge the duties of your function in this college? (*Minutes*, p. 529)

There was prospect of getting the Y.M.C.A. building started and $14,000 was pledged to build Luckett Hall dormitory.

Ten degrees were awarded at 1906 Commencement. Ministerial candidates were required to sign notes to the College, payable with interest if they did not enter the ministry. Sons of faculty members were granted free tuition. (*Minutes*, page 537.)

At the Fall meeting October 16, 1906, Dr. Clyce reported a registration of 112 students; and that only 52 of the eligible 103 of the previous year had enrolled—a loss of 50%. Many

reasons were recorded for this deplorable condition, namely:
(1) Only 50% were from Presbyterian families (2) Lack of
boarding and housing facilities (3) Lack of diversity in curriculum and small faculty.

To remedy this situation it was decided to establish a chair
of Economics and History, of Physics and Pre-engineering;
rush the building program and to increase recruiting by ad-
vertising. Nine men were granted B.A. and B.S. degrees at
the 1907 Commencement. Professor George Case was commended for his training of the Austin College Glee Club the
past two years and for the next year the Board agreed to pay
him $250 to match $250 contributed by a friend. A resolution
on the resignation of Captain C. N. Roberts was recorded,
expressing appreciation and regret.

The College registered 152 students in the Fall of 1907,
largest in the history of the College. Eight came from Mexico
and twenty-two from other states. Income from tuition alone
increased $3,000 over the previous year. Especially notable
was the fact that 86 paid full tuition for the whole year and
37 for one term. There were 20 ministerial candidates and
nine sons of ministers and professors receiving free tuition.

The basement of the Y.M.C.A. was completed and material
on hand to complete the structure. It was soon to be the first
college Y.M.C.A. west of the Mississippi.

Dr. Eagleton was commended for his effective recruiting
campaign and requested to continue. Two private structures,
Togo House and Hardy House were leased to house preparatory students and the following salary schedule accepted:

| | | | |
|---|---|---|---|
| Dr. Clyce | $2,000 | D. F. Eagleton | $1,800 |
| C. C. Scott | 1,500 | R. R. Harwell | 1,200 |
| G. W. Snedecor | 1,200 | T. R. Ludlow | 1,200 |
| Latin Chair | 1,200 | Prep. Department | 1,000 |

On March 16, 1908 Luckett Hall was opened. Thirty-
thousand dollars in college bonds were sold to Rice Institute
of Houston, Texas.

There was one M.A. degree awarded to Wm. Thornton
Read, nine B.A. and six B.S. degrees given — largest in the
history of the College.

Dr. Clyce, who truly had won his nickname "Big Doc" was
authorized to employ a secretary at $60 a month, and was re-

quested to take a summer vacation as a reward for his leadership.

The last year of the Sixth Decade started off with 196 students registered, a 100% increase in five years and highest on record, and of which 141 were college students. There were 33 ministerial candidates, also the largest ever of this group.

Notable additions to the faculty were Dr. Charles R. Pepper, Professor of Latin and French, and Mrs. Sarah S. Collins, Matron of Luckett Hall and first woman employee of the College in its sixty years' history. Dr. Eagleton was given permission to secure funds to endow the English Chair. The decade closed with an enrollment of 202 and the awarding of 13 B.A. and one B.S. degrees.

## THE SEVENTH DECADE

THE Seventh Decade began with an interest bearing debt of $65,000 worrying the College officials. President Clyce notified the Board that he found it impossible to conduct the affairs of his office on the campus and at the same time be a successful financial agent in the field. He pointed out that the executive committee of the Board was given duties that should be shared by the whole Board. The entire time of the Board meetings on February 10 and May 31, 1910 was taken up with measures to renew the interest bearing obligations and for the President of the Board to make an additional loan of $3,000 to pay current expenses.

A minor disaster was the burning down of Togo House, dormitory and main dining hall. The hopes of a successful drive for funds in Dallas were disheartening. President Clyce in his report to the Board was firm in his appraisal of the manner of conducting the financial affairs of the College: "I believe that there should be a central office in the main building in connection with the President's office, through which all the business of the institution should be conducted. In this office should be a good bookkeeper who could act as Treasurer of the College and Purchasing Agent, submitting his work for approval of the President." The year 1909-10 closed with one M.A. degree awarded to Levi Allen Wight and eight

B.A. degrees to John Knox Alexander, Harry Blanding, Roland W. Burchard, Clyde Eagleton, Warren R. Hall, John W. Hickman, Walter E. Long, and Clarence W. Rhea.

The financial strain was relieved temporarily when the Board extended the lease on the MacGregor property in Houston from 1942 to 2042 for an income increase of $3,000 per year net income. A $25,000 loan at 8% was made immediately by mortgaging the lease rentals. A very complex arrangement for the disposition of this $25,000 was made by lending the entire amount at 8% to J. Lewis Thompson, ex–student, Board member and benefactor of the College. Mr. Thompson had endorsed notes of the College at Sherman banks. He agreed to pay off these totaling $22,878 and to pay $125 per month for five years to be applied to the salary of the professor of Chemistry. Mr. Thompson expected to be reimbursed for the $22,878 from money to be raised by the "Committee of Ten" in a Houston drive for funds.

The Stephen F. Austin Fellowship was endowed with a $4,000 gift by the heirs of Austin to encourage the study of Texas history of the period 1829 to 1836. This required a resolution by the trustees that the College would never give up the name "Austin College." These heirs, all nephews of Austin were: Guy M. Bryan, Jr., Guy M. Bryan, Lewis R. Bryan and E. L. Perry. (The Bryan family had four Guy M. Bryans living at this time; one of them left a 11,000-acre ranch to the College in his will. This land on the Brazoria County Gulf Coast is estimated to have a value of two million dollars.)

In 1910 the chair of pedagogy was established. The tuition of the College was increased $20.00 and 216 students registered. John Hardy was placed in charge of Luckett Hall Dining Room and John Alexander was made Bursar and Plant Supervisor. (These two men served faithfully through three decades for the College.)

Improvements on the campus with completion of all YMCA facilities including a swimming pool, basket ball court, barber shop, pressing shop and snack bar gave new spirit to the campus community.

The Austin College Band was organized by Tom M. Cunningham, director and teacher. A paid athletic director, Chester Johnson, was employed at $1000 per year, who would also teach part time.

This 1911 class included a large number of men who were to become famous in their fields. Dr. Clyde Eagleton, son of Professor Dave Eagleton, was a Rhodes Scholar and after Oxford taught at SMU before becoming Chairman of the Department of International Law at New York University. Walter Long was a life long Secretary of the Austin, Texas, Chamber of Commerce. Both of them published several valuable books. The B.A. degree awardees included eleven ministers, four of whom became foreign missionaries.

Important in the 1911–12 seesion was the establishing of separate Chemistry, Biology and Physics Departments. Two hundred and eight students registered. Plans were shaping up for remodelling the Main Building, with new science facilities and a new Library and Study Hall. Dr. Harwell was given two years leave of absence to travel in Europe and do work at Yale University.

The Board mourned the death of a former president, Rev. Henry B. Boude, who was credited with getting Austin College firmly established in Sherman. Fifteen degrees were awarded at the 1912 Commencement, among them J. O. Moseley, who became the second Austin College Rhodes Scholar. Four ministers and two physicians came from this class.

The Board, thinking it important that all students be versed in public speaking, made it compulsory for every student to join one of the Literary Societies. There was one M.A. degree conferred in 1913—to Ernest W. Thompson. Seventeen B. A. degrees were conferred—six became ministers.

Chief among the events of 1913 was the total loss of the Main Building by fire. A student arsonist caught in the act of trying to burn down the YMCA building confessed to setting fire to "Old Main." While the loss was great at the time, the building was entirely out of date and had seen 35 years of rough treatment. Insurance amounting to $15,000 was collected. Very soon thereafter Sherman Hall (auditorium and library) was built by the citizens of Sherman; Thompson Hall (science building) by the Thompson brothers, Hoxie, Louis and Alex; and the Power House (class rooms) by alumni and friends. By 1914 the ten-acre campus had five substantial buildings, and an athletic field and field house on a five-acre tract three blocks north.

Heretofore a quorum required nine out of sixteen trustees to be present and no proxies. By mutual agreement this was changed so that seven members present constituted a quorum.

The Secretary of the Board, Rev. S. J. McMurry, was directed to begin immediately the gathering and arranging of materials for writing a complete history of Austin College. (*Minutes,* Vol. 2, page 3)

Only 18 B. A. degrees and two M. A. degrees (Alexander Gray and George McCall) were granted in 1914, but in it Austin College made another giant stride toward the summit of greatness. With a new library, new auditorium for Chapel, new classroom building, modern science laboratories and new administrative offices, the College strove onward to seek supremacy in the field of education for which its founders had aimed.

One note of sadness—the College lost a constantly loyal benefactor in the death of Mrs. Jewel Link Luckett. A memorial page recording her splendid service to God and man was placed in the Minutes of the Trustees. (Vol. 2, page 31, *Board Minutes*)

During the year 1915 Dr. Eagleton's personal appeal for endowing the English Chair was successful. Master of Arts degrees were awarded to two: M. A. Bryan and W. C. Earheart. Fourteen B.A. degrees were awarded.

A great stride forward toward improving the Christian fellowship and campus spirit came with the selection of Mason L. Cashion for YMCA secretary and Director of Athletics. The YMCA, first on any campus west of the Mississippi, was now complete with bowling lanes, basketball court, swimming pool and gymnastic equipment.

The College future seemed so rosy that Synod at its October 14, 1915 meeting passed a resolution:

> authorizing and empowering Austin College to execute a note in the amount not to exceed Two Hundred and Seventy-Five Thousand Dollars; and it is understood that the members of the Board of Trustees of Austin College shall in no way be individually liable for said sum nor any part thereof. (*Board Minutes*, Vol. 2, page 35)

(Unquestionably, the above action by Synod was to save the College from being closed down 15 years later. In December

1932 the Synod took action to close Austin College in its morning session, but during the lunch period, it was revealed that the Synod alone was legally responsible for $262,000. Paying this debt would take all of Synod's funds for many years and financially embarrass all of Synod's causes).

Eleven men graduated in 1916, among them George Hurst, who became a missionary to Brazil and Lewis J. Sherrill, author of a number of books, who became Dean and Acting President of Louisville Presbyterian Seminary. Another, Mandred W. Comfort, became a famous surgeon with Mayo Clinic.

A pleasant duty for Dr. Clyce on November 30, 1916, was to represent Austin College at the inauguration of President-elect Robert E. Vinson (B.A. 1896) as President of the University of Texas. Dr. Vinson had been President of Austin Theological College.

Sadness prevailed on the campus when news of Dr. Davis Foute Eagleton's sudden death occurred while on a trip for the College. Two brothers, David P. and Paul C. Dean, students of the College, were traveling on the train with Dr. Eagleton when he had a sudden heart attack near Kerrville. They telegraphed the sorrowful news back to the campus. (A gift in 1964 by the Dean brothers enabled the College to build Wm. Dean Hall for men, honoring their father).

At commencement June 4, 1917 Albert Lee Burke and Eugene M. Ellison received M.A. degrees. Among the twelve B. A. degree men were Edward Wells Rugely who later became the second Austin College graduate to earn the Ph.D in Chemistry (Yale 1922). John Morgan Currie became the first Austin College graduate to give his life for his country in World War One. Robert Girard Lowe and Lyndon McCutchen became ministers, the latter serving on the Board of Trustees from 1934 to 1945, and Board Secretary most of that time.

Military training was re-established in the curriculum by action of the Board and preparations were made for implementing the S.A.T.C. (Student Army Training Corp) through contract with the Federal government. Through this action many students were attracted to the College. The government took care of most of the students college expenses including uniforms.

The war year class of 1918 totaled an even dozen. Though small in numbers, this class distinguished itself in many ways. Campbell Butler, Roy McCall, Lardner Moore, Boude

Moore, and Robert Ray became Presbyterian ministers. R. D. Erwin, Wm. K. Furrh, John F. Anderson, Robert Couts Holland, Lloyd Hughes went into the business field; Robert R. Wilson became Professor of International Law at Duke University and Wm. Addison McElroy became an architect in Houston. Most important event in the 1918-19 session was the admission of women students. Much opposition from old grads developed over the conversion of the 70-year old male college into a co-educational one, even on a war–time basis. Only a few girls enrolled for the initial year, most of whom had attended Kidd–Key Junior College and Conservatory; or Carr-Burdette College, sister institutions in Sherman.

The second *war one* class of 1919 was even smaller than the 1918 class. Lardner Moore was the only M.A. degree awardee. (He was the grandson of Dr. H.B. Boude, fifth President of Austin College.) He was born in Japan, son of a missionary and for 42 years he and his wife (Grace Eagleton) served as missionaries to Japan. Only 7 B.A. degrees were conferred to: Roscoe E. Hooker, who entered the ministry and was divested in April 1948. Percy Keith distinguished himself in the field of chemistry. Recognized the world over for his diffusion process in separating the isotopic isomers of uranium hexafluoride, the initial fuel of atomic energy, he can be credited with the abrupt ending of the war with Japan. Homer Rainey and "Charlie" C. A. Robinson were all–round athletes and at first became professional big league baseball players. Rainey soon deserted athletics for the teaching profession, holding the presidency of a number of universities—William and Marshall; Bucknell; Texas University (second alumnus called to Presidency of our State University) and Stephens College. Charlie Robinson was the seventh man in the history of big league baseball to pitch a no–hit, no–run perfect baseball game—with Chicago White Sox against Detroit Tigers in 1922. Lockett Stewart taught physics at Austin College before becoming a physician. Ewell Walker served the Dallas public schools in the administrative field and Jimmy Paxton became an official with a telephone company.

# THE EIGHTH DECADE
### After World War I

FOR some reason difficult to determine, the College quickly overcame many of its difficulties. Students who had been in the war and had survived it, served as a nucleus to invigorate the new students with a desire to make Austin College known not only to Texas but to the Southwest. Among these were Shem and Horace Cunningham, Cortell Holsapple, Ed Grant, Leon Foshee, Nick McCarley, Luther Baker, Guy Estes, Homer Rainey, Zeke Wilson and others.

Austin College began to admit women in 1918, after heated opposition from some of the older graduates, mostly ministers who voiced their opinions in Presbytery and Synod meetings. It was thought that the admission of women would cripple the growth of Texas Presbyterian College for Women at Milford. Co–education won out during the war on the grounds that the College could enroll the necessary students to provide the financial assistance needed while the war was on.

Opinion of Sherman citizens was divided. Some deplored the admission of women at A.C. for fear that Kidd-Key College would suffer. A Methodist Junior College and Conservatory, Kidd-Key had an enrollment as large as Austin College and was apparently flourishing. However, their graduates could now continue at A.C. in the Junior year and arrangements were made to interchange some courses and some professors.

The College in this Eighth Decade began to turn out men for every field—eagerly sought by industry; in education—teachers, administrative personnel, athletic coaches; in public service, and for graduate study for higher degrees in other institutions of learning.

Student organizations of all kinds were a challenge in which to excel, as well as in the laboratories, on the athletic field and in the flourishing literary societies. Campus life was never dull. Pre-medical and chemical societies, tennis clubs, glee clubs, the Ministerial Association, a Strollers Playhouse, and intra–mural sports consumned student energy. Contests between the Philennoian and Athenaeum Literary Societies determined the winners who would participate in the State Oratorical contests. The Junior Class began to win out over Kidd-Key in the annual spelling contest, rarely accomplished in earlier days.

The College intercollegiate athletic teams, always strong, now began to win laurels even over Southwestern Conference teams. Competing as a member of the T.I.A.A. (Texas Intercollegiate Athletic Association) Austin College football teams were winning against S.M.U., Baylor, Rice and T.C.U. Teams coached by E. Y. Freeland, Charlie Robinson, Ray Morehart, Pete Cawthon and Cecil Griggs were feared by every team in Texas.

A strong Y.M.C.A. on the campus, the first college "Y" west of the Mississippi, was not only a strong moral influence under M. L. Cashion, and later under Tom Cunningham, but also sponsored all campus activities with physical, cultural and spiritual programs.

Prior to 1920 all intercollegiate events were at Luckett Field, near the Frisco shops. In 1922 the College acquired 20 acres of land adjacent to its ten-acre campus. This tract known as the Porter property was obtained through the activity of the Alumni Association which chiefly footed the bill for athletics, both intra-mural and intercollegiate. Immortals of this decade were such strong supporters as Pat E. Hooks, Stanly Roberts, Sr., Hoxie Thompson and Arthur Hopkins.

The beginning of this period of excellency in athletics is well presented by James Creighton ('23) in his book *Once Upon a Time*.

As early as 1856 the College had offered the Master's Degree but it was not until the beginning of the Eighth Decade that large numbers of B.A. degree holders began to seek higher degrees. Scholars, particularly in the field of education, chemistry and medicine, and the ministry, were on the increase in numbers and quality.

Among those who were registering in September 1919 was a seventeen–year–old eager–beaver from Somerville, Texas, later to become the author of this book. Also one who for the last half century has been intimately connected with Austin College in one way or another. The history recorded here for the next five decades will be from "within." He arrived with $200 in Liberty bonds, his entire fortune, for which Dr. Clyce generously allowed full value for Board and Room.

Half the student body matriculating for the 1919-20 session were just returning from military service. A few more women registered; all dormitories were full. Intercollegiate athletics

was resumed under Coach E. J. Freeland. Kangaroo Court
which had been abolished as the last act of the Board in the
previous year *was not abolished.* Joe Dickson did a good job
as Judge of the Court. The author doesn't remember who the
two elected Chief Spatters were but he still remembers the
spats. Through the Court and its processes all green Freshmen
were brought up into a knowledge of the true Austin College
Spirit. For intimate information of what went on at the College for this and the next three years, I suggest reading James
"Canary" Creighton's *Once Upon a Time.*

B.A. degrees were conferred on Gladys Marie Cornell and
Lola Belle Perkins, the first women graduates, at the May 31,
1920 Commencement. Thirteen men were in the graduating
class. Horace Cunningham and Jonathan Edwards were the
only two to become ministers. Joe Dickson, Ed Grant, Vernon Guthrie, and Oscar Holsapple entered the field of education. Shem Cunningham and Howard McCarley, business
men, were trustees of the College for many years. John
"Red" Park died while serving as an F.B.I. agent. Fred Hudson, Francis Powell and Clarence Stollings entered business.

Various petitions to abolish co-education were circulated for
signatures, handed to the Trustees and ignored. Campus life
in the 1920–21 year was made less boresome by having such
personalities as Irvin S. Cobb, Miss Anna Case, famous opera
singer and Ex–President John Marshall on the College Ly-
ceum Program.

Coming back strong in athletics under Coach Freeland, the
football team made Texas people take notice by beating
S.M.U. 43 to 0, chiefly due to the running of "Egg" Morehart
and "Choc" Thompson.

The graduating class of 1921 contained two M.A.'s, Joe
Dickson and Vernon Guthrie. Two girls received the B.A.
degree, Grace Eagleton and Katherine Pitman. Of this class
M. L. Baker was the only one to enter the ministry. He also
served as Trustee of the College from Oklahoma Synod. B. F.
Armendt, after doing graduate work in chemistry at Vanderbilt and Illinois Universities, became the first graduate to
teach chemistry at his Alma Mater. Most of the remaining
members of this class began teaching, except Felix Leslie who
became a dentist in Hillsboro, Texas.

The Junior Class began the publication of "The Kangaroo,"
a weekly College newspaper with Leon Foshee editor.

Notable events occurring in the 1921–22 year were: (1) S.M.U. beaten again by a score of 17 to 7, (2) A live mascot— "Pat" the Kangaroo was secured through the efforts of Juniors R. D. Lauderdale, George L. Landolt and other students to be paraded at all athletic contests, (3) Tuition was increased to $137.50 per year and Board and Room in the dormitories to $30 per month, (4) The President and Secretary of the Board of Trustees were authorized to sign a quit claim deed to any and all interest in the estate of the late Guy M. Bryan as set forth in his will (1907), and President Clyce was requested to write a letter to Mrs. Lucy B. Hervey (only survivor) assuring her of grateful appreciation of the loyalty and interest of her father to Austin College (*Minutes of Board*, Vol. 2, p. 71) (Note: This was not the Guy M. Bryan who gave Austin College the portrait of Stephen F. Austin but a nephew.) The will of Guy M. Bryan devised 11,000 acres of ranch land in Brazoria County, the income of which was to be reserved for his daughter as long as she lived and then to Austin College upon her death. In giving this quit claim deed, the Board assumed that Mrs. Hervey would follow her father's wishes for Austin College to own this land after her decease. Mrs. Hervey died in 1958, leaving the entire 11,000 acres to Austin College, now valued at over two million dollars. (5) The Preparatory Department was discontinued for the coming year.

There were six (6) M.A. degrees, six (6) women and twenty (20) men given B.A. degrees in 1922.

The 1922–23 year was the time the Board of Trustees mortgaged the campus for $90,000. Bonds totalling that amount were issued to the Mississippi Valley Trust Company of St. Louis bearing 6% per annum. The service charge by the Bank left a net to the college of $80,000 (This mortgage was later to become a serious problem when the 1929 depression caused the college to default in the regular retirement payments according to contract.)

Austin College beat SMU for the third time in a row in their annual football game (at Dallas). Two seniors, James Creighton and George Landolt met with the Board to request the installation of a Department of Journalism at the College to begin in the Fall of 1923. This request was approved by the Board the following day. The Board voted to rescind the action of 1913 making participation in literary societies optional and voted to require all students to join either the Athenaeum or Philennoian Society and all women to join the Kappa Gamma Chi Literary Society. To stimulate interest the Board authorized an annual sum of money for prizes and awards.

Plans for the Diamond Jubilee Commencement for the next year (1924) were formulated.

Four women and sixteen men including the author of this history graduated with B.A. degrees June 5, 1923. W. W. Tenney was the only M.A. degree recipient.

Chief events of the 1924 year were (1) Abolishing Kangaroo Court (2) In football A.C. team beat Rice 6 to 2, beat Baylor 7 to 3, beat Tulsa 9 to 0.

The new football field was fenced in and painted by the L & L Construction Company (Landolt and Lauderdale) who also erected bleachers.

A new gymnasium was begun on the 22 acre tract, Hoxie H. Thompson donating the lumber from his saw mill at Trinity, Texas. Pete Cawthon was head coach, having arrived on the campus in the Spring of 1923.

The Department of English Bible and Philosophy was established. It was not unusual in the early days of the College to award more honorary degrees than were earned. In celebrating the 75th anniversary of the founding of Austin College, the Board granted 26 earned degrees and awarded 20 Doctor of Laws, 9 Doctor of Literature and 12 Doctor of Divinity degrees. It took nearly two hours to uncap, hood and recap them all.

Rev. Wm. S. Red, D. D. (B.A. 1882), son of charter trustee Dr. George Red, and trustee himself in the Sixth Decade, told of the progress of the College. Thanks were expressed to Dr. Red and to Miss Cornelia McKinney, daughter of Andrew T. McKinney, who taught at Austin College in Huntsville when his father was President of the College for the second time. Miss McKinney secured valuable information relative to the history of Austin College which she prepared for the Diamond Jubilee.

An amendment to the charter of Austin College designated that two of the sixteen trustees should be from the Oklahoma Synod.

The Cawthon Gymnasium was completed in 1925 and Cashion Field improved by the addition of a field house with dressing rooms and showers for visiting teams.

Dr. Charlie Scott, Professor of Chemistry, was given leave of absence on account of illness. B. F. Armendt, B.A. '21, M.A. '22, who was doing graduate work in chemistry at the University of Illinois, was called back to take over the teaching. He was assisted by George L. Landolt (B.A. '23), instructor and graduate assistant returning from Rice Institute. This team began at once to modernize the equipment, laboratory practices and chemistry courses. Five full courses in chemistry were offered. A large number of reference works and chemistry periodicals were added to the department library.

Nine M.A. and twenty-seven B.A. degrees were earned in 1925.

The offer of Rev. W. S. Red to compile and publish a *History of Austin College* was regretfully declined for lack of funds at this time. (*Board Minutes,* Vol. 2, page 102)

Contract for the concrete superstructure of the newly planned three-story Administration Building was awarded to C. D. Hill and Company and work began early in 1926. (This building was not completed until twenty years later).

It was proposed that the College sell the 1232-acre farm given to the permanent Endowment Fund for the purpose of educating men for the ministry. Negotiations with the residuary legatees, J. N. Chadwick and his sister led to the decision to accept one-half of sale price of this property and to give the heirs one-half as well as one-half of all mineral rights. Fortunately the College reserved mineral rights and today receives royalty from oil and gas production.

There were six Masters and thirty-three Bachelors degrees conferred in 1926.

The President's report of May 30, 1927 showed that 242 men and 166 women enrolled with 50 *graduating,* the largest number of graduates in the history of the College. This made a total of 483 B.A. degrees awarded since 1900, — the coming of Dr. Clyce to the Presidency of the College. (*Minutes,* Vol. 2, p. 116)

A committee was appointed to attempt to prevail on the State Legislature not to have the Teachers College at Nacogdoches called "The Stephen F. Austin" college (all efforts failed) on the grounds that confusion would result. (The author knows of one such incident: During the year 1937, a magician of national reputation came to the office requesting student help to assemble his equipment on the stage of the auditorium for a program at assembly time. Investigation of his contract revealed that he was 250 miles from Nacogdoches where he was engaged to perform. A telephone message quickly postponed this for another day and the embarrassed magician was a guest on the campus for a while.)

1927–28 was the first year of the "Skeleton," unfinished Administration Building.

Forty–two B.A. and nine M.A. degrees were awarded. Tuition was raised by the Board to $150 per year for 1928-29. There was sadness on the campus this last year of the Eighth Decade. Elizabeth Clyce, youngest daughter of the President was killed in an aeroplane accident December 30, 1928. She had received the M.A. degree from Austin College in June 1928.

Uneasiness prevailed in the business world foretelling the depression. Synod members were beginning to talk of consolidation of its institutions; Texas Presbyterian College, Daniel Baker and Austin College.

Four M.A. and thirty–eight B.A. degrees were conferred.

## THE NINTH DECADE

THE greatest economic depression of the 20th Century hit the United States early in the Ninth Decade of the College. Efforts to complete the Administration Building came to a complete halt. The Synod was not to be interested in any financial campaign for Austin College as long as the consolidation of colleges was paramount in its plans.

Kid-Key College, a Methodist College, was also having serious financial troubles and a building program half finished. This led to an agreement for co-operative work with Kidd–Key students coming to the Austin College Campus for all science and some second year courses while Kidd–Key afforded art and music courses for Austin College students. This didn't work out sufficiently for either institution. Kidd–Key closed and consolidated with S.M.U. in Dallas. Again Austin College had a record graduating class with 8 M.A. and 57 B.A. degrees conferred on June 2, 1930, this being the largest in its history. For reasons only the faculty were aware of, the Board recalled the B.A. degree of a member of the 1928 class.

The year ended with all academic records and assets of Texas Presbyterian College for Women at Milford, Texas being transferred to Austin College by action of Synod. Mr. L. E. Petty, former president of the closed institution, was elected a professor of economics at Austin College. Dr. Clyce's request was granted and the Board made him President Emeritus, pending election of a President to succeed him.

Because the endowment of Daniel Baker College at Brownwood could be used only in Brown County, Synod released all of its rights to ownership of that institution. Austin College in Sherman thus became the only College operated by the Presbyterian Synod of Texas U.S.

On December 4, 1930, Dr. E. B. Tucker, ex-president of Arkansas College, became president at a salary of $4000 and a home. For some time before leaving Arkansas College, Dr. Tucker had endeavored to consolidate it with Southwestern at Memphis. This failing there was some hope that the Arkansas Synod might join with the Oklahoma and Texas Synods in supporting a tri-synod institution of higher learning. This didn't work out very advantageously. Austin College got Dr. Tucker for its tenth President and Arkansas survived the efforts to merge and move it.

Professor B. F. Armendt was granted a leave of absence so that he might return to the University of Illinois to complete requirements for the Ph.D. in Chemistry. Dr. George L. Landolt was elected Acting Chairman of the department in Professor Armendt's absence. Dr. Landolt took charge in the middle of the summer of 1931. The graduates for 1931 received 13 M.A. and 56 B.A. degrees. The college as almost always before was having no results in employing a successful financial agent. Few of them had ever produced enough results to pay their own expenses and one worked a year and didn't bring in enough to pay his telephone and telegraph bills. Records show that another's work in cash and valid pledges amounted to $140 and when his contract expired he presented expenses accounting for $130 of that, making the net of one whole year's work only $10.

Dr. Tilden B. Scherer, ex–president of King College, was the next financial agent for Austin College, at a salary of $300 per month and expenses, which meant a net of $300 per month to him as the college took care of all his expenses except clothes. The college now became known as the college of Ex-Presidents as, in addition to Dr. Tucker, there were on the payroll Dr. Clyce, Dr. Scherer and Professor Petty. Dr. Scherer didn't raise enough money to pay for the automobile and gasoline he used in his travels. Their failure was not due to lack of reputation or willingness, they just didn't know the alumni and Presbyterians of the State. Their attempt to raise money from people who knew more about the history, needs and problems of the college lessened a real confidence in the College rather than increasing it and in several cases caused the loss of several valuable benefactors of the College. As one Board member said of one such agent, "He gave evidence of compiling a prodigious amount of constructive work which on the whole was a summary of the attitude of the various pastors and churches' concern for Austin College." It would however be incorrect to say that all Synod members "wished us well." There were some in the Synod who wanted to concentrate all the educational work of the Presbyterian church in off-campus student centers at State institutions.

The graduating class of 1932 received 10 M.A. and 43 B.A. degrees.

The depression was really beginning to affect the enrollment. Dr. Steffey was relieved from teaching physics and this work taken over by Professor Armendt, chemistry professor. The Bible and Philosophy departments were combined.

The fourth year of this Ninth Decade started off in the depths of the depression. Unpaid salaries to faculty mounted. The destiny of the College was now in the hands of a few who had loyalty and hope. Among them was Pat E. Hooks who had come on the Board in 1920. Mr. Hooks was an ex-student, not a graduate. He often said that he had passed through the hallowed doors of Austin twice—on entering voluntarily and exiting by order of the faculty. At the July 21, 1932 meeting of the Board Pat E. Hooks, banker of Itasca, Texas, took the shaky helm of Austin College, and was Chairman of the Board of Trustees until 1950.

The first unpleasant task for Mr. Hooks was the report of Dr. D. A. Penick (Greek Professor of Texas University, and Chairman of Synod's Committee on Budget and Audits.) For two years the College had been going deeper and deeper in debt. Pressing bills had been taken care of by Dr. Tucker issuing 8% interest bearing notes, hoping that the end of the depression and good times again were just around the corner. But it got worse rather than better.

At the Joint Meeting of the Board and Synod's Budget and Audits Committee a ten-year program was dreamed up because "serious mistakes had been made (by the college)," the instructions of Synod, through its Committee on Schools and Colleges had not been properly heeded, and obligations had been created which were contrary to Synod's instruction. (To survive, rather than use up more endowment funds, the College had borrowed $30,000 from banks.)

Synod met in Kerrville September 27-29, 1932. Dr. Penick reported for his committee: "Synod's attention must be called to the fact that the College estimated income for the session now opening includes several doubtful items, among them $15,000 expected contributions and gifts and $9,467 for which provision is yet not certain.

"It should be stated further that the present obligations of Austin College are $262, 679.92 and that the net income from endowment is less than $3,500." (*Synod's Minutes*, Vol. VII., No. 3, p. 166.)

Result of this was that Synod called another meeting in Austin, Texas, December 13, to hear another report of the Committee after another conference with the Board of Trustees. Austin College was, however, permitted to operate the current session. The committee suggested that adequate publicity had been lacking:

> "This involves skilled and expert service in addition to expenditures for printing, etc. It may be possible to obtain the service without great cost by using our present force and friends." (This was certainly a paradox.)

Many things happened at the December 13, 1932 meeting, not disclosed in the Minutes. "It was ordered that none of the proceedings of this adjourned meeting be given to the press for publication unless and when authorized by the Special Committee composed of Dr. D. A. Penick, Rev. E. M. Munroe, and Rev. R. F. Gribble."

First item at the adjourned meeting December 13 was prayer for three Austin College professors and Rev. R. A. Partlow who were all in the hospital in Temple, result of a near fatal wreck enroute to Synod to make an appeal for Synod's support. (The professors were C. H. Gillespie, History; J. B. Moorman, Biology and J. T. Jackson, English and Rev. Partlow, pastor of the College Church.) *(Minutes of Synod,* Vol. VII, no. 3, p. 203.)

For the discussion of the report of the Joint Committee of the Board of Trustees and Synod's Budget and Audit Commitee, Synod resolved itself into a Committee of the Whole.

"One observer commented that the College was already *in the hole* and now Synod could appropriately complete the ceremony by burying it." To dwell on Synod's next actions in detail is not appropriate here. Suffice it to say that just before lunch the "Committee of a Whole" were convinced that now was the time to close Austin College at the end of the year, and recessed for lunch. During lunch hour individuals interested in continuing the other Synod's institutions and work raised the question of how that could be done and at the same time pay off $262,000 of debts which would, upon closing Austin College, be automatically assumed by Synod, including the mortgage on its campus and most of its endowment. (Synod at the October 14, 1915 meeting had gone on record to authorize and empower Austin College to execute notes in the amount not to exceed $275,000. According to this Austin College still had $13,000 of good credit.)

The *Minutes of Synod* state that after recess and an hour and a half of discussion in the Committee of the Whole, a special committee was appointed to "digest the report" and to report back their finding to the "Committee of the Whole." This commitee found that the campus was mortgaged with $66,000 unpaid to 55 bond holders; that the college owed back salaries to faculty amounting to $40,000, and interest bearing obligations to banks, real estate mortgages and Sherman business concerns totalling $156,000.

Twice that afternoon the Synod resolved itself unto a "Committee of the Whole," arose and made the following report which was adopted:

> The sense of the Committee of the Whole is as follows, To order the abrupt closing of Austin College by vote of this adjourned meeting of Synod would be disastrous and unwise and is not to be admitted.

Thus, an unusual result had transpired. Many colleges have been closed for debts and lack of funds but a debt was all that saved Austin College on this day. In passing it is worthy of note that from the nine Presbyteries there were only six elders, four of whom were required to be present; and 27 ministers, a total of thirty–three members of the Synod present, who had the power to close Austin College and *did for one hour.*

Even if the College had possessed plenty of capital to survive the depression, which it did not, the survival in the face of unfavorable publicity, lack of faith, confidence and financial support by Synod was considered miraculous by many loyal supporters. The total received from Synod's Treasurer for 1933 for the support of its only college was $2300.

The Executive Committee by order of the Board elected George L. Landolt, Business Manger, on January 13, 1933 at a salary of $2400 per year. Soon thereafter the faculty, library, maintenance and auxiliary enterprise staffs for dormitory operations, bookstore and athletics were adjusted to meet the needs of the decreased enrollment and income. A number of employees were placed on the retirement list with a monthly stipend for their many years of service to the College. This included Dr. Clyce, Emeritus President; John Hardy, Dining room Steward; Mrs. R. R. Harwell, Librarian; and several professors were given leave of absence to complete graduate work.

The Board decided to discontinue the Financial Agent's office under Dr. Scherer.

Mr. Leon Foshee (B.A.'21) was recalled from leave of absence to become Registrar and Dean.

Fifty–five B.A. and six M.A. degrees were conferred June and August, 1933.

The Board approved the plans of Business Manager Landolt to improve and convert the YMCA into a women's dormitory. Further adjustments took place: Rev. Raymond Partlow, pastor of Grand Avenue Church took over the duties of YMCA Secretary. Mathematics and physics were combined. Bible and Philosophy were combined.

The administration was notified that the will of a Dallas schoolteacher, Miss Ruth de Capree, included a bequest to Austin College of $\frac{5}{36}$ interest in her estate. $5,000 was designated for the special purpose of establishing a student loan fund.

Need for giving extension work in surrounding towns resulted in setting up extension centers in Bonham, Denison, Greenville, and Whitesboro.

At the June and August commencements 53 B.A. and 11 M.A. degrees were conferred, a total of 64 for the year (1934).

A great man and teacher over a span of thirty years at Austin College passed away in November 1934. Dr. Charles Carrington Scott had done graduate work in Chemistry at Heidelberg. The author took Dr. Charlie's chemistry course in old Thompson Hall during his Freshman year in 1919–20. The first four men from Austin College to do graduate work for the Ph.D. degree in Chemistry were his students, namely and in order: Dr. Thornton Read, Yale; Dr. Rugeley, Yale; Dr. George Landolt, Pittsburgh; Dr. B. F. Armendt, Texas University.

At the time of Dr. Scott's death he was Emeritus Professor of Chemistry. In his will he established the C. C. Scott Student Loan Fund of $10,000 capital. The S. D. Heard Fellowship in English was established with a gift of $6,000 by Mr. and Mrs. S. D. Heard of McKinney.

Forty–five B.A. and four M.A. degrees were conferred in June 1935. Ten B.A. and two M.A. degrees were conferred in the summer, a total of 61. Mr. Leon Foshee, Dean and Registrar, was granted a leave of absence and Professor J. B. Moorman appointed to succeed him.

Coach E. Y. Freeland returned to the College as Professor of Physical Education and Director of Athletics, the same position he held from 1919 to 1921.

The Board, at the February 19, 1936 meeting, decided to put on a quiet, intensive campaign for gifts from individuals and churches for the payment of the mortgage on the campus and other old debts. Business Manager Landolt was elected Vice President of the College and assigned this additional duty.

Interest in Austin College through the Synod began to pick up. Mrs. T. A. Hervey, daughter of Guy M. Bryan, Jr. established three scholarships. Moderator of Synod, Dr. Robert F. Gribble, personally gave a nice sum, as did also Rev. Thomas H. Pollard, both alumni of the college. Mr. Fred S. Robbins of Bay City and Shem P. Cunningham, (B.A. 1920) began buying the campus mortgage bonds when offered for retirement by the holders. (These two men together retired more than $35,000 of these bonds.)

On account of his father's death, President Tucker was given a four months leave of absence in May 1936. Mrs. Fred S. Robbins left the College $10,000 in her will for permanent endowment of the College and Mr. Fred S. Robbins invested it in two faculty residences near the College. In June 1936 4 M.A. and 28 B.A. degrees were granted.

In August 4 M.A. and 21 B.A. degrees were granted making a total of fifty–eight degrees awarded.

Money from oil leases on several tracts of college land alleviated somewhat the financial strain in 1936-37. The Texas Presbyterian College buildings were salvaged and much of the material used to build faculty homes on college lots near the campus. Money was now being received from the Ruth de Capree Estate. Various trades with and for faculty members had wiped out the $40,000 unpaid salary debt that had accumulated during the depression; and for the first time in four years all salaries were increased by 10% or more.

At the May 31, 1937 Commencement 45 B.A. and 4 M.A. degrees were granted followed by 13 B.A. and 12 M.A. degrees at the close of summer, a total of 74 for the year.

In the 1937–38 session the college received a part of the Isa Y. Miller Estate in Gonzales, Texas.

Mr. and Mrs. J. B. Sawtell made a valuable gift of land to the College through the Presbyterian Foundation.

A tremendous feeling of advancement in the realm of religious education resulted in the acceptance of a call to the professorship of Bible by Dr. Manfred George Gutzke, who with the addition of Dr. and Mrs. Paul Silas, greatly strengthened the Christian influence on the Campus.

Twenty-nine B.A. and seven M.A. degrees were granted May 30, 1938.

The last year of the ninth decade many improvements were made in faculty, equipment and library. The Campus was enlarged by purchase of the Venable property — one half (½) city block adjoining the college.

Mrs. Silas began at once to develop a strong College Choir soon to earn commendation throughout the Synod. The entire Dr. Lillian Stevenson Library, former professor of History at Women's College of Rhode Island, and a large collection of History and International Law books from Dr. Clyde Eagleton, Rhodes Scholar and Professor at New York University, were added to the library.

The Texas Presbyterian College property was sold to the city school of Milford.

Plans were made for a Synod wide joint campaign for funds with the Austin Theological Seminary.

A number of new endowed scholarships were received, largest being the Findley Scholarship established by Mrs. Gus Wortham of Houston with an annual income of $350.

The Ninth Decade closed out with the granting of thirty-eight B.A. and eight M.A. degrees in June 1939 and fifteen B. A. degrees in the summer.

A vote of confidence was brought to the faculty by Rev. Frank C. Brown by request of the Board of Trustees:

> The trustees unanimously expressed a vote of confidence in, an appreciation of, the officers of administration and members of the faculty, for their earnest and sacrificial efforts made for Austin College and for the helpful influences they have wielded upon the young people in the Synod of Texas. (*Board Minutes*, Vol. 2, p. 278.)

# THE CENTENNIAL DECADE

THE Tenth Decade began with a projected income of $83,000 and expected expenses for the same amount. Dr. W. B. Guerrant came on the campus in July 1939. After meeting with a special Committee composed of C. S. Roberts, President E. B. Tucker and Vice President George L. Landolt, Dr. Guerrant was employed as Professor of English Bible and Religious Education. Mr. Garvis Steen was elected head coach and John O. Stephens was elected assistant coach and Physical Education Instructor. Both men were recent Austin College graduates.

The Humble Oil Company finally agreed to drill deeper for oil on the Chadwick farm which already had three gas wells on it with no sales. Soon thereafter there were six oil producers on this property which still continue to produce royalty.

The old T. P. C. property at Milford was sold to the City of Milford. Vice President Landolt arranged to refinance the loan on the Kiam Building in Houston through the National Life Insurance Company at 5% and to pay off $70,000 remaining on the 6% loan made earlier by the Guardian Bank and Trust Company of Houston.

Thirty-nine B.A. and six M.A. degrees were awarded in June 1940.

Fourteen B.A. and four M.A. degrees were awarded August 22, 1940.

As the 1940-41 session began, Austin College was notified by Synod's Secretary that it would benefit to the extent of $240,000 if the proposed 600,000 campaign for Synod's Institutions was successful.

A discussion of the proposed merger with Trinity University resulted in the appointment of a committee composed of President Pat E. Hooks of the Board, President E. B. Tucker, Vice President George L. Landolt, Mr. Thomas E. Craig, T. M. Gribble, Rev. L. L. McCutchen and Rev. C. T. Wharton who were to meet with a similar group from Trinity University to study the proposal and to report back at the next Board Meeting.

The Ruth de Capree Estate of which Austin College received $5/36$ was divided by the legatees. Austin College received $6000 from this Estate, 235 acres of land and $5/36$ royalty under approximately 1200 acres.

The joint committee on Merger met at City Temple, Dallas, February 10, 1941, took note of progress, but no further action. At the June 2, 1941 Board meeting, fifty-two B.A. degrees were awarded; at the August 21, 1941 Commencement sixteen B.A. and four M.A. degrees were awarded.

Insurance on the life of Felix Leslie taken out by his classmates of the class of 1921 was received totaling $1347. (Leslie was the son of a former trustee and the youngest man in his class.)

*Proposed Merger with Trinity University:*
President Pat. E. Hooks and others made verbal reports on the progress of negotiations looking toward the merger of Austin College and Trinity University. A long general discussion ensued, after which the following resolution was passed: It is the sense of this Board that we favor the merger of Austin College and Trinity University, but because of world conditions we do not believe a move from Sherman should be made. (*Minutes*, p. 337, Vol. 2)

The Board met in Dallas September 30, 1941. The report of the Joint committee on merger was discussed—no action was taken. Austin College was very busy with military training, civil pilot training and engineering-science-management war programs.

> *Merger Abandoned:* The following communication to this Board through Pat E. Hooks, President, from Dr. R. Thomson, Chairman and Dean I. M. Gordon, Secretary of the Committee of Ten on the merger of Austin College and Trinity University was read, formally received and ordered spread on the minutes: The two Synods ordered the merger "unless insurmountable obstacles make it impossible."—After several meetings of this Joint Committee of Ten without being able to reach an agreement carrying out the merger of these two institutions, that Committee on January 8, 1942, adopted a motion declaring it to be the sense of the committee that "insurmountable obstacles make it impossible" to effectuate a merger." (*Minutes of Board of Trustees,* Vol. 2, p. 350.)

One of the most important events to take place in this decade was the "Bond Fire" November 23, 1942. At a public ceremony of the Austin College Alumni Association the cancelled bonds held originally by the Mississippi Bank and Trust Company as a $90,000 mortgage on the Buildings and Campus were destroyed. Faculty and visiting alumni were given the privilege of celebrating the event by burning the beautifully embossed green bonds one at a time in the "Bond Fire." (*Minutes,* P. 354) (Many alumni and friends of the college contributed to the retirement of the bonded indebtedness but Shem P. Cunningham., Thos. W. Currie and Fred S. Robbins retired the major share.)

The war was on—many juniors and seniors including almost all of the football team did not return the second semeser—they had volunteered to join one branch or another of our armed services. Only 45 B.A. and 4 M.A. degrees were awarded in May 1942.

For the year, income was $19,000 greater than expenses. Vice President Landolt reported that the $260,418 debt of 1933 when he became Business Manager had now in nine years been reduced $157,000. The plant was free of debt but there was still an obligation of $66,423 the College owed its own Endowment Fund.

The year 1942-43 had hardly gotten started before several Presbyteries were overturing Synod to reopen the merger proposal. The Board of Trustees in regular meeting at Ft. Worth, October 13, 1942 recorded: By a vote of 10 to 2 it is the sense of the Board of Trustees that in view of the improved financial condition of the institution we favor the present location of Austin College.

## TELL IT LIKE IT WAS

IN his splendid *Trinity University — A Record of 100 Years —* Dr. Donald E. Everett, former President of the Trinity University, devotes a whole chapter of his book to "the proposal and final rejection of a merger of Austin College and Trinity University." Chapter Nine entitled "Merger with Austin College?" gives his account of this episode in the history of the two institutions and is for the most part revealing and accurate. I simply want to submit, from the "on the scene" position, additional information especially for the benefit of Austin College Alumni and the Presbyterians of our Church.

The only reason the merger was not consummated was that the Board of Trustees, faculty and alumni of the College and most ministers of the Presbyterian Church U.S. did not want to join forces with the Presbyterian Church U.S.A. in the educational field by merging Austin College with Trinity University at San Antonio.

The facts are that only three of the Board ever voted in favor of the merger. These were Dr. A. B. Boand pastor of a San Antonio church who had been in a U.S.A. church from 1920-27; Dr. Henry Wade Dubose who didn't come to Texas until 1938; and Rev. Raymond Partlow, pastor of one of the Lubbock churches. These men no doubt found good reasons for their stand. Partlow, an alumunus, said later on resigning from the Board, that he had been misled by friends who were proponents of the merger. Dr. Boand also felt constrained to resign soon after the merger failed. Dr. Dubose left the State for a new position in Virginia before his term expired.

Dr. E. B. Tucker, president of the college, the only faculty member on the Campus at Sherman ever in favor of the merger asked for a vote of confidence at the Board Meeting February 9, 1943 at First Presbyterian Church in Dallas. This request was denied by the Board because of certain demands he made. Dr. Tucker was then given a permanent leave of absence with pay until June 10. Dr. W. B. Guerrant, professor of Philosophy and Religion at the College, was made acting President. "The Board expressed its deep appreciation for Dr. Tucker and his service during the troubled years of his official connection with the College and their heartfelt regrets at the termination of this relationship." (*Minutes*, p. 364.)

The resolution to merge "unless insurmountable obstacles prevent" was defeated at a special (adjourned) meeting of the Synod of the Presbyterian Church U.S. at the Broadway Presbyterian Church of Ft. Worth, Texas on January 21, 1943. In the absence of Rev. E. M. Monroe, the moderator, Rev. S. L. Joekel, the last moderator present, called the meeting to order and the Synod was led in prayer by Rev. Robert F. Gribble. The moderator announced that Rev. E. M. Monroe had been detained by death in his congregation. (*Minutes of the Synod of Texas of the Presbyterian Church U.S.*, Vol. VIII, No. 4, p. 189.)

The following communications were received (5) from the student body of Austin College requesting Synod to reject any plan to merge Austin College and Trinity University. Its consideration was postponed until the hearing of the report of the Merger Committee. (p. 192, *ibid*)

> (Here Synod's printed records are exceedingly brief)
>
> Merger Committee Report: The consideration of the report of the Merger Committee was taken up, and after several hours of discussion the report was rejected by a ballot vote of 69 to 67.
>
> The following resolution was offered by Rev. John V. McCall and most heartily adopted by a standing vote:
>
> The Synod of Texas expresses most sincerely its appreciation of the exceedingly generous concessions extended by the Trustees of Trinity University, touching the proposed but rejected merger, and its

> thanks for the kindly gestures and courteous attitude
> in this whole matter. Also the Synod desires to thank
> the committee of this Synod for their sacrificial and
> diligent services. (p. 196, *Synod of Texas U.S.*, vol.
> VIII, no. 4.)

It is difficult to tell why the printed *Minutes* omitted details of what transpired before this ballot of 69 to 67 was taken and what happened immediately afterward. We must give credit to Dr. Donald E. Everett for a more accurate printing of what actually transpired. This he does in his book *Trinity University*. I quote from page 142: "After Synod discussed the proposal merger for several hours, a first ballot resulted in a tie vote 67 to 67. The Parliamentarian ruled the motion lost, and when the Synod balloted again the vote to merge the two schools was defeated by a slim margin of 69 to 67."

There is much missing in both accounts. What actually happened as everyone there knows is as follows:

When the tie vote was announced proponents of the merger immediately called upon the moderator to break the tie. The moderator admitted that he had already cast his vote — on the grounds that he was only acting moderator. Everyone knew that if the moderator's vote was not counted the motion to merge would lose by 67 to 66. The printed *Minutes* of our Synod omits: "The parliamentarian ruled the tie vote lost," as Dr. Everett correctly includes in his account. In order to clear this matter, ballots were redistributed; in the meantime, three additional members arrived in time for the second ballot which resulted in the 69 to 67 second decision not to merge. Immediately thereafter one delegate obtained the floor who stated that he had voted for the merger, having been told that it was a certainty and that even if the motion had passed by and same margin it would have been unwise for Synod to merge the two institutions lacking the support of so large a group, and that he would like the privilege of changing his vote. Numerous hands were upraised for the same purpose and one member actually made effort to get a unanimous voice vote against the merger proposal but this failed by one objection.

Thus ended the whole matter but not without accomplishing much lasting good to both institutions. During the entire four years devoted to the merger proposals, Synod had contributed less than $25,000 from its budget to Austin College. For its part Austin College reported for these four years:

| Ministerial Candidates | Students Graduates | | Debt reduction |
|---|---|---|---|
| 1939 | 22 | 611 | 59BA, 16MA | $11,000 |
| 1940 | 23 | 608 | 52BA, 11MA | 25,000 |
| 1941 | 21 | 693 | 66BA, 4MA | 11,000 |
| 1942 (war year) | 17 | 756 | 45BA, 4MA | 19,000 |

What were the reasons the merger failed to take place? Dr. Everett, former president of Trinity quotes Rev. Robert Bullock in a statement made to him thirteen years later: "One explanation for defeat of the proposal involved Synod U.S. members from South Texas who, certain of the proposal's success, did not bother to make the long trip to Ft. Worth to cast their vote." (*Trinity University,* page 142.)

Dr. Everett quotes from a letter to Dean James M. Gordon from Dr. E. B. Tucker more than a year after Pearl Harbor: "I am convinced that an unequivocal decision is necessary one way or another, now that the matter is reopened. To postpone is but to add to our difficulties and condemn us to slow death at Austin College — I am not an advocate of forced union or union at any price. Self-respect, self-esteem, a mutual trust and a meeting of minds and spirit, at least for the majority, are absolutely necessary." (*Trinity University,* p. 143)

Dr. Tucker had finally begun to realize that the merger was not certain and he began to hedge a bit. It was too late to reverse himself now. In violation of the Board's wishes 13 to 3 to let the matter drop he continued to encourage others to work for the merger. As a consequence he was not given a vote of confidence — only extended leave of absence.

Some of the Austin College Board members could see nothing that Trinity could of itself bring to the merged institution. With her endowment hypothecated, enrollment falling each year, down to 167 by the spring of 1942; placed on probation by the Southern Association of Schools and College in 1936 for low faculty salaries and inadequate library — it was evident that Trinity University must leave Waxahachie. If Austin College would join and move to San Antonio or Houston, Trinity could survive. There were other reasons given for the failure of the merger. For some the Japanese could be blamed or given credit depending upon which side you were on. Pearl Harbor coming when it did was the cause of rapid drop in men students but in most schools this was quickly replaced by men sent by our government for defense or military training. (250 arrived at Austin College in one day.)

Dr. Everett states: George L. Landolt, Vice-President of Austin College described the opposition's point of view in a letter to U.S. Synod Executive James G. Whitten, May 9, 1941:

> There are great expectations in regard to the merger but I think most of it is wishful thinking. A large number of the alumni do not want to merge with Trinity and they substantiate a group who do not see why 66,000 Presbyterians in the U.S. Church operating an institution with all of its history and background, and now rapidly getting out of debt, and going forward in many other ways should take the chance of losing all it has striven for in the past ninety-two years by submerging itself in a merged institution as partner of a school which has lost enrollment for three years and is now losing money yearly. (Everett's *Trinity University,* page 119.)

There are those loyal alumni of the college who believe that Austin College has survived all attempts to change its name and its location and control because God wants to preserve it. He has had plenty of chances to close it. On numerous other occasions its destiny was threatened and always it was the spirit of the faculty, alumni, and determined Board supported by a few benefactors dedicated to attain for it a mark of greatness. As we close the Twelfth Decade and look backwards to the decisions made January 23, 1943, we can truthfully say that few if any are sorry that the merger failed. Certainly Trinity, though maybe not a Presbyterian school anymore, has prospered exceedingly. And Austin College has made giant strides in its Search for the Summit, having acquired a mark of excellence in many of its aims.

Whether we have the Japanese to thank or owe it largely to individuals like Pat E. Hooks, C. Stanly Roberts, Hoxie Thompson, George Landolt or whom, we can only say definitely it was not the Synod for their vote was a tie 67 to 67 on that memorable day.

Synod of Texas, September 1, 1943 Kerrville
Austin College closed its 94th year with 33 B.A.
and 3 M.A. graduates from a student body of 437. The
College classes of regular students have been conducted entirely separate from the Army students on
the Campus. There has been no conflict between
these two groups, and the relationship has been one
of entire cooperation and respect. The academic and
spiritual standards of the College have remained high.

Increased liberality on the part of the Church and
interested individuals along with the war Programs
have made the past year financially one of the best
in the history of the College. The College closed the
year with an operating gain of $34,375.40. (*Synod
Minutes*, page 245, vol. VIII, no. 4.)

Since the last meeting of Synod, Austin College has moved
forward, has improved properties, has rendered a marked
service to the government, and is in the best financial condition in years. (*Synod Minutes*, 1943, page 218.)

It would be natural for one to believe from the above report
that Synod was at last content to let the college rise to its
destiny. The Ad Interim Committee on Synod's Institutions
at the January Meeting in Ft. Worth had recommended:

That Synod put on a campaign for $500,000 of
which Austin College would get $200,000. Dr. C. L.
King, Chairman of the Committee, again presented
the report; followed by Hoxie H. Thompson, Chairman of the special Financial Campaign with a report
on how the campaign could be conducted.

At this point, before adoption was considered,
Synod heard a plan for a Presbyterian College ad-
joined to the University of Texas; prepared and presented by Ruling Elder Hulen W. Black (who was
employed in the Development Office of Texas University). Mr. Black was extended the privilege of the
floor for this purpose. The report (on the Finance
Campaign) was adopted.

Synod expressed its appreciation to Mr. Hulen
Black for his diligent efforts in preparing and presenting the plan mentioned above.

Synod reconsidered and rescinded its action in
adopting the report of the Committee on Financial

Campaign for its institutions, and referred this report
and the plan outlined by Mr. Hulen W. Black and all
matters pertaining thereto to the ad-interim Committee on Synod's institutions with instructions to
bring in a report as soon as possible. (*Synod of Texas
Minutes,* Vol. VIII, 1943, No. 4, page 212.)

The original Financial Campaign as set by Synod October 8,
1940 was for $600,000 of which Austin College would get
$240,000. Three years had passed, the $240,000 had shrunk to
200,000 and that now held up on account of Mr. Hulen Black's
scheme to build a Presbyterian College adjacent to the State
University. It became evident that a determined group in our
Synod saw no need for Austin College and that if the Synod
was going to spend any money on higher education it could
do it cheaper at the door step of the State University. Mr.
Black publicised his idea with the title "A Bold Step Forward."

The Ad Interim Committee on Synod's Institutions, Dr.
C. L. King, Chairman, met again. The committee now recommended holding in abeyance any financial campaign for
Austin College, but that Synod put on one for A & M College
Church, $75,000; and Westminister Encampment a like
amount, and also recommended: "In view of the tensions evident in this meeting of Synod and in fairness to Austin College, we recommend that no action concerning either the
Hulen Black Plan or any merger be taken up at this time."

Thus the Hulen Black plan was shelved when the report
was adopted, (*Synod's Minutes,* Vol. VIII, p. 216, No. 4.) but
the delay caused by it was costly.

Dr. Edward O. Grant, an Austin College graduate of the
class of 1920 "was unanimously and enthusiastically" elected
President at a Board meeting in April 1943, but would not
accept the call because of previous commitments.

In the midst of the war only 21 B.A. and 1 M.A. degree was
awarded in 1943.

In 1944 a campaign in Sherman for $100,000 was begun to
match a like amount to be raised out in the State, this money
to be used to complete the Administration Building (The
Skeleton). A settlement for service in training aviation students for the U.S. Government made it possible to pay off
the obligation on the 22-acre athletic field. Arthur Hopkins,

C. S. Roberts, and O. O. Touchstone held this property in the name of the Austin College Alumni Association. The entire campus and athletic field were now free of debt.

## DR. W. B. GUERRANT
### Elected Eleventh President of Austin College

A T the May 29, 1944 Board meeting, Dr. Guerrant became President of Austin College. George L. Landolt was elected Treasurer, and J. B. Moorman Dean of the Faculty.

Through the efforts of Hoxie Thompson, the Kiam Building in Houston was freed of debt assuring to the college a net income of $5500 per year. Mrs. Fred Robbins in her will gave $10,000 to the permanent endowment fund in 1946. The Administration Building and Coffin Girls dormitory were completed.

Dr. George Landolt assumed a full teaching load as the only staff member in the chemistry department. He had been chairman since 1931. Rev. John R. Clarke from Arkansas College was appointed Business Manager. At the May 1947 commencement 46 B.A. and 5 B.S. degrees were awarded and the John T. Jones memorial Chair of Economics was endowed.

In the summer of 1947, Mr. M. B. Hughey of Charlotte, Texas, a rancher and devout Presbyterian deeded one half of his communal property, mostly oil and gas royalties to Austin College. At the same time Mr. Hughey prepared a will devising the remainer of his estate to the College. His death occurred about one month later. This estate was valued for federal taxes at $660,000. The Board of Trustees increased its number to 22. This increase of six members to the Board was the first change since the charter was granted. The 1947 Board consisted of *Pat E. Hooks*, Ch. *C. S. Roberts*, Dr. Frank Brown, James Fant, Rev. *Gage Lloyd*, *R. L. Morrison, Thos. E. Craig, Eugene Elder, Shem P. Cunningham, R. L. Wood*, Mrs. J. Percy Terrell, Mrs. A. L. Slaughter, R. A. Farnsworth, *W. H. McCarley*, R. R. Craig, Reed Robinson, *John Anderson* and Wm. M. Elliot. (Those in italic are Austin College graduates.)

With the gift and legacy of the Hughey Estate the College was able to make another giant step in its "Search for the Summit." Inspired by the progress of their alma mater following the merger rejection, the Alumni launched a campaign of sufficient proportion to complete the Student Union Building. The Hughey Fund was channeled partly into Endowment and to construct the Hughey Gymnasium.

The 1948 year closed with announcement that the tuition would be raised to $300 per year. Sixty-four B.A. and 21 B.S. and 2 M.A. degrees were issued. Plans were made to apply for an R.O.T.C. unit.

The closing session of the Tenth Decade was marked by a gift by Dr. R. R. Harwell's estate valued at $45,000. Dr. Harwell's house and six other houses suitable for faculty residences and all near the campus comprised this property. A bequest from the estate of Mary Sue Kerr was also received. Coffin Hall, Women's dormitory, was completed and plans were shaping up for a new Campus Chapel.

The centennial year ended with the graduation of 135 B.A. and B.S. degree holders, a number larger than the total number graduating in the first fifty years of the College history.

## THE ELEVENTH DECADE

THE completion of the M. B. Hughey Gymnasium at the start of the Eleventh Decade was a major step in the field of Physical Education. This elegant facility contains bowling lanes, two fine basketball courts, and game equipment for every kind of sport, as well as offices and classrooms for the Department of Physical Education — built with the income from the Hughey Estate.

The citizens of Sherman presented the College with a centennial gift of $110,000 to complete the Student Union Building, which contains the dining rooms, student and faculty lounges, bookstore and game rooms and student affairs offices. The dining room facilities are the largest in Sherman and will accommodate 2,000 persons. The 1950 class was awarded 75 B.A., 25 B.S. and 4 Masters diplomas. There was a great loss to the College and the church with the death of Mr. Pat E. Hooks of Itasca, Texas, ex-student and long-time President of the Board.

The 1950-51 session saw the ROTC Naval Training unit installed. For the first time in twenty years the College was now reporting a heavy deficit, expected to reach $100,000 by May 1952.

There were 39 M.A. and 95 B.A. degrees granted, largest in the history of the College.

In October 1951, the Adams Health Center, gift of Mr. Fred Adams of Austin, Texas, was dedicated.

The faculty Athletic Committee started a plan to gradually make our participation in intercollegiate athletics strictly amateur.

Dr. Louis Winston (B.A. 1915), Dr. George Landolt (B.A. 1923) and Rev. Walter Lazenby (B.A. 1925) appeared before the Board in the interest of Grand Avenue Presbyterian Church and its association with the College, proposing a new church plant that would adequately serve the needs of the student body.

Thirty-four Masters and eighty Bachelors degrees were granted in May 1952. (The deficit this year was $55,000).

On May 11, 1953 Dr. Guerrant requested the Board of Trustees to be searching for his successor. The following resolution concerning Dr. Guerrant was read and adopted:

> Whereas, Dr. W. B. Guerrant has given unstintingly of his energy and spirit to the development of Austin College during the past fourteen years; and whereas, under his able Christian leadership the school has made its greatest spiritual and physical development in its entire history, be it resolved that the Board of Trustees in regular meeting on May the 25th, 1953, expresses herewith the gratitude of the Synods of Texas and Oklahoma and the Board pause in its meeting to pray together in Thanksgiving to God for this Servant of His. Signed John F. Anderson, Jr. and Wm. M. Elliott, Jr.

A Fellowship of Economics and Business Administration was established by Mrs. T. E. Craig with a capital of $9,000.

Twelve Masters and eighty-three Bachelor degrees were awarded in 1953.

Mr. John D. Moseley was elected the twelfth president of Austin College on August 3, 1953. The offer of the Ford Foundation to grant Austin College $10,000 to be matched

by a similar amount by the College was accepted. The purpose
of this grant was to provide a Management Survey. Refinancing of the Hughey Oil Royalties provided funds for much
needed improvement of Luckett Hall and Thompson Science
Building and to have plans drawn for the President's home
and an additional women's dormitory. The destruction of the
field house by fire severely hampered the Athletic Program.

Seventeen Masters and fifty-five Bachelor degrees were
earned in 1954.

Mr. and Mrs. Fred Moore endowed a scholarship with
$20,000 capital.

On March 29, 1955 the Board was increased to twenty-four
members, three classes of eight each; four to come from the
Synod of Oklahoma and twenty from the Synod of Texas. Provision for Honorary and associate Trustees were made.

Ten Masters and fifty-six Bachelor degrees were conferred
May 30, 1955.

Part of the estate of Miss Emma Lillian Keigwin enriched
the College in the amount of $24,000.

The 1955-56 session began with a teaching faculty of forty-five (45); ten (10) professors with Ph.D. degrees, five professors with M.A. degrees, twenty-three associate professors
and seven instructors.

On May 28, 1956, three Masters and fifty-two Bachelor degrees were conferred.

The 1956-57 year brought many lasting improvements to
the campus. College street was closed, thereby making the
thirty-six (36) acre campus much more compact. Dr. Moseley
was authorized to execute contracts for complete plans of two
dormitories, the President's home and a Chapel; and to enter
into negotiations for a 3½% loan to complete the two dormitories, one for men and one for women.

Dr. George Landolt, Chairman of the Chemistry Department was given a three-year leave of absence to supervise the
construction of the Science Buildings and to act as Dean of
the Science College of Tunghai University in the Republic
of China (Taiwan). Dr. Landolt was selected to go out under
the Presbyterian Foreign Mission Board in cooperation with
the Christian Board of Higher Education in Asia.

Two great steps forward in our search for the Summit came
with the munificent gift of Wynne Chapel in 1957. This was

followed by another generous gift from Mr. and Mrs. Bob Wood to build the President's home.

Nine Masters and sixty-four Bachelor degrees were conferred in 1957.

The first large Ford Foundation grant—$243,000—was received in 1957. The Austin College Choir made a European tour, winning a coveted award for a fine performance at a festival in Italy.

The "Great Teachers Program" was inaugurated.

The Cern gift made it possible to completely rebuild the Power House, renamed Cern Memorial Center.

The Failer-Barrett Endowed Scholarship was established to assist in the education of children from the Presbyterian Home and Service Agency.

There were two Masters and eighty-seven Bachelor degrees conferred in 1958.

Shem P. Cunningham (B.A. 1920) and his family endowed the Cunningham annual Lectureship in 1959. That year the College awarded two Masters and ninety-seven Bachelor degrees.

From the Estate of Professor R. R. Harwell there was received $13,000, from the Settles Estate $8,800 and from the Walter W. Vinson (B.A. 1890) $34,800.

The one hundred and tenth year of Austin College began with the dedication of Wynne Chapel at the opening Convocation, September 15, 1958. The year was one of sadness because of the loss through death of several alumni who had served many years on the Board; namely, Robert L. Morrison (B.A. 1917) and Hoxie H. Thompson (B.A. 1901), one of the "Four Horsemen." Memorial resoltuions were also recorded for former Trustees, W. C. Windsor, Opha H. Grissom and Lamar Fain.

There were two Masters and ninety-seven Bachelor de grees granted in 1959. The total number for the Eleventh Decade was 132 Masters and 767 Bachelor degrees.

# THE TWELFTH DECADE

T HE Twelfth Decade was destined to be the crowning period of all the 120 years of the College history. During the period from 1959 through 1969, the Master Plan of Campus and facilities was almost completed. Individuals, many of whom were graduates of the College, began to take an interest in the College through the leadership of President Moseley. Foundation officers were made aware of the excellence of teaching on the campus and the superiority of the graduates coming from it and responded with the financial assistance to further aid the College in its Search for the Summit in the field of higher education. Largely responsible for this was the perpetuation of the Great Teacher Program through which the Sherman citizens channeled their financial support. A steady stream of highly trained men and women for service to God and man flowing into the lite of our country brought recognition of excellence to the oldest Presbyterian College West of the Mississippi (and the oldest College in Texas under its original charter). Truly the College was approaching the long sought for "Summit of Greatness."

The Development Commission set as their goal the completion of the Music Building, the Theatre-Art Center and the Recreation Center.

The Arthur Hopkins Library, completed in 1960, was made possible through gifts from the Hopkins Foundation and from Miss Bessie Heard of McKinney. It contains a micro-film center, Xerox copier, the Hoard Rare Books Collection, over 100,000 books and 700 different periodical titles which are regularly bound. The library maintans a depository collection of U.S. documents. Also finished in the Fall of 1960 was the Louis Calder Stadium, seating 2,500, gift of Mr. Calder of New York.

Craig Hall-Music Center was dedicated in April 1962 and named after the late Thomas E. Craig and Mrs. Craig of McKinney. "Tec" Craig, B.A. 1898, long-time trustee of the College was one of the "Four Horsemen."

Caruth Hall was dedicated during Founders Week October 1963. Named in honor of the late Mrs. Earle Clark Caruth of Dallas, this dormitory with facilities for 162 women, was built with funds from the Hillcrest Foundation.

Wm. Dean Hall, men's residence hall was completed in 1965 with accommodations for 242 men. This building is named for the late Wm. A. Dean, who taught in the Preparatory Department of the College in 1915, and is the gift of his two sons, David P. and Paul C. Dean, who attended Austin College.

The Moody Science Center, completed in the Fall of 1965, was made possible by a $1,000,000 grant from the Moody Foundation of Galveston. The building houses the Departments of Biology, Chemistry, Mathematics and Physics. Included in the building are 22 laboratories, 11 classrooms, 26 offices, shops, reading rooms, and other facilities. The Physics Department and the Hoblitzelle Computer Center with an IBM 1620 digital computer system occupy the first floor, built below ground level. Classrooms, faculty offices, seminar rooms, and a 300-seat lecture hall are on the main, or second floor. The third floor houses the Chemistry Department, and biology facilities are on the top floor. On the roof of the building are a greenhouse and an astronomical observation platform. Among other special facilities of the Science Center are an animal room, an environmental control room, and a laboratory to permit the handling of radioactive materials. Research laboratories are also provided for talented science majors to work with professors on relevant research programs. The Moody Science Center and adjoining Thompson contain the most modern facilities for science instruction and research.

Off the campus proper, but adjacent to it, Windsor House, which has been occupied by the Dean of the College, was completed in 1960 and is a gift from the Windsor family of Tyler and Dallas.

An extremely timely gift in 1962 from George Royal Jordan (B.A. 1915) and his wife, Lucile Jordan, and later augumented by his two sons, Edwin B. and George R. Jordan, Jr. provided the Executive Offices and Board Room in the Administration Building.

On March 12, 1962 the Board agreed to accept a grant of $2,000,000 from the Ford Foundation on the basis of securing $4,000,000 to match it from Austin College alumni and supporters. This was completed in 1965.

An upward swing in financial support from alumni and the citizens of Sherman was immediate. Mr. J. W. "Tobe" Madden, Jr. (B.A. 1924) and his wife, from Denison, Texas, have established provisions for a million dollar increase in the assets of the College which will include a fund for the "Thomas Stone Clyce Fellowship."

Numerous Educational Foundation grants were awarded to Austin College during the last half of the Twelfth Decade. An Institute devoted to the study of human motivation in an educational setting was established at Austin College following a $188,000 grant from W. Clement and Jessie V. Stone Foundation of Chicago. The Austin College Institute of Human Bejavior and Research seeks better approaches toward creating an awareness in students that they should develop and utilize their full potential.

Initially the Institute will serve as a control system for three separate projects: The Institutial Leadership and Creativity Project, the Austin Teacher Program and the Basic Decisions Program.

A third Welch Foundation Grant of $50,000 for student-faculty chemical research raises the total to over a quarter of a million allotted to the College for research projects.

The Brown Foundation of Houston has presented a $200,-000 Scholarship Endowment Grant to the College, given in the name of Rupert B. Lowe, alumnus of the Class of 1919. Mr. Lowe is a retired vice-president of the Union Carbide Corporation. The grant will provide five full scholarships per year as honor awards.

The Research Corporation of New York made the College a grant of $165,000 for program enrichment in May 1967.

Most recently the Hillcrest Foundation of Dallas made a second grant of $300,000 to the Building Program of the College and this gift will be used as part of a launching fund to conduct a thirty million-dollar Fund Campaign, beginning in 1970.

The gifts from all sources, including foundations and grants in the Twelfth Decade, total five and one-half million dollars. Since 1963 Synod has placed $100,000 annually in its budget for Austin College.

# CHAPTER IV

# Special Topics

## Ten Crises of Austin College

1853 (1) Between President McKinney and the Board—the resignation of McKinney accepted.

1859 (2) Between Faculty and Board—Faculty takes over student discipline.

1861 (3) Civil War and epidemics almost close the school.

1876 (4) Removal to Sherman on account of epidemics and lack of support.

1913 (5) Fire destroys newly renovated and enlarged Main Building. Some strong effort to move the college to Dallas.

1931 (6) Synod finally decides to merge T.P.C. and Austin College at Sherman and to give Daniel Baker to Brownwood.

1932 (7) Austin College closed by action of a called meeting of Synod on morning of December 13, 1932 at Austin Texas and reopened again after lunch because no way was found to pay its debts without endangering Synod's other institutions. A case of an institution kept open by its debts.

1941, 1942, 1943 (8) Merger with Trinity University agitated in the Synod and frustrated, first by an illegal tie vote 67 to 67 at Fort Worth Board Presbyterian Church, on January 21, 1943. A second ballot recorded 69 against and 61 for merger with Trinity University. (Some give credit for the merger failure to the Japanese who attacked Pearl Harbor December 6, 1942. Some give credit to George Landolt, Vice President of Austin College who carried six (6) opposing votes to the Synod meeting.)

1943 (9) "From Red to Black"; The Financial Campaign for $200,000 authorized by Synod at Fort Worth held up by Dr.

C. L. King, Chairman of the ad Interim Committee until: (see *Minutes of Synod of Texas,* Vol. VIII, No. 2, p. 212)

"Synod heard a plan for a Presbyterian College adjacent to the University of Texas, prepared and presented by Ruling Elder Hulen W. Black." (Author's thought at the time: This crack-pot idea will sabotage our campaign and may be the end of Austin College.)

"Ruling Elder Hoxie H. Thompson, Chairman of the Financial Campaign, made his report on plans for the immediate launching of the campaign previously authorized. The report was adopted. Synod expressing its appreciation to Mr. Hulen Black for his diligent efforts in preparing and presenting the plan mentioned above."

Synod (then) reconsidered and rescinded its action in adopting the report of the Committee on Financial Campaign and referred this report *and the plan outlined by Mr. Hulen W. Black* and all matters pertaining thereto to the Ad Interim Committee on Synod's Institutions with instructions to bring in a report as soon as possible.

That committee reported the following on the next day (*Synod's Minutes,* Vol. VIII, No. 2, Page 215):

"The Ad Interim Committee has given earnest consideration to the matter referred to it by Synod. It is the judgment of the Committee that a financial campaign including the Seminary and Austin College should be held in abeyance. However, we recommend that Synod put on a campaign for $75,000 for the Church at A & M College and like amount for Westminister Encampment."

"In view of the tensions evident in this meeting of Synod and in fairness to Austin College we recommend that no action concerning either the Black plan or any merger be taken at this time." (page 216 of the *Minutes*)

(10) This space reserved for future use.

## More About Crises

In recent years many crises have occurred on Campuses throughout the world because of militant group demands and ultimatums to Boards of Trustees. When the question was posed in a recent Austin College periodical as to how the Charter Trustees might have repelled these militant protestors, the Author's research revealed:

General Sam Houston, experienced Indian fighter and twice wounded hero of San Jacinto, and Anson Jones, who fought at his side at that battle, were both qualified for markmanship medals. Henderson Yoakum, an artillery expert, was a West Point graduate. Four were officers in the Mexican War. There were three doctors to treat the wounded (John Branch, Anson Jones, and George Red, noted for his practice of blood-letting); three ministers to bury the dead (Daniel Baker, James Miller, and Hugh Wilson); two lawyers to prosecute any survivors (Atchison and Yoakum); and a supreme court judge, Abner Lipscomb, to pronounce sentences.

Finally, the first state prison was located only a few blocks away from the original campus in Huntsville and was sometimes referred to as our sister institution. Because of its convenient location and the fact that several of the trustees were also officers of the prison, one could be assured that all prisoners would be properly handled.

## The Sam Houston Bell

IT is said that Houston admired the Austin College Building and at his request "the executive committee employed a photographer to make a likeness of it from several angles." Houston stressed that a bell tower without a bell was useless and that he would get one. About a year later the "Sam Houston Bell" was freighted from Galveston. It was a brass bell weighing several hundred pounds, made in Belgium. Until 1876 it tolled for classes and the Huntsville people set their clocks by it. When the College moved to Sherman the bell was again housed on the roof of the main building and daily rang for class hours until that building burned in 1913. The fall to the ground caused a small crack ruining the tone, requiring brazing.

The bell was placed in a tower on top of Thompson Hall in 1914 and was tolled for class hours and on all special occasions relating to honors or successes of either faculty or students. It rang for Dr. Clyce when he was made moderator of General Assembly and for Dr. Eagleton when he was made moderator of the Synod of Texas. It rang for football games

won by the Austin College team—one stroke for each point
of the game won. The bell was usually tolled by either the
President of the Student Body or President of the Senior
class but often others stole this honor and it was on such
occasion in 1920 that the bell sustained a larger crack that
required rebrazing. This incident occurred when the bell was
tolled 109 strokes by freshmen after a game with Daniel Baker
College and when tolled again by the rightful bell ringer,
the bell became hot and cracked.

When Wynn Chapel was completed, the Sam Houston Bell
was moved for the last time and no longer tolls for class hours.
A cluster of twenty four finely tuned bronze bells, hand-cast
in Holland, keep the Sam Houston Bell company. This
carillon has usurped the power to summon the students to
classes but old "Sam Houston" still tolls from its lofty position in the Chapel spire at each commencement convocation, one stroke for each graduate.

## Literary Societies in the Campus Life

ENCOURAGED by the professors, and in the spirit of competition, literary societies played a major role in campus
life.

At Huntsville the men belonged to either Clay Union or
Philomathean Societies. Among the great orators who
equipped themselves in these literary societies to win cases
in the courts or to judge on law bench were Joab Banton, Francis C. Hume, Benton Randolph, Norman Kittrell, Lewis Hightower and H. H. Boone, all Judges, and H. L. Storey, Lieutenant Governor of Texas.

Soon after the College moved to Sherman the Philennoian
and Athenaeum Societies were organized and these flourished
until 1918 when the College became co-educational and the
Kappa Gamma Chi was founded by the women. In the early
years of this century several State Oratorical Contests were
won by Austin College and strong debating teams won many
laurels.

**Austin College,**
*Tuesday Evening, June 27, A.D., 1854*

"PERSEVERANDO VINCES."
"EXCELSIOR."

### *ORDER OF THE EXERCISES*
### OF THE
### "CLAY UNION" AND "PHILOMATHEAN" LITERARY
### SOCIETIES.

### PRAYER.

### MUSIC.

A. R. RENICK, P. L. S.—*Texas.* _____
S. A. HUME, C. U. L. S.—*Memories of
the Past.* Original.

### MUSIC.

J. O. STEVENS, P. L. S.—*Rise and
Progress of America.* Selected.
L. O. BLACK, C. U. L. S.—*Motion the
natural state of a Body.* Original.

### MUSIC.

M. B. WOODALL, P. L. S.—*Death of
Daniel Webster.* Selected.
W. A. ALLEN, C. U. L. S.—*Man.* Original.

### MUSIC.

W. J. ALLEN, P. L. S.—*Eloquence.* Selected.
J. H. BANTON, C. U. L. S.—*Bombast.* Original.

### MUSIC.

L. B. LOCKRIDGE, P. L. S.—*Genius.* Selected.
G. W. DAVIS, C. U. L. S.—*Relative
intellectual powers of Man and
Woman.* Original.

MUSIC.

G. W. BARBER, P. L. S.—*Power of the*
  *Press.*                                        Selected.
BENTON RANDOLPH, C. U. L. S.—
  *Education.*                                    Original.

MUSIC.

W. F. SPIVEY, P. L. S.—*Texas.*            Original.
H. H. BOONE, C. U. L. S.—*A Nation's*
*great Men her true Glory.*                 ―――――

BENEDICTION

HUNTSVILLE.
"TEXAS PRESBYTERIAN" PRINT.


## Early Campus Publications

In 1890, under the guidance of Dr. Dave Eagleton, the students began a monthly publication, *The Reveille,* the name no doubt being inspired through the great interest in military training on the campus. The *CHROMASCOPE,* Austin College yearbook, appeared first in 1896 and has continued annually since then except in 1918, suspended on account of the First World War.

In 1902, the *Austin College Quarterly,* with D. F. Eagleton editorial chairman, began publishing under the Act of Congress March 1879. This *Quarterly* contained original addresses, orations, alumni news and news of activities and plans of the College until changed to the Austin College *Bulletin,* published under Act of Congress July 1904. Three professors, Davis F. Eagleton, Chas. R. Pepper and Jeff W. Moss composed the Board of Editors.

The *Kangaroo,* a weekly publication was begun by the Junior class in 1921 and has been the student publication for most of the years since, though not by the Junior class. Leon Foshee, '22 was its editor and guiding star.

The Alumni office publishes a bulletin regularly with a mailing list of about six thousand, and thru it the ex-students are kept informed of what is happening and what is planned at the campus.

*Sid Richardson Center*

*Ida Green Theatre-Conference Center*

# The First National Fraternity in Texas

FIRSTS have always had a fascination for the alert historical mind. Phi Delta Magazine for May 1954 contains an article entitled "Some Early Bits of Fraternity History" which sheds light on the earliest establishment of fraternities in Texas. Judge R. C. Crane of Sweetwater, Texas is the authority supplying the documentary information of the statement: "The first national fraternity to establish a chapter was Phi Delta Theta—at Austin College in 1852—four years later the Kappa Chapter at Baylor University at Independence was established." (*Southwestern Historical Review*, Vol. LVIII, p. 301)

When the Civil War broke out, eight graduates were listed on the Austin College Bond and the war records of six of the eight, according to George K. Shaffer, Historian of ΦΔΘ were:

ALEXANDER McKINNEY RAFTER (Miami-Austin 1855). Head of Shelby Military Institute of Germantown, Tenn., when the Civil War began, he enlisted with his faculty and all his cadets in the Confederate Army in May or June 1861. He was commissioned colonel. Because of imperfect eyesight, he was transferred to ordnance and supply; he stationed the Confederate guns for the battle at Fort Pillow and ended the war in commissary duty below Granada, Miss.

ANDREW TODD McKINNEY (Austin 1858), called a cousin of Col. Rafter. Enlisted in Texas Infantry 1862. Private.

HONESTES H. BOONE (Austin 1855). Major, 13th Battalion, Texas Cavalry, throughout war—1861-65. Wounded in action, 1863.

WILLIAM A. ALLEN (Austin 1856). Private, First Texas Infantry. Killed in action, Gaines Mills, Va. June 28, 1862.

CHAMPION T. HILL (Austin 1858). Private, Fifth Texas Infantry. Enlisted in 1862, discharged for disability 1863.

WILLIAM T. HILL (Austin 1858). Brother of Champion. From private 5th Texas infantry, to captain. Many times wounded and cited. Commanded 5th Texas as senior captain (due to repeated casualties of superior officers) with Gen. Robert E. Lee at surrender at Appomattox, Va. His name at the time had been twice forwarded for promotion to colonel but the surrender prevented the promotion.

An Austin College faculty member, L. J. Mitchell, twelfth man on the Bond of Missouri Beta, sent the General Council petition to re-charter Texas Alpha Prime. When their petition was not accepted, the group as an Austin College local named ΦΦΦ, decided to try a nationalizing move of their own and planted four chapters about, but these lost vigor during the next ten years and the last of them, that at the University of Texas, went bodily into ΦΚΨ in 1904.

Joab Banton was awarded the first B.A. degree (1854), the Bachelor of Law degree in 1856, and the first Master of Arts degree in 1857 from Austin College. These degrees were also the first B.A., B.L., and M.A. degrees issued in Texas. Banton also had the distinction of becoming the first graduate of the College to become a Board of Trustee member (Second Decade). His sudden death at the age of forty cut short the career of the most distinguished lawyer of his time.

A. T. McKinney became an Austin College professor during the war, serving under his father, Samuel McKinney, first President of Austin College (1849-1853) and President the second time in 1863. He became a Fourth Decade member of the Board of Trustees.

The two Hill brothers, Champion and William, were expelled before Commencement in 1858 when the senior class organized a dance party in violation of faculty rules. The students petitioned the Board of Trustees to over-rule the faculty and grant the degrees. When the Executive Committee of the Board recommended leniency the entire faculty resigned until the Board sustained the expulsion, thus ending the second crisis of the decade. A second petition in 1859 was tabled until 1860 when the degrees were awarded to the 1858 class retroactively.

## Austin College in Three Wars

### The War Between The States

SOON after Texas voted to secede from the Union and join the Confederacy, the call for volunteers to support the South was answered by most of the upper classmen at Austin College. At first there was a feeling of the faculty and the members of the Board of Trustees that Texas should stay out of the conflict. However, after Sam Houston was deposed from the governorship, all opposition disappeared and even Houston gave his son, Sam, permission to join the Confederate Army. Young Sam Houston had entered the preparatory department of the College at the age of 12 and was only 18 when he volunteered. He was wounded at Shiloh, captured, was recognized from the Bible he carried and then imprisoned. However, he was well treated and soon exchanged. Many of his classmates did not return from the War. William A. Allen, first to get his B.A. diploma of his class of 1856, was killed in action at Gaines Mill, Virginia, June 28, 1862. James S. Harrison, B.A. 1856, M.A. 1859, was wounded and transferred to the Medical Corp. Sam Houston wrote a letter requesting Harrison's discharge because he was needed at home, but to no avail. Honestus Boone, Wm. T. Hill and his brother, Champion Hill, 1858 graduates, all suffered wounds in battle. John Hill and Bill Hume, sons of two charter trustees, were killed in action. Records have been lost of the others who answered the call and were reported missing in action; as were half the graduates of 1860; namely, James H. Murray, Lucius L. Moreland and Richard Sims.

## World War I

Military training at Austin College, after having been abandoned in 1900, was reestablished in 1918. About three hundred students enrolling at the College became members of the Student Army Training Corp (SATC). This was disbanded soon after World War I ended. Most of the upper classmen and recent graduates were already in military training elsewhere or on battlefields at the time. World War I took a toll of 11 men before it ended.

A live oak tree has been planted in the northwest corner of the College campus as a memorial to each of these Austin College men who gave his life in support of his country in this war and Memorial Scholarships were established bearing their names as follows:

The Robert Jayne Maxey Scholarship, founded by the Class of 1892, in memory of Lieutenant Colonel Robert Jayne

Maxey, D.S.C., Criox de Guerre with palm, who was killed in action at Cantigny, France, May 28, 1918.

The Charles Ignatius Coffin Scholarship, founded by Mr. Pat E. Hooks of the Class of 1903, in memory of Private Charles Ignatius Coffin, who was killed in action at Soissons, France, July 19, 1918.

The Eugene Meek Ellison Scholarship, founded by the Class of 1899, in memory of Lieutenant Eugene Meek Ellison, who was killed in action in France, September 12, 1918.

The John Morgan Currie Scholarship, founded by the Class of 1913, in memory of Lieutenant John Morgan Currie, Croix de Guerre, who was killed in action in France, September 12, 1918.

The Robert Lee Crim Scholarship, founded by Mr. H. H. Thompson, of the Class of 1902, in memory of Private Robert Lee Crim, who was killed in action at Somme-Py, France, October 9, 1918.

The Robert Richardson Scholarship, founded by the Class of 1920, in memory of Cadet Robert Richardson, who was killed off the coast of England, October 11, 1918.

The Gordon Felix Gaither Scholarship, founded by the Class of 1914, in memory of Gordon Felix Gaither, Jr., who died at Camp Pike, Ark., October 11, 1918.

The Robert Waldo Meyer Scholarship, founded by the Class of 1911, in memory of Robert Waldo Meyer, who died from a wound received while assisting a wounded comrade

The Herbert Franklin Wager Scholarship, founded by the Class of 1915, in memory of Rev. Herbert Franklin Wager, who died at Camp Cody, New Mexico, December 15, 1918.

The Louis Wells Scholarship, founded by the Class of 1905, in memory of Private Louis B. Wells, who died in France, December 22, 1918.

The Robert Drummond Scholarship, founded by the class of 1912, in memory of Sergeant Major Robert Drummond, killed in action in France Sept. 29, 1918.

## World War II

Before World War II started Austin College began training air force pilots under the Civil Pilot Training Program of

*Ready for the Spanish-American War 1898*

*Austin College Student Army Training Corp 1918*

*77th Army Air Training Corp*

1939. Two flight instructor classes and nine primary training classes produced seventeen flight instructors, one hundred and twenty-four ground school graduates, and eighty-seven students who went on to advanced training. At the same time, three hundred Engineering, Science, Management, Defense Training students (ESMDT) were enrolled. After the war began, this program became ESMWT, or War Training Program and over three hundred completed this course.

Between Pearl Harbor Day and Christmas of 1942, the entire Austin College football team and many other men students volunteered for military duty. For the first time in the history of the College women students now outnumbered men. This situation did not last long.

The 77th Flight Army Air Training Corp arrived at the College in 1943. With only four hours notice from Major Lindemann, their Commanding Officer, they arrived 250 strong from their Wichita Falls, Texas, camp. They were quartered in the YMCA and two floors of Luckett Hall. Thirty-two girls were occupying the Y dormitory at eleven a.m. that day. With the help and cooperation of the faculty, these were taken into homes around the campus. Eight were accommodated in the author's home. The flight trainees arrived at 3:00 p.m. in time to help the girls move their last load of luggage. A number of romances began that day as a by-product of this moving event. Thereafter, fifty trainees arrived each week, as fifty completed the seven weeks meteorology, air science and elementary flight course.

During the war eleven hundred air crew, paratroopers and flight instructors received training on the Austin College operated airfield.

Because of these additional students and the income from the government contracts, the College was able to maintain its full faculty without disrupting its normal program. The U. S. government officially recognized Austin College, its faculty and administrative officers with a citation for the efficient execution of these training programs in which not a single accident occurred. Vice-President Landolt was coordinator of these war training programs and of the Federal Student Housing Projects erected on the campus after the War ended.

These federal housing projects on the campus provided furnished apartments for one hundred and ten married students. A very large number of the 77th Training Detachment returned to the College to complete their education at the close of the War. Many became Sherman citizens.

Seven hundred and fifty-two Austin College men enlisted in the military forces and twenty-six of these were lost in action.

*Austin College Men Who Gave Their Lives in World War II*

| | |
|---|---|
| Alvin Lee Barker | Capt. USAAF |
| Norman E. Barnes | Private US Army |
| Jack Boggs Bidwell | Private US Army |
| Donald Gladney Boyd | 2nd Lieut. USAAF |
| George W. Firor | Private US Army |
| Ben Prentice Gafford | Engin. Cadet US Merchant Marines |
| Elery G. Gross | Lieut. USAAF |
| La Rue Haralson | Lieut. USAAF |
| Clifford G. Hardwicke, Jr. | Lieut. U.S. Cavalry |
| Harold Hester | Ensign USNR |
| Roswell G. Higginbotham | Lieut. (J.G.) USNR |
| Shepherd Litsey | T/Sgt. USAAF |
| Gordon Duggan McDaniel | Ensign USNAF |
| Guy N. Matlock | S/Sgt. US Medical Corp. |
| Edward Lee Matthews | Lieut. 3rd Armored Div. |
| Alfred Martin Nicholas, Jr. | Seaman 2/c USNR |
| Edwin Hughes Read | C Phm USN |
| Norman Morrow Smith | T/Sft. USAAF |
| Richard E. St. John | Ensign USNR |
| Joseph L. Sory | Sft. US Infantry |
| Donald H. Mebane | Colonel Medical Corp USA |

*Missing in Action*

| | |
|---|---|
| Leonard Alton Page | James Edwin Wood |
| James Edwin Baldwin | Wm. Green Reynolds |
| Billy Deweese Steward | |

## The Road Ahead

IN a speech before the Alumni Association May 27, 1946, the Hon. William A. Vinson of Houston, Texas, a member of the Class of 1896, stated that the "Road Ahead" leading to the summit was always lighted by the inspired leadership of consecrated professors. In answer to his own question (and others many times), "What is the reason for the outstanding achievement of this institution?" Judge Vinson said: "I think God's hand has guided it. The road has been steep, rough, rocky, full of pitfalls and exceedingly difficult. Every place of eminence and prestige carries with it the greatest of responsibilities; one inescapable responsibility of decision, 'that the best today will not be good enough for tomorrow.' " What is the future of Austin College? With God and a host of loyal friends, who needs more?

### Onward Toward the Summit

Evidence of the excellence of teaching at Austin College after the end of the war was quickly realized by students of the Southwest who were looking for a school which had already attained a mark of greatness. Men and women from distant states sought to enroll.

*Lovejoy's College Guidance Digest*, March 1954, includes a report on a recent book by Knapp and Greenbaum entitled, *The Younger American Scholar: His Collegiate Origin.*

A scholar is defined as a recent graduate who went on to earn the Ph.D or who won a private foundation grant, a university fellowship, or a government fellowship based on academic excellence. The time period involved in this study is 1946-51.

Of the nation's 67 institutions producing ten or more male scholars per 1000 male graduates during the period 1946-51 only one institution, Austin College, is located in the five-state area including Texas, Oklahoma, Arkansas, Louisiana and New Mexico.

## Athletics at Austin College

INTRAMURAL sports, especially track and field, were a part of the student life of the College in the Huntsville days — 1849 to 1876. The first gymnasium available to the students was in one wing of the original building on the Sherman campus. At times it was turned into a meeting place for the literary societies, student theatre productions and oratorical contests. The ten-acre campus was ample for baseball and football practice and games.

In 1902 a five-acre tract four blocks north of the main campus in Sherman was given to the College by former President Luckett for an athletic field. Lewis Thompson, who with his brother, Hoxie, and father, Capt. J. M. Thompson, owned a sawmill in East Texas, shipped enough lumber from Trinity, Texas, to build a field house, grandstand and fence around the new athletic field. Austin College publicity in 1905 claimed the best equipped athletic plant of any college in Texas.

Intercollegiate athletics was sanctioned by action of the Board of Trustees in May 1896. The first football game was played that Fall with Texas A & M and was repeated again in 1897.

Austin College became a charter member of the T.I.A.A. (Texas Intercollegiate Athletic Association) participating in football, basketball, baseball and track from the first and later had tennis, golf and wrestling teams in intercollegiate competition. Since 1908 the intramural program has included bowling, volleyball, table tennis and badminton.

The Alumni Association acquired the twenty-acre Porter property adjoining the campus in 1923. Again through the Thompson family, especially Hoxie H. Thompson this time, lumber was given for building a new field house on the enlarged campus and was named after Pete Cawthon, head coach who supervised its construction. It contained a large maple floor basketball court, dressing rooms, two bowling lanes, trophy room and athletic offices. When the new Hughey Memorial Gymnasium was built, the old field house was moved to a new location where it later burned. Cashion Athletic Field was constructed in 1923 also and in the Fall of that year Austin College football games were played there. This facility, named after Mason L. Cashion, long-time Y.M.C.A.

Secretary at the College, served until the new Louis Calder Stadium was built in 1960, the gift of Mr. Louis Calder of New York.

In 1853 the Board of Trustees asserted: "We deem it now not only desirable but urgent that a ball battery be provided for the students to maintain physical fitness to match the intellectual and spiritual life of the young men attending here."

During the year 1970-71 the SID RICHARDSON CENTER, made possible by the Sid Richardson Foundation, is expected to be completed for the above purpose. This center will serve as an important recreational facility. It will include another gymnasium floor, handball courts, bowling lanes and natatorium. Its multiple use for social, cultural and other campus life functions will be featured.

## Football Records of Athletic Coaches at Austin College

RICHARD N. Watts became the first Athletic Coach at Austin College. His team lost to Texas A & M 2 to 0 in 1897.

| Date | Coach | Won | Lost | Tied |
|------|-------|-----|------|------|
| 1896-1903 | Richard N. Watts | 10 | 5 | |
| 1904-05 | Prof. J. W. Culver | 6 | 6 | |
| 1907 | T. W. Currie | | 3 | |
| 1908 | C. A. Richenstein | 6 | 2 | 1 |
| | *Austin College was not scored on in first six games.* | | | |
| 1909-10 | J. Burton Rix | 9 | 6 | 4 |
| 1911-14 | Chester Johnston — His teams beat Baylor three times and tied one, beat Rice 81-0, beat TCU 39-0 and 18-8. | 14 | 13 | 3 |
| 1915 | F. W. Jones | 2 | 4 | 1 |
| 1916 | Webster H. Warren | 4 | 4 | 1 |
| 1919-20 | E. Y. Freeland | 10 | 6 | 1 |
| 1921 | Gene Neely | 5 | 3 | |
| 1922 | Charlie Robinson, Dave Pena, Ray Morehart | 2 | 2 | |
| 1923-26 | Pete Cawthon, Eddie Dyer, Dell Morgan | 22 | 13 | 3 |
| 1927-32 | Cecil Grigg | 13 | 31 | 3 |

| 1933 | Ray Morehart, Wiley Grinnell | 1 | 5 | 2 |
|---|---|---|---|---|
| 1934 | J. B. Head, Bill Pierce | 4 | 4 | 2 |
| 1935-38 | E. Y. Freeland, Bill Pierce | 20 | 15 | 3 |
| | (Richard St. John '36) (Buchanan '37) (Steen '38) | | | |
| 1939-41 | Garvice Steen, John O. | | | |
| | Stephens | 8 | 21 | 1 |
| 1942 | J. W. Nelson, Wannie Miller | 0 | 7 | |
| 1946 | Garvice Steen | 2 | 7 | 1 |
| 1947-48 | Bill Pierce, Byron Gilbreath | 4 | 14 | 1 |
| 1949, 50, 51 | Ray Morrison, Ed Kulakowski, | | | |
| | Gilbreath (Buffington 1951) | 8 | 19 | |
| 1952-53 | Harry Buffington, Joe Spencer, | | | |
| | Gilbreath | 9 | 10 | 1 |
| 1954 | Spencer, Gilbreath | 6 | 4 | |
| 1955-60 | Spencer, Gass | | | |
| | (Ralph McCord after 1955) | 30 | 25 | |
| 1961-68 | Floyd Gass, McCord, Robert | | | |
| | Mason, Wm. Long (Nutt in | | | |
| | 65-68) (Babb 1967) | 43 | 28 | 1 |
| 1969 | Nutt, McCord, Mason, Don | | | |
| | Newsom, Scott Hennington | 7 | 2 | |

Charlie Robertson—famous for pitching the perfect baseball for Chicago White Sox against the Detroit Tigers in 1922—the seventh perfect game in organized baseball was the first alumnus (1919) to become full time coach at his Alma Mater. Others with date of graduation were: Ray Morehart (1922), Odell Morgan (1926), Cecil Grigg (1917), Wiley Grinnell (1935), J. B. Head (1925), Richard St. John (1936), Milton Buchanan (1936), Garvice Steen (1938), John O. Stephens (1937), J. W. Nelson (1943), Wannie Miller (1942), Ralph McCord (1950), Robert Mason (1957), Gene Babb (1958), Don Newsom (1965).

# Austin College Football History

| AC | 1896 | Op. |
|---|---|---|
| 4 | Texas A&M | 22 |

| AC | 1897 | Op. |
|---|---|---|
| 0 | Texas A&M | 2 |

| AC | 1898 | Op. |
|---|---|---|
| 26 | Eastman College | 0 |
| 6 | Fort Worth U. | 0 |
| 6 | Texas A&M | 22 |
| 17 | Denison | 5 |

| AC | 1900 | Op. |
|---|---|---|
| 5 | Sherman Owls | 0 |
| 0 | Baylor | 11 |
| 36 | Wall School | 0 |

| AC | 1901 | Op. |
|---|---|---|
| 11 | South Sherman | 0 |
| 11 | Le. Tellier A. | 0 |
| 5 | Sherman H. S. | 0 |

| AC | 1902 | Op. |
|---|---|---|
| 6 | Daniel Baker | 10 |
| 28 | Fort Worth U. | 0 |

| AC | 1904 | Op. |
|---|---|---|
| 34 | Durant Presby. | 0 |
| 29 | Polytechnic | 0 |
| 21 | Hughey-Turner | 0 |
| 6 | Trinity | 23 |
| 5 | Fort Worth U. | 4 |
| 52 | Armstrong A. In. | 0 |
| 0 | Trinity | 38 |

| AC | 1905 | Op. |
|---|---|---|
| 18 | Daniel Baker | 0 |
| 11 | Texas A&M | 18 |
| 0 | T. C. U. | 21 |
| 5 | Trinity | 6 |
| 0 | Trinity | 33 |

| AC | 1907 | Op. |
|---|---|---|
| 5 | Trinity | 16 |
| 0 | T. C. U. | 27 |
| 0 | Trinity | 5 |

| AC | 1908 | Op. |
|---|---|---|
| 5 | Holy Trinity | 0 |
| 0 | Armstrong Ind. | 0 |
| 15 | Carlisle | 0 |
| 1 | Dallas Hvywts. | 0 |
| 0 | Trinity | 0 |
| 30 | Armstrong Ind. | 0 |
| 25 | Burleson Col. | 17 |
| 11 | Trinity | 5 |

| AC | 1909 | Op. |
|---|---|---|
| 5 | S. E. Okla. N. | 0 |
| 0 | Texas A&M | 17 |
| 0 | Trinity | 0 |
| 18 | Cen. Okla. N. | 0 |
| 3 | T. C. U. | 18 |
| 0 | Southwestern | 0 |
| 10 | Holy Trinity | 0 |
| 3 | Epworth U. OC | 10 |
| 23 | Cen. Okla. St. | 5 |
| 17 | Trinity | 9 |

| AC | 1910 | Op. |
|---|---|---|
| 0 | Baylor | 31 |
| 5 | Texas A&M | 27 |
| 6 | Trinity | 6 |
| 6 | Southwestern | 6 |
| 19 | S. W. Texas N. | 0 |
| 11 | Daniel Baker | 3 |
| 18 | Polytechnic | 16 |
| 37 | Grayson Col. | 6 |
| 0 | Trinity | 3 |

| AC | 1911 | Op. |
|---|---|---|
| 0 | Texas A&M | 33 |
| 9 | Baylor | 0 |
| 39 | T C. U. | 0 |

| | | |
|---|---|---|
| 0 | Polytechnic | 9 |
| 6 | Daniel Baker | 0 |
| 18 | T. C. U. | 8 |
| 3 | Southwestern | 0 |

| AC | 1912 | Op. |
|---|---|---|
| 14 | Dallas U. | 0 |
| 8 | Baylor | 6 |
| 0 | Texas | 3 |
| 0 | T. C. U. | 7 |
| 0 | Texas A&M | 57 |
| 13 | Daniel Baker | 3 |
| 21 | Polytechnic | 0 |
| 81 | Rice | 0 |
| 14 | Southwestern | 0 |
| 7 | Polytechnic | 7 |

| AC | 1913 | Op. |
|---|---|---|
| 41 | Trinity | 0 |
| 6 | Texas | 27 |
| 14 | Baylor | 7 |
| 0 | Texas A&M | 6 |
| 7 | Arkansas | 26 |

| AC | 1914 | Op. |
|---|---|---|
| 6 | Durant Normal | 0 |
| 0 | Texas A&M | 32 |
| 0 | Southwestern | 7 |
| 0 | Baylor | 0 |
| 6 | Trinity | 19 |
| 0 | T. C. U. | 13 |
| 0 | Daniel Baker | 33 |
| 0 | Rice | 0 |

| AC | 1915 | Op. |
|---|---|---|
| 0 | Durant Norm. | 0 |
| 0 | Texas A&M | 40 |
| 0 | Dallas U. | 26 |
| 0 | Denton Norm. | 0 |
| 21 | S. M. U. | 0 |
| 0 | Ouachito Col. | 26 |
| 47 | Trinity | 0 |
| 6 | Southwestern | 7 |

| AC | 1916 | Op. |
|---|---|---|
| 0 | Normal | 10 |
| 0 | Texas A&M | 40 |
| 0 | Dallas U. | 26 |
| 0 | Denton Normal | 0 |
| 21 | S. M. U. | 0 |
| 13 | Hendrix | 0 |
| 47 | Trinity | 7 |
| 6 | Southwestern | 7 |
| 13 | East Texas St. | 0 |

| AC | 1917 | Op. |
|---|---|---|
| 0 | S. M. U. | 20 |
| 0 | Rice | 53 |
| 0 | Texas A&M | 66 |
| 0 | T. C. U. | 59 |
| 8 | Trinity | 20 |
| 13 | Howard Payne | 49 |
| | (Possibly incomplete) | |

| AC | 1918 | Op. |
|---|---|---|
| 0 | S. M. U. | 19 |
| 25 | S. W. Okla. N. | 0 |
| 9 | N. Tex. Normal | 7 |
| 0 | Burleson | 0 |
| 0 | T. C. U. | 25 |

| AC | 1919 | Op. |
|---|---|---|
| 19 | Durant Normal | 5 |
| 0 | Burleson Col. | 0 |
| 12 | Baylor | 17 |
| 0 | Rice | 54 |
| 0 | S. M. U. | 42 |
| 6 | T. C. U. | 0 |
| 1 | Denton Teacher | 0 |
| 46 | Trinity | 0 |

| AC | 1920 | Op. |
|---|---|---|
| 62 | Durant Normal | 0 |
| 0 | Baylor | 9 |

| | | |
|---|---|---|
| 7 | T. C. U. | 9 |
| 109 | Daniel Baker | 0 |
| 0 | Texas | 54 |
| 61 | Hendrix | 0 |
| 26 | Southwestern | 0 |
| 42 | S. M. U. | 0 |
| 21 | Trinity | 0 |

| AC | 1921 | Op. |
|---|---|---|
| 30 | Southeastern Okla. | 0 |
| 13 | Baylor | 17 |
| 0 | Texas | 60 |
| 17 | Southwestern | 10 |
| 17 | S. M. U. | 7 |
| 14 | Henderson-Brown | 7 |
| 14 | Howard Payne | 21 |
| 3 | Trinity | 0 |

| AC | 1922 | Op. |
|---|---|---|
| 0 | Texas | 19 |
| 7 | Howard Payne | 0 |
| 10 | S. M. U. | 7 |
| 17 | Daniel Baker | 0 |
| 14 | Simmons | 0 |
| 20 | T. C. U. | 7 |
| 7 | Southwestern | 0 |
| 0 | Trinity | 9 |

| AC | 1923 | Op. |
|---|---|---|
| 0 | Texas | 31 |
| 0 | Simmons | 0 |
| 3 | S. M. U. | 10 |
| 17 | Henderson Brown | 7 |
| 68 | Daniel Baker | 6 |
| 12 | Howard Payne | 0 |
| 27 | T. C. U. | 0 |
| 17 | Tulsa | 7 |
| 27 | Denton Normal | 0 |
| 48 | Trinity | 0 |

| AC | 1924 | Op. |
|---|---|---|
| 21 | Simmons | 0 |
| 0 | S. M. U. | 7 |
| 21 | Henderson Brown | 13 |
| 7 | Baylor | 3 |
| 0 | Trinity U. | 0 |
| 6 | Rice Institute | 2 |
| 10 | Howard Payne | 15 |
| 9 | Southwestern | 20 |
| 9 | Tulsa | 0 |
| 7 | Hendrix | 0 |

| AC | 1925 | Op. |
|---|---|---|
| 9 | Oklahoma Tchrs | 0 |
| 28 | E. Tex. Normal | 3 |
| 3 | Texas Tech. | 3 |
| 23 | Daniel Baker | 0 |
| 3 | Southwestern | 9 |
| 0 | Trinity | 16 |
| 0 | Howard Payne | 19 |
| 7 | Henderson-Brown | 0 |
| 0 | Texas Christian | 21 |

| AC | 1926 | Op. |
|---|---|---|
| 14 | Oklahoma Tchrs | 13 |
| 14 | E. Tex. Tchrs | 0 |
| 0 | Daniel Baker | 22 |
| 6 | Henderson-Brown | 22 |
| 0 | Texas Christian | 7 |
| 13 | Trinity | 14 |
| 0 | Howard Payne | 3 |
| 13 | Durant Tchrs | 0 |
| 18 | Southwestern | 6 |

| AC | 1927 | Op. |
|---|---|---|
| 19 | Durant Tchrs | 7 |
| 6 | Okla. City U. | 13 |
| 13 | Texas Christian | 20 |
| 0 | Howard Payne | 23 |
| 13 | Trinity | 13 |
| 6 | Simmons | 20 |
| 0 | Arkansas | 42 |

| AC | 1928 | Op. |
|---|---|---|
| 2—Durant Tchrs | | 0 |
| 36—Abilene Christian | | 0 |
| 0—Texas Christian | | 21 |
| 0—Howard Payne | | 21 |
| 6—Simmons | | 0 |
| 6—Daniel Baker | | 13 |
| 6—Southwestern | | 26 |
| 7—Trinity | | 6 |
| 0—Okla. City U. | | 34 |

| AC | 1929 | Op. |
|---|---|---|
| 0—S. M. U. | | 16 |
| 0—Howard Payne | | 22 |
| 14—Southwestern | | 0 |
| 6—Simmons | | 0 |
| 14—Trinity | | 0 |
| 0—St. Edwards | | 6 |

| AC | 1930 | Op. |
|---|---|---|
| 6—Durant Tchrs. | | 7 |
| 7—Texas Christian | | 33 |
| 6—Denton Tchrs. | | 0 |
| 0—S. M. U. | | 34 |
| 7—Howard Payne | | 26 |
| 7—St. Edwards | | 7 |
| 12—Southwestern | | 13 |
| 13—Simmons | | 9 |
| 40—Trinity | | 6 |

| AC | 1931 | Op. |
|---|---|---|
| 13—Durant Tchrs. | | 13 |
| 6—Denton Tchrs. | | 21 |
| 0—Texas Christian | | 38 |
| 13—Howard Payne | | 7 |
| 7—Oklahoma Bap. | | 10 |
| 0—St. Edwards | | 21 |
| 19—Southwestern | | 13 |
| 0—Simmons | | 20 |
| 2—Trinity | | 0 |

| AC | 1932 | Op. |
|---|---|---|
| —S. W. Okla. Tech | | |
| 0—Denton Teachers | | 54 |
| 0—Texas Tech | | 64 |
| 13—Howard Payne | | 47 |
| 0—T. C. U. | | 68 |
| 0—St. Edwards | | 34 |
| 0—Southwestern | | 12 |
| 0—Simmons | | 16 |
| 0—Trinity | | 39 |

| AC | 1933 | Op. |
|---|---|---|
| 0—Texas Christian | | 33 |
| 25—Daniel Baker | | 0 |
| 0—Durant Teachers | | 19 |
| 6—Howard Payne | | 6 |
| 0—Southwestern | | 0 |
| 0—Abilene Christ. | | 13 |
| 0—Trinity U. | | 6 |
| 0—Dixie | | 7 |

| AC | 1934 | Op. |
|---|---|---|
| 7—Durant Teachers | | 6 |
| 0—S. M. U. | | 33 |
| 6—McMurry | | 6 |
| 19—Daniel Baker | | 0 |
| 7—Howard Payne | | 7 |
| 6—Southwestern | | 2 |
| 27—Abilene Christian | | 6 |
| 13—St. Edwards | | 15 |
| 0—Hardin Simmons | | 45 |
| 0—Trinity U. | | 13 |

| AC | 1935 | Op. |
|---|---|---|
| 6—Abilene Christian | | 6 |
| 0—S. M. U. | | 60 |
| 0—Howard Payne | | 0 |
| 25—S.F. Austin T. | | 12 |
| 6—Commerce Tchrs. | | 7 |
| 13—Daniel Baker | | 6 |
| 6—Durant Tchrs. | | 0 |
| 20—McMurry | | 14 |
| 26—St. Edwards | | 7 |
| 13—Trinity U. | | 0 |
| 12—Texas Wesleyan | | 3 |

| AC | 1936 | Op. |
|---|---|---|
| 0—E. Texas Tchrs. | | 6 |
| 19—Durant Tchrs. | | 6 |
| 9—McMurry | | 12 |
| 0—Daniel Baker | | 15 |
| 10—Howard Payne | | 14 |
| 0—Denton Tchrs. | | 0 |
| 58—Abilene Christian | | 14 |
| 20—St. Edwards | | 0 |

| AC | 1937 | Op. |
|---|---|---|
| 25—Daniel Baker | | 15 |
| 6—Denton Tchrs. | | 0 |
| 13—Edmond Tchrs. | | 14 |
| 12—St. Edwards | | 6 |
| 7—Howard Payne | | 26 |
| 41—Trinity U. | | 12 |
| 20—McMurry | | 12 |
| 20—S. E. Okla. | | 6 |
| 20—Texas Wesleyan | | 13 |
| 6—A. C. C. | | 0 |

| AC | 1938 | Op. |
|---|---|---|
| 7—Oklahoma City | | 26 |
| 7—Daniel Baker | | 6 |
| 0—Durant Tchrs. | | 20 |
| 2—N. Texas Tchrs. | | 32 |
| 0—Trinity U. | | 6 |
| 12—Abilene Christian | | 8 |
| 0—Howard Payne | | 13 |
| 0—St. Edwards | | 12 |
| 6—McMurry | | 20 |

| AC | 1939 | Op. |
|---|---|---|
| 6—Okla. City | | 13 |
| 2—McMurry | | 6 |
| 0—Daniel Baker | | 6 |
| 0—Howard Payne | | 20 |
| 13—Texas Wesleyan | | 25 |
| 6—Abilene Christ. | | 32 |
| 0—N. Texas Tchrs. | | 27 |
| 0—St. Edwards | | 19 |
| 0—Durant Tchrs. | | 7 |
| 6—Trinity | | 19 |

| AC | 1940 | Op. |
|---|---|---|
| 0—Durant | | 13 |
| 19—Daniel Baker | | 6 |
| 0—Howard Payne | | 51 |
| 24—O. C. U. | | 0 |
| 6—T. W. C. | | 16 |
| 7—A. C. C. | | 6 |
| 0—Denton Tchrs. | | 14 |
| 19—McMurry | | 7 |
| 7—Southwestern | | 6 |
| 6—Trinity | | 13 |

| AC | 1941 | Op. |
|---|---|---|
| 0—Commerce | | 30 |
| 13—Durant | | 0 |
| 35—Daniel Baker | | 0 |
| 0—Howard Payne | | 20 |
| 7—Texas Wes. | | 48 |
| 6—Abilene Christ. | | 19 |
| 6—N. Texas State | | 26 |
| 6—McMurry | | 0 |
| 13—Southwestern | | 20 |

| AC | 1942 | Op. |
|---|---|---|
| 0—Howard Payne | | 26 |
| 0—Abilene Christ. | | 54 |
| 0—McMurry | | 28 |
| 0—East Texas | | 34 |
| 12—No. Texas | | 32 |
| 6—S. E. Okla. St. | | 20 |
| 13—S. E. Okla. St. | | 27 |

| AC | 1946 | Op. |
|---|---|---|
| 0—Southeast St. | | 12 |
| 0—N. Texas State | | 14 |
| 7—S.F. Austin | | 20 |
| 19—Sam Houston St. | | 18 |
| 0—Howard Payne | | 24 |
| 13—E. Texas Tchrs. | | 33 |
| 7—McMurry | | 0 |
| 0—Southwestern | | 34 |

| 2—Abilene Christ. | | 46 |
|---|---|---|
| 6—E. Central Okla. | | 6 |

| AC | 1947 | Op. |
|---|---|---|
| 0—S. E. Okla. | | 0 |
| 0—Sam Houston St. | | 12 |
| 0—E. Texas Tchrs. | | 13 |
| 14—Howard Payne | | 13 |
| 0—McMurry | | 21 |
| 7—Southwestern | | 6 |
| 7—Abilene Christ. | | 41 |
| 0—Hardin (Midw'n) | | 25 |

| AC | 1948 | Op. |
|---|---|---|
| 14—SW La. Inst. | | 0 |
| 6—Austin | | 39 |
| 0—Miss. Southern | | 41 |
| 0—Corpus Christi | | 25 |
| 0—Howard Payne | | 27 |
| 6—SW Mo. St. | | 25 |
| 6—McMurry | | 19 |
| 0—Southwestern U. | | 28 |
| 6—Abilene Christ. | | 45 |
| 7—Hardin College | | 21 |
| 25—Texas A&I | | 20 |

| AC | 1949 | Op. |
|---|---|---|
| 0—Midwestern | | 28 |
| 12—Howard Payne | | 19 |
| 19—McMurry | | 34 |
| 28—Southwestern | | 0 |
| 27—Abilene Christ. | | 14 |
| 20—Texas A&I | | 19 |

| | Texoma Bowl | |
|---|---|---|
| 27—E. Cent. Okla. | | 7 |
| 0—SW Louisiana | | 30 |
| 0—Corpus Christi | | 14 |
| 33—SW Missouri | | 0 |

| AC | 1950 | Op. |
|---|---|---|
| 26—S. E. Okla. St. | | 0 |
| 27—Midwestern | | 13 |
| 6—Howard Payne | | 14 |
| 0—Trinity U. | | 27 |
| 6—McMurry | | 27 |
| 15—E. Texas Tchrs. | | 40 |
| 14—Abilene Christ. | | 33 |
| 13—Texas A&I | | 18 |
| 7—Southwestern | | 27 |

| AC | 1951 | Op. |
|---|---|---|
| 34—E. Cent. Ok. St. | | 13 |
| 12—Midwestern | | 34 |
| 20—Howard Payne | | 35 |
| 12—Trinity | | 20 |
| 7—McMurry | | 19 |
| 33—A. C. C. | | 50 |
| 7—Texas A&I | | 41 |
| 7—E. Texas State | | 12 |

| AC | 1952 | Op. |
|---|---|---|
| 6—S. E. Louisiana | | 7 |
| 7—Midwestern | | 21 |
| 7—Mexico U. | | 21 |
| 46—E. Cent. Okla. | | 7 |
| 13—Howard Payne | | 14 |
| 6—McMurry | | 27 |
| 13—Abilene Christ. | | 38 |
| 24—Texas A&I | | 20 |
| 7—East Texas St. | | 61 |

| AC | 1953 | Op. |
|---|---|---|
| 41—S. E. Okla. | | 7 |
| 19—Mississippi Col. | | 19 |
| 21—Col. of Ozarks | | 0 |
| 32—E. Central Okla. | | 0 |
| 26—Howard Payne | | 20 |
| 19—Texas Lutheran | | 7 |
| 21—McMurry | | 47 |
| 13—Abilene Christ. | | 25 |
| 18—Texas A&I | | 19 |
| 19—Midwestern | | 18 |
| 38—Univ. of Mexico | | 30 |

| AC | 1954 | Op. |
|---|---|---|
| 35—S. East Okla. | | 6 |
| 26—Mississippi Col. | | 0 |
| 12—S. F. Austin | | 34 |

47—E. Central Okla. ..20
41—Univ. Mexico ......14
0—Midwestern .......... 6
20—Louisiana Col. .....52
62—Arkansas St. .....20
14—Louisiana Tech. ....40
41—South Dakota ...... 6

**AC : 1955 Op.**
19—S. E. Oklahoma .. 0
7—William Carey ....26
6—S. F. Austin .......14
21—E. Central Okla. 0
28—Mexico Univ. ......27
12—E. Texas St. ...... 7
45—Louisiana Col. ....21
19—Arkansas State ....40
21—Lou'siana Tech. ....40
6—Midwestern ..........47

**AC 1956 Op.**
6—Southeastern ......19
20—Henderson St. ...... 0
20—College of Ozarks 6
32—Ouachita Col. ...... 7
7—East Texas' St. . 13
7—Midwestern ..........34
14—U. Corpus Christi 20
52—S. W. of Memphis 20
14—Texas Lutheran ....33

**AC 1957 Op.**
0—Southeastern ........ 6
4—Henderson St. ...... 9
21—Ouachita Col. ...... 7
7—S. W. of Memphis 32
14—East. N.M. U. ....28
0—U. Corpus Christi 27
15—Texas Lutheran ...33
14—East. Cent. St......22

**AC 1958 Op.**
6—Southeastern ......13
20—Henderson St. ......13
27—Mississippi Co. .... 6
33—Ouachita Col. ......10
54—S.W. of Memphis 6
7—East. N. M. U. 13
7—U. Corpus Christ 20
40—E. Cent. St. Okla. 7
19—Texas Lutheran .... 7

**AC 1959 Op.**
13—Southeastern ........ 0
20—Henderson St. ......14
6—Mississippi Col. ....14
35—Ouachita Col. ..... 0
28—S. W. of Memphis 6
21—East Cent. St. 20

33—Corpus Christi U. 7
45—Millsaps ..............20
33—Texas Lutheran ....13
20—Col. of Emporia 21

**AC 1960 Op.**
27—Southeastern .......... 7
14—Henderson St. .....13
20—Mississippi Col. ....18
6—Louisiana Col. .. 16
22—U. of the South ..32
38—East Cent. Okla. 28
29—Millsaps ..............14
20—Arkansas St. .... 39
30—Southwestern ........ 7

**AC 1961 Op.**
6—Southeastern ........20
0—Henderson St. ... 21
0—Mississippi Col. ....29
19—Louisiana Col. ... 20
12—U. of the South ..21
6—Millsaps Col. ........ 0
13—William Jewell ... 14
27—Ark. St. Tchrs. ......21
6—S. W. of Memphis 7

**AC 1962 Op.**
14—Southeastern ........16
13—Henderson St. ...... 6
6—Mississippi Col. ....12
27—Millsaps Col. ......23
10—U. of the South 7
15—Ouachita Col. ......14
21—William Jewell ...24
12—S. W. Louisiana ..38
13—Southern St. ........ 0

**AC 1963 Op.**
7—Southeastern .......... 0
19—Henderson St. ......19
6—Mississippi Col. .... 7
23—Millsaps .............. 0
19—Sewanee ..............39
14—Ouachita Col. ......19
19—William Jewell ...35
37—East Cent. Okla. 54
27—Southern St. .......... 7

**AC 1964 Op.**
21—Henderson St. ......14
19—Southeastern ........28
34—Millsaps .............. 0
16—S. W. of Memphis 7
38—William Jewell .... 7
38—Mex. Polytechnic ..27
27—Ark. Southern ......13
13—Mississippi Co. 16
0—U. of the South 49

**AC 1965 Op.**
32—Millsaps .............. 0
42—Mex. Polytechnic .. 8
14—Henderson St. ...... 20
29—Sewanee .............. 6
21—Wash. U. at
St. Louis .......... 0
41—Missouri Valley .... 0
32—Southern St. .......24
19—Mississippi Col. ...21
48—Southwestern ........27

**AC 1966 Op.**
26—Bishop ..............19
22—Southwestern ........ 7
20—Henderson St. ...... 6
18—Millsaps ..............32
22—U. of the South 0
28—Wash. U. at
St. Louis ..........10
26—Missouri Valley ...28
7—William Jewell ... 21
57 Mex. Polytechnic .. 8

**AC 1967 Op.**
37—Mex. Polytechnic .. 6
14—S. W. of Memphis 7
27—Henderson St. .... 41
27—Neb. Wesleyan .... 0
29—U. of the South .. 6
6—Ouachita ..............22
49—Colorado Col. .....25
14—William Jewell 21
39—Texas Lutheran ....24

**AC 1968 Op.**
41 Northwood Inst. .. 0
40—S. W. of Memphis 0
28—Maryville of Tenn. 7
33—Neb. Wesleyan .... 0
14—U. of the South .. 7
48—William Jewell ....10
50—Colorado College 21
19—Ouachita ..............28
35—Texas Lutheran ....18

**AC 1969 Op.**
9 — Northwood Ins.----------- 7
28 — S.W.Memphis ------------ 7
34 — Maryville------------------ 7
35 — Neb. Wesleyan-----------20
35 — Univ. the South ----------18
7 — Wm. Jewell---------------12
21 — Texas Lutheran-----------20
0 — Ouichita --------------------42
47 — Univ. of Mexico----------15

# AUSTIN COLLEGE ATHLETIC HALL OF HONOR

## Inducted in 1965

Virgil Ballard
Class of 1928
John W. (Red) Carroll
Class of 1917
Peter W. (Pete) Cawthon
Coach, 1923-1927
Shem P. Cunningham
Class of 1920

William H. Keeling
Class of 1928
Charles A. Lingo
Class of 1928
Robert G. Lowe
Class of 1917
Raymond A. Morchart
Class of 1922

Edwin H. (Eddie) Dyer
  Coach, mid-1920's
Henry Frnka
  Class of 1926
Alexander Gray
  Class of 1914
Herbert L. (Hub) Hollis
  Class of 1924
Ralph H. Hollywood
  Class of 1947
Pat E. Hooks
  Class of 1903
Joe M. Joiner
  Class of 1950

John Odell (Dell) Morgan
  Class of 1926
R. N. (Bud) Price
  Class of 1927
Russell T. (Dutchy) Smith
  Class of 1925
Frank G. (Hip) Steen
  Class of 1938
Hoxie H. Thompson
  Class of 1902
Ewell Doak Walker
  Class of 1919
James T. Wilson
  Class of 1950

## Inducted in 1966

Joe D. Coomer
  Class of 1942
H. O. "Molly" Crawford
  Class of 1927
Cecil B. Grigg
  Class of 1917
Joe E. Lillis
  Class of 1933

Ray Morrison
  Coach, 1949-1953
J. T. (Bobo) Nelson
  Class of 1927
Homer P. Rainey
  Class of 1919
James H. Self
  Class of 1958

## Inducted in 1967

Burnett Carroll Cox
  Class of 1934
John Morgan Currie
  Class of 1917
Clyde Eagleton
  Class of 1910
Robert Raymond Landolt
  Class of 1959

Charles Bolanz Miller
  Class of 1961
James Decatur Miller
  Class of 1921
Louis Herbert Monzingo
  Class of 1924
Robert L. Wood
  Class of 1933

## Inducted in 1968

Hiram "Hi" Tuck
    Class of 1917
George L. Landolt
    Class of 1923
Walter O. Miller
    Class of 1926
Leo Wesley "Butter" Allred
    Class of 1927

Wallace T. "Rock" Johnson
    Class of 1938
Sam Curlee
    Class of 1949
Carroll Pickett
    Class of 1954
Willie Joe Carter
    Class of 1932

## Inducted in 1969

J. W. McMurry
    Class of 1930
Albert J. Pruitt
    Class of 1938
Gene Babb
    Class of 1958

Bryan Henderson
    Class of 1931
Don Hulse
    Class of 1955

# CHAPTER V

# The Men Austin College
# Made

## Realization of Daniel Baker's Labor
## Austin College and It's Ministers

WHEN Daniel Baker divided the sixteen charter trustees into three classes there were only two other Presbyterian ministers, Hugh Wilson and J. W. Miller, serving with him.

In his many extended trips seeking funds for Austin College, first as financial agent and later as President of the College, his greatest appeal is expressed in his own words in *Life and Labours of Daniel Baker, D.D.* (p. 388)

> Yes, let it be forever remembered by the Church in Texas — let it be distinctly impressed upon the minds of the Trustees and Faculty of Austin College in all succeeding generations — the one idea of its founders, that for which they wept, and prayed, and toiled, and gave of their means, was that it might be an institution wherein there might be raised up for Texas, generation after generation, a native ministry. For all generations to come, then, palsied be the hand which shall ever cast a ballot to alienate the institution in any way from this, the main purpose of its existence — that sacred purpose which prompted its aged servant to travel and to beg as he did; and which was one motive, at least, which prompted the free contributions of many thousand Christian givers over the land — givers whose eyes will ever rest

upon the institution, watching for the fruits therein of their giving. So long as Austin College shall number one learner within its walls, withered be the tongue of any teacher therein who shall utter a syllable which has a tendency to prevent, in the case of a single student, the accomplishment, of this, the chief and holy object for which, above all others, the College was conceived, born, and reared.

Daniel Baker chose more lawyers than ministers for Trustees because there were very few Presbyterian ministers in Texas in 1849 and Texas was well supplied with lawyers. Before the end of the first decade of the College's existence, there was an increase in number of ministers called to be trustees, eight being appointed by Synod.

Still, Daniel Baker, had he lived until the College was moved to Sherman in 1876, would have been grievously disappointed in the failure of the College to produce a single minister in its twenty-seven years at Huntsville. William Stuart Red and William Harrison McCullough, the entire graduating class of 1882, were the first to enter the ministry.

Rev. Red was the son of charter trustee, Dr. George Red, and nephew of another charter trustee, Rev. J. W. Miller. After graduating from Austin College, he studied at the University of Leipsig; was pastor at Navasota 1890-92; Chaplain at A. & M. College 1892-94; Editor of *Texas Presbyterian 1894-97;* and while pastor of a number of Texas churches wrote *History of the Presbyterian Church in Texas* in 1936, published posthumously. Austin College honored him with the D.D. degree in 1907. Rev. Red was Moderator of the Synod of Texas in 1902 and Trustee of Austin College.

Nathaniel Smylie attended Austin College in 1880-81 and was ordained in 1890. Rev. John V. McCall attended Austin College 1882-83, taught mathematics at the College for two years. Succeeding classes produced Rev. Wm. A. Ziegler 1885-86; Rev. Clarence L. Altfather, 1887; Rev. Walter W. Boone and Albert Sidney Venable, in 1889. The 1892 class produced Rev. Joseph Porter, James Kidd Thompson and William Francis Junkin, also a missionary to China; three ministers of four in the class. The 1893 class has three of the five graduating to enter the ministry; E. B. Fincher, Eugene

T. Lowrance and Wm. C. Tenney. Rev. Robert D. Campbell came from the 1894 class. Five of the nine members of the Class of 1895 became ministers: Brooks I. Dickey, Wm. P. Dickey, Frank Fincher, Lawrence Selfridge and Madison P. Slaughter.

Half of the eight-member Class of 1896 became ministers: Archie Dean Rice who went to China; Joseph Baird; Edward H. Moseley, who later served as President of Oklahoma Presbyterian College; Robert E. Vinson, who became first President of Austin Theological Seminary and later President of Texas University and Western Reserve University.

The 1897 Class produced Rev. James W. Atwood and Walter K. Johnston. Alva Hardie, missionary to Brazil, was the only minister from the 1898 Class of four. Four from the eleven-member Class of 1899 entered the ministry: William Fred Galbraith, James M. Sedgwick, John A. Williams, and Robert Knox.

Though Austin College produced not a single minister from the twenty-seven graduates at Huntsville, it produced twenty-nine (half of the graduates) in the period of 1882 to 1899 which closed the first five decades of Austin College history. The number of graduates entering the ministry later were: Sixth Decade, 25; Seventh Decade, 33; Eighth Decade, 25; Ninth Decade, 40; Tenth Decade, 50; Eleventh Decade, 54; a total of 256 through 1960. Rev. Patricia McClurg, B.A. 1961, was the first woman graduate from Austin College ordained to the ministry and the second woman minister in the Presbyterian Church U.S. However, a very large number of women graduates are serving in the foreign fields and as religious education directors and pastors' assistants. Dr. Robert E. Vinson, B.A. 1896; Dr. Thomas W. Currie, B.A. 1907 and Dr. David L. Stitt, B.A. 1933 have occupied the office of the President of Austin Presbyterian Seminary most of the time since its founding.

Many Austin College men served on the faculties of our Theological Colleges. Dr. Louis J. Sherrill, B.A. 1916 was professor and Dean of Louisville Presbyterian Seminary. Dr. Robert Gribble, B.A. 1911 was professor at Austin Presbyterian Seminary. Dr. Carl Ellis Nelson, B.A. 1937 is teaching at Union Theological Seminary, New York. Dr. Wm. B. Oglesby, B.A. 1937 is teaching at Union Theological Seminary in Virginia. Rev. Shirley C. Guthrie, B.A. 1949 is teaching at Columbia Theological Seminary in Georgia. Revs. Alexander Gray, B.A. 1935 and James B. Storey, B.A. 1940 have been members of the Austin College faculty, and Rev. Campbell Butler, B.A. 1918 was a professor at East Texas State College.

## Austin College in World Missions

MANY graduates have given their lives to World Missions work. Wm. F. Junkin, B.A. 1892 taught Greek at Austin College before going to China as a missionary. He was followed by Rev. Archie Dean Rice, B.A. 1896, who died in China in 1917. A memorial oak tree was planted on the campus and a scholarship established in his honor. John Walker Vinson, B.A. 1903 also served in China until martyred by communist guerrillas in 1931. Wm. A. Venable, B.A. 1907 was an educational missionary to China.

Africa has attracted many Austin College graduates. The zeal of Motte Martin, B.A. 1900 was rewarded by knighthood being conferred upon him by the King of Belgium. Rev. Chalmers Vinson, B.A. 1909 and Revs. Conway T. Wharton, Roy Cleveland and W. F. McElroy, all of the 1911 Class, served in the Congo. Rev. McElroy's daughter, Lucille, B.A. 1941; Mr. and Mrs. Garland Goodrum, 1939 and 1941 classes; Wm. Pruitt, B.A. 1963; Mr. and Mrs. Wm. C. Washburn, Class of 1942; Rev. John Coffin, B.A. 1949; Mr. and Mrs. Paul Donaldson, Class of 1961; Mrs. Lou Ann Hintz Horne, B.A. 1959 and Mary Scott, B.A. 1957 serve the Congo.

Mr. and Mrs. Mac Kyle, Class of 1956 have served in Iraq. Mr. and Mrs. Clarence Bassett, Class of 1943, are missionaries in Mexico.

Rev. Lardner W. Moore and his brother, Boude Moore, of the 1918 Class, served in Japan for forty years. Mrs. Jean Holmes Carrick, B.A. 1946 serves there now.

Mr. and Mrs. Blair Hickey of the 1964 class are serving in Korea.

Dr. George L. Landolt, B.A. 1923 and his wife, Doris Eagleton Landolt, B.A. 1927 were educational missionaries to the Republic of China (Formosa). Rev. Donald McCall, B.A. 1948 serves there now.

Rev. George Hurst, B.A. 1916 served nearly fifty years in Brazil, where Mrs. Paul Coblentz, B.A. 1943 serves today.

## Sciences at Austin College

WHEN the Board of Trustees assembled for its first meeting, the matter of a curriculum became the chief item. One member suggested postponing the matter until copies of courses of study could be obtained from Eastern schools. Daniel Baker and Henderson Yoakum were insistent that there was enough wisdom in the assembled group to provide a study plan without this delay. Consequently, with one exception, the Board unanimously adopted the curriculum listed below and the requirements for admission to the College:

*Course of Instruction in the College — 1850-1851*

FRESHMAN CLASS — First Session
The first six books of the Aeneid;
Xenophon's Anabasis;
Greek Testament; Latin and Greek Exercises;
    Algebra.
Second Session
Odes of Horace; Xenophon's Memorabilia;
Geometry; Latin and Greek Exercises;
    Greek Testament continued;

SOPHOMORE CLASS — First Session.
Satires of Horace; Alcestis of Euripides;
Trigonometry; Mensuration,
Surveying and Navigation;
Latin and Greek Exercises;
    Greek Testament, continued.
SECOND SESSION.
Cicero de Officiis; de Amicitia; de Senectute;
Homer's Illiad; Euripides;
Linear Perspective and Analytical Geometry;
Latin and Greek Exercises;
    Greek Testament, continued.

JUNIOR CLASS — FIRST SESSION
Juvenal; Sophocles;
Spanish or French Languages, *ad libitum;*
Differential and Integral Calculus;
Latin and Greek Exercises;
Greek Testament, continued;
    Natural Theology, and Evidence of Christianity.

SECOND SESSION.
Livy, Tacitus, Demosthenes,
Mechanics, Architecture, and Astronomy, Rhetoric,
    Greek Testament, continued.

SENIOR CLASS — FIRST SESSION.
Persius, Longinus,
Hydrodynamics, Pneumatics,
Electricity, Magnetism and Optics,
With Experiments,
    Mental Philosophy.
SECOND SESSION.
Moral Philosophy, Meteorology, Geology,
Chemistry, With Experiments,
Political Economy, Constitution U.S.A. (Rawle's,)
General Review of Studies.

ADMISSION TO THE COLLEGE
Candidates for the Freshman Class will be examined on
the following studies: —
English Grammar; Geography;
Vulgar, and Decimal Fractions;
Latin and Greek Grammar, including Latin Prosody.
Caesar's Commentaries; Cicero's Orations, and
Jacob's Greek Reader, or THEIR EQUIVALENT.
First Lessons in Algebra.

The subjects to be mastered as a requirement for graduation
were based upon the desire to equip the young men of Texas
with an armamentarium of knowledge sufficient in every
field for battle against the rigors of pioneering life here in
Texas, and to develop leaders for our State and government,
in the church, and in educational fields.

From the beginning the trustees realized the need for strong
science courses in the curriculum. Henderson Yoakum,
Secretary, reported to the Board on February 23, 1853 (page
32 of the *Minutes*): "We have received from the Smithsonian
Institute some valuable works and have the promise of a continuance of like favors. In return for this liberality and for
the advancement of science, we hold with the Institute a
regular meteorological correspondence. This until lately has
been partially done by the present secretary but the want of
time and suitable instruments have prevented a proper cor-

respondence. It should be made the duty of the Secretary to attend to this, or to have it attended to by some of the more advanced students." (Yoakum's request was granted and two seniors were appointed to gather the daily weather reports.)

On December 30, 1853, Henderson Yoakum endowed the first perpetual scholarship to carry on this arrangement between Austin College and the Smithsonian Institute to supply a collection of meteorological data, flora and fauna specimens of Texas in exchange for apparatus, books, science pamphlets, maps and mineral specimens and the Institute's annual Reports. Yoakum, at the request of the Board, made one trip to Washington and New York to secure laboratory supplies.

The Board appropriated in the Spring of 1853 "not less than $500 for chemicals and apparatus" for Dr. Daniel Baker to obtain on his fourth trip to Washington and New York. Dr. Baker reported a gift of $800 from a Mr. Lomax to purchase chemicals and laboratory equipment, a result of his trip in 1854.

The Civil War did not prevent efforts for improving the curriculum for the *Board of Trustees Minutes*, page 121, June 27, 1860 reads:

> The arrangement of the College for the Professor of the Natural Sciences is very difficult and demand immediate provision and in this behalf your committee recommends the adoption of the following Resolution: Resolved, That the Executive Committee be and they are hereby instructed to put the Southeast room of the basement story of the College in suitable condition for conducting the laboratory experiments in the Natural Sciences as early as possible.

Dr. Charlie Scott, on returning from graduate study at Heidelberg, offered the first courses in chemistry leading to the Master's degree in chemistry. Among the M.A. graduates were Dr. W. Thornton Read, Ph.D Yale, first chemistry professor at Texas Tech and later Dean at Rutgers University; Dr. B. F. Armendt, Ph.D, Texas University, successor to Dr. Scott at Austin College; Dr. George L. Landolt, Ph.D University of Pittsburgh and R. D. Lauderdale, M.A., successor to Dr. Landolt at South Park College.

Among the other notable chemistry majors who chose the teaching profession are Dr. Joe Dennis, Chemistry Department Head at Texas Tech.; Dr. Royston Roberts, on the Texas University faculty; Dr. Truman Blocker, President of Texas Medical Branch at Galveston, and Dr. Eugene C. McDanald also at the Medical College; Dr. Robert Mers at Lamar State; P. S. Wharton, at Austin College; Dr. Barnett Guerrant at Texas Tech; Dr. Richard Mitchell, at Arkansas State; Dr. Wha Yul Han, University of Southern California; Dr. Robert G. Landolt, Muskingum College, and Dr. Robert R. Landolt, Purdue University faculty.

Percy Keith, Princeton University Lecturer, has been given credit for the diffusion process separation of uranium 235 resulting in the success of the atomic bomb and nuclear power; and has also become famous for synthetic gasoline by the Hydracol Process.

More than two hundred other chemistry majors are now carving successful careers in industry and high school teaching after doing graduate work in other institutions.

Although Austin College Chemistry Department has complied with all the requirements for full accreditation by the American Chemical Society since 1953, request for action in the matter was made only recently, resulting in the College being added to the approved list.

## Chemistry Department History

MINUTES of the College show the following Chemistry Professors during the 120 years of its history:

| | |
|---|---|
| Washington McCartney | 1851-1853 |
| Rev. A. F. Thom | 1853-1858 |
| B. F. Grady | 1859-1861 |
| Andrew T. McKinney | 1862-1874 |
| W. D. Vinson | 1878-1883 |
| J. C. Edmunds | 1883-1889 |
| Dr. C. C. Scott | 1889-1924 |
| B. F. Armendt | 1924-1931; 1933-34 |
| Dr. George L. Landolt | 1931-1932; 1934-1967 |
| P. S. Wharton | 1934-1961 |
| Dr. W. B. Guerrant, Jr. | 1957-1968 |

The staff of the Chemistry Department in 1969-1970 are:

Dr. Frank Edwards Ph.D., Iowa State University,
Dean—Area Chairman

Charles R. Barr Ph.D., Michigan State University,
Dept. Head

John L. Mackey, Ph.D., Iowa State University

Harry H. Gibson, Jr., Ph.D., Florida State Univ.

Glen A. Wolfe, Ph.D., Univ. of Arizona

Frank A. James, Ph.D., Univ. of Georgia

George L. Landolt, Ph.D., University of Pittsburgh,
Emeritus Professor

Paul Wyatt, Preparations and Stock man for the
Science Area

Samuel P. Zieske, Instrument Technician for the
Science Area

## THE FIRST TEN CHEMISTRY MAJORS AT AUSTIN COLLEGE TO RECEIVE THE PH. D DEGREE
### (From *American Men of Science*)

READ, DR. WILLIAM THORNTON, b. College Station, Tex., Mar. 8, 86; m. 18; c. 2. CHEMISTRY. A.B., Austin Col. 05, A.M., 08; M.A., Texas, 15; scholar, Harvard, 15-16; Ph.D. (org. chem), Yale, 21. Instr. chem, Texas, 14-15; asst. Harvard, 15-16; chemist, bur. econ. geol, Texas, 16-18; instr. Yale, 19-24, asst. prof, 24-25; prof. & head dept, Tex. Tech. Col, 25-30; dean sch. chem, Rutgers, 30-43; sect. chief, Nat. Roster Sci. & Specialized Personnel, 43-46; sci. adv, res. & develop. div, gen. staff, U.S. Dept. Army, 46-57; CONSULT. CHEMIST, 57- Pres, Chemist Adv. Coun. C.W.S., 18, 1st Lt. AAAS; Chem. Soc; hon. mem. Inst. Chem; Inst. Chem. Eng. Composition of petroleum; semi-carbazide, hydrazine and hydantoin derivatives; boilerfeed water; military chemicals. Address: 830 S. Shaver St, Pasadena, Tex. 77502.

RUGELEY, DR. E(DWARD) W(ELLS), b. Matagorda, Tex, Dec. 14, 96; m. 24, 38: c. 2. ORGANIC CHEMISTRY. B.A., Austin Col, 17; M.A, Texas, 21; Ph.D. (org. chem), Yale, 23. From res. chemist to asst. works mgr, Tubize Chatillon Corp, 23-34; res. chemist & supt, res. & develop. dept, Union Carbide Chem. Co, 34-49, tech. dir. textile fibers, 49-60, sr. tech. adv, 60-62; RETIRED. U.S.N., 18-19. AAAS; Chem.

Soc. Synthetic textile fibers. Address: 1006 Highland Rd, Charlestown, W.Va. 25302.

LANDOLT, PROF. G(EORGE) L(IFRED), b. Somerville, Tex, May 19, 02; m. 28; c. 2. CHEMISTRY. A.B., Austin Col, 23, A.M., 26; Ph.D. (chem), Pittsburgh, 30. Instr. CHEM, Austin Col, 24-26; Pittsburgh, 26-28; head dept, S. Park Jr. Col, 28-31; instr, AUSTIN COL, 31-46, PROF, 46-, head dept, 34-57, v. pres. & treas, 36-47. Dean, sci. col, Tunghai, 57-60; vis. prof, Taiwan Prov. Chung Hsing Univ, 63-66. Consult, Hardwicke-Etter Mortar Shell Plant, 42-45. Chem. Soc. Preparation, manufacture and activity of organic flotation reagents. Address: Dept. of Chemistry, Austin College, Sherman, Tex. 75090.

ARMENDT, DR. BRADSHAW F, 102 Tanglewood Dr, Baytown, Texas. ORGANIC CHEMISTRY. Somerville, Texas, Jan. 12, 99; m. 29; c. 2. A.B. Austin Col, 21, M.A, 22; M.S, Vanderbilt, 23; Illinois, 24; Ph.D. (org. chem) Texas, 32. Head dept. chem, Austin Col, 24-34; res. chemist, Humble Oil & Ref. Co, 36-38, res. specialist, 38-62, sr. res. specialist, 62-63; RETIRED. Chem. Soc. Electrolytic reduction of organic compounds; nitrogen compounds in petroleum refining; polymers.

TOWNLEY, DR. R(OBERT) W(ILLIAM), b. Lampasas, Tex, Apr. 28, 07; m. 29; c. 2. CHEMISTRY. B.A, Austin Col, 29; M.A. Texas, 35, Ph.D. (phys. chem), 38. Anal. chemist, First Tex. Chem. Mfg. Co, 31-33; from asst. to instr. chem, Texas, 35-37; bacteriologist, State Dept. Health, Tex, 37-38, chemist, 38-39, chief chemist, 39-41; res. chemist, Humble Oil & Ref. Co, 41-42; indust. hyg. engr, U.S. Pub. Health Serv, Md, 42-44; res. chemist, Ciba Pharmaceut. Prod, Inc, N.J., 44-50; assoc. prof. chem, Drew, 50-54; head res. dept, Personal Prod. Corp, 54-57; DIR, TOWNLEY RES. & CONSULT, 57- Assoc. prof, Fairleigh Dickinson, 58-59. Fel. AAAS; Chem. Soc; Pub. Health Asn; Soc. Microbiol; Indust. Hyg. Asn; Air Pollution Control Asn; Asn. Consult. Chemists & Chem. Eng; N.Y. Acad. Sci. Foods; drugs; water, corrosion; industrial hygiene; biological, medicinal and microbial chemistry, antibiotics; microbiology; analytical methods; physical chemistry applications. Address: Townley Research & Consulting, 470 Long Hill Rd, Gillette, N.J. 07933.

SMITH, DR. PERRIN G(ARY), b. Bowie, Tex, Sept. 3, 12; m. 37. ORGANIC CHEMISTRY. B.S, Austin Col. 34; Ph.D. (org. chem), Northwestern, 38. Abbott Labs. fel, Northwestern, 38-40; chemist, res. dept, Sharples Chems, Inc, Mich, 40-44, develop. dept, Pa, 44!54, asst. to pres, 54-56; asst. to gen. mgr, indust. div, PENNSALT CHEMS. CORP, Phila, 56!65, PROJ. EVALUATOR, Eng. DEPT, KING OF PRUSSIA, 65- Chem. Soc. Amines; rubber chemicals; pharmaceutical intermediates. Address: R.D. 2, Chester Springs, Pa. 19425.

MERS, PROF. ROBERT G(EORGE), b. Merryville, La, Oct. 30, 14; m. 40; c. 4. PHYSICAL CHEMISTRY. B.A, Austin Col, 34; M.A. Texas, 36, Ph.D, 40. Chemist, State Liquor Bd, Tex, 39-40; head, sci. dept, McMurray Col, 40-41; instr. CHEM, Tex. West. Col, 41-43, asst. prof. 43-45; Arkansas, 45-46; assoc. prof, Northwest. State Col. La, 46-48; prof, E. Tex. State Col, 48-51; PROF, LAMAR STATE COL. TECH, 51-, head dept, 51-62. Res. assoc, Oak Ridge Nat. Sci. Found-Atomic Energy Cmn. res. participant, Tufts, 62; Nat. Sci. Found. res. grant, North Carolina, 64. Chem. Soc. Densities and deviation coefficients of gases; partial molal volumes and activities of binary solutions. Address: Dept. of Chemistry, Lamar State College of Technology, Beaumont, Tex. 77704.

DENNIS, PROF. JOE, Texas Technological College, Lubbock, Texas. BIOLOGICAL CHEMISTRY. Sherman, Texas, Dec. 5, 11; m. 35; c. 3. A.B, Austin Col, 33; A.M., Texas, 37; Ph.D. (biol. chem), 42. Tutor biol. chem, sch. med, Texas, 34-36, instr, 36-38; CHEM, TEXAS TECH. COL, 38-41, asst. prof, 41-45, assoc. prof, 45-47, PROF, 47- HEAD DEPT, 50- AAAS; Chem. Soc. Protein denaturation; blood potassium and calcium.

LACY, DR. ROBERT M, b. Coalgate, Okla, Aug. 27, 13; m. 38; c. 2. ORGANIC CHEMISTRY. A.B. Austin Col, 36, A.M, 37; fel, Oklahoma, 41, Ph.D. (org. chem), 43. Lab. asst. chem, Austin Col, 36-37; lab. instr, Oklahoma, 37-42; engr, works lab, Gen. Elec. Co, 42-44, head chem. sect, 44-46, tech. asst. to mgr. works lab, 46-48, mgr. labs, 48-53; tech. dir, Mich. Chrome & Chem. Co, 53-58; mem. staff, adv. eng. & major appliance lab, Gen. Elec. Co, Ky, 59-65; TECH. MGR, PARKER RUST PROOF DIV, HOOKER CHEM.

CORP, 66- Chem. Soc; Soc. Test. & Mat; Soc. Plastics Eng. Polarographic analysis; organic and chemical conversion coatings; plating; chemical engineering. Address: Parker Rust Proof Division Hooker Chemical Corp, 2177 E. Milwaukee Ave, Detroit, Mich. 48211.

ROBERTS, DR. ROYSTON M(URPHY), b. Sherman, Tex, June 11, 18; m. 43; c. 4. ORGANIC CHEMISTRY. B.A., Austin Col, 40, hon. D.Sc, 65; M.A, Illinois, 41, Ph.D. (org. chem), 44. Asst, cmt. med. res, Off. Sci. Res. & Develop, Illinois, 43-45; res. chemist, Merck & Co, 45-46; fel, California, Los Angeles, 46!47; asst. prof. CHEM, TEXAS, 47-51, assoc. prof, 51-61, PROF, 61- Fel, Petrol. Res. Fund, Zurich, 59-60; summer vis. prof, Indiana, 61. Consult. AAAS; Am. Chem. Soc; Brit. Chem. Soc. Organic synthesis; reaction mechanisms; reactions of ortho esters; imidic ester and amidines; new Friedel-Crafts chemistry; thermal rearrangement reactions. Address: Dept. of Chemistry, University of Texas, Austin, Tex. 78712.

## The Biology Department at Austin College

A SEPARATE Department of Biology was established by the Board of Trustees in 1918. Because of World War I conditions, all courses were taught by a senior student, H. Lockett Stewart.

In 1919 Dr. W. L. Porter, a returned missionary from India, joined the faculty and established the first full course in geology. Every Saturday for two years he and members of his classes, including the writer, scoured the creeks and river beds of North Texas and Southern Oklahoma for fossils. This valuable collection is housed today in Moody Science Building.

Professor J. B. Moorman came from Randolph Macon College to take over Geology and Biology when Dr. Porter went to Davidson College in 1921.

Professor Prentiss E. Reid came to take over the Biology Department in 1925 when Moorman went into the insurance business.

Prof. J. B. Moorman returned in 1928 and continued teaching geology and biology until 1964 when he became Emeritus

Professor. Prof. Moorman was also Dean of the College from 1937 to 1960.

Dr. Monroe D. Bryant, a 1927 alumnus, under Professor Reid, became the first Austin College graduate to head the Biology Department in 1947.

J. Forrest Bryant, a 1941 graduate, joined the staff in 1948 and Dr. Wardlow Howard McCarley, a 1948 alumnus, became Professor of Zoology in 1961. The latter three were joined by Dr. Milford Cundiff in 1964, Karl W. Haller in 1965, Jack Pierce in 1966, and Dr. H. Neil Buscher in 1968. These last seven compose the biology staff at the close of the Twelfth Decade. J. Forrest Bryant presently is also Registrar of the College.

Several hundred Biology majors have entered the field of medicine and it would be difficult to find a town in the Southwest that does not have at least one doctor or dentist who got his pre-medical training at Austin College. Another large group is teaching in high schools and colleges. Many others are doing research for governmental agencies.

## Physics Department

THE Physics Department, organized in 1918, was taught by H. Lockett Stewart until 1921. Dr. H. M. Sharp, a Johns-Hopkins graduate, became professor of Physics in 1921 and was succeeded in 1924 by Dr. W. W. Steffey, also a Johns-Hopkins graduate. Dr. Lloyd E. Gourley became Chairman of the Physics Department in 1960 when Dr. Steffey became Emeritus Professor. Dr. Mary Foulks Gourley (Mrs. Lloyd Gourley) has been associated with her husband in the Physics Department during that time. This man and wife team were joined by Dr. Larry Robinson, Ph.D. from Virginia Polytechnic Institute in 1969 and presently constitute the Physics staff.

Most of the Physics majors have joined industrial firms or research groups. Notably among these is George Boyd, B.A. 1930 author of *Autoradiography*, Academic Press 1955. Dr. Billy Jack Marshall, B.A. 1958, is Professor of Physics at Texas Technological University, Dr. Lyndon Taylor, B.A. 1951, is a Professor in the Engineering Department of the University of Texas. These two latter received their Ph.D.

degrees from Rice University. J. T. Krattiger, B.A. 1938, has been teaching at Southeastern College of Oklahoma. Dr. Robert R. Landolt, B.A. 1959, received the Ph.D. degree from Purdue University, where he is Professor of Bionucleonics.

Sam Brooks McLane, B.A. 1942, is teaching at Pennsylvania State College.

## Computer Science

HOBILTZELLE Computer Center—The Hoblitzelle Computer Center, named in honor of Mr. Karl S. Hoblitzelle of Dallas, was first established on the Austin College campus during the construction of Moody Science Center. The Center is now located on the first floor of the new science complex.

The Center houses an IBM 1620 digital computing system and serves as a laboratory for students to do programming and operation of the computer. The computer is used as an integral part of several other courses and research activities. Professor David McBlain is Director of the Center.

## The First Law School in Texas

IT was natural for Austin College to add a law department to its educational endeavors. More than a third of the trustees were lawyers when on October 31, 1854, three were appointed: "A committee of three whose duty it shall be to inquire into the propriety of erecting a law department. . . to report the probable expense for additional buildings, for a law library, number of professors necessary in such a department and probable extent of patronage it would receive."

Henderson Yoakum, the Texas Historian, Abner Lipscomb, Judge of the Supreme Court of Texas and Judge James A. Baker of Huntsville were the three who brought in a favorable report. The Law School was officially opened for student registration in April 1855. Another member of the Board, Royal T. Wheeler, also one of the three Judges of the Supreme Court of Texas, resigned from the Board in order to become Professor of Law in the new department. The other lawyers on the Board of Trustees at the time were Sam Houston,

D. D. Atchison. Texas has further honored these men by naming Houston, Lipscomb, Yoakum and Wheeler counties after them. Anson Jones, the statesman and last President of the Republic of Texas, along with Wheeler and Lipscomb, were honored by having county seats as well as counties named after them.

The law department flourished, graduating four men with the Bachelor of Law degrees in 1856, the first law degrees earned in Texas. They were Joab Banton, Benton Randolph, L. O. Black and L. E. Trezvant. Banton and Black had the distinction of being the first men to earn the Bachelor of Arts degrees in Texas (1854). Banton and Randolph became trustees of the College and District Judges.

The law school as a separate department was short lived. The sudden deaths of Judge Lipscomb and Henderson Yoakum in 1856, the failure to get expected financial aid from the Texas legislature by Dr. Daniel Baker, and his death in 1857, caused instruction preparatory for the legal profession to be phased into the regular curriculum. The strong interest in law was evidenced by the fact that nine of the twenty-three men who graduated prior to the Civil War chose the bar for a career. At least six others, whose college training was interrupted by the war before graduating, became lawyers, and more than one-fourth of all the graduates of the first five decades entered the legal profession.

In an address given by Judge Francis Charles Hume (B.A. 1859), before the Alumni Association of the College June 3, 1903 (*Austin College Quarterly,* Oct. 1903) in speaking of A.C. early alumni said: "Some became judges of our most important courts of original and general jurisdiction—as Joab Banton, Benton Randolph, Normal Kittrell, C. Fred Tucker, Lewis B. Hightower, J. M. Smither and John B. Rector, who at the time of his death presided over a federal court in Texas. H. H. Boone became Attorney General of the State of Texas 1880-1882." Norman G. Kittrell was Judge of the Commission of Appeals Court Dec. 1, 1919 to Dec. 1, 1921.

When the College moved to Sherman interest in law did not slacken. Jacob Fullenwider and H. H. Boone (M.A. and B.A. 1881); Walter Vinson (B.A. 1890); Fred Lowrance (B.A. 1893); Gordon Boone (B.A. 1894); George Butte (B.A. 1895); Joseph Lockett, Oscar Lusk and Will Vinson (1896); A. G.

Barton, John Files, J. L. McCall, Veris McInnes, John Moore (B.A. 1899); Ewing Carter, Harry Cern, John Martin (B.A. 1900) — one third of the graduates up to 1900 chose the legal profession. During the last seven decades the College has trained a host of men for the bar, many of whom have also served on the Austin College Board of Trustees.

For a number of years Ruel C. Walker has served on the bench as Associate Justice of the Supreme Court of Texas.

## Fruit of the Vine

DURING the first five decades 1849-1899 Austin College granted 87 Bachelor of Arts, 11 Master of Arts, 4 Bachelor of Laws, 2 Civil Engineering and 1 Ph.D degrees. Two thirds of these graduates become lawyers or ministers. From 1900 to 1919 the all male college granted 248 more degrees, a total of 352 degrees before women entered the alumni ranks.

In the first year of the Eighth Decade — in the Class of 1920 — two women were graduated: Gladys Cornell Irwin and Lola Belle Perkins Ray. Austin College became co-educational during the First World War in order to have enough students to keep its doors open. Those who advocated going back to men only after the war had little support. Many think the change to coeducational was ultimately to cause the closing of Texas Presbyterian College for women at Milford and the end of Kidd-Key College in Sherman.

Before the end of the Eighth Decade the choice of a profession shifted from law to science. The College began rapidly to produce men of medicine, chemistry and education. Especially did the women graduates choose the fields of education and science, competing exceptionally successfully with the Teachers Colleges of that period.

Albert Sidney Venable was President of Sayre College. A.B. degree in 1889.

Tinsley P. Junkin, B.A. 1893, was twice President of Daniel Baker College.

Edward H. Moseley, B.A. 1896, was President of Oklahoma Presbyterian College.

Dr. Homer P. Rainey was President of Franklin and Marshal and Bucknell before becoming President of Texas University, and later of Stephens College.

Dr. Robert E. Vinson was President of Austin Theological Seminary before becoming President of Texas University and later of Western Reserve. Dr. Thomas W. Currie was President of Austin Theological Seminary from 1920 to 1943.

Dr. Clyde Eagleton and Dr. Edward S. Moseley were Rhodes Scholars; the latter was President of Utah University. Among Seminary Presidents at present are Dr. James I. McCord of Princeton and Dr. David Stitt of Austin Theological College. Rev. Lardner W. Moore, life-time missionary to Japan, organized and became President of Shikoku Christian College. (His grandfather, Dr. H. B. Boude, was President of Austin College 1878-1881).

Numbered among the Junior College Presidents are Dr. Robert G. Landolt of Lees Junior College, Jackson, Kentucky, and John H. Parker, Cooke County Junior College in Gainesville, Texas.

Dr. Truman G. Blocker, world renowned authority on treatment of burns and plastic surgery, is President of the Texas State Medical College at Galveston.

### Summary of Austin College Graduates

| 1849-1876 Huntsville Period | 38 | 1930-1939 | 620 |
|---|---|---|---|
| 1877-1899 | 66 | 1940-1949 | 613 |
| 1900-1909 | 102 | 1950-1959 | 899 |
| 1910-1919 | 146 | 1960-1969 | 1530 |
| 1920-1929 | 329 | | |

Twelve Decades Total 4343

One fourth of the graduates are in the field of education, including ten college, seminary or university presidents; a hundred high school and college athletic directors, a hundred college professors and more than a hundred public school principals and superintendents.

More than five hundred have become doctors, chemists, physicists, biologists, or have entered other branches of science.

Approximately one fourth have entered the business field and three hundred have become ministers or missionaries. Of these latter it is often said that the sun never sets on an Austin College missionary graduate who is not winning souls in foreign fields, for they are serving around the globe.

Of the hundred or so lawyers, ten have become judges, including a Federal Judge, Judge of Supreme Court of the Philippines, Governor of Porto Rico, and Lt. Governor of Texas. Judge Ruel C. Walker is now serving on the bench as Associate Justice of the Supreme Court of Texas.

# GRADUATES BY YEARS

1854   Livingston O. Black
    A.B.; B.L. '56; A.M. '57
    Joab Banton, A.B., B.L. '56;
      A.M. '57

1855   Samuel A. Hume, A.B.

1856   William A. Allen, A.B., A.M. '59
    George W. Davis, A.B., A.M. '59
    James S. Harrison, A.B., A.M.
    L. E. Trezvant, B.S., B.L. '56
    Benton Randolph, B.S., B.L. '56

1857   William Bowles Smither, A.B.

1858   Champion T. Hill, A.B.
    Wm. T. Hill, A.B.

1859   Andrew J. Burke, A.B.
    Francis C. Hume, A.B.
    John T. Hamilton, A.B.
    Samuel Y. Smith, A.B.
    Lewis B. Hightower, A.B.
    Edwin E. Thom, A.B.

1860   Jacob M. Fullinwider, A.B.
    William F. Hardin, A.B.
    Lucius L. Moreland, A.B.
    James H. Murray, A.B.
    Thomas J. Peel, A.B.
    Richard Sims, A.B.

1866   Robert A. McKinney, A.B.

1869   William B. Gillespie, A.B.

1874   William Boyd, A.B.
    William Smith, A.B.

1881   H. H. Boone, A.B., A.M.
    Jacob A. Fullenwider, A.M.

1882   William S. Red, A.B.
    Wm. H. McCullough, A.B.

1883   J. C. Coit, A.B.

1884   Morris Jouvenat, A.B.

1889   W. W. Boone, A.B.
    A. S. Venable, A.B.

1890   Walter Vinson, A.B.

1892   J. P. Hall, A.B.
    W. F. Junkin, A.B. '93 A.M.
    J. K. Thompson, A.B.
    M. K. Thompson, A.B.

1893   T. P. Junkin, A.B.
    E. B. Fincher, A.B. '94 A.M.
    E. S. Lowrance, A.B.
    F. H. Lowrance, A.B.

1894   W. L. Acker, A.B.
    Gordon Boone, A.B.
    R. D. Campbell, A.B.
    Norman S. Cavitt, B.S.

1895   Hugh Gaston King, A.M.
    G. C. F. Butte, A.B., A.M.
      1902
    B. I. Dickey, A.B.
    Wm. P. Dickey, A.B.
    F. E. Fincher, A.B.
    S. J. McFarland, A.B.
    L. E. Selfridge, A.B.
    J. E. Simmons, A.B.
    T. L. Simmons, A.B.
    M. P. Slaughter, A.B.
    Bishop Holmes, B.S.

1896   J. S. Baird, A.B.
O. S. Lusk, A.B.
Peyton Irving Jr., A.B.
E. H. Mosley, A.B.
A. D. Rice, A.B.
R. E. Vinson, A.B.
W. A. Vinson, A.B.
J. L. Lockett, A.B.

1897   B. S. Edrington, A.B.
W. K. Johnson, A.B.
J. C. Stinson, A.B.
G. T. Thompson, Jr. A.B.
Walter Thornton, A.B.
W. D. Mitchell, B.S.
A. G. Thomas, B.S.

1898   Alvie Hardie, A.B.
T. E. Craig, B.S.
C. A. Lanius, B.S.
C. S. Roberts, B.S.

1899   A. M. Barton, B.S.
B. B. B. Brown, B.S.
Guy H. Evans, B.S.
Veris E. McInnis, B.S.
W. Fred Galbraith, A.B.
F. P. Files, A.B.
J. L. L. McCall, A.B.
J. B. Files, A.B.
J. M. Sedgwick, A.B.
J. R. Moore, A.B.
J. A. Williams, A.B.

1900   E. N. Bradshaw, A.B.
E. E. Carter, A.B.
Motte Martin, A.B.
J. R. Stitt, A.B.
W. N. Scott, A.B.
H. G. Cern, B.S.

F. B. Spangler, A.B.
J. W. Wilson, B.S.
J. A. Martin, B.S.

1901   T. O. Perrin, M.A.
E. G. Bell, B.A.
J. L. Read, B.A.
A. W. Kinnard, B.A.
D. P. Brown, B.S.
E. E. McInnis, B.S.
J. B. McFerrin, B.S.
Hoxie H. Thompson, B.S.
H. W. Head, B.S.

1902   C. A. Bissell, B.S.
W. H. Long, B.S.
W. A. McLeod, B.A.
G. C. Moore, B.A.
J. R. West, B.A.
G. L. Smith, B.A.
E. G. Peel, M.A.

1903   T. M. Bogie, B.A.
J. D. Furrh, B.S.
F. E. Hudson, B.S.
T. R. Ludlow, B.A.
E. R. Sims, B.A.
L. C. Smith, B.S.
J. W. Vinson, B.A.
W. J. Kibbe, B.A.
L. W. Roper, B.A.

1904   Nathan Cox, B.S.
Clyde B. Moore, B.A.
Wm. L. Tillman, B.A.

1905   J. P. Cox, B.S.
C. C. Carsner, B.A.
C. L. Cleveland, B.A.

J. H. Ewing, B.A.
W. B. Fitzpatrick, B.A.
B. D. D. Greer, B.A.
H. L. Head, B.S.
T. P. Perkins, B.S.
O. C. Smith, B.S.
W. T. Read, B.A., M.A., 1908
Dewitt Waldo, B.A.
P. E. Wallace, B. A.
Wm. Fred Galbraith, M.A.
L. O. Cunningham, B.A.
C. B. Moore, B.A.

1906 J. D. Blanding, B.A.
F. H. Shaw, B.S.
G. C. Klein, B.S.
R. A. McCurdy, B.A.
G. M. Worthington, B.S.
Henry L. Young, B.S.
W. S. Taylor, B.A.
W. A. Venable, B.A., M.A. '27
C. L. Wilson, Jr. B.S.

1907 F. E. Chamberlain, B.A.
T. W. Currie, B.A.
F. S. Henderson, B.A.
G. H. Lang, B.A.
W. D. Morrell, B.A.
M. B. Pitts, B.A.
O. L. Smith, B.A.
O. O. Touchstone, B.A.
E. V. Moore, B.A.

1908 J. H. Bell, B.A.
W. L. Evans, B.S.
E. L. Fulton, B.A.
J. G. Gregg, B.A.
J. F. Hardie, B.A.
C. L. Hufsmith, B.A.
R. L. Jetton, B.A.
W. H. Lankford, Jr. B.S.

Andrew McCurdy, B.A.
H. R. McLean, B.A.
F. A. Moore, B.A.
J. W. Moss, B.A.
A. H. Spence, B.A.
A. M. Thompson, B.A.
E. A. Lindsay, B.A.

1909 S. R. Coleman, B.A.
R. E. Henderson, B.A.
J. B. Hixson, B.A.
J. E. Ingram, B.A.
C. D. Morrell, B.S.
R. L. Owen, B.A.
E. R. Parker, B.S.
J. G. M. Ramsay, B.A.
J. E. Robinson, B.A.
C. P. Sillman, B.A.
T. C. Vinson, B.A.
H. L. Hall, B.A.
L. A. Wright, B.A., M.A. '10

1910 J. K. Alexander, B.A.
H. O. Blanding, B.A.
R. W. Burchard, B.A.
Clyde Eagleton, B.A.
W. R. Hall, B.A.
J. W. Hickman, B.A.
C. W. Rhea, B.A.
W. A. Riall, B.A.

1911 Clyde Eagleton, M.A.
Walter Ewing Long, M.A.
J. Harvey Gillespie, B.S.
Wm. M. Anderson, Jr., B.A.
J. William Boyle, Jr., B.A.
Roy F. Cleveland, B.A.
James B. Davis, B.A.
Robert F. Gribble, B.A.
J. M. Lewis, B.A.
W. F. McElroy, B.A.

Douglas F. Mebane, B.A.
Edward S. Moseley, B.A.
Charles S. Ramsay, B.A.
J. C. Ramsay, B.A.
Guy T. Roginson, B.A.
Julian S. Sleeper, B.A.
Charlton H. Storey, B.A.
Sidney C. Venable, B.A.
Conway T. Wharton, B.A.
Lawrence H. Wharton, B.A.
Stanley White, B.A.

1912 C. A. Bryan, Jr., B.S.
A. L. Doggett, B.A.
C. K. Holloway, B.S.
C. H. Lang, B.A.
W. C. McDonald, B.A.
J. M. McFarlane, B.A.
S. J. McMurry, Sr., B.A.
John McWilliams, B.A.
Ed D. Mills, B.S.
J. O. Moseley, B.A.
T. H. Pollard, B.A.
B. Smith, B.A.
A. T. Stewart, B.A.
E. W. Thompson, B.A., M.A. '13
D.R. Venable, B.A.

1913 L. D. Amis, B.A.
A. L. Burke, B.A., M.A., 1917
W. P. Clyce, B.A.
Hugh Fitspatrick, B.A.
W. II. Foster, B.A.
Alexander Gray, B.A., M.A. '14
E. S. Gregg, B.A.
W. R. Gregg, B.A.
B. M. Leecraft, B.A.
G. A. McCall, B.A., M.A. 1914
J. R. McElroy, B.A.
S. B. Mclane, B.A.

E. F. Montgomery, B.A.
Robert Morris, B.A.
J. A. Owen, B.A.
C. C. Parks, B.A.
M. A. Smith, B.A.

1914 A. A. Aldrich, B.A.
H. G. Anderson, B.A.
R. B. Anderson, B.A.
Edward Biggs, B.A.
B. T. Brown, B.S.
M. A. Bryan, B.A., M.A. 1915
T. M. Cunningham, B.A.
E. E. Diggs, B.A.
R. M. Donnell, B.A.
W. C. Earhart, B.A., M.A. 1915
H. C. Evans, Jr. B.A.
J. F. Evans, Jr. B.A.
Kenneth Fowler, B.A.
G. F. Gaither, Jr. B.A.
A. M. Gribble, Jr. B.A.
T. M. Gribble, B.A.
R. P. Guitart, B.S.
A. G. Hopkins, B.A.
J. W. Messick, B.A.
J. E. McKinney, B.A.
J. N. McLeod, B.A.

1915 A. P. Caldwell, B.A.
F. H. Clement, B.A.
C. I. Coffin, B.A.
E. Edrington, B.A.
G. M. Engle, B.A.
H. C. Fowler, B.A.
F. J. Iiams, B.A.
F. A. Ramsey, B.A.
H. F. Wager, B.A.
F. F. Wier, B.A.
W. E. Williams, Jr. B.A.

L. S. Winston, B.A.
C. P. Owens, B.A.

1916   J. G. Anderson B.A.
M. S. Brame, B.A.
Clem Calhoun, B.A.
H. E. Chesley, B.A.
M. W. Comfort, B.A.
H. L. Durham, B.A.
E. M. Ellison, B.A., M.A. 1917
G. H. Hurst, B.A.
S. W. McMillan, B.A.
L. J. Sherrill, B.A.
A. G. Sneed, B.A.

1917   V. R. Aston, B.A.
R. C. Bell, B.A.
S. T. Bowers, B.A.
J. W. Carroll, B.S.
A. L. Crable, B.A.
J. M. Currie, B.A.
R. G. Lowe, B.A.
R. S. Mallard, B.A.
L. L. McCutchen, B.A.
R. L. Morrison, B.A.
F. P. Moss, B.A., M.A. 1926
E. W. Rugeley, B.A.

1918   J. F. Anderson, B.A.
D. C. Butler, B.A.
R. D. Erwin, B.A.
R. C. Holland, B.A.
L. B. Hughes, B.A.
R. K. McCall, B.A.
W. A. McElroy, B.A.
Boude C. Moore, B.A.
Lardner W. Moore, B.A.,
   M.A. 1919
R. R. Wilson, B.A.

1919   R. E. Hooker, B.A.

P. C. Keith, B.A.
J. C. Paxton, B.A.
H. P. Rainey, B.A.
C. A. Robinson, B.A.
H. L. Stewart, B.A.
E. D. Walker, B.A.

1920   Gladys Cornell Irwin, B.A.
H. H. Cunningham, B.A.
Shem Cunningham, B.A.
J. L. Dickson, B.A., M.A. '21
Jonathan Edwards, B.A.
E. D. Grant, B.A.
R. V. Guthrie, B.A., M.A. '21
C. K. Holsapple, B.A.,
   M.A. '22
W. H. McCarley, Jr., B.A.
O. K. Holsapple, B.A.
F. M. Hudson, B.A.
J. B. Parks, B.A.
Lola B. Perkins Ray, B.A.
F. M. Powell, B.A.
C. M. Stallings, B.A.

1921   Brad Armendt, B.A.,
   M.A. '22
E. T. Austin, B.A.
M. L. Baker, B.A.
Volney Cavitt, B.A.
Grace Eagleton Moore, B.A.
J. G. Estes, B.A.
T. E. Goff, B.A.
F. H. Leslie, B.A.
J. D. Miller, B.A., M.A. '22
C. A. Moore, B.A.
Kathryn Pitman, B.A.
L. M. Rennolds, B.A.
P. D. Robinson, B.A.
W. R. Smith, B.A.
S. N. Trevino, B.A., M.A.
   '22

1922 W. B. Chapman, B.A.
   B. B. Cobb, B.A.
   V. E. Hebel, B.A.
   E. L. Foshee, B.A.
   J. R. Freeman, B.A.
   J. S. Kimble, B.A., M.A. '28
   A. S. Hurst, B.A.
   R. A. Johnston, Jr. B.A.
   E. J. Dysart, B.A.
   K. M. Larimore, B.A.
   H. L. Lowrance, B.A., M.A. '27
   R. A. Morehart, B.A.
   Alma Peck, B.A., M.A. '30
   J. C. Pyle, M.A.
   P. M. Robinson, B.A.
   R. S. Rodriguez, B.A.
   Sibyl Rudasil McCrary, B.A.
   F. L. Shannon, B.A., M.A. '26
   J. B. Shaw, B.A., M.A. '25
   J. L. Spears, B.A.
   B. N. Taliaferro, B.A.
   Emma Thomas Thornton, B.A.
   W. W. Tenney, B.A., M.A. '23
   Vallie Calhoun Griffin, B.A.,
    M.A.
   Margaret Vest Dysart, B.A.

1923 Rilla Armstrong, B.A.
   W. C. Bain, B.A.
   Mary King Boyd, B.A.
   Geor. W. Case, B.A.
   B. C. Cooksey, B.A.
   James Creighton, B.A.
   U. S. Dalmont, B.A.
   R. C. Dickey, B.A.
   L. B. Eastham, B.A., M.A. '28
   W. H. Fuller, B.A.
   Jewell Hardy, B.A.
   Lena Kidd, B.A.
   G. L. Landolt, B.A.M.A. '26
   W. G. Murray, B.A.

   R. D. Lauderdale, B.A., M.A.
   W. E. Shaw, B.A.
   M. D. Stewart, B.A.
   R P W. Tenney, B.A.
   W. F. Tenney, B.A.
   Grace Vest Hunter, B.A.

1924 T. P. Baker, B.A.
   Grace Bitner, B.A.
   Orbia Blanton, B.A.
   Ruth Caudry, C. A.
   Bessie Cunningham, B.A.
   C. C. Duke, B.A.
   Elizabeth Eagleton Hurst, B.A.
   Nat Edmondson, B.A.M.A. '25
   T. R. Elder, B.A.
   Floy E. Boker, B.A.
   Ivy F. Fain, B.A.M.A. '26
   H. W. Greenup, B.A.
   S. C. Guthrie, B.A.
   E. J. Hunter, B.A.
   Gladys Holliday, B.A.
   Ruth Loftus, B.A.M.A. '25
   J. W. Madden, B.A.
   R. B. Newman, B.A.
   Samye P. Newman, B.A.
   Louise P. Martin, B.A.
   Frank B. Rott, B.A.
   Dorothy Scarborough, B.A.
   W. L. Scott, Jr., B.A.
   Noel Shaw, B.A.
   R. A. Torres, B.A.
   Hattie M. Wharton, B.A.

1925 G. R. Adkins, M.A.
   Jacqueline Bailey B.A.M.A. '28
   S. A. Blackburn, M.A.
   W. W. Bondurant, Jr., B.A.
   B. A. Boyd, B.A.
   J. R. Brooks, M.A.
   O. A. Burk, M.A.

C. E. Burney, B.A.
R. R. Dixon, B.A.
H. D. Fields, B.A.
Alberta Fitzpatrick, B.A.
W. L. Golightly, B.A.
P. D. Hanna, B.A.
John M. Hardy, B.A.
J. B. Head, B.A.
John H. Hill, B.A.M.A. '26
Elizabeth Jones, B.A.
D. F. Kerbow, B.A.
Walter Lazenby, B.A., MA.A '30
F. A. Lloyd, B.A.
Beulah McCaughey, B.A.
R. L. McCutchan, B.A.
Maurine M. Graham, B.A.
C. D. Poe, B.A.
J. B. Polka, B.A.
G. O. Reeves, B.A.
J. S. Robertson, B.A.M.A. '26
J. H. Sheppard, M.A.
R. L. Smith, B.A.
R. B. Taylor, B.A.
D. P. Thompson, B.A.
Frances W. Grady, B.A.
Bettye Boyle, M.A.

1926   J. D. Anderson, B.A.
Lela Armstrong, B.A.
D. W. Bagwill, Jr., B.A.
Augusta Beauchamp, B.A.
J. D. Cox, B.A.
Willie L. Dickerman, B.A.
Elizabeth Council, B.A.M.A. '30
R. L. Currie, B.A.
Dorothy Fincher, B.A.
Adele F. Tucker, B.A.
Marguerite Fletcher, B.A.
Henry Frnka, B.A.
Tom Gallagher, B.A.
J. S. Gilliland, B.A.

N. W. Harris, B.A.
Merrill May, B.A.
Nancy McElreath, B.A.
W. O. Miller, B.A.
L. L. Mode, B.A.
Odell Morgan, B.A.
R. A. Partlow, B.A.
Mary Sanford, B.A.
Harold Schmitzer, B.A.
W. E. Scott, Jr., B.A.
Aline Smith, B.A.
D. E. Temple, Jr., B.A.
J. G. Varner, Jr., B.A.
Marguerite Weems, B.A.M.A.
   '27
Small Weems, B.A.MA. '27
Pauline Yeagley, B.A.

1927   H. C. Akers, B.A.
F. D. Aston, B.A.
T. A. Baker, B.A.
Margaret Bloebaum, B.A.
A. E. Boyd, B.A.
M. D. Bryant, B.A.
Venita Carroll, B.A.
J. W. Bowles, B.A.
Marian Cox, B.A.
H. O. Crawford, B.A.
Varonne Darnell, B.A.
O. L. Dial, B.A.
Verde Dickey, B.A.
Evorie Dillingham, M.A.
Doris E. Landolt, B.A.
Frances Drane Woodward,
   B.A.
Nina Ferrill, B.A.
M. E. Fincher, B.A.
Wm. Gordon, B.A.
Genoveva Hampton, B.A.
Virginia Hanks, B.A.
C. M. Hill, B.A.

Oscar Hutt, B.A.
Lois Jenkins, B.A., M.A.
Gladys Lewin, B.A.
R. G. Lloyd, B.A.
Anna McCampbell, B.A.
Grant McKown, B.S.
T. H. Miller, B.A.
Arne J. Moore, B.A.
Mary L. Moore, B.A.
Ruth Neill, B.A.
J. T. Nelson, B.A.
A. S. Noble, Jr., B.A.

B. Louise Noble, B.A.
Fay Noble, B.A.
Marshall Patterson, B.A.
Virginia Read, B.A.
Maudell Rue, B.A.
C. W. Solomon, B.A.
Rex Strickland, B.A.
Mildred T. Williams, B.A.
C. D. Wallace, B.A.
Frances Werline, B.A.
T. L. Wren, B.A., M.A. '28

## Master of Arts

### 1928

Jacqueline Bailey
Edmonia Elizabeth Clyce
Luther Eastham
Frank R. Hughes
James Smith Kimble

Charles Denison Mercer
Walter Clifton Nash
Richard Nathaniel Price
Thomas Lovell Wrenn

## Bachelor of Arts

Paul Douglas Andrews
Leila Elizabeth Bailey
Maggie Correll Barganier
Ann Louise Benzel
George William Blair
Theodore R. Bomar
Weldon Brown
Andrew Benjamin Byers
George Edward Cauthen
Molloy Oden Cockerham
Octavia Evelyn Copley
Ellen Constance Crook
Eugene Campbell Elder
Dorothy Clare Flannery
Alexander Gullett
Velma Gwyn
Joseph Neill Harling

Haskell Edmone Hestand
Ralph Edwin Hightower
Charles Allen Lingo
Christopher Livingston
Fred Lee McFadden
Bonnie Jane Maxey
Selma Morgan
Delia Mildred Morgan
Walter Clifton Nash
Lillian Neathery
Wilmer Regin Park
Cora Glynn Patterson
Verda Mae Poindexter
Richard Nathaniel Price
Arthur Carson Rubey, Jr.
Edgar Savage
Eula Nelle Scott

John William Stormont
Margie Erline Taylor
Mrs. Vera P. Vaden
Floyd Wharton

Florian Marion Wheat
Bertie Lee Williams
Mrs. S. W. Yeury

## Master of Arts

### 1929

Paul Tyler Brown
George E. Cannon

Otis Lee Hilliard
Gilbert Irwin

## Bachelor of Arts

Donald Adelbert Angus
Florence Arnspiger
Lloyd Duke Aston
Eugene L. Bailey
James Sydney Bargainer
Truman Graves Blocker
George Addison Boyd
Neal Boyd
J. Stratton Brock
Thelma Louise Brown
Mary Connor Bruce
Duer Burton
George E. Cannon
Mary Evelyn Etchison
Lee Sidney Files, Jr.
Lois May Fincher
Winona Helene Fincher
Alton Ray Francis
Willie Greene

Clyde Lamar Houk
Sarah Frances Irving
Inez Jackson
Jenny Aline Lathrop
Everett Bryan Lewis
Wm. Charles Malloy, Jr.
Charles Vastine Rice
Anna Lou Smith
John Richard Smith
Frank Moore Sporer
Arthur N. Springall
Lawrence Irving Stell
Thomas H. Stiff
David Malachi Tate
Frank Mathis Taylor
Wilson Batey Temple
Rayburn Thompson
Robert Wm. Townley
Wayne Walter Welch

## Master of Arts

### 1930

Ellen Crook Armendt
Elizabeth Council
George Addison Boyd
Joseph Wilson Evans

Clark O. Hitt
Walter Lazenby, Jr.
Lyman Donovan Robinson
Mrs. Alma Peck Rutherford

## Bachelor of Arts

Edith Claire Adamson
Amy E. Adrian
Harvard Arthur Anderson
Harry Houston Bidwell
Vannie Marie Bimmerman
Tommy Joe Bradley
Charles Edward Roi Cameron
James Delmar Canon
Everett J. Cappleman
Clem Milburn Carrithers
Iva Estelle Carter
Vivian Robison Clary
Edna Baucom Cornell
Alice L. Craig
Clyde Crimm
Mildred Leuvenia Davis
Sara Garner Drane
Walter Hugh Drane, Jr.
Mrs. Mattie Baucom Elliott
Ernest Leon Farr
F. Marion Files
Alvis Mathew Gaddis
Herman S. Griffin
Leora Guinn
Julia Hayes
Mauldine Graham Hayes
Mrs. E. Hillingsworth
Earl B. Hunt
Fred W. Hunter

Harold Cooper Hunter
Ida Juanita Lankford
William P. Lazenby
John W. McMurry, Jr.
W. Crawford Mearns
Rosemary Meidl
Israel Barnes Milam
Edward A. Miller
Ben H. Moore
Frances Katherine Morris
Jesse T. Muse, Jr.
James Furman Ownbey
Lewis Wallace Pearsey
Lyman Donovan Robinson
Ina Rollins
George Lawrence Rutherford
Tassie Rollins Scott
Cleovis Clifton Smith
John Calvin Solomon
William Johnson Teel
Ruth Leighton Tenney
Mary Alice Terry
Adele Townley
Park Street Wharton
Clara Whitehurst
Percy Earle Worley
Homer H. Young
Morgan Martin Young

## 1931

Mary Connor Bruce, M.A.
Paul William Goff, M.A.
Mrs. Clark C. Haley, M.A.
Mary M. Moore, M.A.
Jessee E. Moxley, M.A.
Minna Klopp Parrott, M.A.
Arthur N. Springall, M.A.
Mary Alice Terry, M.A.

Leora Guinn, M.A.
Thomas Michael Murphy, M.A.
Fay Noble, M.A.
Katherine Estelle Smith, M.A.
Pauline Yeagley, M.A.
Clyce W. Aston, B.A.
Margaret E. Belden, B.A.
Len Spears Allen, B.A.

Herbert S. Bonney, Jr., B.A.
Charles Bruno, B.A.
Fred I. Cairns, Jr., B.A.
Charles E. R. Cameron, B.A.
Vivian Robinson Clary, B.A.
Nathan Albert Cox, Jr., B.A.
Byron A. Crocker, B.A.
Ruth E. Davis, B.A.
Dan C. Deffenbach, B.A.
Ann O. Dickerson, B.A.
Margaret L. Donoho, B.A.
Willis Powell Duff, B.A.
Herbert Paine Edmundson,
   B.A.
Thomas B. Edwards, B.A.
Frances Louise Farr, B.A.
Louise Fuller, B.A.
Mary Larene George, B.A.
Naoma E. Giles, B.A.
Madeline E. Goodson, B.A.
George C. Haggard, B.A.
Mrs. Ethel P. Hanning, B.A.
Bryan C. Henderson, B.A.
Chrystine B. Jared, B.A.
Delphine Jordon, B.A.
Annie L. Lane, B.A.
William L. Mitchell, Sr., B.A.

Blanche Mosse, B.A.
Thomas M. Murphy, B.A.
Minna Klopp Parrott, B.A.
Anna L. Patterson, B.A.
Lola L. Redwine, B.A.
Lloyd A. Rodden, B.A.
Paul H. Sanders, B.A.
Chas. Shoultz, B.A.
Clara E. Steedman, B.A.
Clyde Thompson Stephens,
   B.A.
Vivian E. Tate, B.A.
Cora Mae Thornton, B.A.
Jewel Roberts Wheeler, B.A.
Edith L. Yeagley, B.A.
Lora E. Adams, B.A.
Bennie T. Bennett, B.A.
Bertha Campbell, B.A.
John S. Davis, B.A.
Ruby M. Elliott, B.A.
Mrs. Evie C. Hagood, B.A.
Robert F. Jones, B.A.
James M. Leath, B.A.
Lawrence Malloy, B.A.
Fred G. Schwarz, B.A.
James Edward Teel, B.A.
Henry S. Wilson, Jr. B.A.

## 1932

Marquerite F. Davis, M.A.
Willie Greene, M.A.
Leonard Kamerdiener, M.A.
Arthur Edgar Scott, Jr., M.A.
Dovie Maude White, M.A.
Fred O. Wilson, M.A.
Percy E. Worley, M.A.
James W. Webb, M.A.
Lola Leigh Redwine, M.A.
Pearle Arnspiger, B.A.
Jessee Baxter, B.A.
James R. Bullock, B.A.

Rochelle Canon, B.A.
William J. Carter, Jr., B.A.
Jack R. Connelly, Jr., B.A.
George E. Crosthwaite, B.A.
Elizabeth Donnell, B.A.
Joyce E. Ernest, B.A.
George E. Farriss, B.A.
Mattie Mae Ferguson, B.A.
Wilton Baker Flenwharty, B.A.
Jack Frost, B.A.
Bennie Ballow Gant, B.A.
Ena P. Gregory, B.A.

J. W. Hall, B.A.
Samuel B. Hill, B.A.
Frank Sherwood Hutt, B.A.
Jessie B. Key, B.A.
Mary L. Langford, B.A.
James F. Lockerd, B.A.
Wanda Miller, B.A.
Eula H. Morgan, B.A.
Helen M. Morgan, B.A.
John C. Ownbey, B.A.
Ina P. Patterson, B.A.
Ruth Patterson, B.A.
Arthur E. Scott, Jr., B.A.
Frank C. Siddell, B.A.
Francis Springall, B.A.

Helen O. Stallings, B.A.
Franklin E. Swanner, B.A.
James T. Bryant, B.S.
Robert M. Brooks, B.A.
Alice Bryant Brown, B.A.
Mabel M. Cappelman, B.A.
Ralph M. Davis, B.A.
Casper Dale Landolt, B.A.
Robert H. Leath, B.A.
Dorothy Matlock, B.A.
George Matlock, B.A.
Edna Mosse, B.A.
George L. Rutherford, B.A.
R. D. Lauderdale, M.A.
Blanche Mosse, M.A.

## 1933

Victor Adamson, B.A.
Mary Lee Andrews, B.A.
R. B. Aston, Jr., B.A.
Gladys Belden, B.A.
Dorothy Burns Bomar, B.A.
Charles L. Caldwell, B.A.
Dayton Castleman, Jr., B.A.
William A. Cockerell, B.A.
James Cowan, B.A.
Joe P. Cox, Jr., B.A.
Malcolm DeFriend, B.A.
Joe Dennis, B.A.
Dena Lee Durham, B.A.
Horace Eddy, B.A.
Mary Frances Ferguson, B.A.
James Franklin, B.A.
Jesse S. Freels, B.A.
Campbell H. Gillespie, B.A.
Gerthal Guin, B.A.
Fern J. Hampton, B.A.
Curtis L. Hovell, B.A.
Rebecca Joiner, B.A.
Faye Kelley, B.A.
C. B. Kidd, B.A.

Robert T. King, B.A.
Martha E. Lawrence, B.A.
Louise McCoy, B.A.
Geraldine McFarland, B.A.
Robert Manly, Jr., B.A.
Amos Mullenix, B.A.
Virginia Norris, B.A.
James E. Poindexter, B.A.
Cora Ellen Pos, B.A.
Jean Posey, B.A.
Aletha H. Pugh, B.A.
James D. Richardson, B.A.
J. D. Shelton, B.A.
Dorothy Mae Simpson, B.A.
Hesta Smith, B.A.
Norman N. Smith, B.A.
Mary Kathleen Stevenson, B.A.
David L. Stitt, B.A.
Thomas H. Talbot, B.A.
Billye Faye Thompson, B.A.
Ruth May Walker, B.A.
James S. Kone, B.A.
C. S. Roberts, Jr., B.A.

## Master of Arts

Everett J. Cappleman                    Campbell H. Gillespie

## Bachelor of Arts

### 1934

Howard Angus
Kirk M. Beard
Harry Ormsby Blanding
Isabel Brinson
Beatrice Ann Brittain
James Newton Camak
Martha Jane Clayton
Philip Oden Cockerham
William Burch Cooke
Burnett C. Cox
Dimple Edwards
Frances Fain
Ruth Ferguson
Robert M. Firebaugh, Jr.
De L. Gage
Mrs. Rouelle H. Harrell
Hayden Wilson Head
John Douglas Hensley
Roberta Hollingsworth
Douglas Eugene Jones

Robert G. Landolt
Oscar Fitzallen Landry
Lois Lankford
Holly McLemore
Edward Lee Matthews
Robert George Mers
Hal A. Moody
Arthur Lee O'Mary
Tom Petty
Mardell Pumphrey
Reid Spivy, Jr.
Geraldine Elizabeth Steedman
Frederick William Tyler
Martha Stormont
McKee DeWitt Yant
Elizabeth Alexandra Zogheib
Bertha Katherine Yates
Monroe Wilmeth Orenduff
Perrin Gary Smith
Alfred Allen Rolfe

## Master of Arts

Pearle Arnspiger
Kirk M. Beard
Mrs. N. E. Campbell

Martha Elizabeth Lawrence
Martha Stormont

## Bachelor of Arts

### 1935

William Alan Andrews
Norman Earl Barnes
Edward S. Bayless
Robert Haydon Bullock
Virginia Chapman Burgdorff

Mildred Mae Calhoun
Elizabeth Campbell
Walter H. Carpenter
Mrs. Vera Webb Cartwright
Ulmon Clements

Evelyn Elizabeth Denton
Janet Louise Edmonson
Harry E. Emmerton
John Faulkinberry, Jr.
Hugh Arvin Fincher
Rosalie Fincher
Emily Belle Fitzgerald
Guy Martin Francis
Virginia B. Griffith
Wiley Beall Grinnell
Leon Wade Hampton
J. Lyle Hill
Catherine Howard
John Edward Hutt
Alleyne Kinsey
Curtis Kling
Dorothy G. Kohfeldt

Eugene McDanald
Nannie K. McLemore
Geo. Edwin Mason
Disa-Marie Nelson
Sarah Adelia Perry
Faye Poe
Elizabeth R. Pruitt
Max Shelton
H. Alton Smith
Walter Bruce Thornton
Bettye Turner
A. T. Vestal, Jr.
Grace Louise Vinnedge
Morris P. Wagner
Wm. Lowry Walker
Jeanette Wallis
Martha Lu West

## Bachelor of Science

Leroy Kimbrough

## Master of Arts

Marian Cox
John Douglas Hensley

Inez Jackson
James Edwin Poindexter

## Bachelor of Arts

## 1936

Dorothy Omar Belden
Billie Marie Gilley Breedlove
Farris E. Breedlove
Billy Jerome J. Cox
Talmadge "Doc" Crook
George C. Crowell
Luther Dudley Fletcher
Grover Howell Hight
Helen Frances Johnson
Robert Marius Lacy

Walter Haskell Luck
Doris Matlock
George Edward Mattingly
Marshall Marie McElvaney
Jessie Allene Morgan
Henry Leland Murphy
Roy Allen,
Dovie Mae Arnold
James Edwin Baldwin
Nova May Bowen

Milton Jackson Buchanan
B. B. Christian
Joe Wilson Chumbley
Everett B. Fleming
Will F. Haden, Jr.
May Hill
Richard Edwin Hutchison
Clella D. Kelley
Bertha Knaur
Iris Lightsey
Morriss Mills, Jr.
Ruth Russell
R. E. St. John
Annie Taylor
Elizabeth Carolyn Thomas

Arvel L. Vandergriff
Nell Welch
James Kelly Neal
Beth Deffebach Ownby
Patty Reece Petty
Estela Pina
William Harold Prather
Marion Fletcher Reynolds
Ona Mae Ricketts
Lois Elizabeth Stephens
Edith Stout
Harold Layton White
Clifford Watters Williams
Kenneth Gilmer Williams

## Master of Arts

Jesse N. Hollingsworth
Herbert Lynn Hollis
Christine M. Hotchkin
Evelyn Elizabeth Denton
Fay Trammell Ingram

Monroe Orenduff, Jr.
Max Shelton
Wyncye Lucyle Sanders
Mrs. Vera Pierce Vaden

## Bachelor of Arts

### 1937

Henry William West Allen,
  B.A.
William H. Arnold, B.A.
Wayne E. Atkins, B.A.
William David Blunk, B.A.
Edythe Elizabeth Brame, B.A.
Charles M. Cooper, B.A.
Norman P. Cox, B.A.
Mable L. Craig, B.A.
Edna Lois Daughety, B.A.
Louise E. Dinsmore, B.A.
Juanita Ditto, B.A.
Rosalie Edwards, B.A.
John F. Elliott, B.A.

Annie Mae Francis, B.A.
Guy B. Garner, B.A.
Maurice Harper, B.A.
James T. Hodges, B.A.
William Q. Jamison, B.A.
Creswell C. Jones, B.A.
Joseph M. Keith, B.A.
Winifred M. Key, B.A.
Mrs. R. W. Lewin, B.A.
Esta Louise Linton, B.A.
Margaret Ann Lowrey, B.A.
Lometa I. McAfee, B.A.
Lynn McCraw, B.A.
Carter McKemy, B.A.

Mrs. Addie A. Miller, B.A.
William J. Murdaugh, B.A.
C. Ellis Nelson, B.A.
William Barr Oglesby, B.A.
Wilford R. Penny, B.A.
Carrie V. Preston, B.A.
Helen Edna Rahlfs, B.A.
Marian Ricketts, B.A.
Fay D. Slaughter, B.A.
Corinne Horne Smith, B.A.
Everett H. Smith, B.A.
William Albert Smith, B.A.
John Orlan Stephens, B.A.
Mabel Eugenia Strange, B.A.
Mrs. Charles Spurgeon
   Teague, B.A.

B. Tol Terrell, B.A.
John C. Winfrey, B.A.
Mary Isabel Zimmerman, B.A.
Richard Bailey
G. Todd Crowell
Virgil R. Edmonson
Jaunita Jo Enloe
Mrs. Nana Elizabeth Francis
Mrs. Mina Gunter Harrison
Lola Mae Hensley
Pearl Hill
George Norcross Irvine
Mabel McManus
Beulah Polson
Mrs. Iva Lee Washburn
Mollie Williams

## Master of Arts

B. B. Christian
W. B. Cooke
Luther Dudley Fletcher
Henry Frnka
Maurice Harper
Lutie Lee Heard
Bertha M. Knaur
Robert G. Landolt

George C. LeCroy
Patty Reece Petty
Harold Layton White
Mrs. S. W. Yeury
Robert Marius Lacy, M.A.
M. G. Moreland, M.A.
Robert Reeves Morgan, M.A.
R. E. St. John, M.A.

## 1938

Edith Alexander, B.A.
Christiana Barrett, B.A.
Mrs. Otis Barker, B.A.
C. Y. Bartley, B.A.
Addie Mae Beckett, B.A.
Joe M. Brown, B.A.
Gussie F. Campbell, B.A.
Mary Ella Campbell, B.A.
Jack T. Claybourn, B.A.
Wiley J. Dunken, B.A.
Pauline Ellison, B.A.
Charles M. Gilliland, B.A.

Margaret E. Hawkins, B.A.
Cameron Harris, B.A.
Margaret L. Hall, B.A.
David Lee Hill, B.A.
Joe Hight, B.A.
Jack Jackson, B.A.
Wallace Johnson, B.A.
J. T. Krattiger, B.A.
Davie M. Long, B.A.
James McCord, B.A.
Raymond L. Meyer, B.A.
Doris Ann Neves, B.A.

Lenwood Orick, B.A.
Helen Orr, B.A.
James Franklin Perry, B.A.
Bonnie Mae Pitts, B.A.
Vestice Poteet, B.A.
Albert J. Pruitt, B.A.
Kathryn Reynolds, B.A.
John D. Smith, B.A.
Lucy Ann Snipes, B.A.
Anton J. Van Puffelin, B.A.
Leslie Walden, B.A.

J. H. Webb, B.A.
Linda Wharton, B.A.
Sadie Ball White, B.A.
Marisula Yeargan, B.A.
Dovie Mae Arnold, M.A.
Isabel T. Brinson, M.A.
Mary Ella Campbell, M.A.
Louise Dinsmore, M.A.
Maurice Harper, M.A.
Fred W. Hunter, M.A.
Elizabeth Thomas, M.A.

## Bachelor of Arts

### 1939

Josephine Aslan
Cleveland Barker,
Mrs. Evelyn D. Brent
Millard L. Brent
Murray Robert Byrd
Beverly Basham Carson
Jane LeNoir Cleveland
Kenneth Lawrence Clinton
Robert LeRhea Cowan
Jacqueline Dickson
William Jackson Dobson
Mary Beth Fitch
William Hague Foster, Jr.
Samuel Edgar Gillespie
Garland Woodrow Goodrum
Pearl Marzelle Grafft
H. L. Harding, Jr.
Mary Louise Hawkins
Clyde Vernon Hendricks

Evelyn Welborn Hester
Muriel Anthony Kimbrough
Hervey Lazenby, Jr.
Robert Ellsworth Matthews
John Lewis
Frank J. Little
Myrna Lucas McElroy
Alice Louise Mills
Robert Lee Ratliff
Esley Dean Raulston
Maye B. Russell
Jane St. John
Nancy Shepard
William Paul Simpson
Bruce Grafton Tucker
Fulton Douglas Ware
Mary Lou Weatherall
Dorothy Wilson
Charles B. Yeargan

## Master of Arts

William David Blunk
Charlie K. Davidson
Herman Statham Griffin
Julia Hayes

Emily Virginia Isbell
Mrs. R. W. Lewin
Burton C. McCarley
Lucy Ann Snipes

## Bachelor of Arts

### 1940

Dorothy Mae Abernathy
Edward L. Abrahamson
Redellium Lindley Atnip
Donald Gladney Boyd
Clarice Brashier
Charles Parker Calhoun
Norman Leigh Claybourn
Lottie O'Lena Creswell
Charmon Davis
George Emmet Dodd, Jr.
Pauline Mace Duff
John F. Dunn
Emmett M. Essin, Jr.
J. Cecil Francis
Ward Jasper Francis
Thomas Franklin George
Ozelle Bryant Gibson
William Uklen Gibson
Charlie Fredrick Goff
Morrell Wade Hampton
Mrs. W. H. Hanning
La Rue Haralson
Harold L. Hester
Mary Katherine Hutt
Edward Everett Jenkins
Jo Anne Kalbfleisch

Lucille Leatherwood
D. A. McCall, Jr.
Wm. Frank McElroy, Jr.
Sylvia M. Mercer
G. Loyal Prior
Royston M. Roberts
Perrin Clyce Smith
George M. Staples
James B. Storey
Alex A. Tocquigny
Cecil Hood
Olga Long
Mrs. Lois McAllister
M. F. Mayfield
Mrs. M. F. Mayfield
Malcolm Pate
Mildred Porterfield
Allen Taliaferro
Alexander H. Zogheib
Rebecca Trevino
Roy Andrews
Matthew Bullock
Ruby Burden
Bess Coppin
Cary Head

## Master of Arts

Alice Brown
Helen Orr Christian
Dan McRae
C. V. Hanning
Guy B. Garner

Creswell Carr Jones
Marshall Marie McElvaney
Mae Hill
Lillian Neathery
Edna Clair Mosse

## Bachelor of Arts

### 1941

Wilborn Omer Albright
John W. Alexander, Jr.

Ponnie Ames
John Franklin Anderson, Jr.

Lela Mae (Brannum) Andrews
Walter Angelo Bennett
Gaylord Blue, Jr.
Betty Browne
Luine Guy Bryan
J. Forrest Bryant
Roy Fields Cleveland
Drucilla Dickerson
James Chester Ellis
Edra Faye Ferry
Dorothy Fitch
Lillie Louise Garr
Mary Jim Gee
Lawrence Edmund Gilbert
James Truman Griffis
Isom H. Hale
Severn J. Hallett
Jack Morton Hardy
Charlie Marie Harrell
E. O. Harrell, Jr.
Edith Mae McDaniel
Ruby Haning Hines
Noble J. Hogan
Joan Hunter
Joseph Edward Lawrence
L. B. London
Robert Bruce Lowrance
Eleanor Mae McDaniel
John Laughlin McDonald
Lucile Stone McElroy
Margaret Fern Maul
Vada Mercer
Anna Belle Mitchell

Kent V. Morrison, Jr.
Thomas Davidson Murphy
Thelma Lucille Patterson
Nadine Pearson
J. Weldon Powell
Ouida Maxine Rambin
Irene Lee Richardson
Ople Mills Richardson
Robert Foss Silas
John T. Slusher
George Joseph Tocquigny
Orson Veach Whited
Joyce Cathleen Wilson
Robert Ross Wilson II
Cleo Allen Winkle
Roy Epps
Lucille Beckett
Lucille Wilson Booth
Shelley Edwin Camp
Mrs. Glenn Pratt Chitwood
A. F. DeLashaw
Oma Jewell DeLashaw
Sherman Lee Elliott
Lillian Fox
Lillian McClary Garner
Doris Catherine Harrell
Jesse L. Hendricks
Frances Evelyn Ivy
Sue F. Stephens
M. H. Stockdale
Wilma Moore Whisenhunt
Mozelle Young

## M.A. Degrees

Mrs. Cora Glynn Patterson
  Clark
Woodrow Wilson Elrod

William Dewitt George
J. Lloyd Tarver

## Bachelor of Arts:

### 1942

Mary Muriel Boals
Willie H. Enochs
Myrtle Irene McAllister
Sam Brooks McLane, Jr.
Marian Emily Meadows
Wannie Edward Miller
Jo Priest
Francis B. Voltz
Catherine West
Riley Alton Wooten
David Alexander Zogheib
Noel Ashinhurst
*Robert Leland Bidwell
Allene Brown
Sarah Ellen Carmichael
W. Kemper Fitch, Jr.
Jessie Ann Hamilton
Lyndon Maurice Jackson
Bennett Anderson Joiner
*Nancy Lee Love

Kitty Lus
Jane McGee
Margaret Ann McKinney
*Dorothy Marple
Boyd W. Newman
Lester Combo Newman
William Fay O'Connell
*Helen Edith Orr
William Ray Parrett
Helen Record
Milus Nugent Reed, Jr.
Mae LaVerne Savage
*Zelie Mae Slaughter
Earl W. Smyth
Esther Rose Taggart
Albert Arnott Ward
William Chrisman Washburn
Conway Taliaferro Wharton, Jr.
*Margaret Westerhoff Wilson
Robert Reed Wilson

## Master of Arts:

Louise Marks Goldstein

Tassie Rollins Scott

## Bachelor of Arts:

### 1943

Alexander, Adele
Arnold, William Henry
Att-Kisson, Anjolee
Bassett, Clarence Merritt
Cole, Betty
Ecke, Jr. Max
Gage, William Robert
Hawkins, Clara Vere
McBee, Mable Agnes
Millsap, Harvey Spence
Nelson, Jack W.

Bidwell, Jack
Burdette, Betty Jeanne
Burdette, Mary Clifford
Cleveland, Anne Boyd
Palachek, Joseph A.
Parker, Mrs. Mabel S.
Ratliff, Julia Belle
Shirley, Mrs. Mary Marie
Sylestine, Cora Vashti
Hedgpeth, Mrs. Ora

## Master of Arts:

Shepard, Nancy

### 1944

Henry Edds Acklen
Jane Lewis Boyd
Jacqueline Joy Brooks
Winston Ramsey Bryant
Douglas Elmore Charles
Lena Lea Clausell
Rosario Guevara
Maria Lus Hernandez
Richard Bladworth Hardie
George Ray Hodges

Katherine Askew Myers
*Betty Jane Phinney
Jack Pendleton Powell
Mary Robardey
Kenneth Maxwell Thomas
Dorothy Jean Wallace
William Wiley Warren, Jr.
Lewis Oliver Waterstreet
*Katherine Rachel Wood
Dolores Denton McAfee

### 1945

Virgie Lee Cappleman
Edith Jean Church
Margaret Ruth Clark
Mary French Cook
Patricia Courtney
Joyce Lorene Crane
Spurgeon M. Dunnam, Jr.
Anne Edgar Hart
Frankie Hall
Carol Christine Ivy
Betty Jo Jackson
Mrs. D. W. Jay

Katherine Wood Klunder
Nell Eugenia McCall
C. Rogers McLane
Isabel May
Eleanor Ruth Miller
Jane Morgan
Dorothy Barrett Morris
Lois Annette Powell
Jeanne Louise Rudolph
Susannah Fonda Ruhmann
Grace Wilborn

### 1946

Ray Ayres
Jeanette Barton
Joe D. Coomer
Betty Naoma Covey
James E. Easley, Jr.
William Barnett Guerrant, Jr.
Clyde Lewis Hall
Jean Marie Holmes
Mary Frances Johnson
Jo Ann Korioth

Jean Margaret McClenahan
Helen Williams Miller
James E. Richards
Ryal L. Skaggs
Ross White Stoddard, Jr.
Mary Burnett Thorington
Juanita L. Viers Hardy
Willie Sue Grace
Renee Beazley

## (A. B. Degree)

### 1947

Allen M. Boedeker
Richard Van Bonneau
Marion Bookout
Collie Lee Brigham
Helen Marie Briley
William Joseph Christy
Mary Virginia Coffin
John Wilson Cunningham
Joy Devault
Mary Joe Embrey
Herbert Charles Foster
Robert Lawrence Gilpin
James Robert Hawkins
Ross Wyatt Hester
Ralph Henry Hollywood
William Robert Jarvis
William Robert Knox
John William Lancaster
Kenneth Boyd Lane
George Coleman Luck
Ada Ruth McDaniel
Faries J. McDaniel
Harris Dubose McLane

John Marvin Madison
Linda Miller
Mary Morgan
Oscar Worrell Mueller
Robert B. Patterson
Dorothy Scott Prentince
Byron Thomas Price
Charles Merrill Proudfoot
Elizabeth LaFar Ramsay
James Wyatt Ringgold, Jr.
Mary Frances Robinson
Helen Louise Ruhmann
Anne Marie Smith
Arlie Lee Smith
D. G. Smith
Henry White Sory
Eugene Lee Strickland
George Lee Tuttle
Betty Wheeler
Forrest K. Whitworth
Earl Bernon Wiggins
Ernest C. Young

## (B.S. Degree)

Billy Lee Barnes
Harry King Bean
Howard W. Cogswell, Jr.

Robert Joseph Perkins
Virginia Sturdivant

## Bachelor of Arts

### 1948

Thomas J. Bailey
Mona Ruth Bell
B. Hampton Bowman
Carrol M. Boyd, Jr.
Fred O. Brewton, Jr.

Gusta Stroman Brewton
William A. Brooks
James G. Cameron, Jr.
Alfred C. Casey, Jr.
Lillie M. Combs

Grace Virginia Cook
Juanita Craft
Raymond C. Dean, Jr.
J. Sterling Dimmitt
Dorothy M. Franklin
Wayne Gardner
Billy E. Hardy
Ernest L. Helsley
John William Hughes, Jr.
Warren B. Hunter
Rudolph Inman
Grady Louise Ivy
Horace Lee Jenkins
Joe Wallace Johnson
Nell Karnaghan
Sarah Hampton Kilgore
Alicejean Kent
William C. Kolb
Kenneth W. Kuykendall
Charles T. Kyle
Helen C. Landolt
Doris Ann Lawson
Coy Cecil Lee
Wardlow Howard McCarley
Bobby Joe McWhorter
Jane Douglas Moorman
Jack Myres
Lester G. Nabors
Wilma Carroll Nolte
Frances Park
Taylor O. Perrin, Jr.
Helen H. Pickavance
Anna Todd Reagan
Dean G. Robinson
Anna Binion Scott

Rufus Scott
Betty Pearle Scruggs
Helen Moody Spencer
Abner Reid Steele, Jr.
Verna Stockdale
Jeanette Sutton
Jonelle Sutton
Elizabeth Thorington
R. Hardin Whitaker
Chalice H. White
Virginia Yoder
Robert W. Foster
Donald K. Freeland
Joan Hill Green
Billy Joe Hale
Henry R. Hall
Carl Stanley Hefton
Mary Elizabeth Hess
Tom Malone Hudgins
Sterling A. Kennard, Jr.
Eugene Farris McGlothlin
Charles W. Mitchell
Albert Leon Mulder, Jr.
Randall P. Noe
R. G. Smith
Jack Spears
Joseph Van Ulrich
Harold H. Walker
James B. Manford
Charles W. Owens, Jr.

Dolores Ann Pace
Charles O. Boyd
Letha Haraughty
Jack O. Harless

## Master of Arts

Lewis O. Waterstreet

T. L. Womack

## Bachelor of Science

Claud C. Fincher

Lealon W. Brown

## Bachelor Degree

### 1949

Margaret A. Agee
Samuel G. Barnes
Charles Edward Baxter
Cecil Edwin Biggerstaff
John E. Blevins
Nancy Browne
James Embry Bryan
John Edward Carter
Lee Al Clarkston
Sammie J. Curlee
Herman Ray Feltz
Charles Brayton Fraser, Jr.
George Marshall Gearhart
Johnny T. Goldston
Josephine Gregg
Randolph L. Hall
Charles Richard Heckman
Betty June Moates Lewis
Janis Jayne Horton
Mack Quinn Hunter
Bryan O'Neill Keathley
Tim Fred Kelly
Charles Edward Landolt, Jr.
Betty June Moates Lewis
Elizabeth Jean McClure
Johnny C. MacKey
Evelyn Jo Miller
James Alvin Mitchell
Harry Myers
James William Newton
Claude C. Perry, Jr.
William Harris Pollard
Warren M. Reynolds
Chester P. Rodgers
Geneva Noles Roper
Thomas C. Scheurer
Margaret Anne Silha
Lloyd E. Spencer

Mary Horton Stribling
John Buford Taylor
George T. Townley
S. M. Vaughn
Robert Russell Watkins, Jr.
Fredia Lee Wilson
Hazel Woodward
David Lee Zimmerman
William T. Alexander
William C. Bassett
Carroll Kendrick Baxter, Jr.
Bettye Jane Birk
William Newman Bradshaw
Walter Howard Brownfield
W. E. Burns
Lorabel McLaughlin Casey
John M. Coffin, Jr.
Betty Berniece Dean
Clayton Grimes Forthman
John C. Gallimore, Jr.
Joe Gill
Albert Edwin Graham
Ruby Mildred Grizzard
Ben F. Hardy, Jr.
Don Warren Hefton
Howard A. Hestand, Jr.
Jack A. Hughes
William Doak Jamison, Jr.
Jack B. Keeth
Felix Wilburn Keys, Jr.
Robert Harry Lang
James I. Logan, Jr.
Dan Howard McCown
Echo Griffin Martin
Harold C. Miller
Katherine Ann Moore
Hugh Robert Neill
William J. B. Odon, I

Maebelle Petty
Ben "Bo" Reid
James E. Riley
Howard C. Rodgers
James E. Russell
Lockie Eugene Self
Allan G. Smith, Jr.
Oma Lee Fisher Stephens
John C. Sumner
Barbara Ann Thomason
Stanley Raymond Tropp
Charles Edwin Vincent
Charles T. Weideman
Joanne Wilson
Linus D. Wright
W. Edwin Badgett
James C. Battenfield
Harold Lee Bell
David Burnham Blankenship
Paul Edward Brooks
Stephen O. Bruno
Mary Lou S. Cannon
Eugene A. Castle
Cornelius W. Corcoran
Douglas Duke
George H. Franklin
Rob R. Gattis
Dale R. Glover
Sylvia Grace Green
Shirley C. Guthrie

Leaman Hazelton
Marie Elizabeth Helsley
Billy Carrol Holliman
Carrye Lou Humphries
Wayne Johns
Henry Alexander Keever
Milton Kresse, Jr.
Charlton D. Lawhorn
Jerry Clinton McCann
John Scott McDonald
Lewis Ray Marvin
Robert Thomas Miller
Joe E. Mulkey
Leonard R. Nelson
George W. O'Hara
Clarence E. Phipps
John Reid, Jr.
Richard T. Ringgold
Joseph F. Rogers, Jr.
Jack M. Russom
Billy Vert Sherron
James L. Speck
Sunshine L. Stephens
Austin Golbert Taylor
Emily K. Thurman
Martha Thompson Vandiver
Stanley B. Ward
James Benton Williams
Robert Michael Wilson, Jr.
Roger Q. Wynn, Jr.

## A.B. Degree
### 1950

Cecil Bailey
John G. Barton
Patsy Anita Bilger
Betty Ann Binion
Marjory Bobb
Robert L. Boyd
Billy Jay Calfee
Lola T. Casteel

Viola Louise Cole
Marjorie Crowe
Courtney Dee Culley
Roger Louis Daniel
Robert Moreton Davis
Thomas T. Doss
June Marie English
William Jethro Fogleman

Virginia Foshee
William J. Gerwick
William McIntire Gould, Jr.
Yvonne Guion
John Allan Cuthrio
Margie Ann Hestand
Tommy Hestand
Dan W. Holloway
Rose Marie Holman
Francis Holt
Joseph Melvin Holverson
Robert Anderson Jones
Frank David Kalbfleisch
Thomas E. Kendrick
O'Dell Elliott Knott
William B. Krieg, Jr.
Cecil Herbert Lang, Jr.
Robert Altman Lauderdale
Gus Garland Lewis, Jr.
Kate Moore McCord
Ralph S. McCord
Mary Helon McCurdy
George D. McManus
Frances Eldredge McMenamy
George Robertson McNutt
Troy C. Martin
Willie B. Melugin

Helen Dolores Moody
Philip Raymond Morrow
Price Jackson Parker
Thomas Henry Parsons
Billie Ruth Poe
Harold Lloyd Pryor
Bobbye Evelyn Pyron
Miles Allen Ray
Mortimer Maughs Scholl, Jr.
Billy George Schumacher
Katherine Sherwood
Allen H. Shields
Jessie H. Smith
Delbert C. South
George Raymond Stephens, Jr.
Kenneth E. Stephens
Clifton Leo Thomas
Robert Holland Thompson
Helen Guerrant Thorington
Lois V. Umphress
Ronald Murray Vandiver
Barbara Vann
C. Casey Vett
Ethel Lou Watson
Lou Alice West
Flora Margaret Williams
Jack Elliott Williams

## B.S. Degree

James F. Beasley
James I. Blackmon
Richard E. Brigham
Charles William Browning
William M. Chaffin
Jack B. Dale, Jr.

Charles Paul Giarraputo
George Green, Jr.
Clyde E. Hale
Donald Ray Hatfield

William C. Hatfield
Earl Ralph Hedrick, Jr.
Jack W. Hollensed
John Wesley King, Jr.
Don Ray Martin
Russell W. Oden
Dudley Lee Olds
James H. Parker
Bonnie Adele Powers
James Marcus Ratcliff

Claude J. Sanders                    William Keller White, Jr.
Billy Smith                          Melvin Eugene Wyatt
D. B. Tate, Jr.

## M.A. Degree

J. Weldon Powell                     Joseph Fletcher Rogers, Jr.

## M.S. Degree

William Harris Pollard               James T. Wilson
S. M. Vaughn                         Cecilia Yeargan
Nelda Faye Williams                  Melvia Jo Young
Selwyn Arthur Willis

## Bachelor Degree Candidates

### 1951

Preston Donaghey Allison             Doris Singleton Culley
John Baker                           William D. Dresh
Charles Rex Bates                    Glenn Duke
Rosemary Beachy                      Elaine Rae Dupuy
Joyce Beene                          Diane Osborne Ellis
Mary Carlene Biggers                 William H. Evans
Barbara Janet Biggerstaff            Mary Elizabeth Farley
Eddie Lou Bilger                     Gwyn H. Morton
Harriet Jane Blaney                  James Travis Newsome
Rayford Lewis Bolin                  Billie Earl O'Hara
Harold Wayne Bond                    Kenneth Edmond O'Neal
Jack Davis Braden                    Elizabeth Ann Page
Marlin Sue Shepard Braden            Reuben P. Pearce
William Newman Bradshaw               Lynn Porter
Marilyn Yvonne Bratcher              Robert T. Pulliam
Edward Cahan                         Henry Glenn Reeves
Alice Louise Campbell                Jimmie Garth Reid
Dale Francis Carson                  Joe Haden Robardey
Patrick F. Cogswell                  John Clement Robertson
Eugene Austin Coppedge               Nancy Ruth Roundtree
Raymond Daniel Corbett               Laurence N. Saye, Jr.
John H. Crain                        Billy Byers Sharp
Mary Ann Crews                       Ollie Chisholm Shirley

John J. Sloan
Bill Farrow
Joe Willis Fawcett, Jr.
Wendell Kenneth Francis
Harold Elwood Gibbs, Jr.
Kathleen Franklin Gibbs
Doris Jean Gloff
Paul Hanna, Jr.
Mary Nell Harrison
Barney Brooks Hightower
James Hunter Hill
William Austin Hodges
Grady Hugh Holder
Elizabeth Garland Hopper
Thomas Brents Horne
James Dean Howze
Jack Chriswell Hunnicutt
Billy M. Hutchinson
Roberta C. Jones
Martha Greene Jordan
Henry A. Keever
Ruth Carlene Keller
Roy C. Kerr
Gloria Jean Kershaw
Frances Beckham King

Eula Mae Knox
Janet Lindsay
Rebekah Lloyd
John Robert McClure
Mary Loise May
Thurman Rex Montgomery
Nancy Ellen Slocum
Neilson Amis Smith
Richard Carlisle Smith, Jr.
Bill Stewart
Eugene Vernon Stone
J. P. Talley
Herbert Lyndon Taylor
Joseph B. Thomas
Edward Mack Thompson
Rob Roy Thompson
Jerry R. Tompkins
Richard Lee Turner
Harold H. Vestal
Elva Marie Wallace
Clarence Wayne Warren
Philip Whisenhunt
Joseph Elliott Wilson
Victor Charles Wood

## Master Degree

Robert Dean Bradley
Viola Everett Brice
Lealon W. Brown
Milton Jackson Buchanan
Hazel Legate Buckley
Mildred Elspeth Caraway
Mildred Mattison Carpenter
Margaret Elizabeth Clarke
Ellis Mayo Cleveland
Winnie M. Cowling
Courtney Dee Culley
Albert Forest DeLashaw
Oma Jewell DeLashaw

Grace Bee Littrell Giles
Maudine Graham Hayes
Ora E. Hedgpeth
Wenonah Dyer Hill
Ella Eastham Jones
Elma Lee Knox
Frances Werline Long
Evelyn McCoy
Jane Gray Mayes
Emily Meadows
Clarence Eugene Phipps
Nettie Mae Sampsell
Anna Scott

Marguerite Shankles
Mrs. Ben A. Shaver
Katherine Sherwood
Maggie Sommerville
Henry White Sory
Ernest Sturch
Amos E. Tatum

Geneva Frances Thomas
Mary Johnson Waldrop
Ira Garland Washington
Leslie M. West
Velton Curtis Williams
Virginia Hogg Williford

## Bachelor of Arts

### 1952

John Kinard Alexander
James Edgar Andrews
Marshall Herff Applewhite, Jr.
James Albert Beckerley, Jr.
Anna Margaret Biggerstaff
Fred A. Brooks, Jr.
NaDell Cain
Charles E. Caldwell
Mattie Evelyn Carr
John Buist Chester, Jr.
Bernard Slaton Cohen
Donald Forshee Cook
Lawrence McNeil Correu
Alice Marie Cowan
Walter Montgomery Crofton, Jr.
Betty Ruth Curtis
Paul Emerson Deatherage
Noel Jean DeFord
Helen Diane Deison
James Edward Fromme
Charlie Dillard Grandstaff, Jr.
Katherine Hall Green
Janet Guthrie
Ruth Maud Hatfield
C. John Hinkle
Jessie Elizabeth Hunt
Charles Ray Inman
Roy Reid Jackson
Harry Leigh Johnson
Frank H. Lair

Doris Dell Landolt
Joseph Marvin McCaskill
Patsy Ruth McClure
Billy John McKinney
Mildred Fay Martin
Shirley Ann May
Patricia Ann Meador
Patty Fern Minear
Robin Donald Moffat
Haskell Moorman Monroe
Mariam Joyce Moussa
William Arthur Nobles
James Madison O'Leary
Dorothy Annette Owens
Chester Alvin Patton
Thomas Edwin Patton
William Bryn Patty III
Mary Caroline Purcell
Carolyn B. Schirmer
Richard Henry Schmidt
James Thomas Shelton
Martha Virginia Spurlock
William Henry Storey, Jr.
Irma Louise Sullivan
Clem Fain Sylestine
Hilda Palmer Thomas
Mary Louise Turner
Mary Ella Walker
Victor Charles Wood
Paul Ray Yeager

## Bachelor of Science

Charles Jebez Andrews
Lester David Belcher
Gordon L. Bowers
Elizabeth Bryan Bradish
Billy Glenn Burton
J. R. Chafin
Wayne Lewis Currier
John Leonard Ehrler, Jr.
Ben E. Harmon
Jack Hicks

George Willis Hill, Jr.
Arthur Leland Jackson
Daniel Joe Lewis
Robert Todd Mason
Bobby Wayne Moore
William Graham Reeves
Billy Joe Spann
Vernon Maurice Temple
John Robert Williams
Dewey Leonard Wright

## Masters Degrees

### 1952

James B. Anderson
Gene A. Barker
I. W. Brown
Ruth Davis
Eloise R. Giles
Joe B. Laughlin
Edna Mercer
Paul Owenby
Allan G. Smith, Jr.
Harold H. Vestal
Hazel Woodward
Clem C. Yandel
Orbin Bailey
J. D. Barrett
Harold Cogburn
Floyd V. Ellis
Ora H. Hedgpeth

Inez LeBaron
Wannie Miller
John H. Parker
Wm. Otho Silk
Robert R. Watkins, Jr.
Linus D. Wright
Naomi Baker
William Bassett
Courtney D. Culley
Nana E. Francis
Thomas Horne
Fannie McKinney
Wilma Nolte
Charles N. Pritchard
Sunshine Stephens
David E. Webb
Mozelle S. Wright

## Bachelor of Arts

### 1953

Josie Frances S. Allen
Patricia Bullock Andrews
Daniel Hammond Barfield

Benjamin Haughton Bateman
Quinton Geoffrey Boone
James Graham Brannon

Marianne Broden
Carlos Salazar Buck
James Milton Campbell
Emma Jane Curtis
Lucius Boyden Day, Jr.
Betty Jane Dodson
William Patrick Egan
Peggy Lorene Elliott
Lloyd L. Etchinson, Jr.
James William Ferries
Robert Preston Ferrill
Marvin Cecil Frank
Betty Merle Gayoso
Ben Felan Gutierrez
Betty Jean Harper
Irene Brown Holcomb
Robert Lee Hyatt
Kenneth Marvin Keller
Jeanette Louise Kershaw
Elizabeth Ann King
Lucy Hope Lawrence
Esther Long
Harriet Spurlin Mathews
Jo Ellen Meadows
Morris Joel Molpus
John Wallace Moore

Grace Cornell Newton
Sidney Charles Pruitt, Jr.
Wayne Hal Sebesta
James Robert Sheppard, Jr.
Jo Ellen Sheppard
Mieko Shimizu
Jerry Lee Sims
Eugene Barmore Skinner
Roberta Marilynn Slate
David Hugh Slider
Minnett Rue Steffey
Patricia Mae Stone
Barbara Sturdy
Salita Sudderth
Raymond James Taylor
James Clarence Thrash, III
James Thompson Wilson
Paul Kincaid Wilson, Jr.
Clarence Keith Wright
Dorothy Helene Tucker
Betty Jean Vaught
Jack Bryant Walker
William Oliver Walker, Jr.
Ann Whitworth
Edward Lee Wilbourn

## Bachelor of Science

George James Berlamino
Floyd Allen Cash
O. C. Condon
Bill Davenport
John Edwin Duke
Barbara Fay Dupuy
Arnold Otha Dutton
Shirley Lu Enix
Euwell Eugene Geer
James Stewart Hardy
Roy Earl Harmon
Floyd Albert Harrison
William Roy Hatfield

Jack August Hesse
Jimmy Don Hunt
Herman A. Kanis
Charles Robert McKnight
Russell E. Pelley
Milton Gus Roberts, Jr.
Jack Edward Robertson
Walter Duncan Schirmer
Erwin A. Schroder
William Clark Simpson
James Vernon Stewart, Jr.
Charles M. Stone
Holland Dempsey Watkins

## Master of Science

Eldridge Ancell
John Edward Blevins
Orvetta H. Callen
Ruth Read Ellett
Rob R. Gattis
Ozelle Bryant Gibson

Randolph Lee Hall
Romie Maud Sommerville
Opal Paul Jones
Melva Ruth Reagan
Christine Violet Sanders
Dayle Bartley Sawyers

## Bachelor Degrees

### 1954

George V. Adamson, Jr.
Carol Stetson Anderson
Emily McCune Anderson
Charles Edward Angell
Hulon Eugene Bartlett
Robert Ernest Birk
James Edgar Brock
Joseph Rogers Cooper
Joseph Reeves Cochran, Jr.
James David Craft
Mary DeShazo
Robert Lewis Deutsch
Edward Emmanuel DeWees, Jr.
Alice Stuart Dunn
Doyle Maultsby Dunn
James Rolo Edwards
Grant E. Elwood
Mary Frances Evans
Jimmye Lee Futch
Robert Nelson Hale
Anne Leafe Hardy
Evelyn Louise Hargrove
Ida Dykman Haynen
Goldia Ann Hester
Gerald Lane Hill
George Anderson Hurst
Jorge Braud Lara
Ruth M. DeLara

John Courtenay Laughlin
Albert Franklin Mahaffey
Wallace Newton Meredith
Theron Stanford Nease
Patricia Marie Nelson
Joan Park
Harold Chauncey Parker, Jr.
Ben Peterson
Carroll Lamar Pickett
Dixie Edith Potts
Margaret Ann Purcell
Charles Coe Purdy
Joann Ragan
Mona Lee Roberts
William Harry Schlottman
John Anderson Shelton
James Edgar Sheppard
Martha Anne Smith
Perry Randolph Smith, Jr.
Gene Snipes
Melrose Howard Tappan, III
William Paul Van Pelt
Alice Robinson Vineyard
Bette Miller Watkins
Marian Webster
Barbara Ruth Williams
Walter Lynn Zimmerman

## Master Degree Candidates

Wenonah D. Hill
Frances Marie Alexander
James Edgar Andrews
William Ralph Beckham
Margarette Josephine Boland
Alma Miriam Brown
Donald Burnham Chesley
Mildred Glynn Dishman
Mary-Bess Estess
Van-Noy Hines Gary

Esta Speer Jennings
Clayton Paul Johnson
Pauline Jones
Betty Dean King
Haskell Moorman Monroe, Jr.
Gwen Morrison Shwadlenak
Carl Wesley Stripling
William Earl Young
Victor C. Wood

## Bachelor of Arts

### 1955

Cherry Lee Alexander
Leroy Dewayne Ates
Martha Elizabeth Bartlett
Charles Edison Baum
Raphael Semmes Baird, Jr.
Joan Blake
Bobby Joe Brooks
James Arthur Calhoun, Jr.
William Burdette Chapin
Stanley Lorrain Cobbs
Mary Lois Dalton
Mary Scott Daugherty
Albert Thomas Dyal, Jr.
Charles Raymond Elliott
Shirley Ann Frankel
Billy J. Gleaves
Luther Ray Gohlke
Patricia Merriann Green
Carolynn Jo Hall
Wha-Yul Han
Valton F. Hazelton

Edna Sue Hood
Elizabeth Ann King
Clements E. Lamberth, Jr.
Casper Dale Landolt, Jr.
David Arthur Laverty
Patricia Jean Long
Shirley Ann Martin
Martha Jane Moss
Bobby Ray Richardson
Ruth Lenore Riesel
Roberta Ann Riley
William Risk
Mary Gail Schmid
Marian Letitia Sherard
Joanne Irene Swaidner
Toru Tsukamoto
Carolyn Shaw Waddell
Mildred Ann Williams
Anne Murphy Wilson
Charles William Winfield

## Master of Arts

Juanita Craft
Lloyd L. Etchison, Jr.

Shintaro Tokunaga

## Bachelor of Science

Norman Keith Bennett
Charles Franklin Bons
Davis Kedric Couch
Don Eugene Duke
William Douglas Hamm
Robert Warren Harper
Charles Robert Harrell
Howard Horton Harvey

Don Lee Hulse
Robert Donald Kent
Ronald George Masitis
Harold Burtis Shelley
Minnie Irene Stacy
John Wilburn Taylor
J. T. Yother

## Master of Science

Samuel Taylor Davis
Juanita King
Dorothy Barrett Morris
John Martin Pirtle

Myrtle Vera Pirtle
Owen Rogers
Oscar L. Thomas, Jr.

## 1956
## Master of Science

Paul D. James
Willie Cockburn Penn

Norman Smith Whiteley

## Bachelor of Science

Charles Leon Barnett
Harold Lee Campbell
Orvie Lee Loyd Cantrell
James W. Deatherage
Joseph McAfee Elliott
Ed Gilliam
Thomas Lee Jarvis
Bob Mac Kyle

Billy Van O'Brien
Donald Marvin Pittenger
Billy Byron Redding
Hal Slone Robbins
Donald Edward Sheppart
Wayne Bartlett Smith
Durward Jackson Taylor, Jr.

## Bachelor of Arts

Walter J. Arnold
Fred Herbert Babb
Donald Richard Beeth
Ida Lou Berly
Camilla Elizabeth Bidwell
John Michael Brand III

Barbara Ann Brooks
Mellie Rebecca Brown
Ben Allen Carpenter
Peggy Anne Christopher
James Byrd Crocker
Alfred David Denton, Jr.

Carol Elizabeth Elliott
Virginia Slaughter Graves
Clifford Julian Grum
Kenneth Eugene Hoover, Jr.
H. P. Hosey
Mindy Ann Rogers Hosey
Daniel Brewster Howell, Jr.
Margaret Ann Hunter
Martha Jean Kincaid
Jean Gray Forbes Kyle
Elaine Elizabeth Lubbers
James McGrady McLean, Jr.
William Evans Martin

Robert Wilson Moore
Bernard Edwin Morisette
Richard Dean Munson
John Louis Murad
William Busch Oelfke
Irene Ortega-Castro
Bonnie Jean Pennycuick
Mickey Pfaff
Harry Porter, Jr.
James Earnest Powell
William Mack Reid
Sara Elizabeth Russell

## Bachelor of Arts

### 1957

Emmett Barry Beard
Ben Lawrence Bell
John Leason Bishop
Mrs. Margaret Nell Boozer
Robert Henry Bullard, Jr.
John Hugh Carlbert
Robert Lee Carsner
Mrs. Martha Weems Cheney
Nancy Cunningham
Mrs. Zelda J. DeMilio
Gaylord Howard Dodgen
Charlotte Anne Endress
Carol Franklin Fleming
William Arthur Freeland
Donald Arthur Gloff
Grantland Marvin Groves
Nathalie Virginia Grum
Frances Rae Hardgrave
Harry Edward Hardgrave, Jr.
Carolyn Priscilla Harvey
Watha Jo Henderson
James Francis Jecker
Robert Willem Jurrius

Takao Kitamura
Gloria Ann Lindsay
Frances Rosalie McCall
Beulah Mae McLean
Wallace Eugene March
Robert Glenn Massey
Bernard Reese Mathews, Jr.
Elizabeth Campbell Matson
Frankie Josephine Monroe
Minta Rhea Perry
Vernon Doyle Rheay
Mary Scott
Jack Selman
Mrs. Eva Jane White Somers
Mrs. Carol Dozier Sprinkel
Raymond Keith Sprinkel
Mrs. Marilyn Dunagan
    Stubbeman
Robert Frank Stubbeman
Arra Ann Tolbert
Dixie Estelle Turner
Mrs. Virginia Mathis Wood

## Master of Arts
### 1958

Verrill Wayland Barnes
Mrs. Bonnie Ruth Cleary
Robert T. Mason

Mrs. Mary Loise May
Mrs. Mary Lou Partlow

## Bachelor of Science

James Houston Barnes
Carroll June Bowling
Thomas Lester Cheney
Donald Audrey Correu
John Jacob Egbert
Ormiston Tupper Ellis
David Michael Fox
Fohn Clay Francis
James E. Gaston
Luther Edward Harvey

Donis Kay McBee Henson
Kenneth Willis Homer
Louis Fredrick Lester
Hobert Wade Lytal
Robert E. Maroney
Cecil Jack Miller
James Elmer Owens
John Arnold Streun II
John C. Towles
Lee Roy Weiss

## Master of Science

Mrs. V. Eugenia Tate Chapman
Lee A. Clarkston

Robert Oliver Kidd
Miss Veda Perry

## Master of Arts

Edward Lee Wilbourn

## Master of Science

Dan Read Ellett

## Bachelor of Science

Charles Wayne Arledge
Gerald Lynn Blankenship
Bobby Jewel Clarkston
George Donald Cowden
Mervyn Wilfred Crake
Henry Smythe Groesbeeck, Jr.
Mary Lynne Haynes

Frank Hayward, III
Albert Edwin Jarrell
Lee Waldrop McLane
Weldon Page Rackley
Dennis Burton Redburn
James Earl Sandridge
James Hershell Self

Claudius Ray Smith
Frank Strickland
Clovis Malcolm Swanner, Jr.
Mary Elizabeth Tappan
Franklin Portor Tilghman
Donald B. Watson

James Thomas Bates
Paul Monroe Branum
Clarence S. Dussing, Jr.
Lem Scarbrough, Jr.
Glen Allen Standridge

## Bachelor of Arts

Ira Thomas Anderson, Jr.
Gene Walter Babb
Jerry Thomas Bell
William Walton Bondurant, III
George Nolan Boyd
Dorothy Jane Brand
Lindy Mack Cannon
Harold Layton Clark
Sidney Hall Coleman, Jr.
Clinton Earl Craven
Gail Elizabeth Davis
William Cecil Doyle
Edna Earle Dutton
Kathleen Myrna Finke
Charles Ralph Galbraith
Lila Lois Hall
George C. Herrscher
Ann Carolyn Howard
Patricia Ann Jamison
Mildred Minnett Johnston
Lester Dean Kinkade
John Charles Lamberth
Robert Powers Lehr, Jr.
Gertrude Anne McAlpine
James Douglas McElroy
Billy Jack Marshall
Maurice Ray Martin
Elsa Lu Mickle
Harry Wayne Beard
Ann Leslie Chaffin
Charlotte Anne Frasher

Martha Britt Mixson
Mary Ann Owen
Ernest P. Taylor
V. V. Miller
Richard Sibley Mitchell
Michael Fielding Murray
Lucy Ann Nance
Robert Dixon Nolen, Jr.
Freeman Marcus Payne, Jr.
Lillian Gail Peavy
Laura Kay Peurifoy
Elizabeth Day Poole
Josephine Elaine Russell
Geraldine Sanders
Donald Ray Shepherd
Betsy Anne Slagle
Patricia Ann Smith
Phillip Montford Spencer
Hallie Jane Spragins
Walton Herbert Springall
Jane Marie Staats
James Melroy Thompson, Jr.
Mary Elizabeth Thulemeyer
Joseph Lee Turner
Frank Philip Vogt, Jr.
Earl Fredrick Walborg, Jr.
Donald Quentin Webb
Barbara Ann Whitehead
John Martin Whitfill
Floyd Clark Williams
Vick Franklin Williams

## Master of Arts

### 1959

Linda Miller Peter                Claudius Ray Smith

### Bachelor of Arts

Annis Adele Acrey
Roland Mohler Bagby
Texanita Louise Barsh
William Gregg Berry
Bert Allen Bronaugh
Charles Udell Brown
Wayne A. Brown
Mary Randolph Bullock
Margaret Clyborne
Jack Corzine
Marilyn Virginia Cowles
James Randolph Cumbic
John Christian Danner
Nancy Clay Dennis
Shirley Elizabeth Dirr
John Belton Duncan, Jr.
Andrew Billy Erwin
Lynne Elizabeth Evans
Douglas Brown Finch
Carolee Gollehon
Joan Lucille Grabbe
Margaret Corrine Graham
Doris Geraldine Hanna
Nancy Jean Hatley
Lou Ann Hintz
Barbara Jean Hotz
Phillip Edward Hudson
George Thomas Huser
Richard Phillip Jarrell, Jr.
Billy Wayne Jarvis
Clarence Mike Jousan, Jr.
Dorothy Eleanor Kelly
Johnson Arledge King
Donad Joe Kiser

Fannie Lea Knight
Robert Eugene Lamberth
Robert Raymond Landolt
Lynn Vernon Lawther, Jr.
Giovanno Leo
Martha Neil McAlpine
George Alexander McCall, Jr.
James L. L. McCall
James Clinton McCrary
Donald McKinley McCune
Louis Rushing Manz, Jr.
Leroy Kirk Martin
Patricia Ann Martin
Virginia Stone Mathews
T. DeWayne May
Larry Cullin Miles
Fred Manget Minter
Nancy Ann Mitchell
Charles Edward Morriss
Particia Ann Myers
Jane Nelson
Richard Louis Ortiz
Eddie Jack Polk
Mary Amelia Poole
John Alexander Price
Mildred Robertson
Dorothy Jean Rodina
Thomas Garrison Sauer
Nancy Lou Scallia
Clare Louise Schlegel
Frank Logan Seaman
William Brearly Secor
Mary Edyth Schmoldas
Dorothy Clorine Sims

Lonnie D. Sinclair
Curtis Fred Singleton
Phoebe Alice Slate
Frances Janet Smith
Carl Leon Stone
Howard Lawrence Taylor
Rowena Muriel Taylor

Coy Weldon Teasley
Jean Wilson Travis
James David Wahrmund
Joan Leutsch Watson
Nelma Laverne White
James Clifford Wilson

## Bachelor of Science

L. D. Allison, Jr.
Claude Burton, Jr.
Don Thomas Cantrell
Loyal Delmo Cardwell
William Aaron Cunningham, Jr.
Joe Edward Davis
Raymond Joseph DuPuy
Ronnie Joe Forgus

Kenneth Fleet Kleasner
John Raymond Long
Jim Perry
Wally Frank Reddick
Karl Paxton Sanders
Charles Raymond Sessom, Jr.
Chester William Story
Martha Nell Webster

## Bachelor of Arts

## 1960

Priscilla Ann Abbott
Mary Kathryn Adams
Paul R. Alexander
William Milton Aylor
Bonnie Jean Beardsley
Bruce Richard Blome
Barbara Nell Broyles
Beulah Virginia Burkett
Joyce Thrasher Coney
Charles Randolph Coney
Jerry Dale Dawson
David A. Dickey
Etna Jean Duncan
Jaird Boyd Ellard, Jr.
Rex Lynn Elmore
Marlin Lee Gilbert
Nancy Jane Gracy
Martha Ann Halsted

Wha-Suck Han
James Walter Hanna
Paul Lynn Harris
William Edward Harris
Joe Harold Hurst
Edith Friedlander Kaplan
Mary Elizabeth Kennedy
Fleda Gregory Lambert
Virginia Anne Landers
Evelyn Ann Lare
Jill Ledebur
Jerry Luttrell Loveless
Rupert Walter Lundgren, Jr.
Marjorie Jean McAlpine
James Albright McCullough
Joe Donald Marshall
Roy Lee Merrill
Frank John Meyer

Robert Wilson Minshew
Jon Nelson Moline
Eskridge Ruth Moore
Raymond Carter Morse
Jacquelyn Rhea Nipper
Nancy Carol Nisbett
Margie Ann Noel
Daniel Gregory Page
Richard Blyth Poteet
Sandra Lois Reninger
Charles Leroy Rhodes
Dorothy Louise Richardson
Virginia R. Seaton

Carolyn Marie Smith
Charles Orin Smyre
Catherine Standefer
Barbara Jeanne Steele
Dorothy Louise Stewart
Everett Lavern Sutton
Margaret Edmiston Taylor
Martin Junius Taylor
Daniel Murray Thompson, Jr.
Johnnie Aline Tramel
Roy Laughton Whitehead, Jr.
Earl Hazen Woods

## Bachelor of Science

Jerry Eugene Apple
Ronald Dee Beck
John Bernard Cahill, Jr.
Charles Russell Crowson
John Earl Denton, Jr.
Cletis Gerald Dunn
Gene Eldridge Fike
Robert Glen Gammon
Edith Ann Harper
George Milton Henderson
Thomas Lawrence Huey

James Darrell Maines
Jack L. Manes, Jr.
Barbara Cullison Moore
Kemp Moore, Jr.
Perry Eugene Morris
Earl Gayno Shelton
Samuel Albert Shields
Lawrence B. Smith
Alan Wayne Waldrop
Joe Barry Wood

## Masters Degrees

Anne Martin Johnson, M.A.
Tommie Sue Spaulding, M.A.

Morrie J. Molpus, M.S.

## Master of Arts

### 1961

Ruth Pauline Alexander
Verrill Wayland Barnes
Ruth Crum Entrekin

Virginia Slaughter Graves
Sara Elizabeth Hughes
Lillian M. Myers

## Master of Science

Mabel Louise Craig

## Bachelor of Arts

Jim Tom Ainsworth
William Henry Altman
Elizabeth Ellen Anderson
David Harris Berkebile
Gladys Nadine Blanton
Michael Everett Broyles
Sheila Elizabeth Campbell
William Richard Carey
Virginia Day Carruth
Rebecca Earline Clayton
Saundra S. Copeland
John Gammons Dillard
Anna Elizabeth Doggett
Mary Moore Donaldson
Paul Everette Donaldson
Charles Frederick Due
David Christopher Duncan
James Frederick Dwight
William Warren Dyal
Jean Carol Eberts
Lasandra Sue Fagg
Elizabeth Ann Figley
James Edward Foster
James Alton Franklin
Alma Sarah Gallaher
Bertron Martin Groves
Charles Collins Hendricks
Gerald Howard Holt, Jr.
James Norman Hunt
John Clarence Hunter
Carol Sue Irwin
Kay Irene Jack
Martha Suzanne Jackson
Donald Linous Jarvis
Louis Martin Kluck
Robert George Landolt

Sandra Claire Lavender
Joseph Franklin Lawrence
Carol Jean Lindley
William Wright Lipscomb
Mary Victoria Liscum
Virginia Quay Lyon
Patricia Ann McClurg
Elizabeth Ann McCullough
Elizabeth Hester McCullough
James Lawrence McCullough, J
Lynda Sue Millen
Bonnie Ruth Miller
Charles Bolanz Miller
Carole Ann Money
Phyllis Jo Moore
Ronald Lee Murphy
Jorge Comacho Olguin
Janet Virginia Pearsall
Judith Elaine Pogue
Richard Allen Porter
Daryl Wayne Preston
Donald Gene Pringle
John Malcolm Purcell
Nat B. Read
Robert Wallace Rehmet
Peggy Sue Rheinlaender
Edna Ross Rogers
Sue Schoeneck
Stella Ann Sedgwick
Joseph Taylor Seibold
Barbara Jane Simmons
Billy Eual Smith
John William Solomon
Peter Swain Springall
Donald James Sumerlin
Harold Joe Swafford

Roger Dean Tesch
Doris Jean Tinney
Lottie Nelson Vincent
Edward Louis Wagoner
Nancy Coe Walker
Mary Lynn Watson
Virginia Dale Watson

Sue Pardue West
Madeline Lorraine Whitten
Lois Ann Wilder
John Edward Withers III
Jeanette Love Dunham
Theodore Carl Schirmer

## Bachelor of Science

Walter Neal Ague
Jack Ronald Arwine
Donald William Clark, Jr.
William Waldron Coates III
Jackie Ray Edwards
John Will Gragg
Jerry Leslie Hodges
Glen Raymond Kirk
Karl Dumas Leslie
Carroll Jean May
Michael Walter Mitchell
Clarence Randolph Russell, Jr.

Charles Everett Smith
William Inzer Southerland, Jr.
Barbara W. Stone
Donald Wayne Taylor
Bobby Eugene Thornton
Larry Lee Uland
Jack Gene Walker
Abner Daon Wall
James William Walls
Arthur M. Mosse, Jr.
Charles Ferrell Wright

## Bachelor of Arts

### 1962

Ronnie Robert Aebersold
Sara Lynn Ague
Ruth Anne Alexander
Barbara Sue Aylor
Margaret Ann Ball
Edward Vaughan Bondurant
Margaret Ann Brown
Thomas Finley Brown
Kathryn Bruns
Audra May Calhoon
Carol June Campbell
Kay Curry
Mary Morriss Duncan
Jeanette Love Dunham
Frances Ann Dunn

Nancy Jane Elmore
Trulah Burwell Everett
Faye Dell Farmer
Albert George Fleischer
Lester Gene Furry
Katie Beth Futch
Robert Calvin Galbraith
John Neal Glover
William Emory Glover
Dian Gould
Barbara Adine Gready
Thomas Gerald Gready
Elmer Lee Grisso
Joseph Marshall Groce
Lucetta Ann Harbison

Gloria Jean Harrison
Betty Bevens Hatfield
Helen Marie Hayes
Charlotte Ann Haynes
Rufus Womack Head
Bobbye Jean Harrell
Kenneth Truman Hern
John Charles Hitt, Jr.
Laura Sue Holland
Gerald Eugene Hudson
Carroll Leslie Hughes
Forrest Jack Hurley
Mary Catherine Moses Hurley
Mary Carolyn James
Martha V. Jamison
Murray Lloyd Johnston, Jr.
Brenda Ann Jones
Jerold Baz Jones
Lily Katherine Jones
Karen Keliehor
James Edward Keller
Michael Frederick King
Carol Irene Kingelin
Frederick Wm. Kohlhausen, Jr.
Marilyn Jean Kretsinger
Sharen K. Langston
William Truman Lawrence
Betty Jean Guthrie Lee
Joan Katheryn Leinneweber
Donald Roy Liljestrand
Thomas Fulton Lowe
Robyn Charlotte McChesney
Margaret Gayle McCord
John Scott McMahon
Luis Manueco-Jenkins

Cervando Martinez, Jr.
Michael Joseph Mezzino
Hiromi Morioka
Byron Davis Myrick
William Dewey Narramore
Virginia Rene Perdue
Juan Felipe Perez
Harvey Randall Pierce
Barbara Jean Praeger
Mary Kay Richter
Susan Roberts
Edward Earl Sammons, Jr.
Theodore Carl Schirmer
Carol Schoeneck
Patrick Wilbert Shaw
George Henry Smith
Tinsley Gordon Smith
William Dale Stark
William Rue Steffey
Ronald Eugene Stevenson
Paul Ellis Tatum, Jr.
Anita Alleane Taylor
Ima Jane Taylor
Doris Jean Tinney
William Haywood Tolbert
John Carlton Travis
Robert Warren Trezevant
John Larry Walker
Marcia Ann Wallace
John Thaddeus Wehmeyer
Dan Carlos West
James Marvin Wilbourn
Melinda Claire Witty
Richard Gabbott Wood
Phyllis Ann Wright

## Bachelor of Science

Phillip S. Bailey
Raymond Pace Bennett
Janyce Lanette Benton

Bill E. Cobb
Janet Lemerle Coffman
Reginald Eugene Davis

Norman Edward Dickey
Donnie Howard Duncan
Bruce Emerson Dunn
William Thomas Flanagan
George Wilson Hail
Richard Wayne Hairston
Jerry Mac McBee
Arthur M. Mosse, Jr.
Daniel Wayne Parker
Jerome Louis Reichstetter

Donald Ray Renfroe
Robert Earl Richardson, Jr.
Ronald Lee Sanford
Thurman Eugene Sargent
J. C. Truitt
Bobby Gene Weddle
Charles Edward Williams
Charles Ferrell Wright
Martha Louise Wright

## Masters Degrees

Charles R. Andrews, M.S.
Dixie Louise Bell, M.A.

Billie Ruth Moore, M.A.

## Master of Science

Nonette Camp Kolb

## Master of Art

Daniel F. Manthei

Lottie Creswell Helms

## Bachelor of Arts
## May 27, 1963:

Mary Sue Adams
Ruth Ann Altman
James Michael Atkins
John Lindsey Baker
George Ward Beaudry
Ross William Bedell
Robert Delmer Belew
Janice Lee Bennett
Martha Leone Black
James Emery Blankenship
John A. Bryant
Don Stephen Burket

James Mason Cahalan
Jayne Christine Chamberlin
Jerry Wayne Chapman
Sidney Claire Childs
David DeJarnette Claflin
Lucy Gay Clark
William Lewis Clyborne, Jr.
Harriett Mable Cornelison
Richard Thomas Cowles
John Carlton Dannel
Hugh Clifton Davis
James Ellis DeBerry

Jan Baker Emrick
Mary Sue Farr
Jose Marcelo Garza
Gloria Gaytan
Janie Jo Defee
Karen Ellen Easterly
Judith Carol Edmondson
Mary Lynn Galbraith
Phillips Alton Hanson
Billy Thomas Henderson
Emily Rose Lawhead
Mark Broughton Lindsay
Sharon D. McFarland
Dorthell Grider McKinney
Fredonya McKinney
Geraldine Armon Goleman
Sally Kathryn Goodman
Virgil Boyd Graves
Edith Jean Griffin
Carol Anne Hall
Donna Gail Hardgrave
Lynne Ruth Hartman
Richard Wesley Haythorn
Lawrence Eugene Hedges
James L. Higgins
Michael Adrian Holy
Scherel Horn
David Wallace Hornbeck
Gale Wayne Huckaby
Elaine Mangelsdorf Hull
Richard Thompson Hull
Nancy Jo Jackson
Troy G. Jarvis
Marilou Jones
Mary Jane Langston
Julie Brooks Lawrence
Larry Clinton Ledebur
Ella North Lester
Sally Nixon Lewis
Charles Darrell Locke
Nicholas Lawrence Lund

Wallace Foster McArthur
Richard Ferris McKay
Roy Nolen Markham
John Mitchell Marshall
Harold Fromme Neal
Jay Carter Paul
Carl Milam Peters
Steven Braun Schlosstein
Faith Ainsworth Smith
Karen Stickler
Martha Ann Walters
Jerry Wayne Webb
Jack Hanson McLean
Margaret Donna Madden
Rebecca Reed Maid
Gay Lynn Noble
John Stanley Noble
Carole Margaret Pierson
Barbara Jean Pietsch
Mary Ward Pope
William Franklin Pruitt, Jr.
Roger Travis Quillin
Cheryl Olufs Richardson
Amis Joe Riddles
Carolyn Jeanne Robbins
James Carlton Robinson
Annette Apple Rogers
Jimmy Dan Sanders
Mary Alice Saul
Kenneth Wayne Sebesta
Jerry Glenn Shaffer
Harold Skaggs, Jr.
Sally Jane Smith
Sandra Lynn Smith
Florence Margaret Spragins
David Charles Sprowl
Glen Harry Stanbaugh, Jr.
Robert Eldon Stovenour
Jerry Glenn Strong
Joe Ray Sudderth
Carolyn Kay Teel

Doris Ida VanHooser
Wallis Frederick Westwood
Bruce Howard White
Ramond Hendry William, Jr.
Robert Clifford Williams

Search F. Willis, Jr.
Geraldine Frances Wilson
Glenda Louise Yaughn
Martha Minnette Yeargan

## Bachelor of Science

Jackie Duaine Baker
Tommy Charles Brown
Glen Edward Crisp
Ronald Leon Elsheimer
Edward James Gannon IV
DeWitt Talmadge Greer, Jr.
Kenneth Arthur Krause
Arnold O. Lee
Joe M. Maines
Mack Bradley Pierson
Mary Ann Rath

George Baker Rice, Jr.
Jimmy Orman Rogers
James Leonard Stotts, II
Theodore Robert Thevenet
Sharon Ann Torbett
Charles Dudley Wallace
Charles D. Wiser
Donald Cates Barker
Gary Lee Clark
Dickie Ray Melton
Charles R. Robertson

## Bachelor of Arts

## 1964

Larry Jack Alexander
Rebecca Aston
Vicki Marion Baker
Guy Walter Bayless
Claire Elaine Beekman
Janne Benson
Joanne Lucille Berglund
Howard Ruble Bethel
Jane Elizabeth Brazell
James Washington Buckner
Dan Edward Caldwell
Richie Fernoy Calhoun
James Newton Camak, Jr.
Drake Spencer Cameron
Jean Schwiening Campbell
Margaret Jean Clark
James Stephen Coats

Pamela Sharon Conaway
Carol Marie Cook
Anna Lee Crawford
Nolan Denney Crisp
George Edgar Crosthwaite
David Patterson Dashner
Charles Douglas Davis
Charles Edwin Davis
Eunice Mae Dickey
Emmett M. Essin
Jay Donald Evans
John Ronald Evans
Judith Mary Evans
Malcolm McCollum Feeley
Clifton Donald Finney
David Antoine Frank, III
Norma Jean Fry

John Edward Goodman
Robert Lowry Goodman
Kenneth Floyd Gregory
Pamela Chadill Hemphill
Blair B. Hickey
Joanne Mallett Hickey
Dale LeRoy Hill
Noel Ross Houck
Dorothy Rae Hudgeons
Elizabeth Louise Irwin
William Swaffor Jennings
Polly Ann Johnson
Jim Herschel Joiner
William Edward Kendall
Judith Dorcas Kidd
Robert Barron Lewis
George Ernest Livings
Mary Louise Livings
Ruth Reyes Lizcano
Kenneth Wayne Loyd
Harry Thomas McAlister
John Wilson McKim, Jr.
Fredonya Lucille McKinney
Joan Dae McMahon
David Mercer Martin
William Forrest Martin
Nona Mewhinney
Virginia Ann Miller
Don Eric Moore
Samuel Steele Moore
Marcia Berta Murray
Robert Roy Murray

John Herbert Newton
Helen Deane Owen
Carol Ann Porter
Frank Stephen Powers
Carole Cleveland Price
Susan Qualtrough
Don Robert Read
Sally Carol Robinson
Charles Dimick Robison
David Ross
Linda Jo Rumbel
Charles Richmond Scurry
Michael Gene Sewell
Pierre Shamba
Judith Claire Singleton
Mary Elizabeth Spaulding
Karen Elizabeth Palmer
Paul Edward Pedigo
LeRoy Morgan Poinsett
Harley James Spoon
Henry Merillat Staat
Carolyn Jeanne Sumner
Estelle Stuart Taylor
Marjorie Jean Teel
Wordy Jack Thompson, Jr.
Catherine Upshaw
Sharon Lynn VandeVuss
Patricia Elizabeth Veatch
Richard Wendell Wheeler
Robert Gale White
Ruth Ann Whiteside

## Bachelor of Science

Ronald Dean Beck
Gene Tate Chiles
Charles Reagan Coon
Freddie Michael Day
Robert James Goodman
John Anthony Lawrence
Frederick Otto Lehmann, Jr.

Robert Harold McNay
William Edgar Marion
Will C. Miller
Kearney Clinton Morrow
Dedra Sue Price
Allan Thomas Reeves
John Thomas Young

## Master of Arts

Wm. Lee Crenshaw
Joe Edward Davis
Roy Reid Jackson

Sandra Lavender Tate
Mary Alice Taylor

## Master of Science

Gyneth B. Luby

## Bachelor of Arts

### 1965

Antoinette Elena Aguilar
Andrew Ryan Allen
Roger Kent Anderson
Henry McClelland Bailey, Jr.
Nancy Kay Beinke
Ned Harold Benson
Harry Edward Bilger
Barbara Bolding
Frances Howard Bronson
Kathy Sue Browe
Michael R. Burkett
Robert Jeffrey Caswell
Michael Lee Cauthen
James William Center
Kenneth L. Clayton
Frances Ann Coats
Penny Sue Coyne
Frances Elizabeth Crown
Alice Martin Davis
Jay MacDonald Davis
Nancy Hill Davis
James Elliott Deans, Jr.
Galdino DonJuan
Mary Lucretia Duncan
David E. Easterly
Zelda Faith Easton
Chad Duane Emrick

William Robert Essin
Phyllis Marcia Finkler
Gwenda Lynn Greer
James Allen Hallmark, Jr.
Doris Ellen Hardy
Carolyn Chapin Harris
William Robert Hayes
Sue Ellen Hellmers
Nathalie Ann Henderson
Donna Dee Hollingsworth
Roberta Richey Hunt
Nancy Randolph Hyatt
Kenneth Ward Jack
Evelyn DeMoss Jacoby
Gary Griffith John
Elizabeth Stephenson Johnson
Laurie Ann Johnson
Milton David Johnson III
Charles Christopher Jordan
Frank Hotchkiss Jordan
Dan Charles Kinnard
Frederic George Lahourcade, Jr.
John Charles Landolt
Jim David Little
Paulene Graham Long
Linda Sue Loper
Carol Johnson Lunsford

Eva Jo McGrede
Margaret Ann McKey
James Angus McLeod
Michael John McMains
Craig George MacFarland
Paulette Setzer Martin
Joanna Winchester Maurer
Charles William Miller
Samuel Rutherford Miller
Jack Alan Mims
Jacqueline Lucille Monroe
Richard Lucas Moody
Robert Todd Morriss
William Todd Murray
Donald Ross Newsom
Lou Ray Partlow
William Paul Pearce
Frances Cornette Phillips
Mary Myrnell Phillips
Patricia Sue Pierce
Bernard Joseph Popp
Sandra Helen Preston
Albert Ernest Rath, Jr.
William Warfield Robertson
James Roy Sanders
Thomas Henderson Schmid
John Allen Self
Kenneth Foster Sellers, Jr.

Mary Martia Singleton
Anne Kathryn Smiley
Marilyn Oleta Smith
Ann Coit Sporer
Gail Moore Streun
William Ray Streun
Dianna Lea Tatum
David Jerome Taylor
Frances Leith Taylor
Johnny Stant Terry
David Bacon Thompson
Jeanette Louise Tinney
Don Wayne Trow
Elsie Lenore Tyler
Arlene Faye VanRees
Bedford Mather Vestal
Gerry Luther Waldrop
Michael Claude Walker
Karen Jean Webster
Eric Philip Weisberg
John Dampier Weisinger
Nancy Boyd Weisinger
Nancy Virginia Wilhite
Margaret Louise Wilkins
Weldon Leon Willig
Mary Bob Wilson
McKee DeWitt Yant II
Frank Raymond Yeatman

## Bachelor of Science

Charles Bruce Mauk, Jr.
James Allen Sammons

Paul Michael Sorrells
Akira Yoshida

## Bachelor of Arts

Clifford Keeton Barnes
Joseph James Bonney
Samuel Robert Bonney
William Kenneth Carrell

Teddy Ray Chapman
Patricia Lefforge Davis
Herbert Reed DeWees
Kirk Talmadge French

John Everham Harvey
Mary Louise Jackson
Michael Wayne Jenkins
Wayne Hammer McClure II
Thomas Reed Maid
Felicity Ann Nussbaum
Richard Lynn Pitman

William Russel Pooley
James Allen Rolfe
Phin Sappenfield
Sylvester P. Smith
Charles M. Warlick
Robt. H. Woodruff, Jr.
George W. Tracwick

## Master of Science

Gladyce Belden

## Master of Arts

Marcus Wm. Austin
Dorothy Bonsworth

Barbara Jean Mackey
Thelma Payne Owens

## Bachelor of Arts

### 1966

Carl Verran Aldrich
John Milton Anderson
Gilbert Irenus Anderson, Jr.
Philip Fowler Anthony
John Wayne Baughn
James Oliver Bennett
Robert Wade Bennett
Jerry Glynn Bishop
Stephen Earl Blythe
Woodrow Michael Bonesio
Billy Joe Braly
Michael Kent Braswell
James Daniel Breazeale
Viviane Cecile Chabas Breazeale
Catherine Douglas Talbot Brown
Michael James Brown
Laura Kathryn Bumpass
Leslie Jeanne Burford
Barbara Jane Calhoon
Charles Callendar Carsner III

Irene Clemence Carstens
Robert Paul Carter
Mary Lou Cassidy
Howard Leslie Channell
Jane Kelley Chapman
Gale Rentoul Clarke
Mary Catherine Cloud
Rebecca Ann Cooper
Margaret Ellen Coslett
Cheryl Ann Crist
Mary Lee Cushman
Thomas E. Dale
Robert Clark Dana
Mary Elva Deloteus
Emily Lippke DeWees
William Carroll Dietrich
Margret Rehm Dodge
Jerry Wayne Durham
Caroline Ballew Elbert
Margaret Elizabeth Elder

Cathryn Ann Smith Emrick
Richard Barrett Faulkner
Windell Glenn Ferguson
Dana Sue Fienning
Winifred Anne Flato
James David Fletcher
Jimmie Lee Foreman
John Peter Forney III
Clara Lucille Futch
Fred Gordon Gill
Clark Patton Gillespie
Elizabeth Ann Gleichert
Duane Doyle Gohlke
Kenneth Alan Graham
William J. Haire
Frank Louis Hansen
Billy Wayne Harris
Linda Sue Hart
Ernest Gerhard Harwig
Donald Edward Hayes
Delia Ann Hendricks
Roger Lee Henninger
Dale Alvis Hensarling
Jae Henry Hill
Richard Ballantine Hill, Jr.
Abbey Hintgen
Annadele Holm
Mary Elizabeth Hopper
Lawrence Leggett Huelbig
Mary Christine Isham
Sue Martin Jarvis
Edward Sikes Johnson
Karl Duggan Johnson, Jr.
Mary W. Jones
Robert Earl Karper III
Ayse Koymen
John Frederick Krieg
Laura Alice Coker Lynn
Warren McCain Lynn
Earl Richard McBride, Jr.
Kay Irene McConathy

William Robert McLeRoy
Barbara Ann Malloy
Robert Edward Martin
Edward William Matthiessen III
Nancy Lee Melton
Richard Eugene Merritt
Linda Lea Metcalf
Susan Nelson Mims
Judy Kay Money
Dana Louise Moore
Sara Caroline Moseley
Richard Dean Munson
Lee Brening Murdy
David Rea Musser
Stephen Hughes Nabors
Mary Helen Neal
Willie Michael Nelson
Charles Perry Newton III
Nancy Jane Nickles
Susan Lynne Park
William Edward Peteet
Martha Ead Philbeck
Paul Clark Redman
Susan Mallie Reed
Robert Rex Reitz
Virginia Beth Rennels
Michael George Renquist
Paul Armand Sabatier
Kathryn Janette Sandridge
William Horace Sayre
David Marshall Seaver
Tonelia Hardy Seaver
Lucy Ann Shelton
Emily Sholl
Daniel DaCosta Snider
Linda Jan Speed
Elizabeth Ann Sterrett
Travis J. Stewart
Carolyn Dawn Strickland
Laurence Ellington Sykes
Nancy Jane Robinson Terry

Allen Rupert Thompson
Richard Raymond Thoms
Carolyn Louise Trezevant
Mary Ann Vandergriff
Mary Ann Veirs
John Charles Virden
Ronald Wayne Walden
Robert Logan Ward
Thomas Whelan III
Dianne Sherwood White
Catherine Louise Whiteside
Gary Page Whitfield
George Kent Wilcox
Paul Edward Winkelmann
Nona Bishop Wood
Nancy Nicholls Woodward
Robert Chester Albritton
Charles David Anderson
Mary Susan Begley Anderson
Lee Charles Archie
Virginia Anne Arthur
Sara Lou Bishop
Elizabeth Atkinson Bradshaw
James Travis Brannan
Tommy Roy Brock
Joseph Sidwell Cutlip
Betty Joyce Davis
Tommie Lee Eustace

Barbara Anne Finnegan
Geoffrey Allan Grimes
Gaye Harriet Hewitt
Billy Jack Huebesch
John Michael Jernigan
Doris Coffey Korioth
Ellen Rosalie Krempin
Wayne Lee Langehennig
James Raymond Lawrence
R. Terry LeMaster
Walter Timothy Lewis
Andrea Kay Smith Martin
Robert Rix Martin
Nelson Leon Morris
James Daniel Murphy
Nancy Long Nesbit
Leonard Wayne Parker
James Michael Price
Charles John Rudolph, Jr.
Patricia Lee Smith
Mack Aaron Snider
Herbert Benjamin Spangler
Larry Jefferson Ward
Jack Thomas Whitener
David Charles Winship
Cherrie Louise Wood
Dorothy Louise Young

## Master of Arts

Mary Anne Brock
Dorthell G. McKinney
William Lon Scott

Jo Ellen Sheppard
Archie Edwin Vessels

## 1967

Akil Abdulla Abdulaziz
Kazuko Akiyama
Susan Elizabeth Aldridge
John Robert Asbury, Jr.

Susan Aston
Carolyn Atlee
Thomas Edgar Bachner, Jr.
Linda Ann Bagwell

David L. Baird, Jr.
Donald Earl Barker
William Thomas Bartlett
Jean True Becker
John Wayne Bengel
Nancy Ellen Bickel
Diana Gay Birdwell
Carol Lynn Blackstone
Michael Lee Boyd
Judith Anne Brown
Elva Rebecca Brownlow
David Wattam Bryant II
James Raymond Bryant
Linda Byrd Bryant
Robert Haydon Bullock, Jr.
Robert Lee Bunce
Sally Ann Campbell
Robert Lane Chappell
Caren Clark
Edward Lionel Clarke
Eugene Rex Cooper
Jesse Eugene Covey
George Ernest Crosby, Jr.
Frank Thomas Dean
Deanna Denny
Marie Wakefield Dickinson
Donald Richard Dossett
Joseph Ronald Dowlen
Ione Grace Dyal
David Kraft Eckert
Susan Lee Ellison
Marion Martha Engberg
Cheryl Lynn Finley
Lawrence John Francell
Sara Louise LeTourneau Frank
Joe Marvin Fulenchek
John Yarbro Galbraith
Joe Robert Archie Gay
Ruth Lavelle Gay
Kenneth Hays Gentry
Marvin Kelsey Gibbs

Dan Elliott Goldsmith
Carol Joan Graves
Janet Elizabeth Graves
Pamela Aston Grimes
Michael B. Grizzard
John Sheldon Hacker
Carol Dawn Haehl
John Townes Hairston
David Walden Hall
Carole Madalyn Hamilton
Nancy Mae Hand
Tom C. Hardy, Jr.
Stephen Kenneth Harrel
James R. Harris, Jr.
Diana Sherman Hays
Michael Heistand
Marieulla Sandy Hill
Stephen DaCosta Holt
Joyce Rosalia Howard
Carl Lee Hudson
Harold Cooper Hunter
John Robert Jameson
James Thomas Jarratt
Boyd Abercrombia Johnson
David Russell Johnson
Richard Benjamin Johnson, Jr.
Robert Byron Johnston
Patricia Jane Kaspar
Raymond Reddell Keese
Karen Marie Kendrick
Mary Frances King
Laurence R. Kirk
Carol Alden Kizer
Suzanne Weekley Leach
Dan Henry Lee, III
John Thomas Leftwich
Richard Anton Levacy
Kerry Evans Lewis
Douglas Arthur Lipka
Eric Robert Liston
Thomas Ellis Lockhart III

Susan Goodwin Lowry
Susan Doris Lund
Steven Curtis McAdoo
Eugene Fentress McAlpine
Lloyd Phillip McCarter, Jr.
Jack Hamblin McCubbin
Charles Bruce McNab
Joan Yvonne Mackey
Helen Joan March
Stephen Albert Marx
Edward Orys Mason, Jr.
Hawkins Henley Menefee, Jr.
John Joseph Milligan, Jr.
Stanley Eugene Monroe, Jr.
Claire Louise Moore
Stephen Edward Mosher
Marilee Ruth Munger
Suzanne Murphy
Michael Theodore Nurre
Nira Jo Nussbaum
Dick Alden Pafford
James Mark Paine
Gregg Alan Paris
Gary Wayne Parker
Mary Rebecca Parse
Lela Elaine Peabody
Homer David Peeoples
John Michael Pittman
William Stanley Poinsett
Howard Lee Powell
Edwin Frank Powers
Davis Borden Price
Jimmie Karen Couch Ray
Richard Ivan Readinger
Samuel Pierre Riccobene
Jacqueline Glee Roberts
Marianne Rogers
Marjorie Hume Roth
Richard Elliott Rowland
Lewis Franklin Russell
Mary Rebecca Russell

George Allen Rustay
Charles Clayton Schroeder
William Joseph Sears
John Everman Seay
Thomas Bartlett Sehon
Judith Keith Sikes
Thomas Edward Skipworth
Cynthia Cox Spangler
Judith Wilson Spivey
Carl Celso Stapp
Theodora Anne Sellmacher
Allen Reeves Stockslager
Kathleen Louise Stoddard
Elizabeth Anne Storey
Janet Ann Stripling
Alfred Hugh Summers
Danny Dexter Taylor
Teresa Floyd Thompson
Serena Early Trippet
Cornelius Lycurgus VanZandt
Billy Francis Vier
Nancy LaDue Wallace
Joseph Marion Waller
Stephen Jay Warshaw
Gretchen Weicker
Cheryl Lynn Weinberg
Sara Lucille Weisinger
Aubrey Dwain White
Margaretta Alice Friedel White
Thomas Porcher White III
Katherine Ann Whiteman
John Orville Weiderholt
Edith Anne Williams
Edna Ann Williams
Betty Ann Willis
Betty Gale Barrett Willis
Charles Virgil Wilson
Vicki Ann Wilson
Barbara Jean Wirth
Katherine Townsend Wise
Valena Beth Wofford

Berry C. Woodson
Darrell Weldon Wootton
Carol Lorraine Wynn
Elizabeth Stanley Ash
Patricia Heaney Breazeale
Houston Bryant Campbell, Jr.
Margo Sylvia Cervantes
James Charles Dickson, Jr.
Bobbie Jo Fleming
Elizabeth Dennis Forster
Mona Keffer Gedney
Byron Glenn Goodrum
Anne Ralston Graves
John Robert Kohler
Sara Jane Little

Robert Earl Luther
David E. Melville, II
Alfred William Morgan
Katherine Elizabeth Neel
James Reed Norwood
Rollin Eugene Phipps
Sheryl Stice Ross
Roger Michael Russell
During Stanley Sempala
Gerald William Thompson
Lynda Lou Uphouse
Drusilla Jean von Schweinitz
Kary Meredith Walker
Dennis Roberts Williams

## Master of Arts

Frances Johnson Bailey
Jessie Lou Gill
Donnie Howard Duncan

Anita Alleane Taylor
Mary Meador Moody
Vivian Vorene Muenzler

## Master of Arts
## May 20, 1968

Virginia Anne Arthur
Joyce Wilson Bryant
Don Stephen Burket
Bonny S. Franke
Luna Moore Grimes
Merrill J. Howard
Gary Griffith John
Ima Rose Looney
Elizabeth W. Neel
Mildred Frances Powell

Barbara Lynn Schroeder
Charles Clayton Schroeder
Mary Katherine Smith
Jeanette Louise Tinney
Drusilla Jean von Schweinitz
Antoinette Ball Wyatt
Elizabeth Anne Gooden
Rose Marie Riddle Mayes
Arlene J. Ratz

## Bachelor of Arts
## May 20, 1968

Anne Irene Allen
William Russell Allensworth

Donald Gaines Anderson
S. Joseph Barrett

Brenda Donaldson Barton

David Marsh Barton

Robert Ernest Barton

Cathy DeLoach Baswell

James Harmon Beach III

David Robert Bell

Jerome Carson Bell

Natalie Florine Bencowitz

Barbara Lee Berryhill

James Flimen Biggart III

Judith McArthur Biggart

Elaine Bonner

Roy Boyd Brazell

Kelly Wade Breazeale

Bradford R. Breuer

Richard Dean Brown

Charles Austin Bryant IV

Judy Ann Burrows

Thomas Matthews Calvert

Catherine Kinkler Casey

Charles Kenneth Castle

Mary Gwendolyn Chapin

Charles Madden Chiles

Steven Arbuthnot Clark

David Justin Cochener

William Austin Cochran V

George Mouzon Cox

John Andrew Crosthwaite

Carolyn Adele Cruz

Gregory Allan Dana

Mary Caroline Morrison Dana

Carol Diane Davis

William Jefferson Day

Richard Lane Denham

Charles G. Deppen II

Randall Scott Downing

Mary Frances Downs

David Roach Dowty

Allan Dale Eichenberger

Deane Leslie Sadler III

Eugenia Sue Hargrave Smith

Karol Janet Smith

Suzanne Smith

Linda Gayle Southerland

Robert Kendell Sowards

Mary Ann Spragins

Suzanne Starnes

Jefferson Allen Stewart

David James Tarpley

James Kirby Thomas

Alton Wayne Evans

Gary Wayne Everhart

Karen Faith Fagg

Susan Fekety

William Butler Forbes

Jerry Thomas Foreman

Gordon Fleming Garlington III

Clark Dungan Gedney

Edmund Harrison Gibson

Michael Shiloh Gorman

Maston Lewis Gray

Mary Wheat Hahn

Cheryl Sue Haley

Janet Hansen

Dianne Louise Hardie

Philip Lansing Hays

Donald Alan Henderson

Elizabeth Ellen Henley

Tommy Dennis Hughes

Burl Benson Hulsey III

Susan Lynn Hyatt

Paul Curtiss Ireland

Howard William Jacob

Dennis Pat Johnson

Jean Ann Johnson

Sharon Kaye Johnson

Carol Elayne Johnston

Joe Leland Johnston

Donald Matthew Kass

Joe Wilson Kendrick, Jr.

Tim Ben Kirby

Conrad Epping Koerper III

David Morton Lander III
Janette Charlene Lawhead
Janet Ann Lawrence
Paul Fairbairn Legett
Judith Ann Liggett
Patricia Elizabeth Lillie
Robert Donald Lively
Gretchen Hard Livings
Wm. David Livings
Robert James Lovett
James Scott Thomas
Linda Neil Thoreson
Tomoko Tomita
Anthony Bernard Toro
William Arthur Tribble
Frederick William Tyler, Jr.
Clara Jo Frances Vandivort
Darla Ahnise Varnell
Gloria Ann Waggoman
Barry Hall Wahrmund
Robert Gordon Webb
Victor Ivan Lyday
Linnie Deen Lyle
Karen Marie McCready
Patricia Jean McDaniel
Charles Roger McReynolds
James Hart MacKay
Janice MacPhillimy
Michael Goree Maloney
William Stanley Marietta
Marilyn Margaret Marshall
Guy Neal Martin
Lee Riddle Mayes
Robert Kent Middleton
Ben Wayne Miller
Stewart Ransom Miller
Hilda Marie Mitchell

John P. Molyneaux
John Paul Morris
Jack Morrison II
Candace Ann Mudgett
Charles Bernard Murray
Audrey Sherryl Norman
Cecelia Louise Old
Stephen Joel Oren
Carolyn Sylvia Overstreet
Dimitrios Papadopoulos
Michael Thomas Pennington
Richard Scott Prentice
Joseph Moore Proctor
Lewis Meade Quigg
David Henry Rankin, Jr.
Richard Dana Redington
Thomas Roy Reese
Laura Ann Reilly
Eva Lynn Farr Renfroe
Mark William Rich
Celia Katharine Riddle
William Paul Ridinger
Sharon Eileen Robb
Margaret Lorraine Robertson
Jane Ross
Diane Louise Rumph
Carol Sue White
Stephen Taylor White
Palmer Emanuel Wigby
Michael Charles Wilgen
Nancy Carolyn Wilkins
William Haley Wilson
Harry Edwin Wistrand III
Frederick William Wood
Lawson Allen Wood, Jr.
Lila Mae Woodrow
Stephen Sebring Woodward

## Bachelor of Arts
### August 16, 1968

Michael Lynn Brooks
Emily Austin Bullock

Josephine Lee Crawford
Larry Gene Gaydosik

Mary Harrington Glover
George Myrick Harvin
Wiley Neil Johnson
Thomas Richmond McKinney
Mary Susan Scott McNab
Virginia Bunting Melville

Janet Louise Cook Proctor
James Michael Ross
Patricia Helm Smith
Robert James Smith
Sharon Gail Smith
John Carl Totten

## Master of Arts

### 1969

Marie Kate Davis
Jay Donald Evans
Rosamond Fienning
Carole J. Linsteadt
Karen Faith Fagg
Cheryl Lynn Finley
Kenneth Loyd

Lucy M. Graves
Emma D. Hancock
Janet M. Roy
Kenneth Edward Miller
Rosemary Royse
Leneta Wallace

## Bachelor of Arts

Henry Claude Abernathy III
David Anthony Adams
Barbara Dee Alexander
Charles Frederick Alford
Paula Lynn Alger
Jose Azarias Alvarez
Karl Grove Anderson
Donald Robert Antoniello
Sarah Aston
Margaret Layne Atteberry
Richard Donald Aubrey
Dorothy Sue Aycock
Emily Anne Baker
Thomas Estal Baker
Donald Warne Barker
Robert Baron
Frank William Bassham
John Peter Bievenour
Beverly Ethel Birk
Georgianna Blair
Elizabeth Ann Block

Mary Beth Bolton
Rebecca Lynn Boyd
John Kent Boynton
Shirley Ruth Brooks
Linda Fern Bullard
James Clayton Calhoun, Jr.
William Charles Campaigne
Ronald Hugh Campbell
Stephen Henry Capelle
Gary Bruce Carver
James Davis Clark, Jr.
Susan Elizabeth Clerc
Diana Lynn Connelly
James Allen Cooley
Lorrie Beaumont Cornett
William Lance Corsbie, Jr.
John Parker Craddock
Barbara Jane Craig
William Mark Craig
Michael Wayne Craven
Alma Catherine Crawford

Robert Larry Criswell
Theo Neill Crockett
Henry Baldwin IV
Charles J. Bondurant
Tim Parker Curtis
Sharon Anell Dabney
Richard Allen Davis
Francis Dewitt Dearen
Sandra Susan DeLee
Sherrilyn Olsen Denham
Perry Allen Denning
Charles Grainger Dibrell III
Thomas Alan Dodds
Timothy Evan Drake
Jeana Suzanne Dunn
Margaret Faye Duran
Mary Elizabeth Earhart
Mary Jo Ann Baggett Evans
Thomas Chives Newton Evans
Marilyn K. Facka
Donald Langley Fields
Steven Robert Findlay
Patricia Kay Flanagan
Freida Jean Fleischer
Robert Andrew Forteith
John Carrell Franklin
Ann Vosburgh Frerichs
John Richard Fuszek
Richard Hunt Gateley
John Randolph Gifford
John Thomas Goldston
John Carl Goolsby II
Murry Homer Haber
Susan Cheri Hackney
Anita Harkey
Juanita Sue Harris
Jane Herring
Richard Kelly Hester
Jo Carolyn Hicks
Susan Gregg Hill
Jean Neal Holland

Douglas Warren Holy
Donald Eugene Huey
Randy E. Huff
Michael Lynn Jenkins
James Clayton Johnson
James Noble Johnson
Ronald D. Hagood
Charles W. Jetton
Jemmie R. Kemp
Wm. Evans King
Sandra F. Lamme
Samuel L. Maisel
Julia Ann Johnson
Nancy Everhart Johnson
Edward Lee Jones III
Steven Harlan Josephson
John William Justus, Jr.
Jean Elizabeth Kelley
Danny Joe Kemp
Carol Elaine King
Delane Raye Kinney
Jeanette Elise Kuhn
James Lynn Lamm
Margaret Louise Lang
James Franklin Lee, Jr.
Sandford Leibick
Anne Cynthia Leon
Mary Susan Lynas
John Thomas McCants II
Linda Ann McCown
James Walten McKenzie
Arthur S. Mandell
Freddie Ray Maples
Helen Ann Marmon
Larry Wayne Maroney
Royal Sandford Mason
Martha Ellen Massie
Lynn Marie Mayfield
John Alsworth Menefee
Mary Jean Menefee
James Madison Meng, Jr.

Susan Gay Michero
Jan Louise Mitchell
Alan Duncan Monroe
James Milton Moore
John Dean Moseley, Jr.
Mary C. Nee
Vernon Chris Nyvall
Joan Kathy Pearce
Scott Marshall Phelps
Cathy Lynn Picone
Bill Tom Pierce
Philip B. Plattner
Jonathan Robert Poole
Michael Mamantov
Katherine McCarty
David W. McElroy
John M. McKinney
Jean Marie Mitchell
Robert L. Newman
Larry Wayne Proffitt
Charles Coe Purdy
Travis Roland Rainey
James Wayne Rhoads
Howard Mathew Ross
Donna Joann Russell
Robert Henry Schucany
Kathryn Janice Seddon
Charles Tom Semos
Elizabeth Ann Sewell
Veronica Alleyne Shackleford
Laura Lynne Shelton
Jensie Helen Simms
Joye Ella Simpson
Sherry Johnston Slusarek
Jimmy Lynn Smart

David William Smith
Steven Conrad Smith
Steven Spencer Smith
Joe Clayton Strange
Lynn Meredith Sturgis
Joanne Sutton
Carolyn Sue Synnott
Michael Lynn Tate
James Larry Terral
Donald Newby Test III
William Bateman Vandivort II
Sheila Ann Walker
David Mac Warren
Floyd Larry Wheeler
David Allan White
Pamela Sue Wilkerson
Tommy Ray Wilkerson
Edward Sansom Williams
Ellen Marie Williams
George Harold Williams, Jr.
Michael Eugene Williams
Jo Ann Willis
Carol Augusta Wilson
Edward Winslow Wilson
Margaret Mills Wilson
John Carlton Woods, Jr.
Cynthia Cagle Woodward
John Osborn Wynn, Jr.
Thomas Richard Young III
Elizabeth Reagan
Wm. P. Rutherford
Rebecca Sue Vestal
Alfred J. Weisberg
Don Hall Galgan

## Honorary Degrees from Austin College

1857    Rev. Hugh Wilson, D.D.

1860    Rev. R. H. Byers, D.D.

1869    Rev. A. C. Gukil, D.D.
        Rev. David McGill, LLD
        Rev. James W. Miller, D.D.
        Rev. David Roy, D.D.

1870    Rev. A. R. Baker, D.D.

1871    W. W. Hibbard, LLD
        Rev. W. C. Somerville, D.D.

1878    Rev. J. B. Mack, D.D.

1880    Hon. Richard H. Collins, LLD

1884    Rev. E. O. Guerrant, D.D.

1886    Rev. W. C. Dunlap, D.D.

1887    Prof. J. C. Edmunds, M.A.
        Rev. S. M. Luckett, D.D.
        Rev. D. MacGregor, D.D.
        Rev. R. H. Nall, D.D.

1893    Prof. L. J. Mitchell, C.E.

1894    Prof. Charles C. Scott, A.M.
        Rev. J. H. Skinner, D.D.
        Prof. Allison Thompson, Ph.D.

1895    Rev. Thornton C. Whaling, D.D.

1896    Rev. Wm. H. Leavell, D.D.
        Prof. W. D. Vinson, LLD

1898    Rev. J. H. Zively, D.D.

1899    Rev. W. L. Lowrance, D.D.

1901    A. G. Buckner, D.D.
        M. C. Hutton, D.D.
        J. N. McFarland, D.D.

1903    S. A. King, LLD

1904    Robert Hill, D.D.
        A. H. P. McCurdy, D.D.

1905    Robert E. Vinson, D.D.

1906    R. M. Hall, D.D.
        Wm. F. Junkin, D.D.

1907    H. F. Estill, Litt. D.
        A. A. McGeachy, D.D.
        Wm. Stuart Red, D.D.

1908    Jas. L. Bell, D.D.
        W. S. Jacobs, D.D.
        Jas. O. Reavis, D.D.

1910    Jas. A. Baker, LLD
        E. C. Caldwell, D.D.
        W. I. Carroll, D.D.
        F. C. Hume, LLD
        J. P. Robertson, D.D.

1913    E. Brantley, D.D.
        W. P. Dickey, D.D.
        Tilden Scherer, D.D.

1914    J. M. Clark, D.D.
        W. A. McLeod, D.D.

1916 C. H. H. Branch, D.D.
H. W. Burwell, D.D.
W. B. Morrison, Litt. D.

1917 Henry C. Evans, LLD
E. B. Fincher, D.D.
Jno V. McCall, D.D.
S. M. Tenney, D.D.
Jas. I. Vance, LLD
Joseph A. Vance, D.D.
Walter M. Walsh, D.D.

1918 B. I. Dickey, D.D.
W. F. Galbraith, D.D.
T. O. Perrin, D.D.
Henry H. Sweets, LLD
S. F. Tenney
E. W. Williams, D.D.

1919 T. W. Currie, D.D.

1921 Wm. M. Anderson, Jr., D.D.
Geo. C. F. Butte, LLLD
Guy B. Duff, D.D.
T. L. Green, D.D.
W. R. Hall, D.D.
Jas. S. Hardie, D.D.
Robert E. Vinson, LLD

1922 Watson M. Fairley, D.D.
Pat. M. Neff, LLD

1923 Wm. M. Anderson, LLD
Alva Hardie, D.D.
Arthur G. Jones, LLD
Theodore R. Ludlow, D.D.
Motte Martin, D.D.

1924 Thos. Henry Ball, LLD
Wm. Walton Bondurant, Litt. D.
Henry Clay Brock, D.D.

Samuel Palmer Brooks, LLD
Lewis Randolph Bryan, LLD
John Harmon Burma LLS
Chas. T. Caldwell, D.D.
Thomas S. Clyce, LLD
Wm. Crowe, D.D.
Norman R. Crozier, Litt. D.
Geo. B. Dealey, LLD
Frank C. Dillard, LLD
Thos. B. Greenwood, LLD
Hilton R. Greer, Litt. D.
Robert Gribble, D.D.
Henry O. Head, LLD
John Wm. Hickman, D.D.
John Black Hudson, D.D.
Frank B. Hughes, Litt. D.
John Douglas Leslie, LLD
Eugene S. Lowrance, D.D.
Thos. R. Marshall, LLD
Andrew T. McKinney, LLD
Walter M. Moore, LLD
Robert Paine Pell, LLD
J. Leighton Read, D.D.
Chas. C. Selecman, LLD
Gary L. Smith, D.D.
David Matthis Sweets, LLD
Thos. Vinson, Litt. D.
Wm. Ashton Vinson, LLD
Chas. C. Weaver, D.D.
Wm. H. Whiting, D.D.
Turner Ashby Wharton, LLD

1925 Wm. Ray Dobyns, LLD
Robert L. Marquis, LLD
Louis J. Sherrill, D.D.
Conway Wharton, D.D.
Samuel H. Whitley, Litt. D.

1926 Ebenezer E. Hotchkins, D.D.
Samuel L. Joekel, D.D.

1927    Thos. Watt Gregory, LLD                     Robert A. McCurdy, D.D.
        King Hagy, Litt. D.                         Mary McWhorter Tenney,
                                                        Litt. D.
1928    Wm. Adam Rolle, D.D.                        Samuel Mills Tenney, Litt. D.
        Jas. Kidd Thompson, D.D.

                                            1939    Julien P. Blitz, D.M.
1929    Wm. Addison Alexander, D.D.                 Wm. Alvah Francis, Litt. D.
        Henry Austin, D.D.                          Gibb Gilcrist, D. Sc.
        Caleb Wallace Chambers, D.D.                Malcolm Lee Purcell, D.D.
        Robert Harwell, LLD
        Louis Herman Hubbard, LLD   1940    Ela Hockaday, Litt. D.
        Leandro Garza Mora, D.D.                    Robert A. Law, LLD
                                                    John E. McLean, D.D.
1931    Edmund Marshall Munroe, D.D.                Robert Renbert Wilson, LLD

1933    Edward D. Grant, Litt. D.           1941    R. D. Campbell, D.D.
        Edward Fleming Montgomery, D.                Clyde Eagleton, LLD

1934    Wm. Frank McElroy, D.D.             1943    Martin Luther Baker, D.D.
        Sam B. McLane, D.D.                         Chas. S. Ramsay, D.D.
        Eugene Crampton Scott, D.D.                 David Worth Roberts, D.D.

1935    Franklin S. Henderson, D.D.         1944    Horace Newton Cunningham,
        Pierre B. Hill, LLD                             D.D.
        Raymond Hotchkiss Leach, LLD                Berta Murray, L. H. D.
        Patrick D. Moreland, Litt. D.

                                            1945    Frank C. Brown, LLD
1936    Jas. McFaddin Blanding, LLD                 Edward V. Ramage, D.D.
        Manford G. Gutzke, D.D.
        R. G. Lowe, D.D.                   1946    Percy C. Keith, D.Sc.
        Christopher Matheson, D.D.                  J. D. Miller, Litt. D.
        John O. Moseley, LLD                        Chas. C. King, LLD

1937    A. A. Aldrich, LLD                 1947    Robert F. Jones, D.D.
        A. Lawrence Crable, LLD                     Frank Langham, D.D.
        Wm. Marion Elliott, D.D.                    Arthur G. Hopkins, LLD
        Wm. E. Jones, D.M.                          J. B. Moorman, Litt. D.
        Cecil H. Lang, D.D.
        L. F. Sheffy, Litt. D.            1948    Thomas Timothy Montgomery,
                                                        LLD
1938    L. L. McCutchen, D.D.                       Lawrence Irving Stell, D.D.

Thomas Burke Gallaher, D.D.

1949 George Harvard Hurst, D.D.
Truman G. Blocker, Jr., D.Sc.
R. Matthew Lynn, D.D.
Frank M. Taylor, D.D.
James I. McCord, D.D.
Mrs. C. S. Harrington, D.H.

1950 Pat E. Hooks, D.H.
Charles Stanly Roberts, Sr.,
D.H.
The Hon. Sam Rayburn, D.H.
Louis Calder, D.H.
David Leander Stitt, LLD
Houston Harte, LLD
Ewell Doak Walker, LLD
J. Leighton Stuart
Hubert H. Hopper, D.D.
Harry McClellan Moffett, D.D.

1951 R. Gage Lloyd, D.D.
James B. Boren, LLD
Lamar D. Fain, LLD
Rupert B. Lowe, D. Sc.

1952 R. Bruce Brannon, D.D.
Albert T. Dyal, D.D.
Kim Hyung Mo, D.D.
Thomas H. Talbot, D.D.
Andrew Edington, LLD

1953 John F. Anderson, Jr., D.D.
Thomas W. Currie, D.D.
V. C. Arnspiger, LLD
Arthur Eustace Southon, Litt. D.

1954 Carl Ellis Nelson, D.D.
Sallie Kennedy M. Majors,
LH.D.
Mandred Whitset Comfort, LLD

1955 William M. Logan, D.D.
William B. Oglesby, Jr., D.D.
Wilbur Cunningham Windsor,
LLD

1956 Walter A. Bennett, D.D.
James Martin Singleton, D.D.
Crowdus Baker, LLD
Thomas Powell Baker, Litt. D.

1957 Robert P. Douglass, D.D.
Joseph Thorn Jackson, Litt. D.
David W. Williams, LLD
Joseph Sherrard Rice, D.D.
1958
Mrs. Leighton M. McCutchen,
D.H.
James W. Edgar, LLD
Sherwood H. Reisner, D.D.
Harvard A. Anderson, D.D.

1959 Meril Aubrey May, LLD
Harold C. Kilpatrick, L. H. D.

1960 Jerry McMullan Newbold, Jr.,
D.H.
Paul Hampton Sanders, LLD
John W. Lancaster, D.D.

1961 Eugene Stuart Grett, LLD
Mark Keller Poole, D.Sc.

1962 Toddie L. Wynne, LLD
Henry W. Quinius, Jr., D.D.
Tom B. Anderson, D.D.
Salomon N. Trevino, Litt. D.

1963 William H. Foster, Jr., D.D.
John Erik Jonsson, D. Sc.
William M. Elliott, Litt. D.

1964    Ruel C. Walker, LLD             Cecil H. Green, LLD
        Bruce C. Tucker, D.D.             Edward S. Bayless, D.D.
        R. W. Jablonowski, D.D.           Emmette S. Redford, LLD
        C. Rodney Sunday, D.D.
        Clifford W. Williams, D.D.     1967    Rabbi Levi A. Olan L.H.D.
                                          Robert Haydon Bullock, D.D.
1965    Lucile Anne Allen, Litt. D.        James Storey, D.D.
        Charles Franklin Jones, LLD      Jorge Lara-Braud, D.D.
        John P. Minter, L.H.D.
        John B. Spragens, D.D.        1968    Allan Shivers, LLD
        Joe Dennis, D. Sc.                Ramon F. Adams, L.H.D.
        Royston Roberts, D. Sc.
                                  1969    John B. Connally, LLD
1966    Harry H. Ransom, L.H.D.          James E. Fogartie, D.D.

## Recipients of Founders' Medal

1963    William Barnett Guerrant      1966    D. Elton Trueblood
        E. B. Tucker
                                     1968    Carey Croneis
1964    Homer P. Rainey
                                   1969    James H. Robinson
1965    Laurence M. Gould

## Austin College Distinguished Service Awards

1956    Wm. Barnett Guerrant       1961    Charles L. King

1957    Hoxie H. Thompson         1963    C. Stanly Roberts

1958    J. B. Moorman             1964    Mrs. Thomas Craig

1959    Rollin Rolfe                1968    James A. Fant

## Austin College Alumni Association
## Distinguished Service Citation

1956    George L. Landolt

## Austin College Alumni Association Awards

| | | | |
|---|---|---|---|
| 1957 | Robert L. Wood | 1964 | Edward D. Grant |
| 1958 | Novella D. Little | 1965 | Monroe Bryant |
| 1959 | James I. McCord | 1966 | John F. Anderson |
| 1960 | Mason Lockwood | 1967 | Truman G. Blocker |
| 1961 | Crowdus Baker | 1968 | Noel G. Shaw |
| 1962 | David L. Stitt | 1969 | George A. Boyd |
| 1963 | Charles Lingo | | |

## Austin College Alumni Meritorious Service A

1957 Pete Cawthon, Coach 1923 to
'27
Joseph L. Lockett, '96
Walter E. Long, '10
S. Brooks McLane, '13
W. T. Read, '05
C. Stanly Roberts, '98
Lee Simmons, '93
Hoxie H. Thompson, '01
O. O. Touchstone, '07
Will R. Wilson, '99

1958 James F. Hardie, '08
Lloyd B. Hughes, '18
Euphie Lang, '08
Rupert Lowe, '19
A. T. Stewart, '12
James K. Thompson, '92

1959 Cecil Grigg, '16
Joe Sharp, '25
B. Tol Terrell, '37
Ruel C. Walker, '31

1960 Shem P. Cunningham, '20
George Jordan, '15
V. E. McInnis, '99
T. C. Vinson, '09

1961 Luther Fletcher, '36
James E. McKinney, '14
Elizabeth Zogheib, '34

1962 Ramon F. Adams, '12
R. N. Price, '27
Royston M. Roberts, '40

1963 Charles C. Carsner, '05
Gaston Hallam, '26
Laura Heard Shoap, '24
George L. Landolt, '23
Ewell Walker, '19

1965 Louis S. Winston, '15
James D. Miller, '21
Thomas P. Baker, '24
David P. Dean, '19
Paul C. Dean, '19

| | | | |
|---|---|---|---|
| 1966 | Adele A. Coblentz, '43 | | Paul Sanders, '31 |
| | Bradshaw F. Armendt, '21 | | |
| | Wm. E. Williams, '15 | 1968 | G. Raymond Stephens, '20 |
| | Lucile McElroy, '41 | | Arthur N. Springall, '29 |
| | Cecil Lang, '12 | | James E. Teel, '31 |
| | | | Cora Sylestine, '43 |
| 1967 | Minna Amis Smith, '15 | | |
| | John W. Cowles, '27 | 1969 | Lardner W. Moore, '18 |
| | Wm. W. Bondurant, '25 | | Jane Moorman, '48 |

# The Crimson and Gold

*C. E. Dodge*

1. Today we gladly sing the praise of our dear Alma Mater,
   True sons and daughters may we live that she may know
      we love her;
   To her whose wisdom, power and might has given light
      to men;
   Our dear and fairest mother, A-U-S-T-I-N.

2. To you old school we give our pledge of loyalty forever.
   No thought, no deed or space of time our bonds to thee
      can sever.
   The light of truth which you did give was given not in vain;
   We'll love and serve forever, A-U-S-T-I-N.

Chorus:
   So hail to old Austin Crimson and Gold;
   Long may her colors fly.
   Fight o ye sons and ye daughters too,
   the spirit must not die.
   So hail to old Austin, the Crimson and Gold,
   What care we for the rest,
   We'll do or we'll die for old Austin,
   the school that we love best.

# CHAPTER VI

# The College Today

## Nearing The Summit

THE *Cunningham Lectures* were established at Austin College through a gift of the endowed fund by Shem P. Cunningham and his wife, Cara P. Cunningham, to provide for students of Austin College, Presbyterians generally, residents of the Sherman-Denison area and other interested persons lectures which would further the cause of Christian education and the Christian religion.

*The John T. Jones Chair of Economics* was established by the Houston Endowment Inc. in 1947 and was renewed for a second decade in 1957. It provides by contractual agreement for the annual support of the John T. Jones Professor of Economics. Renewed in April 1967, to be reviewed by the Trustees of the Houston Endowment Inc. on an annual basis.

*The Henry L. and Laura H. Shoap Professorship of English Literature* is being established by Mr. and Mrs. Henry L. Shoap of McKinney, Texas, to provide the students of Austin College with instruction of the highest quality in the composition, understanding and appreciation of the literature of the English language as a part of the liberal arts tradition.

*The Willson-Nichols Lectureship* was established at Austin College through a gift of the endowed fund by Mr. and Mrs. J. M. Willson of Floydada, Texas, in memory of Mr. Willson's sister, Mrs. Geneva Willson Nichols. To be scheduled during a week each Fall, the lectures series will seek to further the cause of Christian education by bringing to Austin College a religious leader and spokesman in the Judeo-Christian tradition.

*Perpetual Scholarships.*

———

Nᵒ 1 .   James C. Smith Issued,  30th Decʳ, 1853.
„  2    Henderson Yoakum   „       Ditto
„  3    John Hume          „       Ditto
„  4    Elizabeth E. Smither „     8th Jan. 1854


*Complimentary*

———

Rev. Benjamin Chase,  Proprietor.
Schol. named as follows: —

Nᵒ 5   Simeon Chase         Issued.  6th April, 1855
„  6   Paine Wingate Chase    „      Ditto
„  7   Susan H. Chase         „      Ditto
„  8   Selah Jean Chase       „      Ditto
„  9   Benjamin Chase         „      Ditto

——————— ° ———————

Nᵒ 10  Hon. Sam Houston  Issued,  10th Sept 1855

——————— ° ———————

James Carroll Smith, Proprietor.      1856
Schol. named as follows: —

## Endowed Fellowships

| | |
|---|---|
| The Stephen F. Austin Fellowship | $ 4,000.00 |
| The Thomas Edgar and Kathryn Heard | |
| Craig Fellowship | 10,000.00 |
| The Doctor and Mrs. J. C. Erwin Fellowship | 5,600.00 |
| The Thomas W. Folbre, Jr., | |
| Memorial Fellowship | 12,150.00 |
| The John S. and Rachel Heard Fellowship | 10,000.00 |
| The S. D. Heard Fellowship | 10,000.00 |
| The Stephen Dudley and | |
| Lillie S. Heard Fellowship | 15,000.00 |
| The Charles Curtis McKinney | |
| Memorial Fellowship | |
| The William B. Steele, Genevieve Wakefield | |
| Steele and Sue Steele Memorial Fellowship | 10,241.00 |
| The P. S. Wharton Memorial Fellowship | |
| in Chemistry | 13,000.00 |

## Endowed Scholarships

| | |
|---|---|
| The John W. Alexander, Jr. | |
| Memorial Scholarship | $ 1,939.00 |
| The Rhodes Baker Memorial Scholarship | 5,881.00 |
| The Albert D. Banta Scholarship | 20,000.00 |
| The Sarah Bell Banta and the Sarah Terhune | |
| Scholarships | 2,500.00 |
| The William Ermon Barker Scholarship | 5,000.00 |
| The Bellaire Presbyterian Church-Robert H. | |
| Bullock Scholarship | 7,500.00 |
| The Martha Nieminen Bondurant Memorial | |
| Scholarship | 2,798.00 |
| The W. W. Bondurant, Jr. | |
| Scholarship Fund | 13,445.00 |
| The E. M. Bramlette Scholarship | 2,500.00 |
| The James Perry Bryan Scholarship | 2,500.00 |
| The Emily A. Coe Memorial Scholarship | 2,730.00 |
| The Chapman Scholarship | 1,800.00 |

The Lieutenant William S. Crawford, Jr.
Memorial Scholarship — $10,000.00
The Mrs. Lora Files Cunningham
Memorial Scholarship — 6,500.00
The C. J. 'Red' Davidson Scholarship — 3,825.00
The Thos. and Pauline Davidson Scholarship — 51,000.00
The Fannie DeLoach Scholarship — 2,725.00
The Diamond Jubilee Class Scholarship — 850.00
The W. C. Eubank Scholarship — 2,500.00
The Failor-Barrett Scholarship — 60,000.00
The Flewellen Memorial Scholarship Fund — 5,250.00
The William E. and Mary R. Foshee Scholarship — 12,500.00
The Emma Pickerell Giddings Scholarship — 2,275.00
The Joseph H. and Betty Gleckler Scholarship — 46,398.00
The J. L. Greene Scholarship — 5,000.00
The Helen Willson Guthrie Memorial Scholarship — 3,000.00
The Edward Stetinus and Elizabeth Houston
Harte Scholarship — 25,000.00
The Charles and Cora Bivins Halsell Memorial
Scholarship — 9,000.00
The John B. Hunt Scholarship — 10,000.00
The Mrs. John B. Hunt Scholarship — 6,666.00
The Miss Manie Heard Scholarship for
Ministerial Students — 1,500.00
The J. R. Hunter Memorial Scholarship Fund — 12,500.00
The Irvin and Ruth Biddle Kennedy Scholarship — 5,050.00
The Murray Steele Kerr Scholarship — 2,500.00
The Kidd-Key College and
Conservatory Scholarship
The Kilgore First Presbyterian Church — $ 2,200.00
The Sallie B. King Memorial Scholarship Trust — 10,000.00
The Anna M. Kuhnle Scholarship Fund — 10,000.00
The Euphie Margaret Lang Scholarship — 2,550.00
The Mary Jewell Link Scholarship — 2,500.00
The Lovejoy Memorial Fund — 3,000.00
The R. S. Lowe Scholarship — 10,000.00
The Roy King McCall Memorial Scholarship — 4,275.00
The Courtenay Marshall Scholarship — 10,000.00
The Miss Hinnie Merriwether
Memorial Scholarship — 3,050.00
The Mid-Texas Presbyterial Scholarship — 3,850.00

| | |
|---|---|
| The Mr. and Mrs. Ferdinand Moore Scholarship | 50,100.00 |
| The Charles Edward Morris Memorial Scholarship | 4,340.00 |
| The R. L. Morrison Scholarship | 1,200.00 |
| The William D. Rembert Scholarship | 2,500.00 |
| The C. N. Roberts Scholarship | 1,500.00 |
| The Roberts-Cunningham Scholarship | 6,000.00 |
| The Russell V. Rogers Scholarship for Ministerial Students | 7,000.00 |
| The Elizabeth M. Sayler Scholarship | 1,070.00 |
| The T. R. Sampson Memorial Scholarship | 1,500.00 |
| The William Marion and Freddie Davis Shaw Scholarship Fund | 2,771.00 |
| The Texas Presbyterian College Scholarship | 4,350.00 |
| The Robert L. Wood Scholarship | 4,630.00 |
| The Addie R. Whitcomb Ministerial Scholarship | 8,000.00 |
| The J. E. Wharton Scholarship | 2,500.00 |
| The Weddell Scholarship | 3,500.00 |
| Mrs. Marguerite Gregg Wills Memorial Scholarship | |
| The Mrs. Dorcas Sheffield Wills Memorial Awards | |
| Alice Wright Memorial Scholarship Fund | |
| The Natalie E. Zogheib Memorial Scholarship | $ 2,525.00 |

## Annual Scholarship Funds

The Austin College Scholarship Fund
Memorial Scholarship Fund
Judge Edward J. Boyles Memorial Scholarship
Mr. and Mrs. R. J. Browning Memorial Scholarship
John A. Huebner, Sr., Memorial Scholarship
Robert W. Knox and Pearl Wallis Knox Memorial Scholarship
Verner Moore Lewis Scholarship

## Other Continuing Scholarships

American Association of University Women Scholarship

E. H. Danner Scholarship
Sherman High School Parent Teacher
   Association Scholarship
Sherman Kiwanis Club Scholarship
Nelson Puett Scholarship Award
Sherman Rotary Club Scholarship

## The Campus

THE Austin College campus is located in a residential area of northeast Sherman. Twenty buildings on 45 acres comprise the campus proper. Additional college owned property adjacent to the campus is used for faculty housing and auxiliary residence halls. The physical plant is valued at $12,000,000, with plans for the addition of a recreation center, theatre-arts center, and an art and speech addition outlined in a master architectural plan. When completed, the campus will provide facilities ideally designed for a student body limited by College policy to 1500 undergraduate students. The enrollment in September 1969 exceeded the previous limit of 1000.

The oldest building on the campus is LUCKETT HALL, completed in 1908. Recently extensively renovated, it serves as a residence hall for 150 men.

THOMPSON HALL is another of the campus landmarks. This building, erected in 1913, was completely renovated in 1957, and in 1965 was further modernized and was functionally related to the new Moody Science Center. (Refer to Moody Science Center in subsequent paragraphs.)

SHERMAN HALL was given to the College in 1914 by the citizens of Sherman to replace the original College building which had been destroyed by fire. Extensive renovation during the past few years has made possible the fullest utilization of facilities in Sherman Hall. On the first floor is located the Shelton Language Laboratory, gift of Mr. and Mrs. E. E. Shelton of Dallas. Also on the first floor are faculty offices, a central secretarial office, and the Vinson Conference Room, named for Mr. Walter H. Vinson, an Austin College graduate of the class of 1890. A bequest from Mr. Vinson enabled the College to remodel and renovate Sherman Hall. The second floor is occupied by classrooms and the

Hoxie Thompson Auditorium, named in memory of the late Hoxie Thompson, a 1901 graduate of the College. The audiorium is used for class lectures, concerts, meetings and public lectures. Faculty offices are on the third floor.

CERN MEMORIAL CENTER is another campus landmark, known to countless alumni as the Powerhouse. In 1957, a bequest from Mrs. Lalla R. Cern of Houston provided for the modernization of the building. Now this building is used as a Learning Center. The TAGER television reception classrooms, the Community Service (Social Sciences) Project and the Austin Teacher (Education Department) Program. The Educational Media Section is on the second floor of the Center.

Of the newer buildings on the campus, the ADMINISTRATION BUILDING was the first to be erected. It was dedicated in 1947 and contains the Jordan Executive Suite, administrative and faculty offices, lecture rooms, laboratories, and classrooms. A gift from the Jordan family of Dallas made possible the redecorating and refurnishing of the executive suite in 1960.

Two buildings, HUGHEY MEMORIAL GYMNASIUM and PAUL COFFIN HALL, were dedicated during the Austin College Centennial Celebration in 1950. HUGHEY GYMNASIUM, built with a portion of a bequest from Mr. and Mrs. M. B. Hughey of Kilgore, Texas, contains a double playing floor equipped with telescopic bleachers, bowling alleys, dressing rooms and dormitory for physical therapy, corrective exercise and instruction, and offices for coaches and faculty members. The gymnasium offers complete facilities for physical training for both men and women. PAUL COFFIN HALL was a gift to the College from Mrs. Paul Coffin of Itasca, Texas, and serves as living quarters for 58 women students.

The modern and well-equipped ADAMS HEALTH CENTER provides facilities for care of boarding students in cases of minor illnesses. The building, erected in 1951 as a gift from the Adams Family Foundation of Austin, Texas, contains reception and treatment rooms, patients' rooms with connecting baths, isolation rooms, kitchen, and an apartment for the Registered Nurse in charge of the infirmary. Expansion and remodeling of the Health Center in 1964 came as a gift from the Adams Best Foundation of Austin. The Etter Student Clinic, a physician's examing office and treatment rooms were also added in 1964 as a result of a gift from the Etter Foundation of Sherman.

THE ALUMNI MEMORIAL STUDENT UNION BUILD-ING is the center of campus social life, housing recreation facilities, and the College dining hall which serves all boarding students. The dining and food preparation area and attractive smaller dining areas for parties and dinners accommodate 1500. A glass enclosed loggia furnishes additional dining space. A post office, snack bar, lounge, TV room, games room, and the offices of the Union Building manager are also located on the first floor. The College Bookstore occupies a separate wing.

The second floor of the Union Building is occupied by offices of the Student Life and Student Counseling Centers and Placement Center, Faculty lounge, student government offices, a record listening room, and several spacious meeting rooms which may be utilized for lectures, meetings, forums, and small parties or dances.

On the southeast corner of the campus is CLYCE HALL, a four-story residence hall accommodating 139 women students, named for Dr. Thomas Stone Clyce, president of Austin College 1900-1932. On the northwest corner of the campus is DANIEL BAKER HALL, a men's residence hall named for the founder, which accommodates 152 men. Funds from the Together For Christ Campaign of the Synod of Texas helped build both Clyce Hall and Daniel Baker Hall.

WYNNE CHAPEL, center of religious life on the campus, was dedicated in 1958. The large auditorium is used for student chapel services and college functions. A smaller chapel is used for student devotions and lectures. The building also contains the offices of the Minister to the Campus, choir room, conference rooms, and a small prayer room for quiet meditation. The Chapel was a gift from the Toddie Lee Wynne family of Dallas. In the spire is the carillon, a cluster of twenty-four finely tuned bronze bells hand-cast in Holland, contributed by the Wynne family. Also in the spire hangs the Sam Houston Bell, a gift of General Sam Houston, who was a member of the first Board of Trustees.

The air-conditioned ARTHUR HOPKINS LIBRARY, completed in 1960, was made possible through gifts from the Hopkins Foundation of Sherman and from Miss Bessie Heard of McKinney, Texas. Arthur Hopkins was an Alumnus of the Class of 1910.

*Resources Available:* The library is an official depository of government documents which now number over 17,000. Other volumes catalogued exceed 90,000. Over 720 different periodical titles are regularly received including newspapers from all around the world. An extensive collection of materials on microfilm is available. To supplement local holdings, interlibrary loans and photocopies of articles are obtained from other libraries all over the country.

*Services Provided:* The highly-trained Library staff includes four professional librarians, eight other regular library workers, and about forty student assistants. Librarians present lectures and demonstrations on how to use the Library and its resources most effectively. Special assistance to readers is provided at the Reference Desk. In preparing to write a research paper students often turn first to the Reference Librarian who can usually save them time by describing approaches and techniques unknown to them.

*Library Facilities:* The Arthur Hopkins Library, a modern, four-level building, contains comfortable seating at tables and study carrels convenient to the open stack arrangement of library materials. The use of the Xerox Copier can save time by eliminating the need to make extensive notes from journals or books. Tape decks are available for listening to tape recordings.

*History of the Library:* The Austin College Library was begun with a collection of books donated by the trustees of the first decade. It was housed in a portion of the first floor of the building erected in 1852. Contributions of books, sermons, lectures and treatises came from Daniel Baker, Henderson Yoakum and Sam Houston; the latter sending items from Washington by friends coming to Texas. Daniel Baker solicited books as well as money on all of his trips seeking aid for the College. Yoakum was the first college librarian and was commissioned to obtain laboratory apparatus and books on a trip to the East. These included proceedings of the Smithsonian Institute obtained by an exchange agreement which required him to record meteorological data for the Institute each day.

Daniel Baker reports that the entire Rev. Twitchell Library including book cases was given to the College by the widow of this first decade trustee. He was minister of the Galveston Presbyterian Church and came to an untimely death by drowning in a shipwreck near New Orleans while returning from a General Assembly meeting.

Among the many private libraries donated to the College are the English library of Professor Davis Foute Eagleton; the International Law Library of his son, Rhodes Scholar, Dr. Clyde Eagleton; the History Library of Professor Stevenson of Long Island University; the Evans Collection and the entire library of Texas Presbyterian College for Women.

The Hoard Collection of Texiana and Southwest Lore to which additions are made annually came from Mrs. Margaret White Hoard of McKinney, Texas.

The library houses a rare books section, a treasure house of ancient volumes, Old Bibles, Maps, and early works of literary art. Among them are the recently acquired "De Alexandro Magno Collection" of Julii Berzunza. This includes nearly five hundred volumes on Alexander the Great in English, French, German, Latin and Greek.

The *New York Times Index* and an accompanying microfilm cabinet makes the earliest years of the New York Times accessible to researchers.

Also finished in the fall of 1960 was LOUIS CALDER STADIUM, seating 2,500. Construction of the stadium was made possible by a gift from the late Mr. Louis Calder of New York.

CRAIG HALL was dedicated in April of 1962 and named for the late Mr. Thomas E. Craig and Mrs. Craig of McKinney, Texas, long-time benefactors of the College. Both Mr. and Mrs. Craig served for many years on the Board of Trustees. Craig Hall houses the Music Department and was specifically designed for this activity. Classrooms, sound-proof practice rooms, faculty office, and a Recital Room accommodating an audience of more than 200 furnish superior facilities for music instruction and for recital and concert work.

CARUTH HALL was dedicated during Founders Week in October of 1963. Named in honor of the late Mrs. Earle Clark Caruth of Dallas, the hall was built with funds from the Hillcrest Foundation established by the late Mr. and Mrs. W. W. Caruth, Sr. The residence hall, with facilities for 162 women, is air-conditioned, has one large reception area and two study rooms, beautifully furnished in Italian Provincial, on the main floor. The lower floor contains a large snack bar, recreation room, kitchen and utility room with washers and dryers.

WILLIAM A. DEAN HALL, men's residence hall, was completed in the fall of 1965. The completely air-conditioned, carpeted building houses 242 men. It contains a recreation room, laundry, kitchen, lounge, typing and study rooms, counselors' quarters, and residence rooms. The building is named for the late William A. Dean, who taught in the College's preparatory school in 1915. The naming was announced in 1964 after David P. Dean and Paul C. Dean, sons of the late Mr. Dean who lived in Fort Worth, made a major gift to the College in honor of their mother and father.

The MOODY SCIENCE CENTER, completed in the fall of 1965, was made possible by a $1,000,000 grant from the Moody Foundation of Galveston. The building houses the departments of Biology, Chemistry, Mathematics, and Physics. Included in the building are 22 laboratories, 11 classrooms, 26 offices, shops, reading rooms, and other facilities. The physics department and the Hoblitzelle Computer Center with an IBM 1620 digital computer system occupy the first floor, built below ground level. Classrooms, faculty offices, seminar rooms, and a 300-seat lecture hall are on the main, or second floor. The third floor houses the chemistry department, and biology facilities are on the top floor. On the roof of the building are a green house and an astronomical observation platform. Among other special facilities of the science center are an animal room, an environmental control room, and a laboratory to permit the handling of radioactive materials. Research laboratories are also provided for talented science majors to work with professors on relevant research programs. The Moody Science Center and adjoining Thompson Hall comprise modern facilities for science instruction and research.

The SID RICHARDSON CENTER is expected to be completed during the 1970-1971 school year. This Center will serve as an important recreational and social facility. It will include another gymnasium floor, handball courts, locker rooms and a natatorium. The Center will feature multiple use of facilities which will provide for auditorium, banquet and social functions. The Center was made possible by a challenge grant from the Sid Richardson Foundation.

Off the campus proper, but adjacent to it, is the PRESIDENT'S HOME, gift of Mr. and Mrs. Robert L. Wood of Midland, Texas, dedicated in 1957. WINDSOR HOUSE, which is being occupied by the Academic Dean, was completed in 1960 and is a gift of the Windsor family of Tyler and Dallas.

## Educational Information

THE degree of Bachelor of Arts is conferred upon students who have completed all of the requirements for graduation.

### The 4-1-4-3 Plan

The 4-1-4-3 Plan consists of a Fall and Spring term of four courses each separated by a four-week January term of one course and a Summer term of three courses. Though students are not required to attend the Summer term, those who desire to complete the college program in less than four years may do so. Other students attend the Summer term to complete additional courses.

The purpose of the new program is to improve the quality of instruction and of learning by concentrating faculty and student effort on fewer courses at a time; by providing an expanded Honors Program for the superior student; by providing experiences outside the classroom both on campus and beyond the campus to supplement the academic course work.

The Summer term is coordinated with the other terms so that by careful planning a student can be graduated in three calendar years.

## The Social Science Laboratory

The Social Science Laboratory is an integral part of the college curriculum and is closely tied to the teaching and learning process. The purpose of this Laboratory concept is to improve and make more relevant the education of Social Science students by stimulating and encouraging the use of field research as a teaching and learning device. Field and laboratory research is incorporated as a regular part of the Social Science curriculum in an interdisciplinary research environment for students and faculty interested in empirical research. Through this Laboratory students are given the opportunity to observe political and social behavior, to formulate hypotheses about human behavior, to test these hypotheses by field research techniques, and to acquire a more immediate and realistic sense of the structure and needs of the community. (The Social Science Laboratory is in part supported by a Community Service Grant received by Austin College for community leadership training and development in local government.)

The Association for Graduate Education and Research of North Texas (TAGER) has the following institutions among its members: Austin College, Bishop College, Southern Methodist University, Texas Christian University, Southwest Center for Advanced Studies, Texas Wesleyan University, and the University of Dallas. This Association makes possible a variety of cooperative programs among the members for the improvement of graduate and undergraduate teaching and research.

Through a closed circuit TAGER television network installed August 1968 Austin College students in two classrooms on campus receive televised programs originating from several TAGER institutions. Included in these are the Southwest Center for Advanced Studies, Southern Methodist University. Austin College has the distinction of being affiliated Dallas. Bishop College and Texas Wesleyan College are also included in the network hook-up, as well as some industries, including Texas Instruments in Sherman.

The TV network has a "talk-back" feature with telephones at each desk over which students can ask questions and converse with the lecturer. Also, two programs can be transmitted simultaneously over the tower at Southwest Center.

This enables students at Austin College to hear a lecturer from one TAGER institution in one classroom while those students in the other room are receiving a program from another TAGER institution.

Initially, the television course offerings will emphasize advanced undergraduate and graduate work in science, engineering, and business administration, but expansion into other areas is expected at a later time.

Austin College also has cooperative programs with the Southwest Center for Advanced Studies, located in suburban North Dallas, to provide selected students in biology, chemistry, mathematics or physics with additional research study or work experiences.

Each summer some faculty and students in the biology department conduct research in a program at the Lake Texoma Biological Station of the University of Oklahoma.

### Junior Year Abroad

In cooperation with specific institutions abroad, Austin College offers qualified students an opportunity to spend a term or an academic year in attendance at a foreign college or university. Austin College has the distinction of being affiliated with the Institute of European Studies. Through Institutes at Paris and Nantes (France), Freiburg (Germany), Vienna (Austria), and Madrid (Spain) students have opportunities for overseas study on a preferred selection basis. Placement in other programs of comparable quality may also be arranged.

Students planning a term or year abroad should apply by April 1 and should have a cumulative grade point average of 2.5. They must demonstrate sufficient maturity and capacity for self-discipline to benefit from such study.

Although these programs are particularly appealing to language concentrators, students concentrating in other subjects such as Art, Government, History, or Philosophy will find such programs attractive. In any case the student must provide evidence of competence in the language of the country to which he plans to go. Each student must provide a plan of study abroad for approval by the chairman of his department and the Chairman of the Department of Modern Languages as well as the Assistant Dean and Registrar.

# Music And Dramatics

AUSTIN College first established itself in the realm of music with the untiring efforts of Prof. George Case, who for twenty years directed the Men's Choral Club which annually toured Texas and Oklahoma from 1905 to 1925. Later Dr. and Mrs. Paul Silas carried on this work with a mixed choir for many years. Then came Dr. and Mrs. Wayne Bedford and there followed the establishment of a full music department now housed in their own quarters, the Craig Music Hall. This acted as a catalyst to bind the College community into a oneness for enriching life on the campus for the talent of student and faculty of the College has been blended with local talent to bring enjoyment to audiences coming from a radius of a hundred miles. The A CAPPELLA CHOIR, now under the directorship of Bruce G. Lunkley, is a highly select group of 60 voices which has toured most of the United States and Europe. The choir has released a number of recordings. It has appeared on national television, radio, and before the legislatures of both Texas and Oklahoma by invitation. The College in cooperation with Sherman Musical Arts sponsors the Civic Orchestra. The Civic Orchestra, Municipal Band, Civic Chorus and other community groups benefit from the participation of members of the College community.

When Mr. Rollin Rolfe came to the College in 1935 he launched the "Little Theatre," and quickly dramatics came to be one of the most enjoyable activities of the college community. Followed by the splendid work of Mr. and Mrs. Paul Beardsley, the "Theatre in the Round" came into being. Now called The Arena Theatre of Austin College, it provides a setting for student creativity in all areas of theatre production including mixed media, films and original scripts.

## Concept of a College of the Church

AS a College of the Church, Austin College has a special role. Not only does it lend the Christian perspective to the learning process, but also it helps to keep alive and to foster the values of Christian humanism in a non-sectarian context. Knowledge is essential for man, but the sacrifice of human values in the quest for knowledge is a dangerous loss which the church-related institution can guard against. On the other hand, Austin College includes in its concept of a College of the Church the practice of tolerance and the process of self-criticism in order to avoid stifling dogmatism and sectarianism.

Affiliated with the Presbyterian Church, U.S., the College has specific obligations to the Church. Just as the Church affords its particular witness, so the College can make its contribution. Austin College recognizes the importance of the creation of educational opportunities for the student that provide a lively encounter between faith and learning, Through its task of pursuing knowledge and truth, the College can give further service as it interprets a changing culture for the Church. Thus, as a College of the Church, Austin College can offer an education with the Christian perspective and can serve the Church by being a resource in times marked by expanding knowledge and increasing demand for informed leadership.

### The Religious Program

Austin College believes that each student's coordinate education program should confront him with the claims and the implications of the Christian faith. Spiritual maturity should accompany and undergird intellectual and physical maturity to prepare him for effective citizenship and good churchmanship. The Religious Program seeks to implement these two convictions.

Services of worship and programs of general interest offer a continuing opportunity for students to understand and appreciate how individuals and groups think through problematic life-situations and how they arrive at a meaningful philosophy of life.

In the fall of each year there is a special series of lectures established by endowment and known as the Willson-Nichols Lectureship. In the spring there is the endowed program known as the Cunningham Lectures. Each of these lectureships enables the College to bring outstanding preachers or laymen to the campus.

*Wynne Chapel*

## Convocation

The Austin College Convocation is held regularly to provide an opportunity for the entire College Community to meet and consider issues of social, educational, and cultural importance. Convocation programs occur at 10 A.M. on Wednesday mornings. The same time period is used by the Sophomore Council to hold forums during the weeks that there is no Convocation. As the Convocations are an important part of the educational program, it is hoped that students will attend all Convocations. ALL full time students are required to attend five Convocations each long term. (The Willson Nichols and the Cunningham Lectures may be counted as Convocations toward the fulfillment of the attendance requirement.) Seniors are required to participate in the Opening Convocation, the Honors Convocation, Baccalaureate, and Commencement.

# The Austin College Graduate Program

### Historical Authority

THE graduate program at Austin College has a long tradition; the first Master's degrees were awarded by the College in 1856. At various times in the history of the College the Board of Trustees, the Administration, and the Faculty have reconsidered the philosophy and purposes of the graduate program and each time, as a result of such evaluation, have reaffirmed its continuance and development at the standard of quality for which Austin College is recognized. Thus, Austin College now offers only the Master of Arts degree with an emphasis on teaching and subject matter content consistent with the liberal arts objectives.

### Philosophy

The Austin College graduate program is based on the premise that thorough subject matter preparation combined with an understanding of the learning process which leads to effective teaching are essential qualifications for the Master of Arts degree. The requirements for the degree include foreign language proficiency, a scholarly thesis, and a comprehensive examination in the field of concentration. The graduate program makes possible a close working relationship between faculty and student, allowing careful individual planning and guidance for each graduate student. This also permits a flexibility in design which allows each student's program to be adjusted to his previous experience, educational preparation, and future plans.

The quality of the total program and of the resulting degree gives to each recipient an education which prepares him to teach in the most competent manner at his chosen level.

### The Graduate Programs and Teacher Education

The specifically designed graduate programs leading to the Master of Arts degree are planned to assist the interested individual to attain certification for teaching in the public schools. Degree programs which lead to certification are available with concentrations in Elementary Education, Counselor Education, and Secondary Education. The teaching fields in Secondary Education are: Biology, Business and Economics, Chemistry, English, and History.

## Student Activities and Organizations

### Student Organizations

MANY opportunities exist for students to participate in activities organized to develop and sustain interest in academic fields, to provide service to others, to recognize achievements, to contribute to the social and intellectual maturity of individuals, and to encourage leadership. All student organizations are under the immediate jurisdiction of the Austin College Student Affairs Division. The Student Affairs Division recommends to the College Council for approval the charters for all student organizations and establishes standards governing the operations of student organizations. Organizations and clubs must have advisers approved by the Student Affairs Division. The organizations are responsible to Austin College for maintaining their activities within the purposes of the College.

## Honors

*Dean's List:* The Dean's List is published following each Fall and Spring term and includes all full-time students in the regular program who during that term achieved a grade point average of 3.25 or more.

*Alpha Chi:* Alpha Chi is a national honor scholarship society, devoted to the promotion and recognition of scholarship and of those elements of character which make scholarship effective among the undergraduate students in the academic divisions of colleges and universities in the United States.

Texas Kappa chapter of Alpha Chi is located at Austin College.

Candidates for Alpha Chi are elected from the top ten percent of the senior class and the top five percent of the junior class. Twice each year the faculty elects to Alpha Chi membership the appropriate number of qualified candidates.

*Sigma Delta Pi:* Sigma Delta Pi is a national honor society in Spanish for advanced students of Spanish literature and culture. The purpose of this organization is to foster a wider knowledge of and a greater love for the Hispanic contributions to modern culture.

The Delta Omega Chapter of Sigma Delta Pi is located at Austin College.

*Eta Sigma Phi:* Eta Sigma Phi is a national honor society in Classics for students who study Greek and Latin. Its purpose is to foster interest in the Classics and to inspire continued study of the classical languages and literature.

The Gamma Upsilon Chapter of Eta Sigma Phi is located at Austin College.

*Pi Gamma Mu:* Pi Gamma Mu is a national honor society in the social sciences and history for junior and senior students who have completed six courses in history, government, sociology, anthropology and economics. On this work a student must earn a 3.2 grade point average and give other evidences of creative or scholarly work.

*Beta Beta Beta:* Beta Beta Beta is a national honor society for students in the biological sciences. Its purposes is threefold: stimulation of sound scholarship; dissemination of scientific knowledge; and promotion of biological research.

The Delta Rho Chapter of Beta Beta Beta is located at Austin College.

# EPILOGUE

Twelve Decades have passed and now Austin College accepts the challenge of the Thirteenth. The guide line motto, "The Best Today is not Good Enough for Tomorrow" still holds. The Summit is never reached by resting on laurels or fame. Each decade requires outstanding leadership and superb performance of Trustees, Administration and Faculty. Financial support, prayers and interest must ever be supplied by the Church and by loyal alumni and friends.

The destiny of the College in this Thirteenth Decade depends not only upon the success of the "Thirty Million Dollar Capital Funds Drive," but very positively upon the zeal and impact of the Christian leadership in the men who hold the future of the College in their hands.

As we strive for the Summit may we all remember well the pungent statement made by its founder, Daniel Baker, 120 years ago:

> For all generations to come, palsied be the hand which shall ever cast a ballot to alienate the institution in any way from the main purpose of its existence. So long as Austin College shall number one learner within its walls, withered be the tongue of any teacher therein who shall utter a syllable which has a tendency to prevent in the case of a single student the accomplishment of the chief and holy object for which, above all, the College was conceived, born, and reared.

## SUBJECT INDEX

# NAME INDEX

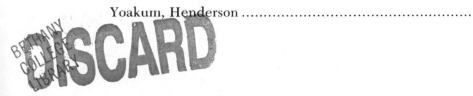